Ten Lessons in Theory

Ten Lessons in Theory

An Introduction to Theoretical Writing

Calvin Thomas

BLOOMSBURY

NEW YORK · LONDON · NEW DELHI · SYDNEY

Bloomsbury Academic
An imprint of Bloomsbury Publishing Plc

1385 Broadway	50 Bedford Square
New York	London
NY 10018	WC1B 3DP
USA	UK

www.bloomsbury.com

First published 2013

© Calvin Thomas, 2013

Library of Congress Cataloging-in-Publication Data
Thomas, Calvin, 1956–
Ten lessons in theory: an introduction to theoretical writing/Calvin Thomas.
pages cm
Includes bibliographical references and index.
ISBN 978-1-4411-5326-5 (hardcover: alk. paper) –
ISBN 978-1-4411-5770-6 (pbk.: alk. paper)
1. English language–Rhetoric–Study and teaching.
2. Knowledge, Theory of. 3. Criticism–History.
4. Literature–History and criticism–Theory, etc. I. Title.
PE1403.T46 2013
808'.042–dc23
2012051555

ISBN HB: 978-1-6235-6989-1
PB: 978-1-6235-6402-5
ePub: 978-1-6235-6304-2
ePDF: 978-1-6235-6164-2

Typeset by Deanta Global Publishing Services, Chennai, India
Printed and bound in the United States of America

For Ihab Hassan

Contents

Acknowledgments

I would first like to express gratitude to all the students who have been open and kind enough to listen to me for the two decades or so that I've been teaching these and other lessons in theoretical writing. I would also like to thank Ian Almond, Rahna Carusi, Tim Dean, Lisa Downing, Janet Gabler-Hover, Chris Kocela, John Lowther (for the expert indexing and sharp eye for infelicity), Randy Malamud, Melanie McDougald, Mark Noble, and Matthew Roudané for their support, advice, assistance, and encouragement in the years that I have been planning this book and writing and rewriting these sentences. Special thanks go to Haaris Naqvi, incomparable senior commissioning editor at Continuum/Bloomsbury, for his splendid support of this project, and to my colleague and climbing partner Mark Nunes, who has so often held my life in his hands. And as always, all my thanks and all my love go to Liz Stoehr.

Preface

"Something worth reading": Theory and/as the Art of the Sentence

Toward the end of Samuel Beckett's novel *Molloy*, the narrator, who calls himself Jacques Moran, encounters a strange man on a lonely road. Words are somewhat nonsensically exchanged, and violence of some extreme sort apparently ensues. For as Moran rather vaguely reports:

> I do not know what happened then. But a little later, perhaps a long time later, I found him stretched on the ground, his head in a pulp. I am sorry I cannot indicate more clearly how this result was obtained, it would have been something worth reading. But it is not at this late stage of my relation that I intend to give way to literature. (1955: 151)

Nor at this early stage of *my* relation do I intend to linger with this bit of Beckettian pulp fiction. But I would like to note the neat definition of "literature" that Beckett's Moran provides—"literature," we are told, is "something worth reading."

Toward the beginning of *Literary Theory: An Introduction*, Terry Eagleton offers a similarly simple definition, a "purely formal, empty sort of definition," of the word "literature"—"Perhaps," writes Eagleton, "'literature' means . . . any kind of writing which for some reason or another somebody values highly" (1983/1996: 8). This "functionalist" definition, as he calls it, doesn't quite satisfy Eagleton, but it works well enough for my purposes here, mainly because it allows me—at the outset of this book, *Ten Lessons in Theory*—to begin troubling the definitional distinction between "literature" and "theory," to begin introducing "literary theory" as a particular kind of writing that "for some reason or another" more than a few people have valued highly (even if others have loathed and reviled it). Taken together, Eagleton's and Beckett's definitions of "literature" give me license to suggest that "theory," like "literature," is "something worth reading," that "giving way to literature" and "falling into theory" (Richter 1999) can be intimately related responses to remarkably similar temptations.

Written as a "literary" introduction to "the activities that have come to answer to the nickname *theory*" (Culler 2007: 1), this book stakes itself upon three major premises. The first premise is that a genuinely productive understanding of theoretical activities depends upon a much more sustained encounter with the foundational writings of Hegel, Marx, Nietzsche, and Freud than any reader is likely to get from the standardized introductions to theory currently available; discourse concerning these four writers thus pervades *Ten Lessons in Theory*. The second premise involves what Fredric Jameson describes as "the conviction that of all the writing called theoretical, [Jacques] Lacan's is the richest" (2006: 365–6); holding to this conviction pretty much throughout, *Ten Lessons* pays more (and more careful) attention to the richness of Lacan's psychoanalytic writings than does any other introduction to theory (that isn't specifically an introduction to Lacan). The book's third premise, already introduced above, is that "literary theory" isn't simply highfalutin speculation "about" literature, but that theory fundamentally *is* literature, after all—something worth reading, a genre of writing that considerable numbers of readers have, for some time now, valued highly, even enjoyed immensely. The book not only argues but attempts to demonstrate that "the writing called theoretical" is nothing if not a specific type of "creative writing," a particular way of engaging with the *art* of the sentence, the art of making sentences that make *trouble*—sentences that articulate the desire to make radical *changes* in the very fabric, or fabrication, of social reality. As presented and performed here, theoretical writing involves writing *about* "writing as the very possibility of change" (Cixous 1975/2007: 1646).

Both the presentation and the performance of the book are consistent with this emphasis on sentence-making as trouble-making transformation. As its title indicates, the book proceeds in the form of ten "lessons," each based on an axiomatic sentence or "truth-claim" selected from the more or less established canon of theoretical writing. Each lesson works by extensively "unpacking" its featured sentence, exploring the sentence's conditions of possibility and most radical implications, asking what it means to say that "the world must be made to mean" (Stuart Hall), that "meaning is the polite word for pleasure" (Adam Philips), that "language is by nature fictional" (Roland Barthes), and so on. In the course of exploring the conditions and consequences of these sentences, the ten lessons work and play together to articulate the most basic assumptions and motivations supporting theoretical writing, from its earliest stirrings to its most current turbulences. Provided in each lesson is a working glossary—specific critical keywords (like "reification" or "*jouissance*") are **boldfaced** on their first appearance and defined either in the text or in a footnote.

But while each lesson constitutes a precise explication of the working terms and core tenets of theoretical writing as such, each also attempts to *exemplify* theory as a "practice of creativity" (Foucault 1983/1997: 262) in itself. And so, while the book as a whole constitutes a novel approach to theory, it also asks to be approached as a sort of theoretical novel. In other words, *Ten Lessons* is a textbook, to be sure, but a textbook written to be read closely, not (or so its writer dares to hope) as yet another routine, academically commodified, and dutifully "historicized" rehearsal of the now-standard "theories of literature," and not as a guide to the practical "application" of theory *to* literature, but rather as a set of extended pedagogical prose poems or experimental fictions or variations on the theme of theory *as* literature, of "life as literature" (Nehamas 1987) and of "the world as text" (Barthes 1968/1977: 147).

The ten lessons are divided into two parts. Part 1 is called "Antiphysis: Five Lessons in Textual Anthropogenesis." The word **antiphysis** actually appears but rarely in the canon of theoretical writing; the word isn't glossed in any of the critical dictionaries that I've employed here to explicate key theoretical terms. And yet the word antiphysis does quite nicely express the core tenet of what's called "historical materialism" —Karl Marx's permanently revolutionary argument that humans distinguish themselves from animals, and that human history as such begins, when people first start *working* to *produce* the very conditions of their human existence. The word antiphysis thus concerns the rudimentary but transformative *labor*—the actual work on or *against* physical nature—that *must* be performed for any "human reality" ever to form itself, bring itself into being. And in this argument, *all* human realities do, in fact, actively and transformatively bring themselves into being; all human realities are restless exercises in **anthropogenesis**, a word that concerns the human causality, the human origins or human geneses, of the human *qua* human. The phrase "*textual* anthropogenesis," then, involves what's called linguistic determinism, or what I'll call semiotic materialism, the argument, also to my mind permanently revolutionary, that any human reality, and any individual subject thereof, must be made out of *language* as a specifically "antinatural"—unreal or "antireal"—form of productive labor. Thus the book's first five lessons, all in various ways, concern "the virtual character of the symbolic order" of language as "the very condition of human historicity" (Žižek 1999/2002: 241); they all concern the difference between human and non-human animals, between human reality and "the real," as well as the constitutive interrelations between historical and semiotic materialisms; they all address the linguistic formations and transformations, the political inscriptions and ideological interpellations, of the specifically human subject, the "animal at the mercy of language" (Lacan 1966f/2006: 525), the animal sentenced to keep making sentences in the purely anthropogenetic, socio-symbolic, textual or virtual reality that is, so to speak, ours.

Part 2 is called "Extimacy: Five Lessons in the Utter Alterity of Absolute Proximity." A key Lacanian neologism, the word **extimacy** mixes "exteriority" with "intimacy," and thereby "neatly expresses the way in which psychoanalysis problematizes the opposition between the inside and the outside, between container and contained" (Evans 1996: 58). The word "extimacy" signifies the unsettling idea that "the innermost, intimate core of a person's psychical being is, at root, an alien, foreign 'thing.'" (Johnston 2009: 86): "extimacy" involves the strange "coincidence of utter alterity with absolute proximity" and "brings us close to what, in ourselves, must remain at a distance if we are to sustain the consistency of our symbolic universe" (Žižek 1999/2008: 368). And so, here, the word "extimacy" marks the various ways theoretical writing tends, rather like the Mobius strip so beloved by Lacan, to turn itself and its readers inside out and outside in; "extimacy" serves to condense the various concerns with alienation, alterity, foreignness, defamiliarization, constitutive otherness, difference, *différance,* queerness, and so forth, which continue to pervade and motivate theoretical writing.

While Part 2 of *Ten Lessons* is similar to Part 1 in that it strives to explicate and perform theoretical writing as a "practice of creativity" in itself, Part 2, despite its alienating title, also serves as a *slightly* more orthodox introduction to and survey of "the history of literary theory," addressing certain "schools" or "approaches" that have by now acquired perhaps a bit too much "name recognition" —formalism, structuralism, semiotics, poststructuralism, postmodernism, postcolonial theory, feminism, gender studies, and finally, queer theory. But what initially sets this section of the book apart from other, more routinely "historicizing" introductions to theory is that it begins with a full lesson devoted to Hegel. Major theorists from Althusser to Žižek acknowledge Hegel's importance to their writing. Jean-Michel Rabaté insists "that a patient reading of Hegel . . . is, if not a prerequisite, at least an essential step on the way to an understanding of theory" (2002: 21) as such. And yet, no introduction to theory to date devotes more than a few sentences, if that much, to Hegel's work. The lesson on Hegel given here attempts to rectify this situation, letting some prolonged exposure to the ever-pertinent Hegel serve the book's readers as "an essential step on the way" to better understanding not only the lessons on formalism, structuralism, poststructuralism, etc., that are to follow, but also, retroactively, the five lessons on "antiphysis" that precede.

"Antiphysis" and "extimacy" are, of course, intimately interrelated matters, so much so that we might here borrow the phrasing of one of our lesson's guiding sentences and say that there is no lesson in "antiphysis" that is not, at the same time, a lesson in "extimacy," and vice versa, so that a productive understanding of this book wouldn't in my estimation be seriously damaged by your reading Part 2 before Part 1. Before getting to either portion of our lessons, however, we have to consider the question of why any of us should even be studying "theory" anymore in the first place; we must work through an introductory chapter that explains why theory isn't dead—even if certain readers have long wished it were. The introduction accounts for this "death-wish" against theory and takes up several descriptions (from Jonathan Culler, Michael Hardt, Slavoj Žižek, Judith Halberstam, Fredric Jameson, and others) of what theory has done and must continue to do to "stay alive," explaining why theoretical writing always attempts to "shatter and undermine our common perceptions" (Žižek 2006: ix), usually by taking any and all "meaning as a problem rather than a given" (Culler 2007: 85). The introduction accounts for theory's necessarily *antagonistic* stances, exploring the various motivations behind theoretical writing as a mode of creative abrasion, a means of relentlessly *writing against* (against common-sense assumptions, against given meanings, against "things as they are," etc.). The chapter concludes with a justification of theory's notorious "difficulty," its discursive warfare against "clarity," and ends by insisting that theoretical writing's inevitable mission is to try "to keep open the difference between things as they are and things as they might otherwise be" (Critchley 1997: 22).

As for the individual lessons themselves, let's let the following serve as a preview:

Lesson 1: "The world must be made to mean"—*or, in(tro)ducing the subject of human reality*

The guiding sentence for the first lesson comes from Stuart Hall. The lesson explains how the sentence's first clause, "the world must be *made*," expresses the principal assertion of historical materialism and then posits the ending infinitive—"to *mean*"—as a sort of semiotic kicker. The lesson presents historical/semiotic materialism (the constitutive interrelation between labor and language) as the grounding "antiphysical" assumption of theoretical writing, the twin foundations of anti-foundationalism, so to speak. Here, we begin to unpack this word "antiphysis," to understand why theoretical writers think that human reality can never be taken "naturally," as a given, and can never be understood as biologically determined or theologically guaranteed. Here also, with a nod to Lacan's insistence on our species' universal "prematurity at birth," are we introduced to the idea that the "subject of human reality"—the specifically human individual—must always be *induced*, must always be brought into being not merely physically, but through labor and language, "work with words."

Lesson 2: "Meaning is the polite word for pleasure"—*or, how the beast in the nursery learns to read*

This lesson's guiding sentence comes from Adam Phillips' *The Beast in the Nursery: On Curiosity and Other Appetites*. The lesson begins with the curiously *unappetizing* assertion that we are never simply "born human" but must always be meaningfully *made* that way. The lesson expands upon Lacan's suggestion of human prematurity at birth and discusses the various "orthopedic" processes by which, as Louis Althusser puts it, the "small animal produced by the union of a man and a woman" must be *turned* into "a small human child" (1971: 205). For a historical/semiotic materialist conversant with Freudian and Lacanian psychoanalysis, this "turn" is always laboriously linguistic—it always involves both the adjustment of the pleasure principle to the reality principle and the sacrifice of animal "being" to human "meaning." Freud, as we'll see, posits that "whoever understands the human mind knows that hardly anything is harder for [us] than to give up a pleasure which [we have] once experienced. Actually, we never give anything up; we only exchange one thing for another" (1907/1989: 437–8). Lacan, as we'll read, casts this exchange of "one thing for another" in terms of a sacrifice of real "being" (*l'être*) for symbolic "meaning" (*la lettre*). Phillips' sentence merges these articulations, revealing "politeness"—the discursively orthopedic politics of self-policing—as that arena of exchange in which the pleasures of animality (such as they are for us) must be traded up for "meaningful" participation in the *polis*.

Lesson 3: "Language is, by nature, fictional"—*or, why the word for moonlight can't be moonlight*

Although it was Nietzsche who first stressed the radically figurative nature of language— the utterly metaphorical condition of any articulated "truth"—our guiding sentence here comes from Roland Barthes' *Camera Lucida*. Readers of Lesson Three are asked to consider the disturbing propositions that we are all "made out" of language *and* that language itself simply isn't real (or isn't simply real). Language exists, to be sure, but it cannot be real; language exists only ever "antiphysically," precisely by virtue of *not* being real, by never quite failing to *negate* the real. Along the lines of Lacan's assertion that "the symbol first manifests itself as the killing of the thing" (1966d/2006: 262), this lesson posits a certain murderous or prohibitory "no to the real thing" as any noun's structural condition of possibility. The lesson rehearses several elementary examples to illustrate the "antiphysical" point (the word "elephant" can't really be an elephant, the word "dirt" etched into real dirt isn't really dirt, a pointing finger must be *read* as something other than just real flesh in order to function as a sign, etc.). The lesson also adumbrates Lacan's take on the linguistic subject as a subject of desire, his "oedipalization" of language acquisition, the way he links language's "no to the real" with the metaphorical "no of the father," connecting the "paternal" prohibition against incest to the figurative "bar" that separates signifier from signified, preventing any word from ever completely *being* the thing that it *means*. The lesson closes with a riff on a passage from Don DeLillo's postmodern ghost story *The Body Artist* and with the suggestion that while it might seem like a "bad thing" that the word for moonlight can never really be moonlight, it's probably a "good thing" that words for excrement aren't really excremental—in other words, the lesson closes by suggesting that we "animals at the mercy of language" should be more gratefully relieved than fundamentally disturbed to be told that we are made out of words, that words aren't really real, and that language is literally nothing.

Lesson 4: "Desire must be taken literally"—*a few words on death, sex, and interpretation*

The lead sentence here is from Lacan, for whom "to take literally" means to take "to the letter," and so this lesson thoroughly unpacks the various structural coimplications of language and desire, starting with the uncanny resemblance between Alexandre Kojève's Hegelian description of desire as "an emptiness, the presence of the absence of a reality" (1947/1980: 5) and Lacan's formulation of the signifier as a literal "presence made of absence" (1966d/2006: 228). In the first section, on words, the lesson maps Lacan's trio of need, demand, and desire onto his three psychic registers of the real, the imaginary, and the symbolic; the lesson also takes up Freud's key distinction between "thing-presentations" and "word-presentations." In the second section, on death, the lesson gets at the notion of the death-drive in the same way Freud did in *Beyond the Pleasure Principle*, by taking up that famous bit of child's play called "the fort-da"; this section also addresses the relation between the death-drive and narrative (as per the analysis of Peter Brooks). The section on "sex" attempts to justify, or at least cogently explain, the Lacanian assertion that human sex is a problem of speech and that speech itself is a sexual dilemma. As the lesson spells out, the English word "sex" itself comes from the Latin *secare*, "to cut." Because the word "sex" shares its root, so to speak, with other "cutting" words (scission, scissoring, sectioning), the "meaning of sex" can be said to involve nothing but "coming to terms" with "the cut" of materialist language, in which not just "sex" or "scissors" but *all* words in *all* languages are serrated, castrating: so much, then, for any retrograde notion of some "completely natural" sexual desire among humans. In this section, however, the problem of sex is "taken to the letter" by being taken as a problem of *writing*, the literal forming of written letters on the page. A few passages of literary writing from Poe and Faulkner that thematize incestuous desire are briefly *interpreted*, and this move takes us into the fourth section, on the relation between *interpretation* and desire. Here, however, we turn away from the explicitly psychoanalytic register, away from Lacan's matter-of-fact assertion that "desire, in fact, is interpretation itself" (Lacan 1973/1981: 176) and toward a consideration of Nietzsche's quip that there are no facts, only interpretations, and his interpretation of the "will to truth" as a form of the "will to death." The lesson ends with Michel Foucault's discussion of the "life and death" of interpretation and his Nietzschean or "aestheticist" insistence on writing as an art of self-transformation.

Lesson 5: "You are not yourself"—*or, I (think, therefore I) is an other*

This lesson explores the politically anti-identitarian strains of theoretical writing. The lead sentence is the slogan that appears on the famous Barbara Kruger text-art photograph (woman's face in shattered mirror), but it also relates to Rimbaud's *"Je est un autre"* or "I is an other" (which insight appears, mashed-up with the Cartesian *cogito*, in the lesson's subtitle).

After introducing some of the ethical motivations behind theoretical anti-identitarianism, the lesson performs a close reading of Kruger's jagged edges, then moves to a thorough explication of Lacan's essay on the mirror-stage. The second section is an extensive explication of Althusser's essay "Ideology and the Ideological State Apparatuses," while the third section returns to Nietzsche and Foucault and to the question of an effective "aesthetics of resistance" to the ideological interpellation of the subject.

Lesson 6: "This restlessness is us"—*or, the least that can be said about Hegel*

This lesson's lead sentence comes from Jean-Luc Nancy's *Hegel: The Restlessness of the Negative*, and the lesson begins with a question: if Hegel is in fact what Nancy calls him—"the inaugural thinker of the contemporary world" (2002: 3)—and if Jean-Michel Rabaté is right to insist that reading Hegel is "an essential step on the way to an understanding of theory" (2002: 21), why do most introductions to theory slight Hegel so drastically, saying very little about his writing, if even mentioning his name at all? This widespread neglect of a crucial theoretical figure is best explained by Fredric Jameson, who warns that "the attempt to do justice to the most random observation of Hegel ends up drawing the whole tangled, dripping mass of the Hegelian sequence of forms out into the light with it" (1971: 306). This lesson attempts to do justice, not to a random observation of Hegel, but to the crucial Hegelian concept of *Aufhebung*, or "sublation." While the lesson doesn't consider the whole Hegelian sequence of forms, it does attempt to chart some of the key movements of the dialectic, taking up, in particular, Hegel's theoretical sublation of Christianity and his rehearsal of the struggle between "lord and bondsman" or "master and slave." The lesson ends with an attempt to demonstrate the political pertinence of a restlessly Hegelian analysis with a close reading of the famous photograph of the 1968 sanitation workers' strike in Memphis, Tennessee, the stark depiction of the "I am a man" placards held up against the fixed bayonets of the state militia.

Lesson 7: "There is no document of civilization that is not at the same time a document of barbarism"—*or, the fates of literary formalism*

The lead sentence here is from Walter Benjamin, but the lesson begins with Terry Eagleton's assertion that all the readers and writers of all the civilized documents in the world basically fall into two groups—those who actually understand Benjamin's dialectical observation and those who simply don't get it. Historically speaking, the latter group tends to be populated by literary formalists, particularly the Anglo-American New Critics, who arguably made attempting to *prevent* our understanding of Benjamin's sentence their critical mission in life. Thus, the first section of this lesson examines the standard definitions of (and political charges against) literary formalism, taking up, in particular, the way the New Critical concern with *formal* control and containment mirrored an underlying and reactionary interest in *social* containment and control. The section also shows how Virginia Woolf practically demolished New Criticism in advance with certain passages from *A Room of One's Own*. The second section of this lesson performs a close reading of two often-anthologized essays by Cleanth Brooks— "Irony as a Principle of Structure" and "My Credo"—demonstrating Brooks' investment in using formalist methods of reading poetry to transubstantiate "new" literary criticism into orthodox religious devotion. The third section pits Russian formalist Viktor Shklovsky's "defamiliarization" against Brooks' new critical "faith," arguing that Shklovsky's resolutely secular (actually, quite Nietzschean) conception of formalism—and particularly, his attention to the distinction between "poetical" metaphor and "prosaic" metonymy—is still quite pertinent to and compatible with contemporary materialist semiotics and poetics.

Lesson 8: "The unconscious is structured like a language"—*or, invasions of the signifier*

In this lesson, we return to Lacan, at least with the guiding sentence, and more or less with a vengeance in Section Three. But the first two sections are devoted to explaining the developments in structural linguistics that made Lacan's trademark assertion possible, to begin with. Here, we distinguish formalism from structuralism and examine the interdependence of structuralism and semiotics. We necessarily spend some time with Ferdinand de Saussure, charting the signifier/signified and syntagm/ paradigm distinctions, mainly as a way of seeing how Roman Jakobson is able to connect metaphor and metonymy to condensation and displacement in Freudian dream analysis (thus enabling Lacan's signature claim). We also spend some time exploring the most radical implications—particularly for considerations of sex, sexual difference, and gender identity—of Saussure's insight that language is a differential system "without positive terms" (1959: 120). This discussion, of course, takes us back to "the structuralist Lacan," to the famous "twin doors" (Ladies and Gents) in "The Instance of the Letter" and, inevitably, to "The Meaning of the Phallus." The lesson ends with an attempt to establish: (1) that the phallus really isn't the penis any more than the word moonlight really is moonlight, and for much the same reason; (2) that Lacan's writings ultimately expose, rather than perpetuate, so-called phallogocentrism, that his writings describe, rather than prescribe, a patriarchal unconscious "structured like a language"; and that (3) we may already find in the allegedly "structuralist" Lacan the strong possibility of what Judith Butler calls "a queer poststructuralism of the psyche" (2004: 44).

Lesson 9: "There is nothing outside the text"—*or, fear of the proliferation of meaning*

The ninth lesson concerns poststructuralism, postmodernism, and postcolonial theory. Poststructuralism and postmodernism have been branded as "trendy nihilisms" that deny life or literature any significance whatsoever. But poststructuralist and postmodernist writers actually fall quite short of affirming that "life" has "no meaning." Rather, such writers examine our pervasive *fear* that human reality generates far *too many* meanings, far *too much* interpretation— they trace and engage with our anxieties about *semiotic excess*, what Jacques Derrida (who is, of course, responsible for the lesson's guiding sentence) calls "the *overabundance* of the signifier" (1966/1978: 290). To see how poststructuralism concerns our "fear of the proliferation of meaning" (Foucault 1969/1998: 222), the first section of this lesson begins with a necessary revisiting of Nietzsche, with specific attention to key moments in "On Truth and Lie in an Extra-Moral Sense" and the *Genealogy of Morals*. We then move through Derrida's deconstruction of metaphysics, his attempted evaporation of "the center" and his abolition of the "transcendental signified," and then to Roland Barthes' and Michel Foucault's interrogations of "the author." The second section gets into postmodernism by way of the Habermas/Lyotard debate, but then more carefully explicates "the postmodern" by considering "the modern" in three aspects—socio-economic *modernization*, philosophical *modernity*, and aesthetic *modernism*. Section three, on postcolonial theory, begins—on what some will, no doubt, consider an inappropriately Eurocentric and "queerly" Foucauldian note—by pointing out the strong similarities between Edward Said's anti-imperialist descriptions of "Orientalism" and Eve Sedgwick's anti-homophobic limning of "sex." We then look at some queerly Orientalist moments in Hollywood film-noir, specifically the Geiger Bookstore sequence in Hawks' *The Big Sleep* and the entrance of Joel Cairo in Huston's *The Maltese Falcon*. We *then* consider the reasons why some postcolonial theorists aligned with Marxism (Lazarus, Ahmed, Almond) would have major problems with what we've just done, why they rail against the "*culturalist* emphasis in postcolonial studies" (Lazarus 2004a: 9), why they think the hybrid intermingling of poststructuralist, postmodernist, and postcolonial theory destroys the very possibility of intellectual *critique* in the sense that Marxism inherits from the Enlightenment. We close, however, by giving Foucault the final word, and his final word is, once again, "Nietzsche."

Lesson 10: "One is not born a woman"—*on making the world queerer than ever*

The lead sentence for this lesson is, of course, from Simone de Beauvoir's *The Second Sex* (while the subtitle hails from Michael Warner's introduction to *Fear of a Queer Planet*). The lesson begins by considering a quite recent objection to Beauvoir's axiom, articulated by Francine du Plessix Gray in the pages of the *New York Times*. Laying waste to Gray's objection, and to other similarly clueless resistances to basic feminist analysis, allows me to pay ironic homage to Cleanth Brooks by posting four "articles of faith" in what I call "My (male feminist) Credo." Here, I argue that to become not a woman, but a feminist theorist, one must learn:

1. *To become relentlessly anti-essentialist, except when it's "strategically" interesting not to be.* (Elaborating on this article takes us to Diana Fuss, Gayle Rubin, Gayatri Spivak, Judith Butler, Martha Nussbaum *contra* Butler, etc.)
2. *To become relentlessly anti-theological: no gods (or goddesses), no masters—no exceptions.* (Elaborating on this article takes us from Marx and Nietzsche, briefly, to Hélène Cixous and Donna Haraway, at greater length.)
3. *To become relentlessly "anti-universalizing" in one's critical endeavors, except when to do so effectively disables critical endeavor.* (This article

involves an extensive and unapologetically non-historicizing critique of Chandra Mohanty's "Under Western Eyes: Feminist Scholarship and Colonial Discourses".)

4. *To do one's part to help "make the world queerer than ever."*

The last "article of faith" takes us directly to the lesson's second section, called "The Future is Kid's Stuff" (after Lee Edelman). The section begins with Gayle Rubin's assessment of the analytical limitations of feminism in her essay "Thinking Sex," charts the way theorists like Edelman, Lauren Berlant, Michael Warner, David Halperin, Eve Sedgwick, Carla Freccero, and others have redefined and redeployed the word "queer," and ends with an extensive consideration of Edelman's rudely worded and identity-disturbing critique of "reproductive futurism" in his incomparably "negative" *No Future: Queer Theory and the Death Drive.*

The last lesson, and the book itself, would thus seem to end on a note of death and destruction. But the book also ends with my resurrection of the claim, first made in the introductory chapter, that theoretical writing, as a vital mode of *writing against*, is not only "not dead," but will most likely "live forever"—or at least, for as long as "the humanities" remain an ongoing concern within a recognizably human reality. For as Jean-Michel Rabaté puts it in his book *The Future of Theory*, theory is that relentless kind of writing that "never stops coming back" (2002: 10).

In the end, *Ten Lessons* is a textbook that never stops coming back to "the basics" of literary theory; it is written to serve as a stylistically performative introduction to the most fundamental assumptions, motivations, tenets, and terminologies of theoretical writing. In other words, believe it or not, *Ten Lessons* is written to *give pleasure*. Of course, the book's overarching aims are pedagogical; these are indeed *lessons* that are made of *sentences* that are written to be *studied*. But these sentences are written quite particularly for those diligent students who can delight in difficult instruction, who can engage in close but identity-disturbing reading, who are capable of learning to relish the experience of letting their common-sense perceptions and assumptions be completely shattered and undermined, and who may be willing to risk "losing their religion" in order to find what they might not have otherwise known they had—not exactly the courage of their convictions, but, as Nietzsche somewhere puts it, the courage for an *attack* on all their convictions.

In other words, the sentences in this book are written for "good students" who aren't so thoroughly "good" that they can't finally bring themselves to "give way to literature." On the one hand, though clearly "instructional," *Ten Lessons* is not written as a facilely commodified "user-friendly guide" to theory or as an overly convenient theoretical "tool-box." On the other hand, while not without its practical uses, the book *is* written to be enjoyed, even if "enjoyment" of the sort *this* writing aspires to provide proves arduous and unsettling. As a professor of theory, I hope that you'll learn to enjoy the genuine difficulties, the "provocative and perverse challenge[s]" (Jameson 2009: 4), of this genre of writing. As a theoretical writer, I hope that you'll simply like the writing itself, that you'll end up falling for it, that "for some reason or another" you'll value it highly. As one animal at the mercy of language writing to another, I hope you'll find "something worth reading" in these *Ten Lessons in Theory*.

Introductory Matters: What Theory Does, Why Theory Lives

I. "Theory is [undead] everywhere"

On the first page of his book *The Literary in Theory*, veteran theorist Jonathan Culler takes up the question of his discipline's decline. Acknowledging that "the heyday of so-called high theory" is over, Culler concedes that "the activities that have come to answer to the nickname *theory* are no longer the latest thing in the humanities" (2007: 1).

Most up-to-date observers in and of the humanities would agree with Culler's assessment. Some have concluded, and not exactly sadly, that theory has had it, that "theory is dead" (2007: 1). Others—who had never been all that fond of "the activities" Culler designates anyway—no doubt believe that "this thing called theory" (Surin 2011: 6) never should have "lived" in the first place, that "the thing" never should have gained its prominence in literary studies, much less its supposed dominance of the field. Thus, Kenneth Surin, reporting on theory's present condition in a special issue of the *South Atlantic Quarterly* entitled "Theory Now," describes the current academic situation in terms of a "presumed or merely posited 'after' of theory, now fashionable in certain parts of the profession (as in 'the days of theory are over, so let's get back to doing literary studies in a way that really focuses on novels, plays, and poems, etc.')." Surin also describes the long-smoldering "ressentiment of intellectual conservatives who detest theory because for them it ensued in the alleged sidelining of Sophocles, Shakespeare, Goethe, and so on (as in 'how dare you place this Egyptian or Pakistani novelist in the same literary-analytical framework as Faulkner or Günter Grass?')" (2011: 3).

Here, Surin alerts us to two related aspects of the death-wish against theory—theory-haters hate theory and are more than happy to think it dead because "the thing" in its heyday debased, degraded, or "decentered" literary studies, spoiling intellectually conservative parties either by taking the focus away from novels, poems, and plays *as* novels, poems, and plays (in order to harp on "non-literary" matters such as popular culture, identity politics, class struggle, etc.), or by staying more or less *in* the literary ballpark, but sidelining the canonical figures of Great Literature's all-star team (Surin's famously named white male players), sticking in a slew of non-white and perhaps non-male "others" in their stead (Surin's unnamed and ungendered Egyptians and Pakistanis).

But let's not fail to mention a third, "aesthetic" or "stylistic" factor in the longstanding resentment against theory—the obstreperous complaints about the sheer ugliness of theoretical writing, its abrasively off-putting opacity, its outrageous dependence on "specialized terminology," on bloated and clunky "in-group jargon," cumbersome "critical keywords" such as "defamiliarization" and "reification" that not only sound unlovely to belletristic ears but refuse all nimble definition.

Little wonder, then, given such unforgiven trespasses against all the finer things in academic life, if no few "intellectual conservatives" think their world a better place for theory's being dead. But while the actual extent of its dominion over literary studies, or the exact duration of its heyday, or the aesthetic or even ethical value of its stylistic infractions against clarity and grace may all be open to debate, it's surely premature for intellectuals of any stripe to mourn or celebrate the expiration of theory, to wring or clap our hands about theory's demise. Like it or not, "the thing" still lives. Theory persists. Theory abides. Granted, the activities that answer to the nickname "theory" may no longer be the *latest* thing in the humanities, but they do seem to have become *lasting* things. They endure—though not, let's note, as stony monuments of unageing intellect or otherwise solidified *things* (after all, resisting so-called **reification** remains one of theory's most vital and pressing assignments). Rather, theoretical activities continue as, precisely, *activities*, actions, restlessly critical *procedures* producing "insights which completely shatter and undermine our common perceptions" (Žižek 2006: ix). Extending its shelf-life beyond any number of sell-by dates, theory survives as a battery of disturbing *questions*, an unsettled and unsettling set of strategies for enabling what Culler calls "reflection on meaning as a problem rather than a given" (2007: 85).[1]

---

[1] **Reification** (from *res*, Latin for *thing*) is a Marxist term designating "the way that commodification reduces social relations, ideas, and even people to things" (Parker 2008: 193). Theoretical writing exposes and opposes this baleful reduction to commodified thing-iness and attempts, against heavy odds, to rescue itself and its objects of analysis from reification, to keep itself *unreified*. For some theoretical writers, this effort against reification actually *constitutes* "theory" as such. In *Dialectic of Enlightenment*, one of the founding documents of contemporary critical theory, Horkheimer and Adorno write that "Intellect's true concern is a negation of reification. It must perish when it is solidified into a cultural asset and handed out for consumption purposes. The flood of precise information and brand-new amusements make [*sic*] people smarter and more stupid at once" (1947/2002: xvii). More recently, in *Valences of the Dialectic*, Fredric

Given reasonable suspicion that "meaning" may never cease to be a "problem," given reasonable confidence that there will never spring from the earth nor fall from the sky some "completely meaningful" and universally satisfying answer that would lay all critical inquiry to eternal rest, given reasonable doubt that "common sense, or even reification itself, can ever permanently be dissipated" (Jameson 2009: 4), one might brashly forecast that "this thing called theory" will go on forever—or at least, for as long as "the humanities" remain an ongoing concern within a recognizably human reality. For even if "theory itself is [no longer] seen as the cutting edge . . . of literary and cultural studies," even if theory is no longer considered "prominent as a vanguard movement" within these fields, the fields themselves nonetheless "take place within a space articulated by theory, or theories, theoretical discourses, theoretical debates." Those of us who still work "in the humanities" are "ineluctably in theory," as Culler writes, for in the humanities, "theory is everywhere" (2007: 3, 2). Or, as Jean-Michel Rabaté puts it in his book *The Future of Theory*, "theory never stops coming back" (2002: 10).

Far from having kicked the bucket, then, theory is resolutely *undead*, permanently relevant and perpetually revenant—if not "everywhere" that

Jameson writes "that theory is to be grasped as the perpetual and impossible attempt to dereify the language of thought, and to preempt all the systems and ideologies which inevitably result from the establishment of this or that fixed terminology." And yet, because the working lexicon of any theory can coagulate into a "fixed terminology"— the word "reification" has, for example, a specific and precise, if not "fixedly" *economic* meaning in the language of Marxist thought—Jameson warns that any "theoretical process of undoing terminologies [can], by virtue of the elaboration of the terminology that very process requires, become . . . an ideology in its own turn and congeal into the very type of system it sought to undermine." Thus, Jameson notes "the hopelessness of the nonetheless unavoidable aim of theoretical writing to escape the reifications [and] commodifications of the intellectual marketplace today" (2009: 9). As these two examples of "theoretical writing" *qua* writing against reification should suggest, to say that theory was ever "the latest *thing* in the humanities" or to characterize theory, as I have above, in the mercantile terms of "shelf-life" and "sell-by dates" is to leave it open to the charge of having failed to stay frosty against reification, as if theory had never been anything more than a steaming chunk of cultural capital, a hotly commodified intellectual amusement, rather like a computer game requiring "advanced" skills, but very little wisdom, a product making "consumers" (teachers and students) at once "smarter" (more technically savvy) and "stupider" (less perceptive about their actual conditions of existence, and hence more compliant with the dominant—reified and reifying—social order). As for theory's hopeful project of successfully "dereifying the language of thought," Jameson soberly suggests that "theory" cannot "expect to supplant the multitudinous forms of reified thinking and named and commodified thoughts on the intellectual marketplace today, but only to wage persistent and local guerilla warfare against their hegemony" (2009: 61).

can be imagined, then at least in and to "the humanities" as they are still being imagined and re-imagined. For in Culler's words:

> the position of theory as an institutional and disciplinary presence now seems well established in the American university . . . It now seems widely accepted that any intellectual project has a basis in theory of some sort, that graduate students need to be aware of theoretical debates in their fields and able to situate themselves and their work within the changing intellectual structures of the professional landscape, and that theory, far from being 'too difficult' for undergraduates, is the sort of thing they ought to explore as one of the most exciting and socially pertinent dimensions of the humanities. (Culler 2011: 224)

This book hopes to serve participants in the humanities at all levels as both an introduction and an inducement to theoretical writing *as* writing against reification, writing against the commodification of writing and of thought. Of course, resisting the commodification *of* writing *in* writing isn't particularly easy these days, especially not if one feels compelled, for professional reasons, to present the putative resistance in a commodified form—to publish, that is, one's writing as a book that one "naturally" hopes will be commercially successful, that is, "widely adopted" as a textbook. And of course, there are many textbooks, many introductions and inducements to theory, available in "the intellectual marketplace today" (Jameson 2009: 61). Most of these begin with matters of definition; they attempt to describe *what theory is* and to provide an historical narrative about how this thing came to be such a strong (or insidious) "institutional and disciplinary presence." In this introduction, however, we'll be concerned less with *what theory is* and more with *what theory does*. Our most vital concern will be with the question of *why theory lives* or *why theory matters*, why theory excitingly pertains not only to students "of the humanities," but to all "the undead"—to everyone, that is, who still actively participates in our specifically human reality, if only in the *spectral* form of writing.

Culler, for one, writes that theory can be understood as an interdisciplinary "genre of works," as a "name for a mixture of philosophy, psychoanalysis, linguistics, aesthetics, poetics, and political and social thought" (2011: 230). But again, we might more productively understand theoretical writing less as an institutionally generic *thing* (even an academically mixed-up thing) than as an "exciting and socially pertinent" intellectual *activity*. For Culler, *what theory is* is the activity of "thinking about thinking"; correspondingly, in his words, the "impetus to theory is a desire to understand what one is doing" *when one is thinking.* Culler thinks that theory, as a particularly challenging way of "thinking about thinking,"

> is driven by the impossible desire to step outside one's thought, both to place it and to understand it, and also by a desire—a possible desire—for change, both in the ways of one's own thought, which always could be sharper, more knowledgeable and capacious, more self-reflecting, and in the world our thought engages. (2011: 224–5)

Here, Culler's thinking (about thinking) about theory in terms of a desire for *change* "in the ways of one's own thought" might make one think of the following bit of wisdom from Michel Foucault—"There are times in life when the question of knowing if one can think differently than one thinks and perceive differently than one sees is absolutely necessary if one is to go on looking and reflecting at all" (1986: 7). But thinking about theoretical writing in terms of desire for change—change not simply in our own individual modes of cognition *but "in the world" itself*—might also bring to mind the revolutionary slogan carved in marble at the tomb of Karl Marx—"The philosophers have only *interpreted* the world, in various ways; the point, however, is to *change* it" (1845/1978: 145). Culler's thinking, however, leads him to quote a somewhat more densely packed sentence from Michael Hardt, who, in an essay called "The Militancy of Theory," writes that "the task of theory is *to make* the present and thus to . . . invent the subject of that making, a 'we' characterized not only by our belonging to the present but by our making it" (2011: 21). Culler goes on to suggest that Hardt here "makes explicit what is only implicit in a lot of theory: the attempt to produce a collective subject, a 'we,' through argument about how things should be conceived or understood" (2011: 225).

Now, while Hardt clearly owes his theoretical militancy both to Marx and to Foucault, his quoted *sentence* might require a bit more "unpacking" than either one of theirs. And indeed we'll be returning throughout this book to the question of what it might mean to argue (1) that what Hardt calls "the present" is never simply *given* but must always be *made*; (2) that a collectively subjective "we" both *belongs to* and is *responsible for* making "the present" historical moment; (3) that the "we" in question must itself be *invented* or *produced*; and (4) that theoretical writing is somehow constitutively involved in this vital activity or *task*, this job of *our* self-actualizing "the world," of our restlessly *producing the very subject of human reality*—in other words, "ourselves."

As I said, Hardt's sentence calls for some strenuous and extended unpacking. Here, though, let's linger on that last phrase from Culler concerning the desired "production" of this collective subject, a certain "we ourselves" that somehow gets produced "through argument about how things should be conceived or understood," and let's ask ourselves how, in theory, things arguably *should* be conceived or understood. What's the difference, after all, between the way things *should* theoretically be conceived or understood and the *normal* or *given* way in which things *are* commonly conceived or understood? Moreover, how does our recognizing this difference—this discrepancy between the good or rich or productive understanding that arguably *should be* and the bad or impoverished or reified understanding that commonly *is*—impel us toward what Slavoj Žižek is happy to call "insights which completely shatter and undermine our common perceptions" (2006: ix)? What allows a theoretical writer like Žižek to propose that "our common perceptions" really *should be* "short-circuited," as he puts it, that they really *ought* to be utterly shattered and undermined?[2]

These questions bring us back to the matter of "reification," as that crucial term is defined above, and to Horkheimer and Adorno's insistence that the "true concern" of any bona fide theoretical work is "the negation of reification" (1947/2002: xvii). For theorists like Žižek and Hardt, who write in the critical tradition of Horkheimer and Adorno, of Marx and of Foucault, "reification" and its "common-sense" confederates pose fairly formidable obstacles to theory's most militant task, diligently working to try to block "our" collective and transformative remaking of the present historical moment. For whenever "we" find ourselves doing the business of "thinking" within an utterly reified social order—the current global capitalist "mode of production," for example, "a world in which corporate Capital [has] succeeded in penetrating and dominating the very fantasy-kernel of our being" (Žižek 1993: 10)—chances are mighty high that "our common perceptions" of that social order, not to mention of "our being," will be pretty much "reified" themselves, and thus the odds of our finding ways to think or dream or use our critical imaginations *against* that order can grow quite dismally slim. Arguably, our habitual tendency to conceive or understand "things as they are" in our given human reality *as things*—specifically, as *commodities* to be purchased (if only we can afford them), and not as productively human and collectively humanizing

---

[2] Žižek explains that "a short circuit occurs when there is a faulty connection in the network—faulty, of course, from the standpoint of the network's smooth functioning. Is not the shock of short-circuiting, therefore, one of the best metaphors for a critical reading?" This critical short-circuiting, writes Žižek, "is what Marx, among others, did with philosophy and religion" and "what Freud and Nietzsche did with morality." Žižek writes that "the aim of such an approach is . . . the inherent decentering of the interpreted text, which brings to light its 'unthought,' its disavowed presuppositions and consequences" (2006: ix).

processes—Is symptomatic of "our" pervasive cognitive and affective reification today. For are we not commonly "encouraged" by "corporate Capital" to conceive absolutely "everything" imaginable in commodified or globally "free market" terms, and to perceive "ourselves," in our very being, as primarily and essentially *consumers* (with or without purchasing power) rather than as subjectively collective *makers* of the present, much less as "citizens of the world" empowered and engendered by the work of our own self-reflective understanding?

Theory, as Culler notes, is indeed driven by the desire for *change* both *in* ourselves and *of* "the world," and so the *task* of theory, as Hardt insists, is indeed to *make* the present—or better, to participate in the radical transformation of the present by negating regnant reifications, by working to shatter and undermine our common and congealed perceptions, particularly the all too common-sense view that "we ourselves" are not the actual (and sole) producers of our present (and future) human realities but merely passive consumers of "things as they are," customers who are "always right" (to think of themselves as customers) and who are thus all too well accustomed to taking or buying into "the world" *as given.*

II. The problem with givens

Describing what he calls "the duty of the critical intellectual," and using the words "theory" and "philosophy" more or less interchangeably, Žižek writes that

> philosophy begins the moment we do not accept what exists as given ("It's like that!", "Law is law!", etc.), but raise the question of how is what we encounter as actual also possible. What characterizes philosophy is this "step back" from actuality into possibility . . . Theory involves the power to abstract from our starting point in order to reconstruct it subsequently on the basis of its presuppositions, its transcendental "conditions of possibility." (1993: 2)

Žižek, then, would pretty much agree with Culler's point that theory's central task is to reflect "on meaning as a problem rather than a given" (Culler 2007: 85). But how might this job-description relate to the more militant claim that theory's most serious business is negating reification? Since both activities would seem to constitute the real *work* of theoretical writing, shouldn't we ask how reflecting on "meaning as a problem rather than a given" and "negating reification" might be practically related? The quickest answer to this question would of course be that "taking meaning as a given" essentially *equals* accepting or "buying into" reification. But since we wouldn't be doing our homework if we were simply to accept that quick answer, take that neat equation as a given, we must rather address it as a problem, must explore its problematic "conditions of possibility."

To proceed with this labor, let's put aside the term "reification" for the moment and focus instead on this tension between "the given" and "the problematic" in the general field of "meaning." What might it mean to reflect on "meaning" as a problem rather than a given? What might it mean to take some specific instance of meaning "as a given" in the first place? Well, even in our common understanding, wouldn't our accepting any piece of meaning as "a given" actually mean our taking its "actuality" pretty easily, with little or no questioning about its conditions of possibility? And wouldn't that "easiness" entail that the more we take a particular piece of "meaning" as "a given," the *fewer* the questions we're likely to raise about it? What "given meanings" would thus seem to *be* given, whenever such easy reception prevails, is a facile sort of freedom from analysis, a reprieve from "thinking about thinking," a sort of well-lubricated immunity from any abrasive "problematization."

In theory, however, no meaning should ever be taken as a given. No piece of meaning, no particular idea, ever gets a free pass. Or, paradoxically, the only idea that might safely be taken as a given is the idea that *no* idea should ever be so taken. The only idea that isn't open to question, the only idea that isn't problematic, is the idea that *any* idea can and *should* be frequently and vigorously problematized, if not completely shattered and undermined.

But let's consider a specific example of a "given" whose license to be taken as "given" theoretical writing has attempted to revoke. For quite some time, "in the humanities" and elsewhere, it was pretty much taken as a given that the word "Man" simply meant all the human beings in the history of the world—the total "horizon of humanity," as Jacques Derrida once put it (1972: 116). The usage ranges from early to late modernity, from Prince Hamlet's "what a piece of work is man" (*Hamlet* 2.2. 303) to Karl Marx's "man makes religion; religion does not make man" (1844/1978: 53) to astronaut Neil Armstrong's moonwalking soliloquy describing, albeit somewhat confusingly, "one small step for man, one giant leap for mankind." The "given" here is (or maybe *was*) that the word "Man" could self-confidently represent *all* human beings *universally*—even though, at any given time, well over half the human beings in the world aren't exactly men, and even though only a minority of actual men resemble the generically "Anglo-European" image that tends to be conjured by the word "Man."[3] Our taking this "blanched" meaning of the word "Man" as "a given" has always tended to involve "our" either ignoring these contradictions or not seeing them as causing "us" any problems.

Another example—for some time, "in the humanities" and elsewhere, it was taken as a given that the word "Woman" could be deployed to designate not some individual woman or the entirety of the human group "women" (and not, to be sure, "the total horizon of humanity") but rather some universal and eternal "essence" of "womanliness" or "femininity." *This* meaning of the word "Woman" could be taken as a given despite rather glaringly evident tensions between this "essential" determination "Woman" (which for some reason usually involved such dispositions as passivity, masochism, or infinite willingness to self-sacrifice) and the characteristics, situations, experiences, or desires of actual women.

Considering these two examples together, then, we might belabor the obvious—that the heretofore "given" meanings of "Man" and "Woman" have involved a pervasive inequality, that what this particular "given" has historically given "us" is the strong impression that the phrase "Man and Woman" has always meant and should forever inevitably mean the hierarchical difference between the one's taking giant steps and the other's being stepped on or over. In other words, here the "given meaning" has done its bit to "naturalize" or "inevitable-ize" or "eternalize" systemic male dominance, sexism, racism, and so on. If the situation today has to some extent been altered—at least "in the humanities," if not elsewhere, and thanks mainly to feminist, postcolonial, and critical race theorists—then the words "Man" and "Woman" are no longer employed quite so facilely in these **essentialized** senses, no longer taken quite so broadly as givens.[4]

As these examples suggest, *what theory does* when reflecting on meaning as a problem rather than a given is to foreground the *contradictions* embedded in the "meaning" under consideration. We might note, for another example, a contradiction in Culler's very phrase, for arguably one *actively reflects* on "meaning" *only* as a problem—that is, *critically* "reflecting on" and "problematizing" are pretty much the same procedure—whereas

---

[3] In *The Location of Culture*, Homi Bhabha nicely specifies one of the key differences between "Man" and actual men by rewriting the phrase "almost the same, but not quite" as "almost the same, but not white" (1994: 89).

[4] In *Essentially Speaking: Feminism, Nature, Difference*, Diana Fuss describes **essentialism** as "belief in the real, true essence of things, the invariable and fixed properties which define the 'whatness' of a given entity." For feminist theory, essentialism involves "the idea that men and women . . . are identified as such on the basis of transhistorical, eternal, immutable essences." Theory is "anti-essentialist" in that it rejects "any attempts to naturalize human nature" (1989: xi).

to take meaning "as a given" is precisely *not* to reflect *on* it but merely to *reflect* it, to repeat and reproduce it, like a mirror, without question, without *friction*. In this sense, a successfully "given" meaning is (rather like a sexually transmitted disease) the gift that keeps on giving. If I myself should take some piece of meaning as given, I will probably expect you to partake as well, to "repeat after me," to join me as I have joined others in a reified set of "common perceptions," a coagulated sort of "common sense," "a stagnant confirmation of inherited thinking, its presuppositions, and its dogma" (Derrida 2008: 120).

Theory, however, isn't going to take it. In *actively* reflecting on meaning as problem, theoretical writing attempts to disrupt or short circuit the reproduction of "common sense." Theory, writes Culler, must always engage in the "critique of common sense, of concepts taken as natural" (1997: 15). Theoretical writers in fact decline to take *any* human activity "naturally," for "as long as one assumes that what one does is natural it is difficult to gain any understanding of it" (Culler 1975: 129). And, as Michael Bérubé has recently put it, "It is very difficult to get a man to understand something when his tribal sense of his identity depends on his not understanding it. But," Bérubé adds, "there are few tasks so urgent" (2011: 74) for theoretical writers and readers—few tasks so urgent or so arduous as trying to get ourselves to understand arguments that our "tribal" or inherited sense of identity, our stable or "naturalized" common sense, necessitates our *not* understanding. Fredric Jameson thus writes of the daunting "un-naturality" of theoretical writing, "its provocative and perverse challenge to common sense as such" (2009: 4). Abrading, then, any and all "natural" or common-sense assumptions, theoretical writing promotes instead an unnatural and uncommon sensibility, an extraordinary or even *anti-ordinary* understanding. Theory, that is, endeavors to **defamiliarize** all the settled normalities of the given world.[5] And this "creative abrasion" (Hall 2003: 71) of "common sense" constitutes the primary reason theoretical writing isn't often "easily understood"— theoretical writing is by definition *hostile* to "normal" understanding and to

---

[5] For Russian formalist Victor Shklovsky, **defamiliarization** (*ostranenie*, or "making strange") defines not theoretical writing but *literary* discourse as such. For Shklovsky, whose 1917 essay "Art as Technique" we'll consider more thoroughly in Lesson Seven, literature "defamiliarizes" in that it "disrupts ordinary language and habitual modes of perception." The term describes "literature's ability to disrupt through its representation of reality the dominant ideas of society" (Childers and Hentzi 1995: 76). For Shklovsky, "defamiliarization" pertains to "literature" and not "theory" per se, but contemporary theoretical writers often employ this word to argue that theoretical writing performs the most radical *work* of literature, as for example, when Jameson writes that the aim of theoretical writing is "to defamiliarize our ordinary habits of mind and to make us suddenly conscious not only of our own . . . obtuseness but also of the strangeness of reality as such" (2009: 50).

the familiar versions of "the normal world" such understanding attempts to secure, and this very hostility makes it difficult for us to *be* secure in our understanding of theory.[6]

We'll return to the matter of theory's alienating "difficulty" anon. Here, though, let's pause to mull over yet another contradiction—this one located in my *own* exposition of theory's self-reflections. A moment ago, I gave you "Man" and "Woman" as examples of meanings that had until recently been taken as givens in the humanities but that had gotten themselves roundly "problematized" at the hands of "high theory." My intent was to offer the following as quick examples of theoretical "problematizations" of these given terms.

In regard to "Man," I intended to quote from the final pages of *The Order of Things: An Archeology of the Human Sciences*, where Michel Foucault writes that "man is neither the oldest nor the most constant problem that has been posed for human knowledge," that "man is an invention of recent date," that the invented convention of man is "perhaps nearing its end," and that the figure of man will someday "be erased, like a face drawn in sand at the edge of the sea" (1966/1973: 386, 387). But I intended to stress that when Foucault heralds the erasure of "man," he isn't predicting or calling for the extinction of the human species; rather, Foucault is signaling that a particular figure of meaning that had for some time been taken as *the* most central and meaningful figure in "the human sciences" and in **humanism** in general now no longer could or should be.[7]

Regarding "Woman," I intended to point out that when Jacques Lacan proclaims that "Woman does not exist" (1975/1998: 7) he is not insanely positing that there are no *women* in the world. Rather, he is asserting

---

[6] To make this difficult point more or less understandable, let's borrow and alter some language from Jean-Luc Nancy and write that "If the strictest [and strangest] formulations of [theory] often inspire perplexity, annoyance, and refusal, it is because . . . these formulations . . . wish to make understood that they cannot be, as they are, understood by [our normal] understanding, but rather demand that [such] understanding relinquish itself." (2002: 63) Nancy's language will appear again in unaltered form in a footnote in Lesson Six.

[7] Childers and Hentzi write that "in current critical debates **humanism** usually refers to an anthropocentric view of the world that asserts the existence of a universal human nature informing all actions and decisions." (1995: 140) "Anti-humanist" theorists don't hate humans, but question the existence of any such "universal human nature" or at least reject "Man" as this universal's standard-bearer. Specifically, "feminists, black activist, postcolonial critics, and gay and lesbian critics have argued that the 'man' at the heart of humanism is not free of the limitations of limiting interests resulting from the specifics of a particular gender, class, race, or sexual orientation; on the contrary, this 'man' is male, white, middle-class, Anglo, and heterosexual. For these [anti-humanist] critics, the attempt to pass off such a limited viewpoint as universal is covertly, if not overtly, oppressive." (1995: 141) Anti-humanist writing thus desires, as Derrida puts it, to "pass beyond man and humanism" (1966/1978: 292).

that "Woman"—specifically, *the* eternally, masochistically self-sacrificing Woman—is "essentially" a fiction, if not a pathologically self-serving male fantasy.[8] I also intended to explain that when Monique Wittig avers that a "lesbian" is "*not* a woman" (1981/2007: 1642), she doesn't mean that "lesbians" are not "chromosomally female" or don't "have vaginas," and so on and so forth, but rather that "woman" is a *political* category invented by men for the purpose of maintaining systemic male dominance, and that lesbians, by definition, refuse the category as well as the system (not to mention the men).

But here's the problem. By introducing these particular examples, I basically wanted to tout my investment in feminist, psychoanalytic, and queer disturbances of the "given" meanings of gender and sexuality as among the most excitingly and politically pertinent *activities* that theoretical writing brings to the table. And yet, in the very gesture of offering these examples, I unintentionally reproduced one of the primary "givens" of masculinist privilege itself. I trotted out "Man" *first*, because, for some strange reason, that example *occurred* to me first. And in maintaining this particular order of introduction, I unconsciously repeated—and effectively reinforced or "re-reified"—an ancient order of male priority, a dogmatic fable as old as Adam. In attempting, that is, to *conscientiously* reflect on "Man" as a problem rather than a given, I *unconsciously* reflected "Man" as *the* given rather than as an outdated problem.

Now, upon recognizing my own *complicity* with the very order of systemic male privilege and priority that I was ostensibly writing against, I could have easily revised my writing, resituated the examples, let "Woman" come first, given Wittig the first or only words, and so on. I could have neatly hidden the traces of my being unconsciously in cahoots with patriarchy, and no reader of my work would have been any the wiser. But since I should aspire to make my readers at least somewhat wiser—or, since theory's purpose is to "negate reification," and reification can be defined not only as commodified "thingification" but "as the removal of traces of production from the product" (Jameson 2010: 124)—I've chosen to let these infelicitous "traces of production" stand and to call your attention to them. I do so not to make myself momentarily look "bad" for having made the mistake and then "good" for having "politically corrected" it but rather to attempt further to illuminate *what theory does*, to describe theoretical activities while attempting in the process to *do* some theory, to attend to a contradiction and elucidate (but not exactly solve) a problem. "Theory," writes Culler, "is reflexive, thinking about

---

[8] In *Mythologies*, Roland Barthes diagnoses what he calls "this disease of thinking in essences, which is at the bottom of every bourgeois mythology of man" (1957/1985: 75).

thinking, enquiry into the categories we use in making sense of things, in literature and in other discursive practices" (1997: 15). But theoretical writing is also always necessarily *self*-reflexive critique; it devotes considerable energy to thinking about (its own thinking about) thinking. Reflecting on meaning as problem rather than as naturalized given, theoretical writing is given or driven not only to reflect upon but also to interrogate, if not to torture, its own reflections—apparently to cause yet more problems.

But why keep causing problems? Why this endless "problematization" of "meanings" that might just as well be taken for granted? Why not let just a few things go without saying? Why keep trying to make sense (or mincemeat) of the categories we use to make sense of things? Why not just keep using these categories if they have heretofore served us well? In regard to "literature and other discursive practices," why all the "complicated fuss about things that really should be simply consumed" (Culler 2007: 251) or unproblematically enjoyed? Why not simply relish reading for the sake of reading, literature for the sake of literature? Why not gratefully accept "the pleasure of the text" as *gift*, pure and simple?

A short response to these questions would be that there is really no such thing as *pure* enjoyment, or *simple* pleasure, much less *simple* meaning, for any specifically human being. To say so is not bleakly to proclaim that there is absolutely no enjoyment, pleasure, value, or meaning ever to be had (contrary to rumor, that is, theory is not a thoroughly anhedonic nihilism); rather, it is "simply" to say, with Jacques Derrida, that "things are very complicated" (1994: 110); it is "simply" to say, with Jean-Luc Nancy, that "the given *always gives itself as something other than simply given*" (2002: 52), that human experiences *qua* human are never pure or simple, if only because in reality a human being is "an animal at the mercy of language" (Lacan 1966e/2006: 525) and "language being what it is, we shall find nothing simple in it" (Saussure 1959: 122). In other words, given this radical *absence* of simplicity in language, given the irremediable *loss* of immediately natural life for any speaking being as such, the *gift* of the text can never be a simple *present*, for "what opens meaning and language is writing as the disappearance of natural presence" (Derrida 1967/1997: 159). Or, in the words of Marjorie Garber:

> Language is not a secondary but a primary constituent of human nature . . . Language is not transparent, though fantasies of its transparency, its merely denotative role, have always attracted and misled some of its users, both writers and readers. (2003/2008: 437–8)

So much, then, for any short sweet reply to the question of simple enjoyment; evidently, a more extensive response is needed. And indeed, this more extensive response, which must account for *why* all of the preceding might actually be the case, which must explain *why* writing involves the disappearance of natural presence, why simplicity has gone forever missing from language, why speaking can be said to necessitate a loss of immediacy, why the transparency of language is an attractive but misleading fantasy, why the terms "human," "being," "meaning," "nature," "presence," "language," "text," "writers," "readers," "enjoyment," and so on, must all ceaselessly be called into complicated question—"dereified into a complex set of human acts" (Jameson 2009: 47) rather than simply taken as natural givens—will take up the remainder of *Ten Lessons in Theory*.

III. Just being difficult/difficultly being just

If language itself "is not transparent," as Marjorie Garber stresses, theoretical writing is rather notoriously not so even more so, and in his introduction to *Critical Terms for Literary Study*, Thomas McLaughlin provides some clear and compelling explanations for theory's abrasive complexities and opacities. McLaughlin writes that "the very project of theory is unsettling. It brings assumptions into question. It creates more problems than it solves. And, to top it off, it does so in what is often a forbidding and arcane style." But McLaughlin maintains that "theory isn't difficult out of spite." Rather, theoretical writing is always rough going

> because it has proceeded on the premise that language itself ought to be its focus of attention; that ordinary language is an embodiment of an extremely powerful and usually unquestioned system of values and beliefs; and that using ordinary language catches you up in that system. Any discourse that was to uncover and question that system had to find a language, a style, that broke from the constraints of common sense and ordinary language. Theory set out to produce texts that could not be processed successfully by the commonsensical assumptions that ordinary language puts into play. There are texts of theory that resist meaning so powerfully . . . that the very process of failing to comprehend the text is part of what it has to offer. (1995: 2)

For Culler, as we've seen, *what theory does* is reflect on meaning as a problem rather than a given. McLaughlin, however, puts Culler's case more strongly, asserting that theoretical texts do not merely *reflect* on meaning but sometimes go so far as to "powerfully" *resist* it. And these texts don't just resist some specific *instance* of meaning; rather, theoretical texts "resist meaning" altogether, resist meaning *itself*. They attempt to break free from those "constraints of common sense and ordinary language" that systematically regulate the ostensible given-ness of meaning, that work to make sure "our common perceptions" pretty much *stay* common. Theoretical texts attempt to liberate us as readers from these commonly normative constraints since our very use of ordinary language is said to catch us up in this disciplinary system. Moreover, in their attempted break with conventionalized meaning, these texts endeavor to provoke in their readers a salutary *failure* to comprehend the very discourses that are offered up for comprehension. Promising a strange sort of freedom through cognitive failure, theoretical texts attempt to engage us in what Gayatri Spivak calls "moments of productive bafflement" (1999: 273).

Should readers, then, take these baffling texts up on their offers and feel licensed to give up even trying to comprehend their meanings? By no means, for the unsettling "freedom through failure" of which I write above has nothing to do with the normalizing "freedom from analysis" to which I earlier alluded. Theory, that is, never gets us out of *work*, never frees us from the responsibility to *read*. Even in their most rebarbative moments of unreadability, theoretical texts mean not to repel readers but rather to *encourage* us to take the risk of getting caught up in the potentially productive process of unsuccessful processing. Theoretical writing offers us the opportunity to reflect not only on comprehensible meaning but on the very conventions of comprehension that make "meaning itself" possible. Ceaselessly questioning what it means to mean, theory provocatively and perversely encourages us to challenge "the categories we use in making sense of things" (Culler 1997: 15), to inquire into the origin of these categories and of our places within them, to ask about *their* conditions of possibility as well as our own. Theory encourages such inquiry even if it involves the risk of comprehensive failure, the risk of "not getting it," of losing certainty, losing "clarity," losing the ability to "make sense" in the ways to which we're *normally* accustomed, the ways in which we've in fact been *formally* trained. I repeat the word "encourages" here because I believe it requires something like courage to go against one's training, to risk losing or disrupting one's ability to "make sense of things" in one's accustomed or inherited or "tribal" ways. But what makes the risk worth taking is the possibility of discovering new and different ways of making sense of things—of the world, of the text, of oneself, of one's life—in this "unprocessable" process. For once again, "There are times in life when the question of knowing if one can think differently than one thinks and perceive differently than one sees is absolutely necessary if one is to go on looking and reflecting at all" (Foucault 1986: 7).

Before going on with these reflections, however, I'd like to touch on two theses regarding the way theoretical writing disturbs our normal procedures of "making sense" and provokes us to "think differently," to see "things as they are" otherwise. The first thesis—to my mind, a permanently and radically "de-reifying" one—is that "sense" must indeed always be *made,* must always be fashioned or fabricated or produced, and by none other than our own all-too-human hands. Making sense—like "making the present" in Michael Hardt's theoretically militant sense—is nothing if not human labor; human reality is nothing if not a piece of *work.* To employ a sentence from Stuart Hall that will be put to much more strenuous labor in this book's first lesson—"The world must be made to mean" (1998: 1050), which means that neither "sense" nor "meaning" ever grows on trees or falls from the sky, that there's nothing "natural" or "supernatural" about these phenomena. To be sure, *common* sense and *given* meaning have often relied upon ideas of "nature" and/or the Deity to guarantee, legitimate, or otherwise prop up their own reproduction, to stabilize or "fix" themselves as steadily lucid signs. Be forewarned, however, that theoretical writing constitutively refuses "nature" and "God," emphatically rejects both "biological determinism" and "divine will" as causal factors or explanatory solutions to any of the problems of human meaning. If it weren't for the fact that theoretical writing also jettisons "Man"—erasing that little stick-figure "like a face drawn in sand at the edge of the sea" (Foucault 1966/1973: 387)—we might say that theory is a form of secular humanism. Of course, theory is nothing if not secular; it is "firmly and rightly committed to renewing the necessary conviction . . . that thought only begins on the further side of religion" (Gibson 2006: 5); but theoretical writing is often just as resolutely "anti-humanist" as it is decidedly "antinaturalist" and deicidally "anti-theological" (Barthes 1968/1977: 147).

Designating these antagonistic stances as such leads to my second thesis, which is that "theory" is most productively encountered as a "practice of creativity" (Foucault 1983/1997: 262) in itself, a genre of so-called creative writing, an interventional exercise in the art of the sentence. Theoretical writing, that is, warrants being read in the same "close" way that "defamiliarizingly" imaginative literature demands to be read. Indeed, the main premise of this book is that the risk we take in engaging with theoretical writing, the risk of losing the ability to "make sense of things" in our normalized, habituated ways, is intimately related to the risk we take in that "encounter with strangeness" (Bloom 1994: 3), which is (or can be) "the literary experience" itself. Theory, my friends, assumes "the world as text" (Barthes 1968/1977: 147). It engages with a world that must be made to mean as a problem to be interpreted or thought through rather than as a given that "just naturally" goes without saying. Theory is a de-reifying procedure of reading and writing that "refuses to fix meaning"

(Barthes 1968/1977: 147) and which, by virtue of that refusal, *affirms* a world that can only ever be experienced as text, affirms "the very text of your existence" (Lacan 2008: 78), affirms a subjective existence that can only ever be lived "extimately," inter-textually, as "interpretive experience" (Derrida 1988: 148).

But these affirmations can never be purely "positive." Theoretical affirmation always depends upon *active* negation. Theory, that is, *enacts* or *actualizes* itself by being antinaturalizing, anti-humanist, anti-theological, anti-essentialist, anti-normative, anti-**metaphysical**, and so on.[9] But to the extent that "negativity can be positively exhilarating" to "a properly literary understanding" (Culler 2011: 228), this actively negative dependence marks theory's radical affinity with "creative writing," with "literature." Theoretical writing, perhaps like all *actually* creative writing, only ever agonistically affirms. It must negate or say "no" to a host of "givens" in order to say "yes" to what it takes to be the fundamental problem.

But what, for theory, *is* the fundamental problem? McLaughlin has already told us by pointing out that theory's enabling premise is "that language itself ought to be its focus of attention"; he further specifies that "the *experience* of theory . . . ought to engage the reader in a struggle over language and with language" (1995: 3). But we should hastily add that much more is at stake in this "struggle over language" than just some "ivory tower" tussle with terminology. For theoretical writers, this *wordy* conflict is intimately connected to *worldly* struggles involving relations of *power*. Theoretical writing, that is, conceives and understands the fundamental problem as the human power-struggle over meaning, the conflictually "interpretive experience" of all our struggles with and over *signs*. This *agon* among animals at the mercy of language is always, at the same time, *both* a real power-struggle *and* a "matter of interpretation," for power, as theoretical writing interprets it, "is both part of material, social reality, and also available to comprehension as a profoundly complex textual structure, operating differentially and discursively" (Wolfreys 2004: 197). In examining and challenging the workings of power, theoretical writers conflate these complex textual or discursive structures with more self-evidently "real world" forms of social, economic, political, and historical striving and strife, those forms of *real* human suffering, those matters of *real* life and death, that don't "normally" seem to have much to do with sentences or textuality or

---

[9]   **Metaphysics** "usually refers to philosophical attempts to establish indisputable first principles as a foundation for all knowledge" and involves belief in "the existence of absolute entities" (Childer and Hentzi 1995: 186). Metaphysics also involves "belief in something unconditioned, i.e., something which would be true, absolutely and unconditionally, outside of all temporal and perspectival conditions" (Pearson and Large 2006: xxxi).

semiotics or **discourse**—the really important matters that "people in the real world" typically don't like being "reduced" to "mere words."[10]

For theoretical writers, however, the fundamental problem is precisely that these down-to-earth *agons* never *cease* to have to do with words, have never been *exterior* to language, are "always already" irreducibly semiotic. For theoretical writers, the struggle over meaning—a problem as old as *polis* and papyrus and as new as Derrida's "*there is nothing outside the text*" (1967/1997: 158)—is what constitutes *any* human **subject**, individual or collective, and *all* human reality *as such*.[11] Theory, that is, interprets the whole of human reality as a "signifying structure" constituting itself through the social production, proliferation, and exchange of signs. But because this totally interpretive experience of socio-symbolic reality is seen in terms of "real-world" struggles over power, most theoretical writing situates a "**political** perspective" on language, literature, and culture as "the absolute horizon of all reading and all interpretation" (Jameson 1981: 17).[12]

Although postmodern theorists tend, as we'll see, to abjure any "universal," "totalizing," or "absolute" claims about human reality, we might note that the preceding paragraph describes little else *but* universalizing absolutes.

---

[10] "Real-world people"—a category normally understood to exclude academics in general and "English majors" in particular—dislike having *themselves* "reduced" to mere words as well. Even students of literature, who supposedly "love language," don't always relish the thought that that's the stuff all people in the real world are made of. But such radically "linguistic determinism" is pretty much the message of **semiotics**—the study of signs and signification—as it regards all selfhood or subjectivity or "personal identity" whatsoever. As for **discourse**, Wolfreys defines it as "the work of specific language practice: that is, language as it is used by and within various constituencies (e.g., the law, medicine, and the church) for purposes to do with power relations between people" (2004: 65). He also writes that "human subjectivity and identity itself is produced out of various discursive formations as a result of the subject's entry into language always already shot through and informed by figurations and encryptions of power, politics, historical, cultural and ideological remainders organized through particular relationships and networks" (2004: 66).

[11] Theoretical writers use the term **subject** to designate the human individual as constituted by linguistic, discursive, and sociocultural practices (which is to say, the human individual as such); in theory, humans or "subjects" exist only by virtue of being "subjected" to these practices—hence, as Louis Althusser puts it, "the ambiguity of the term *subject*" (1971/2001: 123). The term "subject" sometimes refers to "the rational, active mind of the human individual" and is "defined in opposition to the object—that which is other than consciousness" (Malpas and Wake 2006: 256). But what interests most theoretical writers is the weird permeability of the boundary between conscious and unconscious, subject and object, self and other, particularly, as we'll see, in ambiguous moments of "writing or self-representation" when "the *I* is the self-present subject of the sentence as well as the subject 'subjected' to the symbolic order of the language in which [it] is writing" (Gagnier 1991: 9).

[12] The **political** in the theoretical sense exceeds our "normal" (and hence impoverished) concepts of electoral politics, political parties, and so on. Rather, theoretical writers "understand *political* in its deeper meaning, as describing the whole of human relations in their real, social structure, in their power of making the world" (Barthes 1957/1985: 143).

Indeed, the word "theory" itself might be considered a "nickname" for all the critical activities that begin to crank up at that moment when, as Derrida puts it, "language invaded the *universal* problematic and *everything* became discourse" (1966/1978: 280, my emphases). The "moment" or "event" that Derrida describes is sometimes called "the linguistic turn in the human sciences," and we could probably do worse than consider the historical emergence of "theory" itself in terms of this all-encompassing "turn." Jameson, for example, tags the linguistic turn as the very genesis of theory when he writes that "theory begins . . . at the moment it is realized that thought is linguistic or material and that concepts cannot exist independently of their linguistic expression." Jameson thus describes theory's inauguration as well as its continuation "as the coming to terms with **materialist** language" (2004: 403).[13] The postcolonial theorist Rey Chow also commemorates the linguistic turn when she uses the term theory "to mark the paradigm shift . . . whereby the study of language, literature, and cultural forms becomes irrevocably obligated to attend to the semiotic operations involved in the production of meanings, meanings that can no longer be assumed to be natural." Chow, like Jameson, defines theory as a coming to terms with materialist semiotics, as a way of paying "tenacious attention to the **materiality** of human signification" (2002/2007:1910).[14]

Arguably, then, it is through pushing "the linguistic turn" to the extreme—through trying to grasp the most radical consequences of the idea that

---

[13] For Jameson, "coming to terms with materialist language" involves the "attempt to dereify the language of thought" (2009: 9) and entails that "the traditional relationship between language and thought is to be reversed . . .: not language as an instrument or a vehicle for conceptuality, but, rather, the way in which the conditions and form of representation (speaking and writing) determine the concepts themselves, and constitute at one and the same time their conditions of possibility and also their limits, inflecting their shape and development" (2006: 365).

[14] The words **materialist** and **materiality** deserve some definition here, but I am going to defer elaborating on them until the next chapter's discussion of the sentence "The world must be made to mean"—a "materialist" assertion, if there ever was one. Here, let it suffice to say that one is well on one's way to being "materialist" or "coming to terms with materialist language" when one attends to the production of meaning in a way that no longer assumes meaning or sense to have any "natural" or "supernatural" guarantee, when one begins to grasp the whole of human reality as an ongoing historical process of materialization or dynamic realization or actualization that originates in and depends upon nothing other than human productivity. Conceptualizing a world that must be made to mean, materialism "has to do with the humanization of that world and its de-naturalization, that is to say, with our recognition of that entire post-natural world [i.e., human reality itself] as the product of human praxis and production" (Jameson 2010: 108). Now, if this brief explanation of materialism doesn't suffice, see Žižek's long response to Adrian Johnston's question "*What does it mean to be a materialist in the early twenty-first century?*" (Johnston 2009: 214), or consider the "antinatural" implications of the following from Catherine Malabou's *What Should We Do With Our Brain?*: "A reasonable materialism, in my view, would posit that the natural contradicts itself and that thought is the fruit of this contradiction" (2004/2008: 82).

"everything" has *become* discourse, has always *been* discourse, will always *be* discourse—that theoretical writing both universalizes its political claims and politicizes its universal claims (even its paradoxically universal claims against universalization). Tenaciously attending to the materiality and historicity of *all* human signification whatsoever, assiduously connecting "all aspects of life and consciousness to the material conditions of existence" (Childers and Hentzi 1995: 181), theoretical writing attempts to respond to the contradictions and conflicts embedded in the variously discursive ways in which the world must be made to mean. But responding *responsibly* to the ways our world means *means* more than just subjecting it to gnarly "academic" analysis. For Marx, as we've read, philosophers have only interpreted the world, while the point must be to change it. In the text called *Specters of Marx*, however, Derrida writes of "the dimension of performative interpretation, that is, of an interpretation that transforms the very thing that it interprets" (1994: 51). For theoretical writers, then, to interpret the world *really* can mean to change it—that is, to substantially *rewrite* it—for the "real world" is "always already" nothing but actively and collectively performative interpretation. If theoretical interpretation involves *transformative* "thinking about thinking," theoretical writing involves writing *about* "writing as *the very possibility of change*, the [discursive] space that can serve as a springboard for subversive thought, the precursory movement of a transformation of social and cultural structures" (Cixous 1975/2007: 1646).[15]

With such subversive thoughts in mind, let's return to the question of theory's difficulty, to what we might call its guerilla warfare on "clarity." McLaughlin, as we've read, asserts that theory "isn't difficult out of spite," but, to be quite honest, when considering all the possible motivating factors involved in theoretical militancy, I'm not so sure we should rule out "spite" altogether. Nietzsche no doubt had our number when, in the *Genealogy of Morals*, he linked our most rigorously "objective" intellectual procedures to extremely *personal* feelings of pique and *ressentiment*. And no doubt there are some really mean-spirited theoretical writers out there who like nothing better than to shatter your poor common-sense perceptions simply because

[15] A major caveat here: please note that the operative word in Cixous' promising phrase about "writing as the possibility of change" is *possibility*, not "certainty" or "inevitability." Nor can theoretical writing guarantee in advance that any "changes" wrought by your "coming to terms with materialist language" will necessarily be useful or progressive in any conventional political sense or that letting your common-sense perceptions be shattered and undermined will be "good for you" in any conventional moral sense. As we'll be exploring, there are ethical as well as aesthetic and political dimensions to theory's attempt to "de-reify the language of thought," but the ethics of the attempt aren't always transparent. And so, please recall this caveat—"change" is neither painless nor necessarily "for the common good"—anytime that I seem in this book to be crowing too loudly about the "transformative" potential of theory.

they *can* be shattered. But setting aside as much as I can my own considerable meanness of spirit, I would like to suggest that theory's opacity, while perhaps partly rooted in all-too-human *ressentiment*, also involves ethical obligation, a sense of political responsibility or social justice. I would like to suggest that what animates most theoretical writing is not a spiteful insistence on "just being difficult" but rather a strenuous commitment to *difficultly being just*.

To explain this suggestion, I turn back to Horkheimer and Adorno's *Dialectic of Enlightenment*. I have already quoted this resolutely "difficult" duo to the effect that "Intellect's true concern is a negation of reification." Now, on the same page in which they express this concern, Horkheimer and Adorno also write that "False clarity is only another name for myth" (1947/2002: xvii). By *this* claim, the authors mean that we may never be more mystified, more benighted by our "primitive" or "tribal" mythologies, than during those still moments when everything seems perfectly obvious, completely unproblematical, when our "common sense" tells us that some premise or perception is *clearly* absolutely right and true. By the word "myth," the authors refer specifically to the sort of fearfully reactionary and religious/superstitious worldviews that "enlightenment" thinking (ostensibly rationalist modern philosophy) sought to escape, defeat, or crush (as per the slogan "*écrasez l'infâme*"—we must crush the infamy!—with which the arch-*philosophe* Voltaire reportedly signed his letters). In *Dialectic of Enlightenment*, Horkheimer and Adorno are concerned with what they call "enlightenment's relapse into mythology" (xvi), the way purportedly fearless modern rationalism devolves into a fear-based "instrumental reason" as bloody and oppressive as anything practiced under any *ancien regime*. Other than mention that the authors see both the rise of European fascism and standardized post-World War II American mass culture (particularly the Hollywood film) as expressions of this intellectual and moral disaster, we can't rehearse their arguments about enlightenment's mythological relapses here.

We *can* note, however, that Horkheimer and Adorno consider "myth" the symptom *par excellence* of reified thinking. If *critical* intellect's true concern is to *negate* reification, and if "clarity" can function as the calling card of reifying myth, then critical intellect should always be prepared to challenge "clarity" itself. Because in an utterly reified social order, any instance of "clarity" stands a splendid chance of being a myrmidon of "false consciousness," a promoter of "mass delusion," the critical intellectual is always obliged to try to kick "clarity" in its transparent pants. In other words, in any culture in which reification reigns, the "duty of the critical intellectual" is to learn to suspect an ideological shell-game at work in the very insistence upon linguistic transparency, to smell something fishy whenever words and sentences appear "to mean" all too axiomatically, all too unproblematically, "all by themselves." Obviously, then, since "clarity" itself can be the symptom of reification, it follows that one's attempt to negate reification, to de-reify the language of thought, isn't likely to be very clear. Indeed, one's articulation is obligated to be strategically difficult, baffling, defamiliarizing, resistant to facile processing or immediate comprehension.

Of course, for Horkheimer and Adorno, not every single instance of "clarity" in the world of discourse is necessarily "false"; for these guys, clarity is mythological, and hence false, only when it aids and abets reification. But we might understand clarity's abetting function more clearly if we momentarily drop "reification," Marxism's preferred term for the undesirable "fixing" or coagulation of cognitive processes, and employ another word (viz. **sedimentation**), drawn from a different intellectual tradition (viz. **phenomenology**), instead. This terminological shift might give us some clarity about what's at stake in both the formation and the attempted negation of clarity.[16]

Imagine, if you will, a firmly sedimented foundation at the bottom of some body of standing water. To call this foundation "sedimented" is to say that over a period of time a certain amount of particulate matter has settled down and become stably impacted therein. A direct *result* of this sedimentary process is that the water above the foundation remains relatively clear. Clearly, however, the water's *present* transparency is an *effect* dependent upon the accomplished sedimentation, upon the previous "settling of matters." In other words, "clarity" (figured here by the unclouded water) depends upon the sedimentation of complexity (figured here by these particulate "matters" which have been put out of sight, which seem to have just "naturally" gotten themselves "settled"). But if this sedimentary foundation were to be in some way unsettled or *de-sedimented*—if some trickster were to poke a stick into this soggy bottom and give it a vigorous stir—then all the gritty matters that had long been settled down would come swirling back up into *play*. And the necessary consequence of this agitation would be the water's corresponding *loss* of clarity.

Theory, if you hadn't guessed, is the stick that stirs this dirty analogy, which is why we should stick with thinking of the very project of theory

---

[16] **Phenomenology** involves the analysis of "human consciousness as 'lived experience'" (Childers and Hentzi 1995: 227) and is usually associated with "the canonical three H's of German philosophy" (Rabaté 2002: 47)—Hegel, Husserl, and Heidegger. The phenomenological term **sedimentation** appears in the later work of Husserl and, somewhat like "reification," refers to a sort of spatial transformation of active perception into "settled" knowledge. David Carr writes that Husserl's "geological metaphor suggests that which has sunk below the surface [of human consciousness as lived experience] but continues to support what is on the surface. Husserl availed himself of this metaphor in his later work precisely to elucidate what has the status of knowledge or belief rather than perception, but which recedes into a position comparable to a spatial horizon. It is that which *figures* in my awareness of the present, frames or sets it off without my having to think about it explicitly" (1987: 263).

as unsettling—theoretical writing involves de-sedimenting or disturbingly
deconstructive thinking about thinking.[17] But contrary to the scatological
allegations of those who despise theory and rejoice at the thought of its
demise, the main impetus behind the theoretical "movement" in literary
studies was never simply to dump a load of "fashionable nonsense" into the
ordinarily clear and calm waters of thoughtful minds. Despite appearances,
theory does not aspire to foul placidly apodictic streams of consciousness,
but it very much desires to disturb the waters, to stir up matters seemingly
long settled, all the better to "completely shatter and undermine our common
perceptions" (Žižek 2006: ix). Or, in somewhat ruder words, originally issuing
from the lips of queer theorist Judith Halberstam, theoretical writing really
just wants "to fuck shit up" (2006: 824), and so this writing sticks its abrasive
questions and irritating keywords deep into the sedimented foundations and
mythological fantasies that underpin ideational clarity—which means that we
can basically stick "anti-foundationalism" pretty high up on our expanding
list of theory's antagonistic stances.

  In the following pages, we'll explore the dire consequences of what is no
doubt theory's most radically "anti-foundational" insight, emerging directly
from the aforementioned linguistic turn—this would be the "structuralist"
perception that signs "do not have essences but are defined by a network
of relations" (Culler 1975: 5), that "in language there are only differences
without positive terms" (Saussure 1972/1986: 118), that "no signification can
be sustained except by reference to another signification" (Lacan 1966e/2006:
415), and so on. For now, we'll "simply" observe that, from a theoretical
perspective, no single instance of linguistic or ideational "clarity" can ever
just simply, transparently, meaningfully *be*; nor can "meaning" ever securely
rest upon a naturally or supernaturally firm foundation, some reassuringly
"real bedrock" of metaphysical truth. Rather, from a theoretical perspective,
a perspective which always desires to bring about "a desedimentation
of . . . encrusted determinations" (Smith 2002: xi), mythological clarity,
ordinary language, plain common sense, given meaning, absolute truth, and
so on—this whole crusty and determined gang—are all only the ideological
effects of a naturalizing, essentializing, familiarizing, or normalizing

---

[17] Although I defer describing **deconstruction** until later pages, I will here share David
Richter's story that Derrida at one point wanted to replace the word deconstruction
with "de-sedimentation"—although "that word never caught on" (827). In fact,
early in *Of Grammatology*, Derrida uses the words interchangeably: he writes of an
"enlarged and radicalized" writing that "no longer issues from a logos" (that is, from
any consciously rational center of intention, either human or divine), and he writes that
"this writing inaugurates the destruction, not the demolition but the de-sedimentation,
the de-construction, of all significations that have their source in that of the logos.
Particularly the signification of *truth*" (1967/1997: 10).

suppression of *other* meanings, the repression of *extraordinary* signs. These assorted "betrayals of repressed human possibilities" (Derrida 2008: 105) work together as an active forgetting, a forced amnesia about *alternative* intelligibilities. While *no* meaning is sustained except by reference to another meaning, *some* meaning—namely, clearly given meaning—sustains itself through the *erasure* of competing interpretations. Such an erasure, such a removal of the traces of production from the product, is the very work of reification, of sedimentation, the underlying goal of which would be obviating the very possibility that "things as they are" might be imagined otherwise.[18]

Theoretical writing, then, must always attempt to negate reification, must always work against the erasure of imaginative alterity. Through its restless de-sedimentations, theoretical writing attempts to help bring *alternative* intelligibilities into circulation, to help bring *other* ways of making sense, other ways of "making the present," into play. At its productively baffling best, theoretical writing "never stops coming back" to challenge, resist, or disturb all the sedimentary operations that are required to reproduce "ordinary understanding," to stabilize "given meaning," to reify all human reality, and to *normalize* a world thus insulated from discomfort, protected from interrogation, shielded from interpretation, contestation, and change. This "normalization" is what theory fights. This fight is what theory does. And what theory does is why theory lives.

Coming to Terms

Critical Keywords encountered in the Introduction:

reification, essentialism, defamiliarization, humanism, metaphysics, semiotics, discourse, the subject, the political, materialism/materiality, sedimentation/de-sedimentation, phenomenology, deconstruction

---

[18] I've repeated the phrase "things as they are" a number of times now without giving proper attribution, so here, at last, are two—In *Very Little . . . Almost Nothing: Death, Philosophy, Literature*, Simon Critchley writes that for Adorno, "the task of thinking is to keep open the slightest difference between things as they are and things as they might otherwise be" (1997: 22). Meanwhile, in the poem "The Man with the Blue Guitar," Wallace Stevens writes that "things as they are are changed on the blue guitar" (1937/1982: 165). I take "the blue guitar" to mean for Stevens the poetic imagination itself. But I also imagine that in some venues, performing the task of thinking, keeping open the possibility of change, theoretical writing can play a pretty mean blue guitar.

Part 1

Antiphysis: Five Lessons in Textual Anthropogenesis

"The world must be made to mean"

—or, in(tro)ducing the subject of human reality

I. Work with words

So what in the world does it mean to say that "the world must be made to mean"? How does this sentence help us begin the hard work of "coming to terms with materialist language" (Jameson 2004: 403), of getting a handle on materialist semiotics? And why is this morsel of semiotic material an appropriate starting point for "in(tro)ducing the subject of human reality"— for *introducing* the idea that this "subject" must always be *induced*, as other processes, like labor or vomiting, must occasionally be induced? Like all properly "materialist" questions, these cannot be simply, briefly, or tidily answered, but we can learn a great deal about the most basic assumptions of theoretical writing by "coming to terms" with their terms.

The sentence was written by the **Birmingham School** cultural theorist Stuart Hall.[1] To say that Hall's sentence concisely expresses the most basic assumption of "materialist semiotics" is to locate it within the tradition of Marxist or "historical materialist" cultural studies. The initial clause of the sentence—*the world must be made*—is pretty much the foundational *premise* of historical materialism, while the final infinitive—*to mean*—is our semiotic *kicker*. Taken together, premise and kicker basically boil down to *labor* with *language*, or *work* with *words*, or, if you'll forgive me, *Marx* with *marks*.

What marks Marx as an "historical materialist" is his conviction that humans must always make or produce their "world," their "history." In other words, Marx concurs with what Edward Said calls Giambattista Vico's "great observation that [people] make their own history, that what they can know is

---

[1] What Hall actually writes, in "The Rediscovery of Ideology," is "The world has to be made to mean" (1998: 1050), but for a number of reasons, including the hard time I have resisting alliteration, I've changed "has to" to "must." **Birmingham School** is short for the Birmingham Center for Contemporary Cultural Studies, founded in 1964 at Birmingham University, UK. Hall was director of the Center from 1968 to 1979 (Childers and Hentzi 1995: 28–9).

what they have made" (1978: 4–5). For Marx and other historical materialists, that is, "the world" is nothing but "the history of the world," and that history is only ever "anthropogenetic," only ever humanly fashioned, fabricated, or caused—humans only are responsible for it.[2] In *The German Ideology*, Marx sets his materialist analysis of anthropogenesis against philosophically idealist or mistily theological accounts of "the origin of the world." He writes that human beings

> can be distinguished from animals by consciousness, by religion or anything else you like. They themselves begin to distinguish themselves from animals as soon as they begin to *produce* their means of subsistence . . . By producing their means of subsistence [people] are indirectly producing their actual material life. (1932b/1978: 150)

For Marx, then, specifically *human* history begins, antinaturally enough, when the earliest humans first distinguish themselves from immediately *natural* or merely *animal* life by actively *producing* the real material conditions of their existence, their human reality, their *world*. For Marx, only humans "think, act and fashion [this] reality" (1844/1978: 54); only humans *produce*, actively and materially *create*, this world—which is why some Marxists, such as Antonio Negri in *Time for Revolution*, speak of historical materialism as "creative materialism" (2005: 166).

Here of course the word "world" doesn't mean the physical planet (crust, mantle, magma, molten core, etc.), which Marx doesn't for a minute think that humans "created" (though he doesn't believe that some almighty, otherworldly deity cooked it up either); rather, by "world" an atheist historical materialist like Marx means the untranscendable horizon of human social existence in its historical totality, from the most rudimentary tribal forms in the dark backward and abysm of time to the most developed and digitally

---

[2] Commenting on the link between Vico and Marx, Fredric Jameson notes that Marxism "stakes out what may be called a Viconian position, in the spirit of the *verum factum* of the *Scienza Nuova* [1725]; we can only understand what we have made, and therefore we are only in a position to claim knowledge of history [which is our work] but not of Nature itself, which is the work of God" (2009: 7); thus "Vico's *verum factum* in effect sunders history from nature as an object of possible human knowledge" (2009: 217n21). But where Marx's materialism surpasses Vico's is less in the act of sundering history from nature as an object of human understanding and more in understanding human history itself as our permanent sundering of ourselves from nature, understanding history as the ongoing and productively human or "anthropogenetic" process of "antiphysis." Marx further surpasses Vico in rejecting the idea that nature is "the work of God" and positing instead that "God" is the creative or imaginative work of "man"—for the militantly atheist Marx, that is, "the criticism of religion is the premise of all criticism," and "the basis of irreligious criticism is this: *man makes religion*, religion does not make man" (1844/1978: 53–4).

fast-forwarded cyber-societies. Specifically *human* history or "the world" *begins* for Marx not when some deity says "let there be light" but when "the first humans" begin *working* on the raw materiality of their immediately natural environment in order to *transform* it into something starting to resemble specifically human or social existence—thereby becoming, anthropogenetically speaking, "the first humans." In other words, probably because "living like animals" wasn't working out all that well for them anyway, the proto-people who are our most distant ancestors gave up trying to live a "merely natural" life—they stopped seeking shelter in the nearest natural formation (the proverbial cave or some other hole in the ground) and starting building huts and hovels out of the available sticks and mud; they stopped being merely hunters and gatherers, as some animals merely hunt and gather, stopped grubbing on whatever happened to be growing or grunting nearby, and started raising flora for harvest and fauna for slaughter. As these quite basic examples might suggest, the materialist gist here is that human reality or human history even at its most "primitive" level never "just naturally" (much less supernaturally) happens, never just grows on trees, or falls from the sky; a certain amount of *work* or productive activity is required in order to get human history up and running—to begin wrangling a realm of specifically human *freedom* from the merely natural realm of *necessity*.

"Antiphysis," then, isn't a bad name for this anthropogenetic activity, this totally human and—potentially, at least—totally humanizing *work* on and "against nature."[3] For an historical materialist account, there is no beneficently divine creator watching over us, and nature is completely indifferent to our survival, much less to our "cause" (freedom, autonomy, dignity, etc.). Nature, that is, doesn't really give a damn whether or not we're protected from its elements, doesn't care if or, most importantly, *how* we live or die. If I live like a king or die like a dog, it's all the same to nature. And the fact that nature is completely indifferent to Operation Human Freedom, the fact that raw and immediate physical nature *must* be transformed, worked on, worked *against*, if this project of antiphysis is ever to get off the ground,

---

[3] I write here that human history as our ongoing work on and against nature is only *potentially* "totally humanizing" because, so far, history hasn't exactly worked out this way for everybody—in other words, we haven't yet reached what Jameson calls "the human age itself," the *utopian* age of our totally mutual recognition of ourselves in a "fully human and humanly produced world" (2010: 107). The "world," to be sure, is still only ever "humanly produced," but for many, the work itself is anything but "fully" humanizing. For many producers, that is, labor is still "alienated" in the four-fold sense Marx describes in the *Economic and Philosophical Manuscripts of 1844*. We will discuss Marx's theory of alienated labor more fully in Lesson Seven. For now, let's just say that from a Marxist perspective, "the human age itself" can't and won't come about until the age of global capitalism is superseded.

constitutes the basic or primordial reason why "the world" must always "be made"—and always only by us. Because we, the people, first distinguish ourselves *as* people by anthropogenetically differentiating ourselves *from* animals in the practical act of *producing* our means and conditions of existence, human reality must always be distinguished from natural reality, from merely animal life.

II. Post-oceanic feelings

Or, as psychoanalyst Jacques Lacan might put it—in terms no less laboriously "materialist" than those of Marx—human reality must be distinguished from nature because each and every *subject* of this reality must be set apart from **the real**, must separate or free itself from the real's oppressively immediate *hic et nunc* or "here and now." Lacan describes "human reality" as a "montage" of **the imaginary** (the register of images) and **the symbolic** (the register of language). He distinguishes this imaginary and symbolic montage from another register, which he calls the real. In Lacan's account, the real both *precedes* and *exceeds* human or "socio-symbolic reality," precedes and exceeds any individual subject *of* this reality, any particular human being. The real *precedes* reality insofar as it relates to "the very young child's experience of itself," which, Lacan says, "develops on the basis of a situation that is experienced as undifferentiated" (1966c/2006: 91); Lacan characterizes this "precedent" real as a perceptual state or experiential stew in which "things . . . at first run together in the *hic et nunc* of the all" (1966d/2006: 229). Because the inarticulate infant mired in this undifferentiated real literally can't "tell the difference" between its "experience of itself" and everything else, it in effect experiences itself as "everything." Thus the real as "the *hic et nunc* of the all" relates to what Freud in *Civilization and Its Discontents* calls the infant's "oceanic" feeling, "a feeling of an indissoluble bond, of being one with the external world as a whole" (1930/1989: 723)—a "feeling" that we all of course must one day *lose*. For, eventually and inevitably, each and every "very young child" must be pulled out of the "oceanic" real and *installed* in properly human reality, *framed* in the imaginary/symbolic montage, must become an individual human subject, an "I," a *parlêtre* or "speaking being," as Lacan puts it, "an animal at the mercy of language" (1966f/2006: 525). Thereafter, the real is what *exceeds* human reality and "resists symbolization absolutely" (Lacan 1991: 66).

We'll be returning to Lacan, to "infantile" experience, and to the real's resistance to language's tender mercies, later in these lessons. Here, let's say that for Lacan, human reality must be distinguished from the real because, in the real, there is nothing to distinguish the human from the merely natural/ animal "here and now."[4] While for Marx, *labor* pries humans loose from nature, for Lacan, *language* separates reality from the real. Taking Marx and Lacan together, materialist semiotics asserts the "labor of language" as the specifically and exclusively human mode of antiphysis that *produces* human reality as such. The world must be made, to be sure, but it must also be made to mean. Human reality is only ever the product of human work with words.

But how do these laboriously linguistic matters relate to the idea that "the *subject* of human reality"—the individual human being—must be "induced"? Here, we begin to approach a materialist assumption that many self-respecting human beings find unpalatable—the assumption that, like "the world," each and every one of us must also be "made to mean." To paraphrase Lacan—humans make meaning, but only because meaning makes us human.[5] Antinaturally enough, this quip means that none of us is ever actually *born human*; rather, universally and transhistorically, we must all be *turned into* human beings through the antinatural labor of language. What does this mean? How does this work? How could this possibly be?

Well, consider all the abilities or activities by which we tend to "distinguish" ourselves from animals. Make a list of everything we can do that a non-human animal, a monkey or a lobster, cannot.

---

[4] Let's also say a little more about Lacan's triptych—the imaginary, the symbolic, and the real. It's true that Lacan distinguishes human reality, as imaginary/symbolic montage, from the real. It's also true that Lacan gives us a sort of developmental narrative in which the infant starts off in the undifferentiated real, leaves that mess behind, and enters "the imaginary order" via the so-called mirror stage (which we'll be discussing quite thoroughly in a later lesson), and then supersedes the imaginary by entering "the symbolic order" of language. But Lacan doesn't want to suggest that any distinction drawn between the real and reality is absolute; nor does he want us to put all our psychoanalytically interpretive eggs in the developmentally narrative basket; rather, Lacan stresses the structural permanence of real, imaginary, and symbolic interconnections within human reality as such. In fact, he famously represents the real, the imaginary, and the symbolic with the diagram of the so-called Borromean knot, "a group of three rings that are linked together in such a way that if any one of them is severed, all three become separated" (Evans 1996: 18) and the whole "subject of human reality" falls apart. So, while it's accurate to say, as I have above, that "the real" in Lacan's sense *precedes* and *exceeds* human reality, it's probably *more* accurate to say that the real precedes, exceeds, and yet never ceases to *invade* human reality. This sense of invasion can produce a feeling of "extimacy" for the subject of human reality. As explained in the Preface, the word extimacy "neatly expresses the way in which psychoanalysis problematizes the opposition between the inside and the outside, between container and contained" (Evans 1996: 58); the word opens us up to the unsettling suspicion "that the innermost, intimate core of a person's psychical being is, at root, an alien, foreign 'thing'" (Johnston 2009: 86).

[5] Or, to quote him directly: "Man thus speaks, but it is because the symbol has made him man" (Lacan 1966d/2006: 229).

Seriously—make a list.

Now consider whether you could perform any of these constitutively human tricks immediately upon the moment of your birth, or even for several *years* thereafter. Sure, you may have first popped out with the innate *potential* to *learn* these operations eventually, to *acquire* these characteristics one fine day. But a moment's reflection will inform you that you, in fact, *had* to be *taught* each and every single one of them because in the inert facticity of your neonativity, you basically couldn't do *squat*.

In fact, from this rather unflattering perspective, our most "species-specific" characteristic as newborns is our utter *inadequacy* not only as humans but even as little animals. This lack of sufficient animality stems from what Lacan calls our species' "*specific prematurity at birth*" (1966b/2006: 78), a matter we'll consider more carefully in the next few lessons. For now, however, let's see if we can cut through all the "ideological labor of cuteness" (Edelman 2004: 137) that is normally and normatively performed upon "the baby" and behold the human neonate as a "small animal conceived by a man and a woman," a little creature that will not just naturally become but must actually be *made* into "a small human child" (Althusser 1971: 205). If we can swallow this queerly materialist description, then we might begin to digest the radical proposition that humanness itself, while a *conceivably* innate or hard-wired *potential*, is *actually* only ever a hard-scrabble *acquisition*, that we are each born as inadequate little animals, rough beasts that must be *turned* into human children through laborious linguistic processes of *socialization*. Like the world that must always be made to mean, we ourselves must always be made to mean and must always continue to make meaning.

But while being "made" here denotes being *manufactured* or *fabricated*, the word also suggests being *compelled* or *forced*, just as the word "must" implies an inexorable, and hence, vaguely sinister imperative. What are we to make of this more ominous meaning of the phrase "must be made"? Here, it might help to know that Lacan refers to human reality as **the symbolic order**. In Lacanese, the symbolic order is the underlying set of grammatical and syntactical structures that regulate the material production of meaning that *is* social reality itself. For Lacan, the *symbolic* order pervades and supports any actually existing *social* order. The *symbolic* order is the "grammatically correct" organization of signs and symbols that *gives* us our "politically correct" position within the *polis*, within the prevailing *social* order (our properly *gendered* position within a legitimated exogamous marriage or kinship system, for example). To become a *social* subject, one must first assume the symbolic position of the *grammatical* subject. One must first agree to designate oneself in terms of the first-person pronoun—to say "I" and really mean it.[6] But this seemingly casual agreement to "be oneself" in words is actually "made" under a bit of psychic duress. For the symbolic order isn't merely an ordered row of symbols, an organized concatenation of words. It's also an order *to* symbolize, an officially issued *directive* to mean—or else. To *enter* "the symbolic order," to participate in human reality as one's own personal "I," one must first *follow* "the symbolic order," the order to symbolize, the relentless imperative to mean. Non-participation in "meaning," exclusion from the privileges of the "I," would be the aforementioned "else"—and you *really* don't want to end up *there*.

Now, like everything else involving the production of human reality, the symbolic order doesn't grow on a tree or fall from the sky. So, where does it come from? How is it maintained? Suppose I don't really want to enter or follow it. Can I take or leave the symbolic order, as I please? Is it possible to refuse? Or, does the symbolic order "make me" (as) an offer that I can't refuse without somehow refusing myself *and* participation in human reality in the bargain? These questions take us into our next lesson, which explores the *socializing* mechanisms by which we are initially "made to mean," first inducted into the "politics" of meaning.

Coming to Terms

Critical Keywords encountered in Lesson One:

Birmingham School, real/imaginary/symbolic, the symbolic order

---

[6] With this phrase—"to say 'I' and really mean it"—I am playing on the literal meanings of Freud's German *das Ich* and *das Es*—"the I" and "the it"—which appear in Strachey's English translation of Freud's work as "the ego" and "the id." Thus, Freud's famous motto *Wo Es war, soll Ich werden*—"where id was, there ego must be" (1933/2001: 80)—can be read more literally as "where it (*das Es*) was there I (*das Ich*) must come into being." Thus, "to say 'I' and really mean it" can mean: (1) to say "I" and sincerely intend to represent oneself as a subject, a self-identical person, but it can also mean (2) to say "I" but *unconsciously* refer to something else, something "other," an "it," an object, "an alien, foreign 'thing'" (Johnston 2009: 86). This second and much stranger meaning points us to what Lacan calls "the truth of 'I is an other,' less dazzling to the poet's intuition than it is obvious from the psychoanalyst's viewpoint" (1966c/2006: 96). We'll have more to say about this dazzling truth in Lesson Five.

Lesson Two

"Meaning is the polite word for pleasure"

—or, how the beast in the nursery learns to read

I. Bungle in the jungle

In our first lesson, concerning how "the world must be made to mean," we encountered the rather rude proposal that none of us is born altogether human, that each of us comes into this world as an inadequate little animal that—not *who*, mind you, but, more precisely, *that*—must be *turned* into a small human child. We also encountered the unflattering suggestion that our entire species universally and transhistorically experiences a "*specific prematurity at birth*" (Lacan 1966b/2006: 78). This prematurity is called upon to account for our woefully insufficient animality, for what Lacan calls the "organic inadequacy of [our] natural reality" at the experiential get-go, "a certain dehiscence at the very heart of [our] organism, a primordial Discord betrayed by the signs of malaise and motor uncoordination of [our] neonatal months" (1966b/2006: 77, 78).

But what accounts for our prematurity, for our allegedly over-early launch out into this world that must be made to mean? How does it happen that we as a species don't take as much time in uterine space as we apparently "should" and so seem "biologically determined" to endure a period of abject immobility and helpless dependency considerably longer than that of any other animal neonate? A conjectural explanation for our endemic "organic inadequacy" at birth is that premature birthing developed as a strategy of evolutionary adaptation—when our primate ancestors first assumed an upright gait, this postural shift precipitated a skeletal pelvic contraction in proto-human females such that heads of fully formed fetuses were suddenly too big to be born. But whatever its speculative prehistorical cause, the ongoing effect of our prematurity—and thus, our dehiscent historicity—is that, *unlike* other animals, born simply as small versions of what they already organically are, we are *not* born human but have to be *made* that way. In other words, while any non-human animal that survives its neo-nativity will spontaneously grow to become an adult of its species, the infant of *our* species, congenitally inadequate to its own animality, requires careful assistance, orthopedic correction, extensive training, and prolonged cultivation if it is ever actually going to become a human being, a viable participant in extra-uterine human reality. If the neonate, for some reason, never receives its "basic training," if nobody ever "does any work" on it or with it, if nobody ever orders or induces it to mean, then this organism may somehow survive in the purely physiological or "animalistic" sense, but, bluntly stated, it won't become "one of us." It won't, simply by virtue of growing larger, just naturally and spontaneously develop the characteristics that distinguish us—or, that we cultivate in order to distinguish ourselves— from non-human animals.

In a way, this problem, the primordial discord of our species, is registered in the quirks of our vocabularies. Consider, for example, how fairly commonplace such English words as "humanization" and "dehumanization" can seem, while nonce words like "caninization" or "deporcinization" seem fairly absurd. And the reason for the absurdity is clear enough. You might be able to teach a puppy some nice tricks, but you don't exactly have to "caninize" your mutt in order for it to become a dog. And because the individual oinker is completely identical to its own porcine life, the only way to completely "deporcinate" a pig would be to kill it.

Humans, however, do have to be humanized, or socialized—worked on and put into words—in order to become certifiably human. And while, unlike non-human animals, we have proven ourselves particularly adept at genocide and self-slaughter, it is of course quite possible to "dehumanize" people and peoples without actually having to go so far as to kill anybody— indeed, we've been performing this nasty trick on ourselves and each other for pretty much all of our history. It is sometimes said, though rarely anymore, that people should study "the humanities" so as to become "more fully human." But as far as I know it has never been suggested that a horse should study "the equininities" to become more fully equine, or that an ass needs to throw itself into "the asininities" to become more completely asinine.

But let's sum up the idea that I've been braying about here, an idea that may come as a kick in the pants to any self-respecting common-sense adult, but which, I would venture, most very young *children* intuitively understand— the idea that we "adulterated" human beings are actually only ever *relatively humanized* beings, never anything other than *anthropomorphized* animals in a world that must be made to mean. Now, when I suggest that *children* basically get this, that they actually understand humans to be socialized or anthropomorphized animals, what I mean is that children at a certain age can probably sense what's really going on with them, what's really happening

to them, even if they couldn't articulate the ordeal in such sophisticated
language—children, that is, may unconsciously register the fact that their
"animality," such as it is, is being *transformed* by and into "sociality," that
their already quite limited "animal joy" is being further *sacrificed* to the
socio-symbolic, that their "animal being" is being *exchanged* for intelligible
meaning.

Of course, this exchange isn't really the worst existential bargain in
the world, for the child no doubt painfully perceives the extent of its own
helpless dependency, the sheer inadequacy of its otherwise enjoyable
animality. Ambivalently, then—grudgingly *and* gladly— the child, in order
to become "a child," a "who" instead of a "what," accepts induction into "the
human club" as a sort of consolation prize for not having been a particularly
successful beast. But this child, I speculate, unconsciously (and, again,
ambivalently) may very well register the *cost* of following the symbolic order.
At some level, at some other frequency, so to speak, the child *knows* that
something is being lost as well as gained in its mandatory morphing from a
"what" to a "who," from an "it" to an "I," from "bad" little animal to "good"
little boy or girl.

Evidence for this awareness on the child's part might be found in the
enduring popularity among schoolchildren of a certain species of animation.
I refer to the *pleasure* that children take in watching animated cartoons that
feature *nothing but* anthropomorphized animals—dogs, cats, mice, birds,
bears that/who are capable of walking upright, can engage in relatively
polite (if rather inane) conversation, and so on. Very young spectators
probably wouldn't long enjoy watching a realistic cartoon canine that could
only bark, growl, bite, eat from a bowl, crap on the sidewalk, and so on;
they would be bored, dismayed, or possibly even frightened by animated
adults who behaved just like their parents (and thus, their own futures).
But children *do* psychically invest in and gain *representational pleasure*
from animatedly anthropomorphized animals. They find *meaning* in these
figures simply because, as small animals that/who are in the process of being
anthropomorphized themselves, they *identify* with these "funny" forms.
These "silly" characters correspond *profoundly* to their own transitional
state—no longer specifically animal, not yet certifiably human. Such cartoons
compensate children for their acquiescence to the symbolic; they make good
the *little* human animal's *huge* animal loss.

But let's be clear about the "nature" of this loss. It of course involves a loss
of nature, a loss of animal enjoyment, a disappearance of *real pleasure.* But
it also involves a gain in and of *meaning.* But what, or how much, does this
loss-as-gain actually amount to? How does this cost/benefit analysis open
the question of meaning's initiation as a *subtraction* of enjoyment, a *sacrifice*

of pleasure, a *renunciation* of the real? Note that in the preceding I write that children "gain *representational pleasure*" from cartoons. Since cartoons are nothing but representations (i.e., they're "not real"), the pleasure gained from them is clearly representational. But the phrase is tricky, implying a distinction between merely *representational* pleasure and some immediate *non*-representational enjoyment of "the real thing."

And here's where *language* rears its head, so to speak, for what is language if not a "mediating" system of representations in which *words* are called upon to re-present real *things*, to symbolize or signify the various matters of the real? But then again, what if language itself in its entirety were nothing but a *massive* and *total* substitution *of itself* for every really enjoyable thing, for any immediate enjoyment of the real? What if representational "meaning" turned out to be our very young child's *reward* for having abjected or "cast out" real enjoyment? What if "meaning" were *really* only another word for "pleasure"—a single word for all the words that substitute themselves *for* pleasure, and thereby effectively *block* our ever really having any ever again?

Solemn adults who respect all meaning and suspect all pleasure—who both *insist* that life be Meaningful (with a great big honking capital M) and *despise* the thought of anyone's being alive just for the heck of it—would likely be displeased by these questions (or rather, they would find them "meaningless"). But children, again, arguably understand the questions quite well—and perhaps even get a kick out of them. Indeed, in his book *The Beast in the Nursery: On Curiosity and Other Appetites*, the child psychologist Adam Phillips goes so far as to suggest that "for the child, meaning [itself] is the polite word, the sophisticated word, for pleasure" (1999: 11). What does Phillips mean by this impolite suggestion?

For Phillips, I think, the word "pleasure" must pertain to what Freud calls the **pleasure principle**, a primary type of psychical functioning that Freud contrasts with the **reality principle**. As we'll see in the following elaboration of these two principles, their negotiation is the crux of what I've called above the very young child's "existential bargain"—the initial anthropogenetic exchange of "bad" young animal *being* for "good" old human *meaning*. In other words, the negotiation between the pleasure and reality principles is the very condition of possibility for that little animal's being brought "into the fold" of human historicity, for its becoming a subject of human reality.

Now, you may be surprised to learn that by "pleasure," Freud does not mean "stimulation" of any sort (sexual, emotional, neurological, etc.), but rather just the opposite—by "pleasure," Freud means the *reduction* of *excess* stimulation, the subtraction of *unpleasurable* tension. By "pleasure principle," then, Freud designates a process of mental functioning that demands and depends upon unpleasure's immediate reduction. The basic goal of the pleasure principle is to retreat from unpleasurable tension and return to a psychic equilibrium or quiescence, an ideally tensionless homeostasis. Whenever it loses homeostasis, whenever it experiences unpleasurable tension in any form—hunger, diaper-rash, fear of the dark or of strangers or of being all alone—the helpless infant wants to get its "pleasure" back, wants the tension to go away, wants its homeostasis restored, *immediately*. But in reality there will always be some discrepancy between the infant's immediate demand and two interrelated and mediating factors (factors which mediate in that they "come between" infantile demand and its fulfillment). One significant factor is the time it actually takes for homeostasis to be satisfactorily restored (if ever it is); the other significant factor is the form in which the satisfaction actually materializes (if ever it does, and the object eventually obtained may very well differ in form from the object irritably anticipated or psychically reached after). Reality, then, constitutively involves the "factoring in" of significantly temporal delay and significantly formal alteration (so much so that, as we'll see, temporal delay and formal alteration become the twin bases of significance itself). The discrepancy between immediate, formally self-identical gratification and satisfaction temporally delayed and/or formally altered is pretty much the difference between pleasure and reality. And every "little animal" must deal with this difference in order to factor itself into human reality, to become a small human child, a good or *polite* little girl or boy.

Now, the infantile psyche—ragingly impolite (and arguably ungendered) at this juncture—is completely under the "inhuman" dominance of the pleasure principle. Whatever it wants, whenever it wants it, its infantile majesty wants exactly what it wants and it wants that now. It knows no reason to endure *waiting* for pleasure's homeostatic restoration; it knows no reason to accept any substitute gratification whatsoever. Too bad for this completely unreasonable infant that it's also utterly powerless, helpless, and dependent, a miniscule tyrant incapable of actually *doing* anything to remedy its "wanting" situation. Under the pleasure principle's dominance, then, the infant having a bad time attempts to reduce anguished temporality in the most immediate way possible—by mentally summoning (i.e., fantasizing, hallucinating reaching after) the missing object (e.g., the mother's breast). But since this instant fantasy image fails to satisfy, provides merely representational pleasure, but never the real thing, the infant who wants someday to be more and other than an infant must eventually give itself over to the mediations of the reality principle. The infant, that is, must actively substitute a real demand for the merely imagined delight, must *actually* cry out for the missing object, which *in reality* may only eventually appear, may show up in a disappointingly diminished form (pacifier instead of breast), or may never materialize again in any form whatsoever—the toughest tit of all, so to speak.

The psychoanalytic gist here is that reality necessarily *impels* the infant's acquiescence to *waiting* and *substitution*, to *temporality* and *exchange*. To the infant's fantasmatic demand for the *real* thing, right *here*, right *now*, reality or "the adult world" comes back with a prohibitive or retarding counter-offer. Reality "responds," so to speak, with a rather tragicomical "promise of happiness," with a "not that, not here, not now, not yet; something else, somewhere else, some other time, maybe—we'll just have to wait and see." Given adult-world's promisingly negative response, the infant, completely dependent upon adult-world, has little choice but to *renounce* the fantasy of *immediate* enjoyment and *accept* the adulterated, delayed, partial, altered, *substitutive* gratifications that reality offers—or rather, that human reality essentially *is*.[1]

Outside of accepting reality's counter-offer—a frustratingly vague "promise of happiness" in place of the real thing—the infant's only other "option" would be to remain a kicking and screaming infant *for all time*. The word "infant," of course, means "without speech," so, psychically speaking, remaining an infant (even while physically outgrowing the nursery) would mean "going without" speech. But without speech one isn't likely to go very far with the grown-ups. For the reality principle, whose interests the adults represent, offers its promising gifts mainly in the *form* of speech, or even *as* the very *structure* of language itself. For language, like the reality principle—or perhaps *as* the reality principle—always involves temporal delay, formal alteration, partiality, substitution, displacement, and exchange. While *real*, natural, animal, or infantile experience is always immediate, *reveling* in the here and now, human *reality*, *revelatory* linguistic *meaning*, must always unfold in time (for "meaning" is never instantly "revealed" through parting clouds but actually only ever appears in *sentences*, and even the shortest sentence imaginable isn't exactly instantaneous, while some—like those I write, as you

---

[1] In "Creative Writers and Daydreaming," Freud writes that "whoever understands the human mind knows that hardly anything is harder for [us] than to give up a pleasure which [we have] once experienced. Actually, we never give anything up; we only exchange one thing for another. What appears to be a renunciation is really the formation of a substitute or surrogate" (1907/1989: 437–8). In *Civilization and its Discontents*, however, Freud describes perhaps the most "universal" form this "existential bargain" takes when he writes that "Civilized man has exchanged a portion of his possibilities for happiness for a portion of security" (1930/1989: 752).

may have noticed—seem to drag on forever). Language, linguistic meaning, always takes time, always takes us *out* of the present, always *tears us away* from the here and the now. As Lacan writes, language,

> by its very nature, always anticipates meaning by deploying its dimension in some sense before it. As is seen at the level of the sentence when the latter is interrupted before the significant term: "I'll never . . .," "The fact remains . . .," "Still perhaps . . ." Such sentences nevertheless make sense, and that sense is all the more oppressive in that it is content to make us wait for it" (1966e/2006: 419).

Always making us "wait for it" (whatever "it" may *be*), language oppressively substitutes its "promise of happiness" for happiness itself. And language, with its negatively promissory or "differential" structure, always "exists prior to each subject's entrance into it at a certain moment in his psychic development" (Lacan 1966e/2006: 413). Initially, upon entry into language, "each subject" is saddled with the responsibility of substituting words for withdrawn gratifications, for prohibited pleasures, for unsettled homeostases, for lost or missing *things*; consequently, as reality's "life-sentence" goes on, "each subject" *must* ride out the relentless *substitution* of words *for* other words, *must* follow the potentially infinite *combination* of words *with* other words.

For each and every subject of human reality must be made to mean— that's the symbolic order.

II. *L'être pour la lettre*

The negotiation between pleasure and reality *is* the symbolically ordered sacrifice of an insufficiently animal *being* for properly human *meaning*. Lacan calls this animality-overcoming exchange *l'être pour la lettre*, by which phrase he designates the anthropogenetic act of swapping "being" (*l'être*) for "the letter" (*la lettre*). But call it whatever we please, call "it" by some name we must, for barring this mandatory change-up, our infant can never become a "meaningfully" human being. If the infant "chooses" against reality, goes on hunger strike, opting for its internally conjured image of the mother's breast to the point of refusing the externally real thing, it could starve to death, lose its very *animal life*. If it refuses to trade its demand for immediate gratification for its desire for the other's recognition, for the *promise* of a more significant, meaningful, important pleasure in the *future*, then our infant will refuse (to be made) to mean, refuse to work (or be worked on) with words. It will never obey or accede to the symbolic order, and "it" could thus lose its opportunity to "fully" participate in properly *human life*, to be a subject of human reality, an "I."[2]

Now, Adam Phillips suggests that the child sacrifices pleasure to meaning not to "be a subject of human reality," but rather, and seemingly more simply, in order to be "polite." The word "polite" does seem relatively simple, but it actually gets quite complicated if we play a bit rough with its etymology. For being "polite" involves more than simply refraining from talking with one's mouth full, or interrupting the grown-ups, or loudly farting in their general direction. Of course, polite "participation in human reality" *does* largely entail learning how and when to keep our asses covered and our pie-holes shut, learning how to be well-behaved in the *polis*. But such excellent comportment doesn't just develop spontaneously; rather, it results from our being rather relentlessly *policed*. The most profoundly *political* meaning of "meaning is the polite word for pleasure" is that proper "meaning" always means being subjected to "police" investigation. "Meaning" means being disciplined or corrected, not simply by Miss Manners or some overly prescriptive grammarian but by the symbolic order itself—the "Big Other," as Lacan also ominously calls it. "Meaning" means pleasure's being put under the Big Other's surveillance; it is the *political* consequence of having subjected oneself and one's pleasures to the normative *policies* and prohibitions of the socio-symbolic order. If these policies are properly enforced, then the polite or "politicized" child will have taken its *rudely animal being* and "turned it in"— given it up, informed upon it, betrayed it to the authorities, had it arrested—in exchange for *literally human meaning*. The wild child becomes a wise child when it trades up the animalistic *demand* for immediate gratification for the anthropogenetic *desire* for the other's recognition.

To illustrate how this trade works, I turn back to that rudimentary example—the baby at the mother's breast. At the *animal* level, the infant *needs* this overflowing "object" not merely for "ideal" psychical homeostasis but for *real* physical survival. At this level of sheer physiological *need*, there's no *real* difference between the proto-human animal and any other udderly feeding

---

[2] To get the "fullest" picture of what this thoroughgoing refusal might amount to, consider that the little animal that refuses *linguistic* training may very well decline other forms of "basic training" as well—toilet training, for example. Here, I suppose, would be the appropriate place to let drop what Žižek calls "Lacan's thesis that [the] animal became human the moment it confronted the problem of what to do with its excrement" (1994: 179).

beast—we all must nurse or die. What sets our "beast in the nursery" apart is that it *demands more* from the breast than mere mammalian sustenance. The "wannabe human" infant demands to be given the breast-giver's gift not only as an indispensible "life-line," but also as an excessive sign—a signifier of what else but love. In other words, just as Marx's very early workers "distinguish themselves from animals as soon as they begin to produce their means of subsistence" (1845/1978: 150), so the very young child distinguishes itself from its own suckling animality as soon as it accomplishes the work of letting the sign-value that attaches to the appearance of the breast exceed the merely animal "life-value" that flows directly from it; in yet other words, the very young child distinguishes itself from itself when it first begins to learn how to *read*. For what else but *reading* would we call an activity in which a sign of life somehow becomes more important than immediate life itself, which thereafter seems strangely to lose significance? No non-human animal ever can be taught to "read" in this sense or to this extent; no non-human animal can ever allow a mere sign, a mere look of love or recognition, to become more important than itself, more significant than its own animal life; no non-human animal can ever consider losing life for love. A platypus couldn't manage it.

But our little animal turns human not by literally losing life, but by symbolically exchanging *l'être pour la lettre*, not by really dying but by metaphorically sacrificing the "inner animal" that is unwilling to sacrifice itself, unwilling to metaphorize, that recalcitrant beast that needs to be fed and demands to be pleased, but can't quite bring itself to "come to terms," can't quite agree to defer pleasure, or accept substitute gratification, the animal that can't stand being in a state of sustained desire because it is incapable of ever "dying to be loved"—the animal, in other words, that can't be *made to mean*. The fledgling human sacrifices or renounces or distances itself from its bad animal being in a bid to be recognized, to be meaningfully loved, or belovedly "read." For to be read/recognized as being meaningful is to be loved, wanted, approved, applauded, to be the deserving recipient of some (typically parental) hymn of praise. Reading/ recognizing as desiring to be read/recognized means desiring not only to "find meaning" in the other (rather than just demand pleasure from the other); it means desiring to be *found meaningful* (rather than merely animal) by the other, to rise in the other's esteem, to become not a "what," but a recognizably human "who" who would literally rather die than go without meaning, would rather die than remain an animal "it," a mere thing, in the estimation of others. The anthropogenetic desire for recognition trumps merely animal need and merely infantile demand when the very young child recognizes that it is significantly more pleasurable to have certain others be pleased with it than it is for "it" to have whatever pleasure it wants whenever it wants it.[3]

The "beast in the nursery" begins to learn to read when it starts allowing the metaphorical incept of desired signs to become more important than the material intake of needed sustenance, when it starts perceiving substitutive "signs of life" and reality's "promise of happiness" as being somehow better than immediate life itself—"even better than the real thing." When the real thing in question is the breast, what the infant must learn to read is not that real pound of flesh, much less its milky issue, but rather the telling expression that "overflows," so to speak, from the breast-giver's face. When the needy infant demanding the breast accepts in its stead a disappointingly diminished substitute—the cold dry plastic pacifier instead of the warm and softly seeping thing—it accepts this diminution only because a surplus of meaning provides symbolic compensation, makes good the loss of real enjoyment *qua* enjoyment in the real. The mother's completely approving facial expression, her milky look of love, along with any unconditionally soothing sounds she might manage to make—all work to compensate the infant, make up for the difference in pleasure-yield between breast and pacifier. These significant sights and sounds partially "paper over" the discrepancy between the enjoyment anticipated and the enjoyment obtained.

But if the infant does feel fairly compensated, it does so only because it senses what it damned well better get used to sensing—to wit—that it is "better" to "take in" these rewarding sights and sounds of approval than it is to obtain immediate gratification. At the end of the day, reality's primary lesson is still Freud's famous motto *Wo Es war, soll Ich werden*—"where id was, there ego must be" (1933/2001: 80), or, more literally, where an "it" was, an "I" must come into being. Reality's lesson, in other words, is that it will have been much more significant for me, *das Ich,* to obtain recognition (for having sucked it up and been polite) than it would have been for it, *das Es,* to have gotten exactly what it wanted, exactly when it wanted it (back in the prehistorical miasma of the real, the merely natural/animal *hic et nunc*). If the infant doesn't learn this "history lesson," if it doesn't on a very basic level grasp "the virtual character of the symbolic order [as] the very condition of human historicity" (Žižek 1999/2002: 241), if it doesn't figure out the terms of this existential bargain—if it clings to its pure pleasure principle in the real and doesn't allow itself to be worked over by virtual reality, if it simply continues to cry like a baby until it gets what it wants, refuses any substitutive

---

[3] I allude here to the distinctions Lacan makes among *need, demand,* and *desire*, which roughly and respectively correspond to his three "registers" of psychic life—the *real*, the *imaginary*, and the *symbolic*. We will return to the "knotted" relations among these two trios in our fourth lesson.

pacification and never learns to give a big happy damn what any significantly "Big Other" thinks of it—then this beast isn't going to get very far in the *polis*. It probably won't make it out of the nursery.

III. Happier endings

Adulterated reality, then, must supersede pure pleasure if "*das Ich*" is ever to displace "*das Es*," if anything resembling anthropogenesis is ever to occur. But reality can't simply eradicate pleasure altogether; rather, reality modifies, redirects, *transforms* pleasure. Reality can't "just say no" to any and all enjoyment. Reality "says no" to *immediate* and *self-identical* gratification, to be sure, but because no animal responds well to unmitigated negativity, the reality principle must always hold out the future promise of greater, more important, more significant gratification.

The paradoxical crux of the matter, however, is that, throughout their negotiated conflict, the pleasure and reality principles still share the same overriding goal—the reduction of unpleasurable tension, the restoration of homeostasis. And since the goal does remain the same, pleasure still pretty much rules the roost, despite reality's encroachments on its terrain. What must *fundamentally* change in the transition from *pure* pleasure to *accomplished* reality is the question of what actually constitutes the *source* or *cause* of the unpleasurable tension that demands to be reduced. Back in the day of the *pure* pleasure principle, what caused unpleasurable tension was whatever forced us "to wait for it"; in our quest to have our homeostasis restored a.s.a.p., we psychically withdrew like the heads of frightened turtles from whatever threatened to make us wait—that is to say, whatever threatened to *make* us *mean*. In the *accomplished* reality principle, however, unpleasure involves whatever disturbs the *reassuring stability of meaning*, whatever threatens the formally established coherence of *das Ich*. The stray memory of *non-meaning* (the "purposeless" animal enjoyment of inarticulate babble); the emergence of *bad meanings* (impolite or "perverse" gratifications that "I" might feel sick even thinking about); the appearance of *strange meanings* (unfamiliar articulations that disturb my normal understanding, anxiogenic "foreign elements" that "terrorize" my psychic equilibrium) —all these "bad" things become the unpleasurable tensions that "I" have to deal with—that is, *repress*—if *meaningful* homeostasis (the "homeland security" of my own private Idaho) is to be maintained. In the pleasure principle, it is the very thought of *repression*, the thought of my having to renounce a satisfaction, of my not getting what I want, that precipitates unpleasure; in the reality principle, however, it is the thought of *the return of the repressed*, of getting *more* than I bargained for, that does the trick. As Freud writes in the essay called "Repression," a specific satisfaction might be "pleasurable in itself" (i.e., in the pure pleasure principle), but "irreconcilable with other claims and intentions" (e.g., those of the reality principle). Thus the same thought can "cause pleasure in one place and unpleasure in another" (1915/1989: 569). Psychoanalysis, which studies psychic conflict, which explores the ways the same thought can generate antithetical feelings, has thus been called "the science of ambivalence."[4]

But speaking of ambivalence, and of tricks, the one that my "I" is about to play on yours really isn't very nice. For I can imagine that your "I" could without too much difficulty imagine itself *as an infant* sucking with great satisfaction at its mother's breast. Your "I" might even be able to imagine *that* infant being seriously displeased to have this breast suddenly pulled away. You *as an adult* "I" can probably imagine fairly easily that you *as an infant* "it" would want to banish immediately the very thought of the nipple's disappearance. OK, so far so good. *Now* let's see if you can imagine yourself *at your present age* sucking away at the wet and erect nipple of your own mother's breast (not just *any* old nipple, mind you, but specifically, unimaginably, unspeakably, *your own mother's*). I imagine, I would even heavily bet, that your "I" can bring *that* image to mind only with *extreme* difficulty, if at all, that the very idea provokes feelings of queasy disgust, unbearable shame, painful embarrassment, horrible incestuous weirdness, homophobic revulsion (particularly if you're a good girl), considerable anger at yours truly for even trying to stick the hideous thought into your head, etc.—in other words, *massive psychical unpleasure.* You *must* want to get this sick thought out of your head as quickly as possible. But while you're busy trying to restore your disrupted homeostasis, let's at least note what's illustrative here—to wit, back when you were a little "it," completely under the dominance of the pleasure principle, it was the thought of the object's *disappearance* that you wanted immediately to get rid of; now that you're a great big "I," long under the sway of the reality principle, it's the unwelcome thought of the object's *return* that you want to beat back, exclude, expel, repress, *tout de suite,* for "the essence of repression lies simply in turning something away, and keeping it at a distance, from consciousness" (Freud 1915/1989: 569–70).

In Freudian and Lacanian psychoanalytic theory, the term **unconscious** marks the "extimate" space of "otherness within" each of us, the traumatic thing or "unbearable truth" (Žižek 2006: 3) within each subject's psyche from

---

[4] I have to apologize for the fact that I can neither remember nor discover who coined this phrase—I'm beginning to think that I dreamt it.

which normally constituted consciousness tries—pathetically and bathetically enough—to keep its distance.[5] So, when I write that anthropogenesis depends upon repression, that anthropogenesis begins to kick in when impolitely animal *being* is "sacrificed" to properly human *meaning*, I don't mean to suggest that the sacrificial beast vanishes into thin air, flies, or slithers, or waddles off to die. For "to be sacrificed" doesn't necessarily mean "to be killed"; sacrificing an object can involve making it "sacred" by setting it apart, excluding it from the mundane, the everyday, the familiar, the easily accessed, the readily known. The strangely animal "it" of the pure pleasure principle is not terminated, but repressed, distanced from normal everyday consciousness, from the standard operating procedures of "common sense." Upon repression, it—*the* it, *das Es*—is relegated to the unconscious, where it doesn't expire but rather remains a lively but covert participant in the psychic life of the I, *das Ich*, sometimes coming back to bite my polite or "politicized" ego in the ass.

As this rather rude turn of phrase might suggest, *its* most vital activities are *fundamentally incompatible* with normal, conscious, proper meaning and manners, homeostatic good housekeeping, all the rules and regulations of fine upstanding citizenship, freedom, dignity, self-respect, impeccably clear writing, and so on. The fundamental psychoanalytic thesis about anthropogenesis is that none of us ever neatly exchanges *l'être pour la lettre*, pleasure for reality, wild being for civilized meaning, our pitiful portions of real happiness for the Big Other's tenuous portions of security. There is always for each of us an "unbearable truth," an ego-traumatizing *remnant* or *leftover*, unconscious but still unceasingly productive, the impolite if not unspeakable "stuff" that our darkest dreams of light are made of.

Freud, of course, called dreams the "royal road" to the unconscious. But for any theoretical writing that is informed by psychoanalysis, *all* the lost highways on the map of human reality lead to and from that strange location as well. For the gist of psychoanalysis is that the unconscious plays *its* part not only in the production of baffling dreams, neurotic symptoms, and embarrassing slips of the tongue; it determines and undermines the very production of meaning itself, all the work with words that *makes* the world that *must* be made to mean. Unconscious desire haunts *all* the forms

[5] In *How to Read Lacan*, Žižek writes, "The unconscious is not the preserve of wild drives that have to be tamed by the ego, but the site where a traumatic truth speaks out. Therein lies Lacan's version of Freud's motto *Wo es war, soll ich werden* (Where it was, I am to become): not 'The ego should conquer the id,' the site of unconscious drives, but 'I should dare to approach the site of my truth.' What awaits me 'there' is not a deep Truth that I have to identify with, but an unbearable truth that I have to learn to live with" (2006: 2–3).

of symbolic compensation or substitute gratification that we can imagine, or that have been pre-imagined or prefabricated for us, in this world or "the next." Cartoons and other forms of child's play can, of course, "count" as such imaginary or fabricated compensation. But then, so can all the really important grown-up stuff as well—literature, art, cinema, culture, politics, philosophy, science, religion, not to mention theory itself—in short, pretty much everything of which it pleases us to say that it all "has to meaning something," that it *must* be *meaning* and not just pleasure.

Coming to Terms

Critical Keywords encountered in Lesson Two:

pleasure and reality principles, the unconscious

Lesson Three

"Language is by nature fictional"

—or, why the word for moonlight can't be moonlight

I. Down to earth

Thus far in our introduction to theoretical writing we've seen some fairly large claims being made for *language*. We've been instructed that theoretical writing demands nothing less than our radically "coming to terms" with linguistic determinism, our bowing down, as it were, to *language* as invader of the universal problematic, surrendering to *language* as constitutive power behind all human reality, accepting *language* as origin and limit of all personal identity, and so on. But now we're being asked to swallow the pill that "language is, by nature, fictional" (Barthes 1981: 87); we find ourselves being told that almighty *language*—"this alien and inhuman force . . . which tortures and scars our existence as human animals" (Jameson 2006: 393)— isn't even really *real*.[1] This claim would seem particularly counter-intuitive, since we are obviously *really* using language at the present moment to communicate, or because the very assertion that "language is by nature fictional" must be made *in* language, therefore language *must* exist, and so on. So where does theory get off, telling us, on the one hand, that we're made out of language and then, on the other, that language is nothing but fiction?

To understand the real significance of the claim that significance isn't real, to grasp "the virtual [fictional or unreal] character of the symbolic order [as] the very condition of human historicity" (Žižek 1999/2002: 241), we need first to situate *fictionality* between relative *unrealness* and absolute *non-existence.* To say, with Roland Barthes, that language is nothing but fiction, to say, with the structural linguist Ferdinand de Saussure, that language is "*a form and*

---

[1] When Roland Barthes makes this remark in *Camera Lucida: Reflections on Photography,* he is specifically reflecting upon language's problem with authentication as compared to the camera's capacity for more veridical documentation (i.e., the now dated, pre-Photoshop idea that the camera doesn't lie). Compare the evidentiary value of a sworn statement such as "I was the man, I suffered, I was there" with an undoctored photograph that might conclusively prove that I was really a woman enjoying myself elsewhere.

not a substance" (1959: 122), is *not* to say, absurdly, that language doesn't exist; it *is* to say that language is not a substantial thing, but it's *not* to say that there's "no such thing" as language. For after all, *fiction* obviously exists—it's demonstrably not the case that there's "no such thing" as fiction, and I could give you a fairly substantial list of not too shabby examples thereof (*Antigone, Beloved, Candide, Disgrace, Ethan Frome, Germinal, Hamlet, Infinite Jest, Kangaroo, Lolita, Molloy,* and so on). So, since there clearly *are* such "things" in the world as "pieces of fiction," to say that language is by nature fictional is *not* to say that language doesn't exist.

But to assert language's "natural" fictionality *is* to foreground its unnaturalness, its "virtual character," and, in that quite specific sense, its antiphysical *unrealness.* For "fiction," by definition, isn't real. Just as human beings must distinguish themselves from non-human animal nature in order to live *as* human beings, as subjects of human reality, so "fiction" must bring itself into existence *as* fiction by formally *distinguishing* itself from the really real. Fiction's very existence *as fiction* definitionally depends upon this *separation* from the real, this active *negation* of the real. If a little piece of fiction, like that bit from Henry James that he calls "The Real Thing," were somehow to become the real thing, to become real, to become "fact," it would thereby cease to be fiction, no?

Well, in much the same way, the existence of language *as language* depends upon a similar separation from and negation of the real. So, we might venture to rewrite and expand upon Barthes' claim that language is by nature fictional as follows—language exists, but it's *not real.* It *cannot possibly be* real. In order to *be* language, to *exist* as language, language must *separate* itself from the real thing, cut itself off from the really real. If language were somehow to *become* real, to *merge* with the real, to become *identical* with the real, it would, by definition, cease to exist—or, at least, it would no longer be language (though whatever it would be I really can't say). Language, in other words, comes into existence not by positively but vaguely "saying something," but rather by negatively but specifically *having* "said" *no* to the real. Whatever language affirmatively says, it says only by virtue of this primordially prohibitive *no.* This negation of the real, this prohibition against identity with the real, *is* language's existential condition of possibility.

Some examples drawn from the realms of words and things might help us out here, so let's say that in order to *mean* "elephant," the word "elephant" cannot *be* an elephant. A complete merger of the meaningful word with the elephantine thing would not be possible, would not be meaningful. Of course, nothing prevents me from saying the word "elephant" in the real physical presence of a pachyderm or even from painting the word "elephant" on the said elephant's hide. The word's *meaning,* however, in no way depends upon that real, hidebound *presence* in order to mean. Rather, the word's meaning depends upon the real thing's *absence*, its disappearance, its *non-being*. In language, in other words, there can never *be* a completely real *coincidence* of *being* and *meaning*. For "to mean," as Barbara Johnson writes, "is automatically *not* to be. As soon as there is meaning, there is difference" (1981: ix).

But let's get "down to earth" here and literally (that is to say, figuratively) run this point into the ground. Let's say that even if I were to trace the word "dirt" into actual ground, into an actual spread of real dirt, the fingered *word* "dirt" still wouldn't *be* dirt; it would merely *mean* dirt. What allows the *meaning* of the word "dirt" to emerge *from* the dirt is nothing other than the four letters, the purely *formal* delineations of *non-dirt* that I've traced into the dirty surface. These formal delineations, these narrow defiles of *non-dirt* within otherwise unfurrowed substance—these *non-substantial fissures* within formlessly real soil—become the existential openings (the very *souls*, if you like) of meaning itself. *Meaning* must formally or soulfully separate itself out, must cleanse itself *of* and distinguish itself *from* formlessly real *being*, in order to raise itself up out of the really real *as* clear or distinct meaning. *Meaning* must mean non-merger with murkily real *being*. The veritable "law" of meaning *means* quite precisely that the word for "elephant" must not be elephant, that the word for "dirt" *must not* be dirt.

We can take the letter of this "law" back to our previous lesson. Its significance is not simply that "*meaning* is the polite word for pleasure." Our lesson's actual significance is that *pleasure* itself is a polite word for pleasure, that *any* meaningful word (pleasure, elephant, dirt) is a "polite" substitute for and separation from the real thing or experience that it names. To *mean* "pleasure," the word "pleasure" is prohibited from *really being* pleasure. I *don't* mean to say that saying the word "pleasure" can't be pleasurable, can't be a *form* (however attenuated) of enjoyment. I do mean to say that saying "pleasure" never necessarily *depends* upon one's *really experiencing* pleasure; rather, the word "pleasure" depends upon the possibility of our *not* really enjoying ourselves, of our *not* experiencing real pleasure; it depends upon the possibility of pleasure's *non-presence*. If one could *say* "pleasure" and really *mean* it *only* if one were at the precise moment of enunciation really experiencing a pleasure that was not only completely identical with the word but in fact caused one to say it, then the word "pleasure" *as word* would not be possible. The word "pleasure" need not be caused or accompanied by real pleasure any more than the exclamation "ouch" need be caused or accompanied by actual pain—we can say "ouch" even when we're not being bitten or stung or insulted, and we can say "pleasure" even at moments, such as perhaps this very one, when we're not having any fun at all.

II. Giving (up) the finger

Again, what *makes* the *presence* of any word possible is nothing but the possible *absence* of the real thing or experience that it names, which is precisely why Lacan characterizes the word as "a presence *made* of absence."

> In order for the symbolic object freed from its usage to become the word freed from the *hic et nunc* [here and now], the difference resides . . . in its vanishing being in which the symbol finds the permanence of the concept. Through the word—which is already a presence made of absence—absence itself comes to be named . . . And from this articulated couple of presence and absence . . . a language's world of meaning is born, in which the world of things [must] situate itself (1966d/2006: 228).

For Lacan, the ways by which language is "by nature fictional" are intimately related to the rules and regulations that make "meaning" the polite word for pleasure in a world that must be made to mean. In other words, for Lacan, our linguistic *separation* from and *negation* of "the real" has everything to do with what he calls "the symbolic order"—the imperative processes of anthropogenesis that we belabored in our first two lessons. To demonstrate the relations among these lessons even further, however, I'm afraid I'm going to have to give you the finger.

That is to say, I'm going to have to ask you to imagine that you are a very young child, in the very last stages of your infancy, not yet "in language" but on the cusp of "learning to read" in the sense described in the previous lesson. Imagine that I am the adult standing before you, trying to give you one of your first reading lessons. In this imaginary scene, I am using not my middle but rather my *index* finger to indicate something "over there" to which I want to direct your attention, some real thing *other* than my finger that I *employ* my finger to point out to you. You, however, continue to stare at my pointing finger, blissfully unaware that "pointing" is what I'm attempting to do with this digit. I can therefore jab and gesticulate as much as I please, but you simply won't get the picture; you won't get the point of my pointing. Illiterate infant that you are, you don't yet know how to "read," so you don't understand that this finger *isn't* merely a finger, a column of flesh moving back and forth in space, in a relatively undifferentiated, pointless, or meaningless "here and now." Incapable as yet of meaningful speech, you don't realize that, in giving you the finger, I am giving or trying to give you a **sign**. Not yet up to speed on your structural linguistics, you don't comprehend that this "indexical" sign is comprised of a **signifier** (the index finger as *pointer*) and a **signified** (the *point*, the "concept" I'm trying to convey, which in this case is "hey, look over there"). Nor do you yet grasp that the function of a sign (signifier and signified combined) is to *refer* to something *else*, something *other*, a **referent** (in this case, whatever the stupid or wonderful thing "over there" is that I so desperately want you to look at).[2] Because you don't yet "get" any of these points, because you're not yet in any position to take pointers, you won't take your eyes off my finger. I might as well be gesturing to a gerbil.

Now, if all I really wanted from this exercise were simply to get you to "look over there," then I could finally resort to just picking you up and pointing your little eyes in the thing's direction so that you would finally really see it. But we would have accomplished very little by these merely physical acrobatics. Therefore, because what I *must* want is for you to learn to read, *not* just see, I must *make* you see *this* thing (my finger) *not* just as a *real* thing floating around in this immediate space but as a veritable *sign* indicating some *other* thing *elsewhere*. To *give* you the finger as mediating *sign*, I must gently or sternly *deny* you the finger *as finger*. To *teach* you to "read" finger as a sign, I must, as it were, *wean* you from finger *qua* finger. And this weaning denial will no doubt initiate itself in the form of the prohibitive word *no*, as in, *no, don't look at my finger, look over there; no,* dumbass, not this stupid thing but that one; *no,* you *cannot* just keep staring at my finger; no, you *must* tear yourself away from the real flesh and look to that "other scene" to which the flesh is pointing; *no,* our flesh and bone can't just be pointless boney flesh, it all *must* signify something; *no,* our fingers can't just *be*, they must *mean*, must be ordered, must be named. And the same thing goes for you too, sweetie.

Not that sweet little infant you would actually take *in* any of these words, even though according to Lacan you've "always already" been taken in *by* them insofar as language always "exists prior to each subject's entrance into it at a certain moment in [its] psychic development" (Lacan 1966e/2006: 413). But, if you're ever going to become anything more than a sweet (or squawking) little animal, you must begin to hear that sour *n*ote; you must begin to understand the "negating" function of the *first* word in each of my prohibitory but literacy-enabling phrases (no, don't look at my finger; no, not here but there, and so on); moreover, you must, on some level, "understand" that this singularly prohibitive and negative word *no* actually precedes and precipitates *all* the words and *all* the phrases that you're ever going to understand in your life. The world that you are sentenced to enter must be made to mean, but it's precisely this primordial "*no* to the real" that *first* makes

---

[2] All of these terms—**signifier**, **signified**, **sign**, **referent**—pertain to the structural linguistics of Ferdinand de Saussure, which we will explore at greater length in Lesson Eight.

any meaning happen, that initially gets any sentence in any language up and running, by *preventing* any word you can imagine from ever really being the real thing that it names. Erecting, so to speak, a permanent and irreversible divide between real *being* and significant *meaning*, this primordial *no* is built into and basically *causes* or makes possible any articulation whatsoever. In order to signify anything, a sign *can never be* a simple, indivisible, absolute "thing in itself," but must always *separate* itself into a signifier and a signified, a pointer and a point. In order to *be* a *meaningful* word, a word can never simply remain what it "really" is—a certain quantum of sheer materiality, of ink on a page, or chalk on a board, or pixels on a screen. No, it must articulate a message, and back behind any articulation lurks the *fundamental imperative* of the symbolic order, which is simply this word—*no*. No, you can't keep looking *here* for your pleasure; no, you can't simply remain in the pure pleasure principle of the immediate experience of real being; as per the final words of Beckett's *The Unnamable*, no, you can't stay here; no, you can't even stay there; no, you must "go on" (1955: 414).

III. Thanks for nothing

The real *being* that *meaning* must leave behind in order to "go on" meaning is "the real" in Lacan's sense, the "oceanic feeling" in Freud's—a formless, limitless, undifferentiated experience of the "all" of the *hic et nunc*, the immediately *here and now*. Meaning, as such, formally *cuts* into and incisively *removes* us from our experience of that simple "immediate" being and "sends" us, *as if we ourselves were letters*, on our limited, grammatically regulated, and politely articulated way. For it's the real function of any meaningful word to *tear* us away from immediate being, to *deliver* us from the undifferentiated darkness of "the Real always lurking dimly in the background" (Jameson 2006: 376), and send or carry us in a brighter, more promisingly significant direction. Any meaningful word must point us away from itself and prod us to "go on" to the next word in the chain of signifiers (so please imagine my exemplary finger as pointing from left to right, the direction in which we in English *read*). The word "the," for example, the so-called definite article, seems to say something positively "in itself" to its reader—something affirmative, like "My name is '*the*' and I *am* the definite article." But even if it *is* the definite article, which it is, "the" *still* isn't simply the real thing; because it's a word, the word "the" *still* must always say "no" to whatever real thing or stuff (like ink or sound) that it might substantially be. In other words, the word "the" can never allow its reader to *stay* with it. Like the fallen grunt in the military action film who waves his comrades on, heroically urging the

rest of the squad to keep going, the word "the" must always *impel* the reader
to abandon it, to leave it behind, to keep moving on—if only just one more
space . . . to . . . the . . . right. In other words, the word "the" must always
carry out *its* symbolic orders and *the* symbolic order itself— the word "the"
must prod the . . . reader to move on to the . . . next word in the . . . temporal
sequence of meaning that we . . . call . . . the . . . sentence.[3]

As these annoyingly retarded articulations might help me suggest,
"language is by nature fictional" not only because, like fiction, it isn't really
real, but also because, like fiction, it usually involves something resembling
narrative design, the formal manipulation of merely chronological revelation
upon which the craft or sullen art of **narration** depends.[4] Certain exercises in
the art of the sentence—consider the hard work of a Henry James or a David
Foster Wallace—can read like gnarly epics. But even the briefest of complete
and fully predicated sentences, even those completely innocent of craft, still
manage to tell a little story, unfold a tale, relate the dramatic adventures of a
grammatical subject, verbalize an action, enact a beginning, stage a middle,
and struggle toward an end, providing, perhaps, a relatively satisfying sense
of narrative closure.[5]

But if language is "fictional" not only because it de-realizes but also
because it "narrates," just what *sort* of story does language actually tell?
For Lacan, the story of language always at some level involves Oedipus, or
Oedipal desire. Lacan, that is, rather tirelessly (and, for some, tiresomely)
relates language acquisition to what Freud famously dubs the **Oedipus
complex**.[6] But Lacan "Oedipalizes" our accession to language not simply
for psychological reasons, not simply because language acquisition and

---

[3] Unless of course the "the" in question is that last word of Joyce's *Finnegans Wake*, in which case the reader is compelled to circle back to the text's first word, "riverrun," and begin the fiction all over again.

[4] "The **narrative** theory of Russian Formalism distinguishes between story (*fabula*) and plot (*sujet*), between the story and the way it is told. *Fabula* . . . refers to the story as it might have occurred in real time and constitutes the raw narrative material awaiting the formal manipulation of the author. *Sujet* . . . designates the authorial transformation worked upon the story" (Childers and Hentzi 1995: 106).

[5] "Structurally, narrative shares the characteristic of the sentence without ever being reducible to the sum of its sentences: a narrative is a long sentence, just as every constative sentence is in a way the rough outline of a short narrative" (Barthes 1966/1977: 84).

[6] The **Oedipus complex** involves the idea that every child unconsciously desires complete "possession" of the mother and thus jealously and aggressively regards the father as a rival. Freud names this complex after the tragic title figure in Sophocles' play *Oedipus Rex*, the man who consciously attempts to avoid his "fate" (an oracle tells him that he will murder his father and "marry" his mother) and thus unwittingly blunders into it. Freud also offers an Oedipal interpretation of Shakespeare's *Hamlet,* suggesting that Hamlet can't bring himself to kill Claudius because Hamlet unconsciously identifies with the man who has done in fact what Hamlet himself desires to do in his dreams—dispatch the father and "marry" the mother.

the onset of the Oedipus complex can be said to "happen" at roughly the same time in the child's psychological development; rather, Lacan links language to Oedipus for "structural" reasons. He posits, that is, a structural analogy between the primordial "no to the real" that *initiates* all access to language and the "paternal" prohibition against incest that *bars* all sexual access to the mother's body and thereby founds any exogamous social order whatsoever. Obviously, Lacan's analogy goes against the grain of consciously common sense; after all, it's pretty hard to grasp what our conventionally grammatical desire to make complete sentences might have in common with our unconsciously Oedipal desire to "make it" with the mom. But if you can understand how "the symbolic order" *as the "law" of meaning that separates you from your immediately real being and subjects you to conventional rules of grammar and syntax* might be analogous to "the symbolic order" *as the "law" against incest that separates you from the maternal body and subjects you to the conventional regulations of normative heterosexuality*, then you basically get the Lacanian picture. If you can understand that "meaning" means both that you can no longer simply be in the undifferentiated real and that you can no longer "be with" your mother in the exclusive way that you might unconsciously desire, if you can understand that "the symbolic order" is an "order to symbolize" your mother (and everything else in the world) rather than "totally" be with her as if you and she were "everything" and there really were nothing or no one else out there—then you're well on your way to speaking basic Lacanese (whether you want to be or not).

But let's leave Lacan, not to mention our poor mothers, out of this discussion for the moment and return to the question of "real being" and of language's fictive negation thereof. I've suggested that linguistic meaning tears us away from the pure unmediated "here and now" of real being and sends us on our intelligibly articulated way. I've insisted that, consequent to this "tearing," there is an irrevocable split or rupture between *being* and *meaning*. A word, as I insist (or as the very pronoun "I" insists), can never *be* the thing that it names (elephant, dirt, me, etc.), and a thing (like my dirty finger) can never *remain* a simple, self-identical *thing* if it is ever *made* to function as a *sign*.

But is it a "good thing" or a "bad thing" that "the word" can never be "the real thing"? It depends, perhaps, upon the specific word in relation to the particular thing. To illustrate this "moral relativism," we can note a rather interesting thing that happens late in Don DeLillo's short novel *The Body Artist,* a sort of postmodern ghost story that, like most of DeLillo's fictions, meditates upon the strange and (in DeLillo's view) occasionally miraculous things that can happen in contemporary (fictional) encounters between language and the real. The story concerns a woman, Lauren Hartke, a performance or "body artist" who, while mourning the death of her film-maker husband, apparently discovers a strange quasiperson living in her (formerly their) house. This male semipersonage may be the embodied ghost of Lauren's husband, or he may be an imaginary figment that Lauren is cooking up for one of her embodied performance-art pieces, or he may simply be "a retarded man" (2001: 102) who has wandered away from some nearby institution. Whatever he may be or mean, this figure—nameless, though Lauren for reasons of her own calls him "Mr. Tuttle"—is presented to us as suffering from a disorder of speech, a sort of linguistic indeterminism. Mr Tuttle speaks, utters intelligible and even uncannily familiar words, but he is still paradoxically caught up in what the narrator calls "the not-as-if of things" (2001: 92). We are told a number of things about Mr Tuttle, but the most pertinent for our purposes here is that he "hasn't learned the language. There has to be an imaginary point [says our narrator], a nonplace where language intersects with our perceptions of time and space, and he [Mr. Tuttle] is a stranger at this crossing, without words or bearings" (2001: 101). Because he is so alien to this linguistic crossing, because he cannot quite successfully use good old words to cognitively map his "being in the world," Mr Tuttle, we are told, "violates the limits of the human" (2001: 102).

This description of Mr Tuttle's loss of bearings makes it sound "as if" he's in an unbearably inhuman spot. And yet, despite (or perhaps because of) his strange violation of human limits, Mr Tuttle manages to say some lovely, brilliant things. For example:

> He said, "The word for moonlight is moonlight."
> [And] this made [Lauren] happy. It was logically complex and oddly moving and circularly beautiful and true—or maybe not so circular but straight as straight can be. (2001:84)

Now, bear in mind that Mr Tuttle isn't simply being tautological here. He isn't just elliptically claiming that the word that we use to designate the phenomenon called moonlight is this specific word, "moonlight." Rather, he claims, flat-out, "straight as straight can be," that the word moonlight *really is moonlight*. This "poetical" merging of word with wave strikes Lauren as "beautiful" and thus makes her "happy," thus reminding us of Stendhal's tragicomic characterization of "beauty" as "the promise of happiness." But even though it makes her happy because she finds it beautiful—and even though a line from Keats's "Ode on a Grecian Urn" instructs us that the "articulated couple" or aesthetic/veridical copulation of beauty with truth is all we know and all we need to know—is Lauren "right" to consider Mr Tuttle's statement "true"? Doesn't this "logically complex" statement logically contradict everything we've learned in this lesson about the impossibility of a word's meaning merging with its real being? If "elephant" can't be an elephant and "dirt" can't be dirt and "I" can't be me, how can "moonlight" possibly be moonlight? Truly, maybe sadly, but in the end, I think, quite fortunately, it just can't be; it can't possibly simultaneously *mean* and *be.*

But why the hell not? And what's so "fortunate" about this *sad* impossibility of the *said*? Why might it be a "good thing" that linguistic meaning both makes and breaks the so-called promise of happiness? OK, so Mr Tuttle's blurting out that "the word for moonlight is moonlight" makes Lauren happy—fair enough. But we might ask if Lauren would have been made just as happy if Mr Tuttle had proclaimed that "The words for internal hemorrhage *are* internal hemorrhage"? The sentence is far from beautiful, you'll agree, but it could only quite disastrously be "true." For if the statement *were* "literally" true, then no "body artist" could ever produce the words "internal hemorrhage" without her body's internally hemorrhaging. Or, to take the art back out of the body, what if Mr Tuttle had asserted that "the word for excrement is excrement"? It's hard to imagine that Mr Tuttle's pressing *those* little words out of his uncanny hole would have made Lauren or DeLillo or Keats or any lover of beauty and truth radiantly happy.

So, yeah, maybe it's a real shame, on the one hand, that the *word* for moonlight can never really *be* moonlight, that we can't just utter this enchanting word and *be* instantly bathed in lovely lunar lucidity. But on the other hand, maybe it's a relatively good thing that you can ask for a "concrete example" of the difference between being and meaning without having a cinderblock fall on your head. Maybe it's a good thing that words for real excrement aren't really excremental things. Maybe it's a good thing that we're all able to utter our favorite excremental words without finding our mouths filled with you-know-what, that we can read Eliot's *The Waste Land* without actually landing in waste, and so on.

Maybe, at the end of the day, there's something to be said for our just saying "no" to non-differentiation, for our being able to distinguish ourselves from the real, simply by saying "no, not really what we had in mind." Maybe there's something to be said for being's being said, even if saying so means forever losing all our oceanic feelings. Maybe there's something to be said for our being able to say, which is to say, our being able to lie, to fabricate, to negate "the not-as-if of things" by making metaphors, by reading and writing, telling the stories of our so-called lives, proliferating ourselves quite precisely as fictions. Maybe we readers and writers and would-be lovers of literature should be enormously *grateful* that language *is* by nature fictional, even if its unstable fabrications actually turn out to be the stuff that we're made of, even if such gratitude puts us in the exceedingly strange position of having to say thanks to no one for nothing. Yes, the "no to the real" that makes the phrase "real significance" nonsensical, that makes language, and hence we ourselves, possible, may *prevent* us from getting *all* that we might really *desire*. But such negativity also *protects* us from getting *more* than we might really *deserve*. We may be "real-losers" in the sacrificial exchange of our being for a meaning that can never be completely real again, but, considering what we get out of it, and considering what it gets us out of, we might just have to say that "radically linguistic determinism"—our being sentenced to sentences, to being nothing by nature if not fictionalized characters, anthropomorphized animals at the mercy of language, male and female impersonators in a world that must be made to mean—can't really be the dirtiest trick that was ever played on us, can't really be the crappiest thing that ever happened to us. While the slogan "language is by nature fictional" might seem like the worst bit of "ontological bad news" (Butler 1999: 198) ever to hit the fan, it really can't be the unhappiest headline, the most unpromising piece of prose, that any real fan of writing has ever encountered, that any really appreciative reader of fiction has ever really read.

Coming to Terms

Critical Keywords encountered in Lesson Three:

sign, signifier/signified, referent, narrative/narration

"Desire must be taken literally"

—a few words on death, sex, and interpretation

I. "a few words"

We often abuse the word "literally," claiming that we *literally* died laughing or *literally* jumped out of our skins when we actually only ever *figuratively* accomplish such maneuvers. How literally, then, can we take Lacan when he insists that "desire must be taken literally" (1966f/2006: 518)? What would it mean, and where would it take us, if we were to take Lacan at his word?

In Lacan's own words—as registered in "The Instance of the Letter in the Unconscious, or, Reason Since Freud"—to take desire "literally" means to take it "*à la lettre*" (1966e/2006: 413), to the letter. And the "letter" to which Lacan takes us here would seem to follow the same script as the letter we find in *l'être pour la lettre*, the slogan Lacan uses to describe our exchange of *being* for *meaning*, the *loss* of *real being* that we all incur upon our anthropogenetic *gain* of recognizably human significance.

So when Lacan writes that "desire must be taken literally," to the letter, he means that "desiring" and "lettering" are pretty much the same thing, or rather the same *non*-thing, that *desire* and *signification* are both precipitated by the same "no" to the real thing, the same *negation* of the real that we encountered and belabored in the previous lesson. Because "for Lacan, human desire (in contrast to animal instinct) is always, constitutively, mediated by reference to Nothingness" (Žižek 1999: 126), we should take his phrase "desire must be taken literally" to mean *both* that "desire" itself is literally nothing—"the revelation of an emptiness, the presence of the absence of a reality" (Kojève 1947/1980: 5)—*and* that the signifier itself is, again, literally nothing, "a presence made of absence" (Lacan 1966d/2006: 228), never (again) the completely real thing. Insisting that desire means incompletion, that *in* desire, as in signification, something real always goes missing, Lacan means that *meaning* always means the *loss* of the real thing, that language presupposes a radical subtraction of being, that signification is always constituted around a central and defining *lack*. And since we ourselves—as distinctly human beings, or non-animal animals—are always constituted in and by signification, we ourselves must be subjects of this very lack.

For better or worse, Lacan chooses to speak of this situation, of *our* situation (in contrast to the non-human animal's *completely* instinctual situation), in terms of *symbolic castration*—in terms, that is, that are not to be taken anatomically or biologically, but are to be taken, quite literally, "literally."

Taken literally, then, *desire* involves our significant (albeit unconscious) attempts to get the missing real thing *back*, to overcome our symbolic castration, strenuous efforts animated by nostalgic fantasies of "totally" returning to the lost homeland of the real. But because these attempts and efforts are totally *fantasmatic*—imaginary and symbolic, not "really real," but only ever the signifying traces of the real's inexorable withdrawal—nothing is more *impossible* than our desired recovery of the real thing. Because the word "must" in the slogan "desire *must* be taken literally" corresponds intimately to the same imperative in the axiom "the world *must* be made to mean," nothing is less possible, nothing is less meaningful—and, finally, paradoxically, nothing is less desirable—than our desired restoration of really real being, our desired return to the real. It's literally the last thing we'd ever want to happen.

To begin to hash these matters out, let's return not to the real, but to Lacan's distinctions among *need*, *demand*, and *desire*, touched upon but lightly in a previous lesson. Let's see if we can see how these three modalities might instructively be mapped onto Lacan's three registers of the *real*, the *imaginary*, and the *symbolic*. Let's see if we can see how *need* seeps into *the real*, how the *imaginary* reflects *demand*, and how the *symbolic order* provokes and perpetuates—but never fully satisfies—*desire*.

Since I desire to interpret these inter-knotted trios under the general rubric of anthropogenesis, or the question of what "makes us human," let's begin by noting that at the most basic level of organic *need*, there's *really* nothing that radically distinguishes us from nature, from animals and plants, from eagles and oak trees or earthworms and algae. Fish, flesh, or fowl; flora, fauna, or fledgling folk—all organisms *need* air, water, food, maybe a little light, to live and not die. At this basic or beginner's level of sheer nutritional *need*, then, we're all pretty much in the same boat. Or rather, since at this level "we" living organisms are all missing the meta-phorical boat—missing, that is, if we're plants, animals, or human infants, any firmly differentiated ego-coherence or buoyant personhood or ship-shape sense of self—let's say that at the level of *need* "we" all seem to sink, swim, or "run together" in the undifferentiated "ocean" of the biologically determined *real*.[1]

But there is *one* particular aspect of incipient *human* existence that does distinguish us from every other chicken in the sea, and that's the fact that *we* really *need more* than all those other organisms in the real, thanks to the "vital insufficiency" (Lacan 1966b/2006: 72) stemming from our specific prematurity at birth, discussed at some length in Lesson Two. The fact that our earliest needs *are* more pronounced (compared to those of the more vitally sufficient neonates) inevitably compels us to have to *pronounce* them, to make them *known* to others, even if, as newborns, we can't yet make them *nouns*. In terms of the Lacanian registers, we might say that our capacity while as yet still mewling infants to *express* without *nominating* our *real needs* situates us at the *imaginary* level of *demand*. Demand allows us to make our first feeble movements out of the oceanic real, where all things run together, to crawl up and flop around on relatively drier land. The capacity for demand, that is, separates us, though only partially, from the swirling stew of sheer

[1] There are a number of sources for all this "nautical" talk about the undifferentiated real, this "sea of yolky enjoyment" (Žižek 1992: 40) where "things . . . at first run together in the *hic et nunc* of the all" (Lacan 1966d/2006: 229). For Freud, as we've seen, the infant in the "primary narcissism" of the real experiences a putatively "oceanic feeling," the overwhelming sensation of "an indissoluble bond, of being one with the external world as a whole" (1930/1989: 723). Freud's "oceanic feeling" of course *precedes* anyone's sense of ego-coherence, predates any firm "sense of self"; in *Civilization and its Discontents*, Freud writes that "originally the ego [*das Ich*] includes everything, [but] later it separates off an external world from itself. Our present ego-feeling is, therefore, only a shrunken residue of . . . an all-embracing . . . feeling which corresponded to a more intimate bond between the ego and the world" (1930/1989: 724–5). For Georges Bataille, this all-embracing and relatively ego-free world is both dissolutely oceanic and saturated with animality; in the "Animality" chapter of his *Theory of Religion*, that is, Bataille writes that "every animal is *in the world like water in water*" (1973/1989: 19), and in Bataille's thinking, the difference between animals (thoroughly saturated with their own being) and humans (relatively dessicated by their own meanings) involves the difference between *continuity* and *discontinuity* with this water-world. Anticipating Freud and Bataille, Nietzsche, in *The Birth of Tragedy*, discusses the formation of the *principium individuationis*—the Apollonian "principle of individuation," as opposed to Dionysian self-dissolution—in notably nautical terms, quoting Schopenhauer, "As a sailor sits in a small boat in a boundless raging sea, surrounded on all sides by heaving mountainous waves, trusting to his frail vessel; so does the individual man sit calmly in the middle of a world of torment, trusting to the *principium individuationis*" (1872/2006: 44). Arguably, Nietzsche's "frail vessel" and Freud's "shrunken residue" and Bataille's all too human "fish out of water" are all figures for ego-coherence or ego-syntony, for the firm "sense of self" that the pre-linguistic "little human animal," like any other piece of yolky flotsam in the real, *lacks*. It's this lack of a discernible "sense of self" that I'm addressing when I suggest that, in the realm of *real need*, "we" are all "missing the boat." Correspondingly, those of us organisms who come to possess a sense of self, who are "on board" and thus no longer "missing the boat," are, by definition, missing the real. In other words, persons *qua* persons are always missing the real, and the real is always *missing persons*.

mute need—demand-capability, that is, distinguishes us from all vegetable matter (from seaweed, for example, which as far as I know can't demand anything) but not from all animals. For just as human infants can and do issue demands, quite vocally, in the form of grating inarticulate bleats and squeals, so can certain non-human animals let *their* pressing needs be known. My dog Joni, for example, never fails to let me know—and in "terms" that are no less certain for not being put into words—when her canine highness needs to be fed or petted or taken out for a walk.

Demand, then, like need, remains an aspect of animality; it is not yet *desire*, which, in this interpretation, exclusively involves the human. Demand, that is, can be said to correspond to the register of the *imaginary*, the embodied realm of the *visible* world (in which all animals with eyes take part), but demand does not yet coordinate with the *symbolic*, which organizes or structures specifically human reality. Animals can of course not only see but communicate, can send and receive "vital signs," signals that (again, as far as I know) pertain *only* to the protection-enhancement-continuation of their biological species-life, *with* which they are (again, arguably) *completely identical*, as per Georges Bataille's claim that every animal is in its world "*like water in water*" (1973/1989: 19). But even "signaling" animals, from warblers to whales, lack language in the "vitally mortifying" sense that is specific to human reality; *their* signals, that is, can neither separate them from nor ever become more significant than their immediately animal life, whereas *our* signs not only can and do but *must* separate us from our purely corporeal existence, our simply anatomical destiny, our merely animal instincts. Unlike human desire, which must be taken literally, to the letter, animal instinct is never "mediated by reference to Nothingness" (Žižek 1999: 126). Unlike us, animals don't have to repress or negate some aspect of their animality in order to become or remain the animals that they are. Unlike us, animals shake off nothing of their "real being" in their ecstasies of communication, while we non-animal animals can be said to lose everything *but* our symbolic meaning—lose our sense of being (lost in) everything—when we first find ourselves distinctly located in language. This "total loss" as loss of totality *turns* us from organisms of real *need*, or animals of imaginary *demand*, into symbolically ordered *subjects* of *desire*.[2]

---

[2] If we lose our sense of being (lost in) everything by finding ourselves cohering *as individual selves* in language, then we can regain that sense only by "losing ourselves," losing our singular and isolated sense of self-coherence, escaping our enclosure in what Nietzsche in *Birth of Tragedy* calls "the miserable glass shell of human individuality" (Nietzsche 1872/2006: 82). We can experience loss of self as *ecstasy* (sex, drugs, rock n roll, sports, mysticism, religious fervor, or some combination thereof) or as *trauma* (war, assault, natural disaster, animal attacks, etc.). But the line separating ecstasy from

Now, it should be fairly easy to see how *need* corresponds to the organic *real*, how animal *demand* can be distinguished from botanical need, and thus how human beings are a bit closer to monkeys than we are to moss. But other than the fact that irises don't have eyes, what decisively links *demand* to the *imaginary*? To grasp this connection, let's momentarily bracket the difference between *need* and *demand* and consider instead the difference between the *imaginary* and the *symbolic*. And, to use a few terms from Freud, let's say that the difference between *imaginary demand* and *symbolic desire* involves the difference between "thing-presentations" and "word-presentations."[3] As we should be able to see, both physically and psychically, "thing-presentations" function as visual *images* in a clear-cut, *either/or* sense—whether in perception or apperception, whether in the eye or in the mind's eye, a "thing-presentation" exists in such a way that "now you see it, now you don't." Thing-presentations, that is, are typically *either* present *or* absent; basically, they're either *there* or they're *not there*. And it is in *this* respect that images, as thing-presentations, might be said to correspond to *demand*, at least insofar as demand, in Lacan's book, is always "for a presence *or* an absence" (1966g/2006: 579, emphasis added). In other words, what the organism that *can* demand *does* demand *of* a needed or unneeded thing, of some wanted or unwanted thing-presentation, is *either* for it to "be there" *for* the organism *or* for it to get the hell away *from* the organism. What the "organism of demand" most basically demands is that the image/thing-presentation *either* appear *or* disappear, *either* come closer *or* keep its distance. Thus, barring some complex visual effect or *tromp-l'œil* in which "objects may be closer than they appear," thing-presentations are always

trauma is easily transgressed (when great rough sex gets too rough to stay great, or when we overdose on drugs or religious fervor and turn into fanatics, or when the drunken crowd in the "Dionysian" mosh pit or sports arena riots and "Apollonian" people get their "principles of individuation" crushed to bloody pulp). The point here is that "you" as a point, as a *coherent self*, can *never* return to the real as such, mainly because you were formed *as* a "you" by being separated *from* the real by the symbolic order. Like language, "you" exist, but you're not real; if "you" were to become real, to merge with the real, "you" would cease to exist, lose your "personal identity." The real, again, is always "missing persons," and persons *qua* persons are always missing the real, so if anything returns to the real, it's not going to be "you personally." Any return to the real would involve a violation of human limits, an ecstatic/traumatic encounter with the "not-as-if of things." The great benefit of language, art, and other cultural forms of *representation* (high and low, tragedy and Wagnerian opera or theatrical S&M, war and horror films, porn) is that they allow spectators to *approach* a close encounter with the ecstatic/traumatic "not-as-if" of the real without ever really being blown away or torn apart. So Nietzsche argues in *Birth of Tragedy* (minus, of course, the bit about porn).

3   According to Laplanche and Pontalis in *The Language of Psycho-Analysis*, these are "terms used by Freud in his metapsychological works in order to distinguish between two types of 'presentation'—between the (essentially visual) type which is derived from things and the (essentially auditory) one derived from words" (1973: 446).

clearly *either/or*—they are never *both/and*—for the organism of demand. Animal or infant, barking dog or squealing kid, the organism *physically capable* of demand is nonetheless *psychically incapable* of sustaining the ambiguity and/or ambivalence that the simultaneous *both/and* of *presence/absence* demands (of us).

And so here's the crux of the matter—very much *unlike* imaginary "thing-presentations," "word-presentations" are *nothing but* ambiguous instances of the *both/and* of *presence/absence*. To re-present Lacan's and Derrida's presentations of the "absentations" of words, a word is always a "presence made of absence" (Lacan 1966d/2006: 228); a meaning is always the appearance of the "disappearance of natural presence" (Derrida 1967/1997: 159). A "word-presentation" is *both* a "thing-presentation" *and* a "non-thing-presentation" at the same time. This *both/and* condition obtains for the word because, as we've read, the word presents or shows itself as *a* thing but can never be *the real* thing that it names. Thus a word, rather like a king in Prince Hamlet's bitingly low estimation, is always ever a "thing of nothing." And the reference to Hamlet—for whom the famously soliloquized question is "to be or not to be"—isn't exactly infelicitous here:

> For the signifier is a unique unit of being which, by its very nature, is the symbol of but an absence. This is why we cannot say of the . . . letter that, like other objects, it must be *or* not be somewhere but rather that, unlike them, it will be *and* not be where it is wherever it goes. (Lacan 1966a/2006: 17)

Now, we should be able to recognize that *real need, imaginary demand,* and *symbolic desire* all bear on the question of the *satisfactions* necessary to sustain "life" and/or human reality. And because to be or not yet to be or not at all to be (satisfied) is indeed the question, we should be able to imagine how the tensions among real need, imaginary demand, and symbolic desire coordinate with the conflicts between the pleasure and reality principles that we examined in our earlier lesson. But we should also be able to understand the following distinctions among our inter-knotted trios:

In the *real, all* living organisms have *needs.* Moreover, organic *need* can actually be completely *fulfilled.* The orchid in the swamp, the mollusk in the shell, the fetus in the womb, can all really, naturally, or umbilically obtain amounts of nutrition vitally sufficient to their days, however numbered, without having, or even being able, to ask.

In the *imaginary, some* living organisms *do* have to ask and are quite capable of *demand.* Moreover, *some* demands can be fully *met*—for if demand is always for a presence *or* an absence, all things or thing-presentations can either be (seen) or not be (seen), can either be brought closer or chased away, killed off or kept at the ready.

But while in the imaginary any given organism may demand a presence *or* an absence, once the *human* organism is ensconced in the *symbolic,* once the fledgling *human* organism finally learns to turn its *needs* into *nouns,* what this non-animal animal gets, and gets to be, is *only* ever a presence *made* of absence—a "letter" (like the letter "I") that will both be (a thing) and not be (the thing that it is), wherever it (or "I") may go. And the "letter" in question here is of course *the* letter to which we're taken if we "take desire literally," as Lacan insists we must. The letter thus reveals all of human reality as not-all, as never completely here or there, as nothing but the problem of desire. The letter turns all incipient subjects of human reality from demanding organisms with merely real needs into symbolically ordered subjects of anthropogenetic desire. I don't mean that upon this transformation the subject of human reality no longer experiences any real need, or that it completely gives up on all its merely imaginary demands. I mean that in entering/following the symbolic order the subject of desire suppresses and surpasses its own real needs and imaginary demands *by symbolizing them,* putting them into words, taking them literally, to the letter. *Only* by taking its needs, its demands, and itself "literally" can it "truly" (i.e., *not really*) become a subject of human reality/desire—a being *driven,* to be sure, but driven much less by animal instinct than by an ongoing reference to (its own) nothingness.

It is not *not* for nothing, then, that Lacan writes that language "grabs hold of desire at the very moment it becomes humanized by gaining recognition" (1966d/2006: 243). For Lacan, that is, the desire for recognition, the desire of meaning, is the meaning of humanized desire. If desire is the presence of the absence of a reality, and the word is the presence of the absence of the thing, then linguistically determined or humanized reality is nothing but the appearance of the disappearance of natural presence, the presence of the absence of the real. To insist, then, that "desire must be taken literally" is really only to reiterate our first three lessons (in reverse order), to say once again that "language is by nature fictional," that "meaning is the polite word for pleasure," and that "the world must be made to mean." And having repeated these lessons as often as we now have, we should be better positioned to return all the way back to our "introductory matters" and to better appreciate "what theory does," to better understand why theoretical writing *must* reflect on "meaning" as a problem rather than as a given, why theory *lives* to denaturalize and defamiliarize the desire for meaning as the meaning of desire—*particularly* when theoretical writing gropes and grapples with the meanings of human *sexual* desire.

OK, you might be thinking, it's about fucking time—all this "theoretical" chatter about "pleasure" and "desire" with only the slightest mention of "real sex"! Well, yes, it *is* about "fucking time," so to speak, and we *are* finally going to say a few words about desire in relation to "real sex" and in relation to real death.

But we're going to have to let death come first.

II. "on death"

You might have already noticed its shadow falling upon this discourse. Back in the first lesson, for example, when I asked you to list everything you could think of that separates humans from, say, roosters, you might well have included "awareness of our own mortality" on your roster.

Or maybe you got a whiff of the necrotic back when I was giving you the low-down on the pleasure principle's prime directive. When you read that this principle's goal is to "reduce unpleasurable tension," to restore homeostatic quiescence, the thought might have crossed your mind that it's hard to be much more quiescently homeostatic than stone-cold *dead*. Freud himself reached the same conclusion, by which I don't mean that he died, though of course he did, but rather that, in his attempts to think through the problems of the pleasure principle, Freud ends up speculating on *Thanatos*, the unconscious **death drive**, which, along with *Eros*, the unconscious sexual drive, works to shape human psychical reality.[4]

Well before trotting out the couple *Eros* and *Thanatos*, however, Freud begins his great study *Beyond the Pleasure Principle* by addressing the phenomenon of "repetition compulsion" and by posing the following thorny question—if the goal of the pleasure principle is to avoid unpleasurable tension and restore homeostatic quiescence, why on earth would we compulsively repeat *unpleasurable* activities or *disquieting* memories of tense or even traumatic experiences? Freud provisionally answers this question by speculating that we compulsively repeat unpleasure in the attempt to gain a sort of ideational *mastery* over it and so to *recover* our lost equilibrium,

---

[4]   According to Laplanche and Pontalis, *Thanatos* is the "Greek term (=Death) sometimes used by analogy with 'Eros' to designate the death instincts; its use underscores the fundamental nature of the instinctual dualism by lending it a quasi-mythical sense. This name is not to be found in Freud's writings, but according to [Ernest] Jones he occasionally used it in conversation" (1974: 446).

fantasmatic endeavors fundamentally in keeping with the pleasure principle's overriding goal.

Freud bases this "masterful" hypothesis upon a number of clinical observations, but what particularly leads him to posit an unconscious death drive is his interpretation of a seemingly simple game played by his 18-month-old grandson, Ernst. In what is now called the *fort-da* game, little Ernst—a "good boy" who "obeyed orders not to touch certain things or go into certain rooms" and who "never cried when his mother left him for few hours" (1920/1989: 599)—would be observed (by Freud) fooling around with a wooden reel tied to a piece of string. The child would repeatedly throw the reel away while holding onto the string, making urgent staccato sounds (rendered in the text as "o-o-o-o") that for Freud approximated the fully fledged German word *fort*, meaning "gone." Then, typically, Ernst would pull the reel back in and greet "its reappearance with a joyful '*da*'" ['there']. "This, then, was the complete game—disappearance and return" (1920/1989: 599). And, in Freud's view, the "interpretation of the game" is, at least initially, "obvious":

> It was related to the child's great cultural achievement—the instinctual renunciation . . . he had made in allowing his mother to go away without protesting. He compensated himself for this . . . by himself staging the disappearance and return of the objects within his reach. (1920/1989: 600)

But this interpretation, if obvious, is also complicated for Freud by the fact that Ernst sometimes throws the reel away *without* reeling it back in. This repeated pattern of disappearance and no return contradicts any purely happy reading of the ludic reel as *unambiguously* representing an *unambivalently* desired maternal object (since Ernst would ostensibly *always* want *that* object back, constantly *da* rather than ever distressingly *fort*). As Freud explains:

> The child cannot possibly have felt his mother's departure as something agreeable or even indifferent. How then does his repetition of this distressing experience as a game fit in with the pleasure principle? It may perhaps be said in reply that her departure had to be enacted as a necessary preliminary to her joyful return, and that it was in the latter that lay the true purpose of the game. But against this must be counted the observed fact that the first act, that of departure, was staged as a game in itself and far more frequently than the episode in its entirety, with its pleasurable ending. (1920/1989: 600)

Now, the fact that in the observed performances of the *fort-da* game, the *fort*s sometimes outnumber the *da*s leads Freud to posit "another motive" behind the *Liebestod*dler's staged loss of the reel.[5]

> At the outset he was in a *passive* situation—he was overpowered by the experience; but, by repeating it, unpleasurable though it was, as a game, he took on an *active* part. These efforts might be put down to an instinct for mastery . . . But still another interpretation may be attempted. Throwing away the object so that it was 'gone' might satisfy an impulse of the child's which was suppressed in his actual life, to revenge himself on his mother for going away from him. In that case it would have a defiant meaning: 'All right, then, go away! I don't need you. I'm sending you away myself.' (1920/1989: 600)

Freud's interpretation of this pint-sized revenger's tragedy subtly connects "play" in the *ludic* sense, as *game*, to "play" in the *literary* sense, as *dramaturgy* (note the references to staging, first acts, taking on parts, etc.). And the main piece of dramatic literature Freud has in mind here is pretty obviously *Oedipus*, for the evidence of Ernst's being a "good boy" includes his never crying when his mother goes away and his obeying orders not to "go into certain rooms" (forgive me, if you possibly can, but one has only to imagine *Fudd* rather than *Freud* reading *that* line to get the Oedipal gist of which chambers Ernst has been symbolically ordered not to go back into).[6]

Somewhat less obviously, but perhaps no less Oedipally, the *fort-da* also plays out the whole three-act drama of real need, imaginary demand, and symbolic desire. The game thus leads us, as it led Freud, to the death drive, to the radical idea that "*an instinct* [or drive] *is an urge inherent in organic life to restore an earlier state of things*" (1920/1989: 612) and to the fateful conclusion that "*the aim of all life is death*" (1920/1989: 613). We are taken to this conclusion literally—that is to say, figuratively. For figurative language allows us to suggest that the earliest "state" of little Ernst's big ocean of "things" is immersed in the real (if only by virtue of the homonymic coincidence that

---

[5] I claim full responsibility for this atrocious word "*Liebestod*dler," which mashes up the English "toddler" with the German "*Liebestod*," or "love-in-death" (taken from Wagner's opera *Tristan und Isolde*)—all the better to adumbrate Freud's argument that the desire for love *and* the desire for death are disturbingly merged in the playful dynamics of the little boy's *fort-da*.

[6] "Loony Tunes" cartoon character Elmer Fudd, hapless hunter and principal adversary of Bugs Bunny, is represented as having a speech impediment that causes him to pronounce "rabbit" as "*w*abbit," just as Ernst in *Beyond the Pleasure Principle* is represented as pronouncing "front" as "fwont" (1920/1989: 600). The really bad Oedipal joke here is that in a Fuddian/Freudian reading the word "room" would sound like "womb."

one of these things is in English called a reel). If the aim of the death drive is to return to an "earlier state of things" that resembles being in the real, then, we might argue, Ernst expresses his desire to return himself to the real when he returns the reel to himself. We might also argue that Ernst "masterfully" manipulates the real reel *both* to vocally register imaginary demand (for an absence *or* a presence, a *fort* or a *da*) *and* to aggressively negate real need (as in the puny and punitive ad-lib "all right, then, go away! I don't need you").[7] But what separates Ernst's anthropogenetic antics with the reel from a puppy's fetching a stick or a kitten's toying with a piece of string is the fact that in Freud's reading *this* reel *means* something *other* to the boy than what it *really is*. In this sense, the reel is *symbolic*, and as we are significantly told, the "good boy" manipulates this symbolic object all the better to *compensate* himself for the very "instinctual renunciation" by which he becomes "good" in the first place, by which he becomes *un*demanding, able to allow "his mother to go away *without protesting*" (1920/1989: 600).

But it takes more than throwing real things around in the *play-pen* to turn imaginary demand into symbolic desire—it takes, so to speak, a figurative *ink-pen*, the magical "wand" of *words*, to perform that anthropogenetic trick. For what's actually decisive in the *fort-da* game is not any physical manipulation of real objects but rather the way little Ernst must literally "write" his way out of the real, must linguistically *designate* his own relationship to any real object's disappearance and return. To "literally" free himself from the here and now, Ernst must irrevocably bind his fate to that of the letter. In other words, whatever he may or may not *have* in his mitts, nothing will be anthropogenetic for Ernst until language grabs hold of the nib of his desire. And, to tell the truth, anthropogenesis just isn't going to be happening for Ernst until it finally occurs to him *to lie*—to fabricate, to make stuff up, make the real "go away," to turn his back, as it were, on "the not-as-if of things." For it *really is as if* language will have "truly" grabbed hold of Ernst's desire only when he becomes a playful liar, a bit of a poet, a ludic little "man of letters" (even if the first letters attributed to him are but the compulsively repeated revelations of an emptiness, an empty set of naughts, a meager series of zeroes

---

[7] To grasp how Ernst's *physical* manipulation of the reel expresses *imaginary* demand, we can note two details. The first is that when Ernst plays *fort-da* with the reel, he throws the object "over the edge of his curtained cot, so that it disappear[s] into it" (1920/1989: 599). Significantly, the game of disappearance/reappearance stresses the visual over the tactile. The second detail is that Ernst would sometimes be observed playing *fort-da* or "Baby o-o-o-o" with his *own* image in a mirror, "the child had found a method of making *himself* disappear. He had discovered his reflection in a full-length mirror which did not quite reach the ground, so that by crouching down he could make his mirror-image 'gone'" (Freud 1920/1989: 599n2).

strung together in a hyphenated line—"o-o-o-o").[8] *Only* when simulation and dissimulation become vital sources of stimulation—only when he realizes that he doesn't have to have a thing in his little hand to give birth to a *da*, or that he can at any time let out a *fort* without having cast out any actual reel—does little animal Ernst "literally" begin becoming human.

But Ernst enters human reality not simply by using words—presences made of absence—to designate the *tangible* alternation *between* presence and absence that he himself causes. No, Ernst *liebestod*dles into the big empty house of fiction, the world of desire—becomes, again, figuratively speaking, human, a non-animal animal at the mercy of language—only when he accepts that it *is figuratively speaking*, not *really* having, not *really* being, that constitutes the only true "habitat for humanity" in which he or we will ever meaningfully live. In this interpretation, it is only ever language that builds what Martin Heidegger calls "the house of being" (1947/1977: 193), only ever the "world of words that creates the world of things" (Lacan 1966d/2006: 229).[9] *This* world, the only world there is, must always be made to mean, and "to mean" must always mean to *lose* real things, to *lack* real being—in other words, to *desire*.

But I've yet to toss out a compelling interpretation of how this interpretation of desire relates to the death drive. To grasp this relation, we need to return, not to an earlier *state of things* but to some earlier *statements about nothing*—specifically, to Kojève's neat description of desire as the "revelation of an emptiness, the presence of the absence of a reality" (1947/1980: 5) and to Žižek's assertion that "for Lacan, human desire (in contrast to animal instinct) is always, constitutively, mediated by reference to Nothingness" (1999: 126). Taking these lines of thought literally, we can better comprehend

---

[8] How many o's does it take to make a *fort*? In Freud's first inscription of Ernst's approximation of the German word for "gone," there are four letters, or four instances of the same letter: "o-o-o-o." But in a second inscription, there are, perhaps not insignificantly, only three—as Freud reports, "When this child [Ernst] was five and three-quarters, his mother [Freud's beloved daughter Sophie] died. Now that she was really 'gone' (o-o-o), the little boy showed no signs of grief" (1920/1989: 599n2). What to make of this emotional no-show, of the fact that here, in Freud's writing, one lower-case "o"—which can already be read as a zero, a hole, a sign that something's missing—is itself quite conspicuously missing, no longer "*da*"? Insofar as that "o" might be read as representing the departed Sophie (not for the son Ernst, who showed no signs of grief, but for the bereft father, Freud), we might speculate that by letting that "o" be "gone" from his writing, by himself staging the absence of a particular presence made of absence, the "philosopher" Freud is showing by not showing the very sign of his grief—"o."

[9] Although some theoretical writers, like Derrida, consider Heidegger to be terribly important, and despite the clear relevance to the present discussion of Heidegger's notion of "being towards death," I am omitting any further mention of Heidegger's philosophy in this book for this simple reason—I really really hate Heidegger. I've just never been able to get past the whole business of his having been a Nazi. Concerning Heidegger's Nazism, see, for example, Farias (1991). For what passes for a critique of Derrida's "retention" of Heidegger, see the chapter on Heidegger and Derrida in Thomas (1996).

not what desire *literally is* (because it literally *isn't* any *thing*) but rather the way desire *formally works* (with "formally" here meaning without regard to any particular content, any specific *object* of desire).

Formally, then, if there *is* desire, if desire *exists*, if desire is "present," then some reality or object of desire *must* be absent. If the desired reality weren't absent, then desire wouldn't be present—the desideratum's "full presence" would spell desire's complete cancellation. Desire as emptiness, as nothingness, would necessarily *terminate itself* in its utter fulfillment. Thus, in the purely *formal* sense, the desire of desire must be to end itself, to cancel itself out, as desire. By definition, then, desire desires to kill itself; structurally, desire desires suicide, and so on.

But if there's something structurally and constitutively "self-destructive" about the desire of desire, there's also something animatedly "self-protective" about it as well. Desire, that is, may very well desire to end itself, but at the same time desire desires to *sustain* itself, to go on and on, to continue to make its presence felt by literally "staying hungry," by *remaining* insistently empty, dissatisfied, dis*content*ed, constantly deferring or negating or "sending away" the absent but approaching "reality" whose fully satisfying presence would inevitably bring desire to its (un)desired conclusion. Desire in this sense desires to keep playing *fort/da*—it is nothing but the longing to *keep on longing* to reach the end, the longing to keep on longing to grasp the thing at the end of the line. Formally, then, desire "literally" self-perpetuates by putting off its ending, by only ever *circling* but never *seizing* its object, remaining the garrulously *active* revelation of its own emptiness or nothingness or restless discontent.

It is in *this* sense that desire can be conflated not simply with "death" or "the dead" but, more strictly speaking, with the death *drive*. And the vital irony of the *death drive* involves this very discrepancy between merely "being dead" and actively "being *death*"—the tension between, on the one hand, the idea of "death" as necrotic *state*, as passive *stasis*, an "earlier" state of things where we all "eventually" end back up (ashes to ashes, womb to tomb), and on the other hand, the idea of "death" as an eternally destructive, "reicidal" *force* that *actively* negates all *things* (I take the word "reicide" from "reify," from the Latin *res*, for "thing") but just keeps going and going because it's always already "nothing" itself and negates everything *but* itself. Death in the latter sense is actually quite *lively*—it apparently "lives" forever. This "death" can never ever die, which is why we rarely personify "Death" as unlucky stiff or motionless cadaver—we imagine "Death" as the grimly *active* reaper, never one of the grimly *reaped*.

Now, we might desire to grimly *read* the difference between death and death drive, between being *dead* and being *death*, as the difference between an "earlier state of things" and our active (albeit unconscious) desire to return *to* that "state." Or, to put the death/death drive difference in somewhat more "literary" terms, we might think of it as the distinction between "lying in state" and *lying through our teeth.* We might read the desire to return to an "earlier state of things" as a desire to return to the real, to the "not-as-if of things" that all run together, a desire to dissolve that isolated and desiccated residue called "the self" back into the greater "sea of yolky enjoyment" (Žižek 1992: 40) that we fondly remember as lost oceanic feeling. But the law of language can only ever tear us away from real dissolution; the law can only ever say "no, not really" to the yolky enjoyment of the not-as-if of things. Real death—not the active death *drive* but the passive *state* of dissolution—would be the only conceivable result of language's becoming really real, of its no longer lying, of its ceasing to be fictional and fatally merging with the real. Stirred to the only life it knows by its "no" to the real, language can stay alive only by keeping the real at a distance, maintaining its actively *destructive* stance toward the thing. "All right, then, go away! I don't need you." Such "reicidal" labor—the very work of *antiphysis*—is the ludic, liberatory, and transformative "fiction writing" that makes and keeps all human reality (all too dishonestly) human.

Let's remember, though, that, in the interpretation of desire being pushed here, it is not language *per se* but language's specific and "vitally mortifying" *fictiveness* that allows us to conflate it with symbolic desire and the death drive, that arguably sets it (and us) apart from natural need, corporeal demand, animal instinct, or any merely "biologically determined" method of "communication" between physical bodies (those of "the birds and the bees," for example). As we learned in Lesson Three, language is constitutively fictional both at the level of the solitary word and in the sequential or "narrative" dimension of the sentence. At the level of the word, language is fictional because of the word's necessary separation from and negation of the thing. Literally, the word both *lacks* and *kills* the thing. This linguistic "reicide" is what leads Lacan to refer to words as "lethal symbols" (1966d/2006: 249), what compels him to comment upon "the profound relationship uniting the notion of the death instinct to the problems of speech" (1966d/2006: 260), what causes him to insist both that "the symbol first manifests itself as the killing of the thing, and [that] this death results in the endless perpetuation of the subject's desire" (1966d/2006: 262).

Taken literally, however, desire tends to be perpetuated mainly in the form of *sentences*, seldom in random strings of murderous words but more typically in grammatically organized and syntactically ordered *patterns* of meaning that are, again, arguably *narrative* in structure. As suggested in the previous lesson, every completely predicated, grammatically correct sentence "tells a story," narrates an action, features a beginning, middle, and end, and so on. But insofar as they do participate in narrative, sentences also implicate themselves in the death drive, for, like the beginning of any well-told story, the beginning of any minimally well-crafted sentence presupposes its ending and literally provokes a reader's *desire for* closure, her desire for "the end." According to this interpretation of desire, we "readers" at a very basic level want the same "thing" from our sentences, our stories, and our lives—that by the time we reach their and our conclusions, they and we will have "totally" *meant* something.[10]

But believe it or not, this notion that we all desire to obtain a satisfying sense of "totality" or "completion" from syntactical, narrative, and auto-biographical "closure" is what finally connects "the problems of speech" to the problem of . . .

III. "sex"

If taking desire "literally" means anything at all, it means interpreting language and sex as the same k*not*ty problem—to take desire literally means to read all language as "sexual" and all *human* sexuality (the avian and the apian won't count for much in this discussion) as linguistically rather than biologically determined.

As befits an argument based on linguistic determinism, what justifies this theory of linguistic sex *qua* sexual linguistics is neither empirical research involving microscopic investigation of physical, chromosomal evidence nor exhaustive ethnographic research quizzing every child, woman, and man in the history of the world about the minute particulars of their actual "sex lives." Rather, what justifies the assertion that human sex is (and has always been) a problem of speech, and that speech itself is (and has always been) a sexual dilemma, is the purely etymological "fact" that the English word "sex" comes from the Latin *secare*, meaning "to cut." Because the word "sex" shares its root, so to speak, with other "cutting" words (scission, scissoring, sectioning), the "meaning of sex" can be said to involve nothing but "coming to terms" with "the cut" of materialist language, in which not just "sex" or "scissors" but *all* words in *all* languages are (strictly speaking) serrated.[11]

---

[10] This interpretation was first and most famously developed by Peter Brooks in the essay "Freud's Masterplot," in which Brooks employs *Beyond the Pleasure Principle* to conflate our desire for narrative closure with the death drive.

[11] Of course, not all languages derive from Latin, nor is it likely that the word for "sex" in each and every language in the history of the world derives or derived from some primordial word for "cut." But these historicist objections are actually quite immaterial to the properly structuralist argument that *antiphysis*, this reicidal "cut" or lacerating "no to the real" that I've been yammering about in these lessons, is not simply a "secondary characteristic" of one or more languages but is rather *the condition of possibility* for human language (and human sexuality) as such.

For here, the sexual "cut" is to be read as nothing but the "no to the real" that initiates (us into) the symbolic order, tearing us away from the here and now, turning our oceanic world of runny things into a more sharply defined world of articulated phrases, routing our **polymorphous perversity** through the defiles of unimorphous normality, and so on.[12] Just as Marx alerts us to the fact that "to be radical means to grasp things by the root" (1844/1978: 60), so too a radically linguistic account of human sexuality holds that language *cuts us off* at the natural root, scissors or sections us away from the real, tears us a new hole—*castrates*, so to speak, every one of us who manages *to speak*, regardless of any merely anatomical origin or destiny.[13]

While actual castration in the "anatomically correct" sense would seem to make it impossible for some people to really "have (a) sex," *symbolic* castration—always articulated, never anatomical—is for Lacan the very condition of possibility of "sex" of *any* kind for *everybody*—yes, everybody. For if human sexuality can be described in the universal terms of a desire for *some* form of erotic merger, union, or more-or-less lubricated orificial friction between one desiring/desired body and some other(s), then this description presupposes a *division* between such "bodies and pleasures," however infinitely varied they all might be (for if there were no division, no separation, there would be no desire to speak of). Human sexual desire thus presupposes a certain incompletion or "missingness"; it presupposes our being "cut off" from others with whom we were "originally" merged, from others to whom, mythically or umbilically, we were "originally" attached—others back into whom we would like ourselves to melt, others up against whom we would like to rub ourselves or some part of ourselves again (and again).[14] In other words, in contrast to

---

[12] Freud characterizes infantile sexuality as **polymorphously perverse**, which means that for the infant erotogenic stimulation comes from many different sources and that its various component drives are not yet fixed in relation to any orifice or object. For Freud, the infant's polymorphous perverse disposition entails an original bisexuality and is part of what the child loses when subjected to the social prohibitions that produce "unimorphously normal" erotic experience/fantasy/object choice.

[13] Toril Moi ends her splendid essay "Is Anatomy Destiny?: Freud and Biological Destiny" with this observation—"psychoanalysis is a form of thought that attempts to understand the psychological consequences of three universal traumas: the fact that there are Others, the fact of sexual difference, and the fact of death. Freud might have said that it is our destiny to have to find a way to coexist with others, to have to take up a position in relation to sexual difference, and to face death. To say so is not evidence of biological or any other kind of determinism" (2000: 88). I would add that Lacan might have said that *language* is the universally traumatic condition of possibility for all three of these "universal traumas," that language is our specifically human way of coexisting with others, of taking up positions in relation to sexual difference, and of facing up to death.

[14] In one of the richer moments in *Beyond the Pleasure Principle*, Freud turns to "myth rather than ... scientific explanation" to trace "the origin of an instinct to a *need to restore an earlier state of things*" (1920/1989: 622). After having dwelt at tedious length on the topic of germ-cell division, Freud abruptly trots out "the theory which Plato put into the

animal instinct, human sexual desire presupposes a sort of "personological" discontinuity with the totality of "things [that] at first run together in the *hic et nunc* of the all" (Lacan 1966d/2006: 229); it presupposes a radical separation not only from designated "others" but, back behind them, and more primordially, from that anonymous "sea of yolky enjoyment" that both "resists symbolization absolutely" (Lacan 1975/1991: 66) and saturates our earliest experience-of-ourselves-as-everything in the undifferentiated real.

Note that in this interpretation of desire, *Eros* and *Thanatos* are disturbingly indistinguishable. The two become "as one," so to speak, insofar as both the *erotic* and the *thanatical* can be imagined as a *single* drive, "*an urge inherent in organic life to restore an earlier state of things*" (1920/1989: 612). Just as all desire, regardless of particular object or orifice, is structurally suicidal, always urging self-cancellation, so, as Lacan comments, "every drive is virtually a death drive" (1966h/2006: 719). This interpretation of desire thus couples the idea that "*the aim of all life is death*'" with the notion that the aim of all *sex* is *jouissance*.[15] In this interpretation, both *Eros* and *Thanatos* aim to dissolve themselves into their "others." Both desire to erase the boundary that separates each into its own discontinuous confines.

But what if this boundary demarcating "the limits of the human" person were *initially* nothing but the "no to the real," the no to nondifferentiation, that first installs any speaking subject into the symbolic order? If "the moment at which desire is humanized is also that at which the child is born into language" (Lacan 1966d/2006: 262), then the initiating *law* of language dictates that words must be separated from real things in order to symbolize them, that signifiers must be divided from signifieds in order to join together

mouth of Aristophanes in the *Symposium*, and which deals not only with the *origin* of the sexual instinct but also with the most important of its variations in relation to its object. 'The original human nature was not like the present, but different. In the first place, the sexes were originally three in number, not two as they are now; there was man, woman, and the union of the two . . .' Everything about these primeval men was double: they had four hands and four feet, two faces, two privy parts, and so on. Eventually Zeus decided to cut these men in two . . . After the division had been made, 'the two parts of man, each desiring his other half, came together, and threw their arms about one another eager to grow into one'" (1920/1989: 622–3). Note how in this myth whoever is subjected to the sexual drive desires to return to a state before "the cut." Note also how neatly the myth accounts for variations in regard to sexual object—accounts, that is, for male and female homosexuality and heterosexuality for we obviously should read the three sexes in the mythic time "before the cut" not as "man, woman, and the union of the two," but as man–man, woman–woman, and man–woman.

[15] *Jouissance* is a "French term derived from the verb *jouir*," to enjoy, to play, and to come. *Jouissance* "denotes an extreme form of pleasure: ecstatic or orgasmic bliss that transcends or shatters one's everyday experience of the world" (Malpas and Wake 2006: 211). *Jouissance* thus relates to *la petite mort*, or "the little death," as French writers have been known to refer to orgasm.

and become signs. This law decrees that the very letters comprising signs must be separated from each other, must not occupy the same space at the same time, so that each individual letter might be "more productively" organized and combined with other letters in properly spaced, grammatically correct, *normatively sequential* and thus *socially consequential* ways.

In this "legal" interpretation of human desire—in which all merely "animal instinct" is always already trumped by a "law" that isn't simply "of the jungle"—language structures and enforces the anthropogenetic *social norms* that make *all* versions of *human* reality *everywhere* possible. For Lacan, however, the most rudimentary law and most constitutively social norm that language enforces is the "paternal prohibition" against *incest*. As we rehearsed in the preceding lesson, the "no to the real" that *separates* words from things is for Lacan *structurally analogous* to the "Oedipal" law that separates moms from their spawn. Just as a word cannot immediately *merge* with the real thing that it names but must "wait" to be *combined* with other words in order to form a grammatically correct and complete sentence, so the child cannot "merge" with its real mother as illicitly desired sexual object but must wait to grow up in order to be legally "combined" with some more appropriate "other" in a institutionally sanctioned matrimonial alliance. Intimately bonding syntax to kinship, Lacan marries the *syntactical* rules that establish which *linguistic combinations* are permitted and which are proscribed to the *sexual* regulations that establish which *erotic combinations* are legally recognized or encouraged and which are abominated, reviled, or (in some cultures even capitally) punished.[16] As Lacan insists:

> The primordial Law is . . . the Law which, in regulating marriage ties, superimposes the reign of culture over the reign of nature . . . The prohibition against incest is merely the subjective pivot of that Law . . . This law, then, reveals itself clearly enough as identical to a language order. For without names for kinship relations, no power can institute the order of preferences and taboos that knot and braid the

---

[16] In 2010, for example, the government of Uganda, after hosting a series of anti-queer talks by visiting American "evangelicals," got to work proposing "a bill to impose a death sentence on homosexuality" (see "After US Evangelicals Visit, Uganda Considers Death for Gays," *The New York Times*, 4 January 2010, A1). In 2011, however, "after receiving overwhelming criticism from across the globe, Uganda's Parliament . . . let the time expire on a contentious anti-homosexuality bill that had threatened this East African country's international standing. The Anti-Homosexuality Bill sought to impose the death penalty for a number of reasons, including being a 'serial offender' of the 'offense of homosexuality.' The bill also called for Ugandans to alert the government to known cases of homosexual behavior within 24 hours. Religious leaders said they had obtained more than two million signatures in support of the measure" ("Antigay Bill in Uganda is Shelved in Parliament," *The New York Times*, 14 May 2011, A4).

thread of lineage through the generations. And it is the confusion of
generations which, in the Bible as in all traditional laws, is cursed as
being the abomination of the Word and the desolation of the sinner.
(Lacan 1966d/2006: 229–30)

But, outside of the fact that some infractions of the sexual laws of a given
society are punishable by execution of the desolate "sinner," how might
these syntactical/sexual analogies relate to the death drive?[17] As it turns out,
they are quite intimately related, for, in a sense, all three (*Eros, Logos,* and
Thanatos) involve our old friend—perhaps our *oldest* friend—*antiphysis*;
all three involve the initial and ongoing separation from the real "reign of
nature" that is human reality's "cultural" condition of possibility; all three
intimately involve the *social* question of the various ways in which we must
psychically deal with this *physical* separation.

Let's pause to consider this intimate involvement in the light of the
distinction between the *physically impossible* and the *socially prohibited.* As
we learned in Lesson Three, it is *physically impossible* for the word "elephant"
ever to be an elephant, or for the word "moonlight" ever to be moonlight.
Analogously, it is *physically impossible* for "the little animal produced by the
union of a man and a woman" to "unproduce" itself back into that woman,
to disappear up into its mother's womb, to physically re-occupy that "real
place" with the entirety of its miraculously re-fetalized body (umbilicus
reattached, placenta stuffed back in to boot, all needs met before they can
even be experienced as needs, much less turned into demand or desire,
and so on). Both of these "mergers" (word with thing, tot with mom) are
physically impossible, not just *socially prohibited*—in other words, there's
no "law" imposed from elsewhere, the "repeal" of which could allow these
events to transpire.

On the other hand it is physically possible for an experimental writer
to unseparate words and letters and to omit punctuation altogether and
yet still have written some thing more or less readable albe it not without
some difficulty. It is even physically possible, in some graphic media, to
"do away" altogether with the spaces separating individual letters (like,
say, the letters i, n, k, s, t, a, i, and n), so that they all can be made to occupy
the same space at the same time. Nothing physically prevents a writer from
"experimentally" superimposing in one single space all the letters in an

---

[17] I refer in the first part of the sentence not only to legally sanctioned hangings of convicted
"sodomites" in early modern Western Europe, and the stoning to death of homosexuals
that is permitted under some contemporary Islamic law, but also to the extralegal (but
still ideologically encouraged) murder of homosexuals and transsexuals in the United
States (Matthew Shepard and Brandon Teena, for recent historical examples).

independent clause— such as, for example, "the word for ink-stain is ink-stain"—thus breaking the "law" that "says" that individual letters "must" be divided from each other. Such a real merger is *prohibited* (by the symbolic order) but not *impossible*. Our "experimental writer" will have really taken these letters down, transgressively merging one with another, aggressively destroying the discrete individuality of each; s/he will have really negated the prohibitory "no to the real," the no to "sexual" undifferentiation, that makes "normal" human reality possible. But the end result of this scoff-law experimental writing will be only a real but unreadable stain, a dark spot of **abjection**, a traumatic/ecstatic *blotch* marking the "place where meaning collapses" (Kristeva 182: 2).[18] In other words, our experimental writer's "ink-stain" will have achieved *being* a real ink-stain but only at the expense of ever legibly *meaning* "ink-stain" or anything else at all.

Analogously to this botched experiment in transgressive writing—it is quite possible to really break the law against incest and actually "return to the mother's womb" by having honest-to-god sexual intercourse with said mother, whether "wittingly" or not.[19] The trouble here, however, is that our "wits" are constituted in such a way—through socio-normative regulations and prohibitions—that to *really* and *wittingly* have sex with our own mothers could very well cause us to lose them (our wits, that is). If the very structural coherence of consciousness is established through being made to mean, through an ordered separation from or loss of the real, then to lose the loss of the real and re-merge with it could mean to lose ourselves, lose our meanings, lose our minds. In other words, overcoming the social prohibition against incest, negating this particular *form* of the prohibitory "no to non-differentiation" that initiates human reality, may very well be *physically possible*, but it may not be *psychically viable*.

---

[18] From the Latin *abjectus*, meaning "cast out," **abjection** involves the acts of psychic, social, and corporeal exclusion and expulsion by which symbolic order, cultural identity, and personal hygiene are maintained. The abject, writes Kristeva, is thus that which "disturbs identity, system, order. What does not respect borders, positions, rules" (1981: 3). Thus "filth, waste, pus, bodily fluids, the dead body itself are all abject," for "the abject represents what human life and culture exclude in order to sustain themselves" (Childers and Henzi 1995: 1).

[19] Oedipus was unwittingly incestuous, had no idea that Jocasta was his mother when he was once again inside her. Nor does Hamlet seem to know what he's asking with the line "How stand I, then, that have a father kill'd, a mother stained?" (IV.iv.58–9). Ambiguously mixing possession with commission, this line is usually taken as the clincher for the Oedipal interpretation of the play, for though Hamlet is consciously stating the obvious—that he *has* a father who has been killed (poisoned, by Claudius) and a mother who has been "stained" (inseminated, by Claudius)—Hamlet inadvertently owns that he himself has *done* the killing/staining in his unconscious.

Now, since the adjective "viable" relates to life and the liveable—the word literally means "capable of living outside the uterus"—what the preceding examples suggest is that neither experimental *ink-stain* nor accomplished *incest* can be a viable subjective or "authorial" enterprise. Literally speaking, one might say that both spell *death*, the collapse of conventional *meaning*. In other words, "incest" might be *read* as a name for "the place where meaning collapses," but insofar as the *word* "incest" itself remains a *legible* name for that unspeakable stain, a "lethal symbol" that can be used to murder that murderously meaningless "place" *from a distance*, the *word* "incest" is *not* that place, says *no* to the "**primal scene**" of undifferentiation.[20] In other words, the word "incest" can *mean* incest, can designate whatever incestuous desire we might unconsciously harbor, but the word "incest" can never finally *be* incest—and we have nothing but the "sexual" cut of the symbolic order to thank for that.

But let's flesh these analogies out a bit by considering a few pieces of fiction that thematize incest as symbolic death-match, watery silence, structural collapse, and so on. At the end of Poe's "The Fall of the House of Usher," for example, Roderick Usher's "eroto-thanatical" tussle with his own freshly "unencrypted" sister precipitates the crumbling collapse of his "House" (a gothic mansion of a metaphor for both his psyche and the Usher "family line")—at the moment of narrative climax, the whole show fissures and falls back into the miasmic "tarn" from which it seems to have emerged.

In Faulkner's *The Sound and the Fury*, the suicidal Quentin Compson—obsessed with temporality, mortality, and thoughts of having sex (or of claiming to have had sex) with his sister Caddy—takes a little time before drowning himself in the Charles River to think "If I'd just had a mother so I could say Mother Mother" (1929/1984: 197). But if I were to rewrite Quentin's line to let it support the interpretation of desire being developed here, I would have him think instead, "If I'd just really *had* mother, I never would've *had to say* Mother, not even once." For if Lacan is correct to say that the prohibition against incest "reveals itself clearly enough as identical to a language order," then it's the fact that Quentin *has to say* "Mother"—is *ordered* to *symbolize* Mother, to put her and everything else into words, to "matri-reicidally" *mean* her rather than uninterruptedly *be* with her—that keeps him from ever "really" having "had" her in the first place. If he had never been separated from that "first place," he wouldn't have to think about

---

[20] Normally in Freud's discourse the phrase "**primal scene**" refers to the real or imagined observation of one's parents having sex. I am misusing the term here by letting it represent the image of one's having sex with one's parent.

tossing himself into the body of water that finally substitutes for it. If he had just *had* Mother, had never been expelled from the oceanic/maternal real, he wouldn't have had to *say* Mother or any*thing* else at all.[21]

But of course the symbolic order insists that we all *do* "have to say." Even if we don't all get to have our say, "our say" is, in this interpretation of desire, all we ever really get to have, all we ever really get to be. The linguistic "limits of the human" ensure that we never *really* get to *be* but must always be made to *mean*. It is nothing other than the radical unavailability of *being* to *meaning* that guarantees that desire must be taken literally. As whorish as it all may seem to Prince Hamlet, this interpretation of desire tells us why we can only ever unpack our hearts with words.

IV. "and interpretation"

Now, I keep unpacking *my* theoretical heart with the words "in this interpretation of desire" because, *in* this interpretation of desire, "desire, in fact, is interpretation itself" (Lacan 1973/1981: 176). In fact, my own heart's desire at this juncture is nothing but to marry Lacan's matter-of-fact statement about desire's being "interpretation itself" to Nietzsche's radical claim that there *are* no facts, only interpretations.[22] In other words, the "fact" that I have been

---

[21] You can add Usher's tarn and Quentin's river to your list of bodies of water that represent "self-destructive" immersions in the oceanic real. You can also throw (yourself) in Buffalo Bill's bathtub in *The Silence of the Lambs*. In Jonathan Demme's 1991 film, Buffalo Bill (Ted Levine) is a serial killer and all-too-real gender-bender who "wears" the skins of his female victims. He also sports lipstick and eye-liner and poses "self-castratedly" naked in front of a mirror, penis tucked between his legs, etc. When FBI agent Clarice Starling (Jodie Foster) ventures into the killer's basement, she obeys the literary/cinematic convention that misreads *un*conscious as *sub*conscious and compels the protagonist to enter some subterranean space in order to confront her own unconscious fears and desires. And what Clarice finds in the cellar is of course a horrific scene of sexual undifferentiation, a place where meaning has collapsed because the primordial "cut" separating the symbolic from the real, life from death, one sex from the other, has been inhumanly "sutured." The money-shot of this sequence comes when Clarice beholds a bathtub filled with some "unspeakable" dark gunk, from which protrudes what appears to be the "iceberg" tip of a submerged skull. This tank is of course the acid bath in which Buffalo Bill dissolves the remains of his victims, and it is the last hideous thing Clarice sees before the lights go out and she loses herself in the darkness. A good cinematic example of the bad oceanic feeling, the sequence does a neat job of depicting the ecstatic/traumatic "kernel" of the real.

[22] In *The Will to Power*, Nietzsche writes, "Against positivism, which halts at phenomena— 'There are only facts'—I would say: No, facts are precisely what there are not, only interpretations. We cannot establish any fact 'in itself'—perhaps it is folly to want to do such a thing . . . In so far as the word 'knowledge' means anything, the world is knowable;

giving this account of desire in a language that is by nature fictional means that what I am offering here is not "the truth" about desire, but "merely" an interpretation. And yet, as Nietzsche would have it, any *competing* set of truth-claims about desire can't finally amount to anything more or other than interpretation, either. For in this interpretation, there is no empirical, objective, or absolute "truth" about desire or about anything else in human reality to be had; there is only ever a potentially infinite set of competing, more or less engaging, more or less *lively*—but never anything other than *perspectival*—interpretations.

Of course, it may come as no surprise to read that what you're reading *here* purports to be nothing more than an interpretation, given from a particular perspective, and not an objective report on absolutely axiomatic conditions. But if reading this stale news leaves you unsatisfied, wanting more—not because you want *fresher* revelations but because you are at heart a reader who hungers after *timeless truth* and aren't likely to be content with "trendy" artifice—then you may already have an unconscious sense of what links interpretation to desire (and hence, to sex and death). For what, one might ask, *is* "interpretation itself" if not the revelation of a certain emptiness, the presence of the absence of certainty or finality, the limning of one's lack of some satisfyingly conclusive explanation? And what would we *want* "*the* truth" to *be* if not the final answer to all our interpretive prayers, the explanation to *end* all explanations, the "absolute knowledge" that would bring the restless *activity* of interpreting to its final destination?

But here, our "prayers" can pretty much be damned—for in "the end," our *actively* "interpreting the text" of human reality must presuppose that some firm and final knowledge of its significance will always remain *missing*. The phrase "interpreting the text" of course implies our *wanting* to know "*the* truth" about it, *wanting* to know exactly "what it all means." But what does "wanting to know" mean except *not* knowing? And what would *knowing* "the truth" or the "total meaning" of anything *mean* if not *being* in a state of *no longer wanting* to know, no longer *desiring*, no longer interpreting, no longer restlessly *reading*?

but it is interpretable otherwise, it has no [single] meaning behind it, but countless meanings.'" (1901/1968: 267). Anticipating this theme in "On Truth and Lies in a Non-moral Sense," Nietzsche writes, "What then is truth? A movable host of metaphors, metonymies, and anthropomorphisms: in short, a sum of human relations which have been poetically and rhetorically intensified, transferred, and embellished, and which, after long usage, seem to . . . be fixed, canonical, and binding. Truths are illusions which we have forgotten are illusions" (1873/2006: 117).

Paradoxically, then, Roland Barthes knew exactly what he was talking about when he wrote that "literature is the question minus the answer."

> What do things signify, what does the world signify? All literature is this question . . . but it is this question minus its answer. No literature in the world has ever answered the question it asked, and it is this very suspension which has always constituted it as literature. (1964/1972: 202).

And because Barthes is, ironically enough, perfectly correct—"literature" *is* the right answer to the question of the missing right answer—*literary* interpretation might be read as the very "restlessness" of the *active* death drive itself. However, such articles of faith or kisses of death as "*the* answer," "*firm* knowledge," "unshakeable belief" in "*absolute* truth," etc., could be considered the *anti-literary* tropes *par excellence*, representing the necrotic "state of things" that interpretation may *think* it desires to restore (since interpretation ostensibly "wants to know," wants to have knowledge) but which interpretation may "literally" want to defer. In other words, active interpretation ceaselessly puts off possessing the knowledge it supposedly wants to have because the *vital* process of interpretation *ends*, cancels itself out, when its "revelation of emptiness" fills itself up (with satisfying "truth"); interpretation dies when the restless negativity of *being death* settles into the pure positivity of *being dead* certain, *being dead* right. In a literally *literary* interpretation of desire, then, desire desires *only* desire, *not* absolute knowledge; interpretation interprets only interpretation, minus final answers, minus the honest truth.

Now, I have written the words "*literary* interpretation" above as if there were some other kind. But if we buy Derrida's interpretation that "fictional" language has "invaded the universal problematic" and everything become "discourse" (1966/1978: 280), if we subscribe to Lacan's interpretation that all human "desire must be taken literally" and that "desire, in fact, is inter-pretation itself" (1973/1981: 176), then might we not also want to submit ourselves to the interpretation that all interpretation is literary, fabricative, creative writing? If the beating heart of any interpretation must be unpacked with words, expressed in language that is by nature fictional, then might not "interpretation" be most richly interpreted as an *aesthetic* rather than *veridical* or *moral* phenomenon, a strong exercise in the art of the sentence emerging from a strong *aversion* to any honest-to-god "truth"? Interpretation, in this radically *Nietzschean* interpretation, wouldn't desire the intuition of "truth" or the acquisition of "knowledge"; it wouldn't want answers at all but rather the *strength* to live *without* final answers so as to proliferate more engaging *fictions about fiction* in a world that must be made to mean.

I call this interpretation Nietzschean because it was Nietzsche's radical claim that "only as an *aesthetic phenomenon* are existence and the world *justified*" (1872/2006: 58). Well before Freud or Lacan got around to it, it was Nietzsche who first interpreted interpretations as matters of life and death (drives), as particularly dense transfer points for libidinal energy and relations of power. It was Nietzsche who first framed the arts of interpretation as perversely erotic, even sadomasochistic, but in any event always richly *aesthetic* endeavors, and it was Nietzsche who correspondingly considered the "will to truth" as an austere and *impoverishing* form of priestly *asceticism*, a pacifying renunciation of interpretation grounded in a rancorous hostility to sensuality, to art, to sex, to violence, to "life" itself. Perhaps the first philosopher wise enough to love fiction more than "wisdom," it was Nietzsche who first desired to call the *value* of "truth" into question and who first connected the epistemological drive, the "will to truth," to the "will to death."[23]

For Nietzsche, there is neither "absolute truth" nor "divine will," only competing and "all too human" interpretations. All interpretations are humanly "embodied," situated in individual perspectives, and all perspectives are contingent upon, and determined by, the relative strength or weakness of the interpreter's "will to power" or "instinct for freedom." The relative strength or weakness of any interpreter's "will" depends in turn upon the *type* of "instinct for freedom" it expresses in relation to "life" interpreted as perpetual change or *becoming*, as a (not exactly painless) process of *self-transformation*—the ecstatic, self-shattering, "Dionysian" reality of *creatively human suffering*. Nietzsche, that is, pretty much endorses the Buddha's first "noble truth," that "life is painful," but he veers away from Buddhism or any other "world religion" in terms of the question of what to do with or about the pain. For Nietzsche, *strong* interpretation not only "takes the pain" but eagerly *uses* it to express itself as the instinct for freedom *for* "life" as perpetual *becoming*, while *weak* interpretation flees the pain, flinchingly expresses an instinct for freedom *from* "life," conducts itself as a "spiritual retreat" into hypostasized *being*. A strong or "noble" interpretation "masochistically" enjoys the pain of vital self-transformation, finds a constitutively *aesthetic* "happiness in great tension" (1886/2006: 356); a weak or "slavish" or "herd"

---

[23] In Book V of *The Gay Science*, Nietzsche writes that the "will to truth . . . might be a concealed will to death" (1887/2006: 364); in *Genealogy of Morals*, he writes that truth-driven ascetic idealism entails the "renunciation of any interpretation (of forcing, adjusting, shortening, omitting, filling-out, inventing, falsifying and everything else *essential* to interpretation)," and that "on the whole, this [renunciation of interpretation] expresses the asceticism of virtue just as well as any denial of sensuality (it is basically just a *modus* of this denial). However, the *compulsion* toward it, that unconditional will to truth, is *faith in the ascetic ideal itself*, even if as an unconscious imperative" (1887/2006: 431).

interpretation, however, finds its "promise of happiness" only *anesthetically*, in conventional "truth" or the congregationally "fixed idea" (1887/2006: 396) and in whatever "slackening of tension" (1887/1992: 474) such "fixings" can provide.

Rather obnoxiously, at least from our contemporary perspective, Nietzsche frequently depicts the difference between "noble" and "slave" moralities, between strong and weak modes of interpretation, in explicitly gendered, racialized, or nationalized terms. More interestingly and productively, however, Nietzsche, anticipating Freud, also suggests that this "prepositional" conflict of interpretive wills—desiring freedom *for* life vs. desiring freedom *from* it—can obtain within a *single* individual's psyche.[24]

Now, the idea that a mode of interpretation can be grounded in an instinctual desire for "freedom *from* life" allows Nietzsche to link a certain type of interpretative "will" to the death drive. But Nietzsche also appreciates the difference between death *drive* and death itself; he understands the difference between active and passive annihilation. Nietzsche thus posits that although the "will to truth . . . might be a concealed will to death" (1887/2006: 364), even the weakest will in the world "still prefers to will *nothingness* than *not* will" (1887/2006: 435). In other words, though interpretive desire may desire to complete or "end itself" as desire, it also desires to perpetuate itself *as* interpretive desire, as the continuing revelation of emptiness, as an ongoing "reference to Nothingness" (Žižek 1999: 126), an indefinitely literal and literary *suspension*.

Little wonder, then, if, after Nietzsche, the "essential incompleteness of interpretation" becomes one of the most prominent "postulates of modern **hermeneutics**," as Michel Foucault writes in the essay "Nietzsche, Freud, Marx."[25] Foucault suggests that in Nietzsche's work in particular "it is clear that interpretation is always incomplete."

> What is philosophy for him if not a kind of philology continually in suspension, a philology without end, always farther unrolled, a philology that would never be absolutely fixed? Why? As he says in *Beyond Good and Evil*, it is because "to perish from absolute knowledge could well form part of the basis of being." (1967/1998: 275)

---

[24] In *Beyond Good and Evil*, Nietzsche writes, "There are *master moralities* and *slave moralities*. I would add at once that in all higher and more complex cultures, there are also apparent attempts to mediate between the two moralities, and even more often a confusion of the two and a mutual misunderstanding, indeed sometimes even their violent juxtaposition—even in the same person, within one single breast" (1886/2006: 356).

[25] **Hermeneutics** is generally understood as "the study of understanding" (Malpas and Wake 2006: 201), is generally interpreted as "the theory of interpretation in general" (Childers and Hentzi 1995: 132).

In Foucault's strongly Nietzschean interpretation, any strongly Nietzschean interpretation refuses to fix meaning or be fixed by it; such an interpretation declines "to perish from absolute knowledge." Rather, interpretation in the Nietzschean mode suspends and sustains itself, persists in perpetually *becoming* rather than finally or completely *being* (itself), and it pulls off this hat-trick of modern hermeneutics by reveling in *language's* vital but brutal *fictionality*. In Foucault's "violent" interpretation of Nietzschean violence:

> Interpretation can never be completed . . . quite simply because there is nothing to interpret. There is nothing absolutely primary to interpret, for after all everything is already interpretation, each sign is in itself not the thing that offers itself to interpretation but an interpretation of other signs . . . so that it is as much a relationship of violence as of elucidation that is established in interpretation. Indeed, interpretation does not clarify a matter to be interpreted, which offers itself passively; it can only seize, and violently, an already-present interpretation, which it must overthrow, upset, shatter with the blows of a hammer. (1967/1998: 275)

Interpretation "with a hammer" enacts its "will to power" *against* certainty, against the fixity of non-fiction, against the self-cancellation of desire, against reification, positivism, or any absolute truth. This interpretive desire expresses—and always in a language that is by nature fictional, always in words that negate real things, always in symbols that are reicidally "lethal" (Lacan 1966d/2006: 249)—an instinct for freedom *for* rather than *from* "life":

> The death of interpretation is to believe that there are signs, signs that exist primarily, originally, actually, as coherent, pertinent, and systematic marks. The life of interpretation, on the contrary, is to believe that there are only interpretations. (Foucault 1967/1998: 278)

In the end, then, taking desire "literally" requires a suspension—not of disbelief, but of belief itself; for if taking desire literally requires "believing" that there are, originally and ultimately, only all-too-human interpretations, it also requires believing that this very belief is "only" an interpretation as well. But while this interpretation of interpretation is, no doubt, radically atheistic, it is not an expression of so-called "nihilism"; rather, believe it or not (and if you're trained to believe that atheism equals nihilism, then you'll probably not), radically incredulous interpretation maintains itself as a way of *overcoming* nihilism, as a way of saying *yes* to "life"—or at least to what Nietzsche calls "everything strange, unusual, and questionable"

(1887/2006: 368) in the interpretive experience of life.[26] For Nietzsche, and for Foucault, the "death of interpretation" (and hence of desire) would indeed be the wages of believing "in the absolute existence of signs" (Foucault 1967/1998: 278), of believing that such signs can actually ground objective knowledge, faithfully represent absolute truth, finally decipher the real's big secret, and so on. This faith in some *firm* and *final* significance, in what Derrida calls "the transcendental signified" (1966/1978: 280), expresses a weak interpretation that completely "abandons the violence, the incompleteness, the infinity of interpretations" (Foucault 1967/1998: 278). Faith in the "transcendental signified" signifies a spiritual retreat from "life"—it enacts or "wills" a veritable "freedom *from* life." But the "life" of "faithless" interpretative desire, as the perpetual revelation of human (and cosmic) emptiness, as the ongoing reference to our own nothingness, the perpetual presence of the absence of the answer—as, in other words, *literature*—involves affirming that signs only ever signify more and other signs. In this interpretation, saying "yes" to *this* "life" means nothing but affirming that "everything is [always] already interpretation" (Foucault 1967/1998: 275).

Ultimately, then, taking desire literally involves affirming human reality as a montage of the imaginary and the symbolic, as a rich tapestry of ambiguous and conflictual fictions—suspended over the void. To affirm (rather than bemoan) this "empty" or "aesthetic" reality means learning, with Nietzsche and other bad company, to savor the unsettling of sedimented ways of making sense of the world, to affirm that it is "only as an *aesthetic phenomenon* [that] existence and the world [are] *justified*" (Nietzsche 1872/2006: 58). Such affirmation involves refusing the comforts of fixed meaning, swearing off absolute knowledge, swearing to tell anything but "the truth," lying with a good conscience, even dancing at the edge of the abyss. It involves nothing less and nothing more—and, for Nietzsche, nothing more *becoming* of a "free spirit"—than affirming "life as literature."[27]

---

[26] Overcoming nihilism for Nietzsche means getting over the "death of God," getting over "monotonotheism," getting over one's disappointment and hurt feelings that *an* interpretation turned out not to be *the* one—"One interpretation has collapsed, but because it was considered *the* interpretation, it appears as though there is no sense in existence whatsoever, as though everything is *in vain*" (1887/2006: 386). For Nietzsche, our overcoming nihilism and affirming life mean our allowing "the world [to] become 'infinite' for us all over again, in as much as we cannot reject the possibility that *it may include infinite interpretations*" (1887/2006: 379).

[27] In *Genealogy of Morals*, Nietzsche designates "art" as the realm "in which *lying* sanctifies itself and the *will to deception* has good conscience on its side" (1887/2006: 431–2). In *Gay Science*, Nietzsche writes that "one could conceive of such a pleasure and power of self-determination, such a *freedom* of the 'will' that the spirit would take leave of all faith and every wish for certainty, being practiced in maintaining himself on insubstantial ropes and possibilities and dancing even near abysses. Such a spirit would be the *free spirit* par excellence" (1887/1974: 289–90). "Life as Literature" is the subtitle of an excellent book on Nietzsche by Richard Nehamas (1987).

But taking desire literally also involves affirming or asserting *oneself* as literature, accepting one's own "textual anthropogenesis," reveling, so to speak, in the revelation of one's own emptiness, the referential nothingness of subjective desire. Not that there's anything particularly self-assuring about such "self-relating negativity" (Žižek 2006: 64). Indeed, affirming one's own textual condition or symbolic castration takes a sort of existential courage, or perhaps just a strong sense of irony, a willingness to put the self at risk, if only by virtue of not being cocksure about identity, not taking one's own or anyone else's dead-seriously. Perhaps taking desire literally requires taking all identity ironically, for both forms of "taking" require that we "recognize ourselves as always already altered by the symbolic—by language"; both forms invite us to "hear in language that basic incompleteness that conditions the indefinite quest of signifying concatenations." Taking desire literally, taking identity ironically, affirming "life as literature," interpreting the self as text—all these linguistic endeavors finally add up to nothing but "joying in the truth of self-division" (Kristeva 1982: 89), engaging in the work of *antiphysis*, the violent art of self-transformation. As Foucault puts it in "The Minimalist Self":

> For me intellectual work is related to what you could call aestheticism, meaning transforming yourself . . . I know that knowledge can transform us, that truth is not only a way of deciphering the world (and maybe what we call truth doesn't decipher anything) but that if I know the truth I will be changed . . . This transformation of one's self by one's own knowledge is, I think, something rather close to the aesthetic experience. Why should a painter work if he is not transformed by his own painting? (1983/1988: 14)

Or, to change the medium, but not the self-divisive aesthetics of the experience in question, why should writers desire to write if "writing" isn't actively interpreted "as *the very possibility of change*" (Cixous 1975/2007: 1646)? Why would we ever find ourselves dying to write if we didn't think we were going to be transformed, turned on and torn apart—literally—by our own writings?

Coming to Terms

Critical Keywords encountered in Lesson Four:

need/demand/desire, Eros/Thanatos, fort-da, polymorphous perversity, jouissance, abjection, hermeneutics

"You are not yourself"

—or, I (think, therefore I) is an other

I. Missing persons, bodies in pieces

Unlike Jesus in the popular bumper-sticker slogan, theory doesn't love you. Theoretical writing *is* of course keenly concerned with the social, psychic, and political *processes* that allow or compel you to become a "you" or me to become an "I." But theoretical writers generally don't believe in any *real* "you" or "I"; they don't believe in any essential or abiding core of identity for any one of us, don't believe that there's some truly "true self" trapped within, lurking behind, or floating above these socio-symbolic processes. "Anti-identitarian" theorists never claim that "we" don't exist at all, you, and I; rather, they argue that none of us ever manages to abide in the purely self-identical, fully self-present way that we might be pleased to think. Given our irreducibly linguistic and representational condition, we can never quite seamlessly coincide with ourselves; we are always "extimately" alienated "strangers to ourselves," always *more* or *less* or, in any case, *other* than what we (might like to) think (of ourselves).

But just so we're clear—in this interpretation, it's not as if anyone of us ever *originally* possessed some *naturally* "true self" back in the day, some organic or authentic identity that we managed to lose through some blunder, trauma, or trespass, some historical misfortune, social injustice, or original sin, an essentially "real core of self" that's somehow been highjacked by malign forces and that we might actually *recover* some bright dawn through therapy, prayer, meditation, heroic intellectual effort, divine intervention, spiritual retreat, or worker's revolution. No, sorry, fat chance of help for one's "true self" from any of those redemptive quarters—in this interpretation "you are not yourself," you've never *been* yourself, and you're never going to *be* yourself, no matter what. So you might just as well get over it.

Now, this last piece of theoretical advice may seem cynically flippant, less sage than sour. For "alienation" is commonly recognized as a genuinely human malaise, a source of considerable human suffering. And according to no less of a theoretical writer than Theodor Adorno, "the need to lend a voice to suffering is the condition of all truth" (1966/2007: 17–18). But truth be told, this seemingly cynical counsel about our self-alienation—that maybe we should just get over it—might also be taken as well-intended, user-friendly, even generously meant. This "anti-identitarian" idea of constitutive and irreparable "loss of self" could even be taken as a sort of "glad tidings," as an invitation to throw off the burdens and constraints of consistent self-identity. In other words, the "ontological bad news" (Butler 1987/1999: 198) that we'll never really *get* to be ourselves, you, and I, is offset by the more promising assurance that we don't *have* to really be ourselves either (given that there's never been any "real self" for any one of us to be). At the end of the day, the ardent identity-busters of "anti-humanist" theory aren't simply callous misanthropes indifferent to personal suffering or spiteful nihilists who think nothing valuable about anyone's humanity has ever been damaged or denied through assault, addiction, objectification, state-sanctioned violence, terrorist attacks, alienated labor, religious intolerance, racial oppression, colonial subjugation, the predations of consumer capitalism, or any other indisputably *real* source of humanly caused human misery—theorists just don't think it's some inherently "true self" that gets banged up on these avenues of immiseration. And actually it's often in the interest of protecting or enhancing our potential for self-transformation—for developing richer and suppler modes of human agency, dignity, creativity, well-being, and freedom—that theoretical writers resist or reject the notion of the absolutely "true self." For on this view, there's already been enough damage done to human life in the service of mandatory selfhood; there's already been enough impoverishment of human reality in the name of compulsory identity.

So while "the need to lend a voice to suffering" may well be "the condition of all truth," as Adorno proclaims, the actual *articulation* of specifically *theoretical* "truth," as Fredric Jameson describes it, "must always be accompanied by the shock of defamiliarization and demystification, and of the revelation of repressed or forgotten realities" (Jameson 2006: 369). And the shocking revelations that must always accompany radically theoretical truth-claims must also come as pain-causing kicks in the pants for our reified common sense, our clarified understandings of identity, our oldest and strongest feelings of familiarity with ourselves and our surroundings. Theoretical truth-tellers, then, demote or deride "the true self"—and stress identity's *contingency* and *fluidity* (as opposed to its *necessity* and *stability*)—for a whole host of ethical, political, aesthetic, or even secularly "spiritual" reasons. Because they discern *ideology* busily working behind the scenes of all "identitarian" imperatives, theoretical writers see liberatory potential in hatching new strategies for subverting, abusing, or otherwise defamiliarizing and demystifying "identity." Theoretical writers, that is, suspect that it's invariably some representative of the "regulatory regimes" of "the Political Father" that encourages you to "be yourself" or commands you to "be all you can be" (to quote an old recruiting slogan for the United States Army); they suspect that it's always some instrumental agent of the normalizing *law* that demands to see your dog-tags, your identity papers.[1] So the question of whether and how successfully you can "play tag" with yourself and produce "your papers" before the law is always already political. But because the name-game of "identity politics" does involve the production of "papers" (or, in the broadest "**cultural**" sense, of *writing*, of inscribing and re-inscribing ourselves into our various "documents of civilization"), the question of what it means to be (or not to be) "all you can be" is always already "literary" to boot.[2] Our purpose in this lesson is to investigate why this is the case. Or better, our purpose in this lesson is to consider how a "literary" response to the "political" question of our being or not being "really and truly" ourselves—a response that, *as* "literary," is necessarily *ambivalent*, mixing anxiety and exhilaration as well as memory and desire—relates to both Adorno's and Jameson's truth-claims about "truth."[3]

[1] In "Imitation and Gender Insubordination," Butler writes that "identity categories tend to be instruments of regulatory regimes . . . the normalizing categories of oppressive structures" (1991/2007: 1707). In *The Pleasure of the Text*, Barthes writes that "The text is . . . that uninhibited person who shows his behind to the Political Father" (1975: 53). But the patriarchal figure being mooned here is for Barthes not necessarily your own personal daddy but rather whoever or whatever attempts "to fix meaning." Thus, for Barthes, the uninhibited text "liberates what may be called an anti-theological activity, an activity that is truly revolutionary since to refuse to fix meaning is, in the end, to refuse God and his hypostases—reason, science, law" (1968/1977: 147).

[2] With the phrase "documents of civilization," I'm alluding to the title sentence of our seventh lesson (which concerns the fates of literary formalism)—Walter Benjamin's axiom "There is no document of civilization that is not at the same time a document of barbarism" (1950/1968: 256). As for the term **cultural**, in his essay on "Culture" in *Critical Terms for Literary Study*, Stephen Greenblatt characterizes **culture** as "a system of constraints" and describes **cultivation** as "the internalization and practice of a code of manners" (1995: 227). Noting that in literary studies the concept of culture is "closely allied" to that of ideology, Greenblatt writes that "the ensemble of beliefs and practices that form a given culture function as a pervasive technology of control, a set of limits within which social behavior must be contained, a repertoire of models to which individuals must conform" (1995: 225). The use-value of "culture" for literary studies involves recognizing that "Western literature over a very long period of time has been one of the great institutions for the enforcement of cultural boundaries through praise and blame" (1995: 226).

[3] Since both Adorno and Jameson are resolutely Marxist intellectuals, both of their truth-claims about truth are consciously and conscientiously "political." But while Adorno's straightforward stance on the "condition of all truth" is *morally* or *ethically* political, Jameson's description of what must *accompany* the *practice* of "truth" is, one might argue, *aesthetically* or *poetically* political as well, not because the claim itself is particularly beautiful or aesthetically pleasing, but if only because of the way the claim couples those

Taken in full, this lesson's title is a mash-up of three sentences, one from a contemporary feminist visual artist, one from a seventeenth-century rationalist philosopher, and one from a nineteenth-century symbolist poet. The title's first words—"You are not yourself"—are taken from a 1983 Barbara Kruger photograph, upon which they appear prominently and in Kruger's trademark **futura bold italic** font. The "subject" of the photograph is a woman's face reflected in a broken mirror. A densely reticulated circular shape appears in the top portion of the frame, and lines of fracture radiate from this point of presumably violent impact (perhaps the woman threw some blunt object at the mirror, or perhaps she hit it with her own forehead in anger, frustration, or disgusted self-hatred). The letters of the words "**You**" and "**are**" are scattered across the top of this scene of disintegration, those of "**yourself**" are strewn about the bottom, while the three comprising the word "**not**" are positioned in a straight line at the exact center of the visual space.

The photograph positions its spectator, you are looking at it, as the "**You**" addressed in its textual overlay, so that in viewing this shattered image, you are prompted to see "**yourself**" *in* and *as* the fragments of the woman, of this "other" who—unless you just happen to be she who posed for the

unsightly terms "defamiliarization" and "demystification." The first term, as we've read in this book's introductory chapter, and as we'll consider more fully in Lesson Seven, hails from the poetics of the Russian formalist Viktor Shklovsky; this "lit-crit" term also relates to the "alienation effects" intentionally wrought upon the audiences of the theatrical productions the German Marxist dramatist Bertholt Brecht. But the term "defamiliarization" is also quite relevant to the philosophical hammerings of Friedrich Nietzsche, who, as we read in the previous lesson, issued the famously "anti-moral" and paradoxically "anti-veridical" truth-claim that "only as an *aesthetic phenomenon* are existence and the world *justified*" (1872/2006: 58)—and who for this and other reasons isn't exactly a Christian or Marxist saint. As for "demystification," *that* critical procedure has pretty much been the prime directive of all rational "Enlightenment" thinking since Kant, and it remains an indispensible weapon in the Marxist arsenal for any assault against "false consciousness." And if *reification* is still the principal method of "mystifyingly" maintaining "false consciousness" within the ideological machinations of late capitalism itself, "demystification" would have to equal "dereification" for Jameson and would have be a crucial aspect of *theory* insofar as theory must involve our "attempt to dereify the language of thought" (2009: 9). But here, returning to this lesson's focus on "personal identity," is the rub, the point of seeming tension between Adorno's stance and Jameson's. Many people, particularly among the global poor and working class, the dispossessed and wretched of the earth, utterly depend upon forms of mystification and reified "false consciousness" to make their sufferings bearable—they depend, in other words, on faith, on religion, on a strongly familiarized sense of self-identity recognized by parents, priests, and despots, blessed by a beneficent deity, etc. Such people do not "suffer" from reified "false consciousness" so much as they enjoy and benefit from it, psychically and spiritually. To subject such people to abrasively dereifying, defamiliarizing, and demystifying revelations or "truths" would surely only *increase* their sufferings. And so if Adorno's "lending a voice to suffering" is taken to mean *alleviating* picture—is "**not**" exactly you. As for the imaginary woman, she isn't quite herself either. Nor does she seem to be particularly "joying in the truth of self-division" (Kristeva 1982: 89). Her expression sorrowed, her gaze downcast, a teardrop clinging to a piece of broken glass, "she" appears to be looking not at you or "**You**" or even at her own face within the frame but down and out, past "**yourself**," perhaps at her own body, **not** shown, or perhaps at some missing shard of reflection that has fallen away from the frame and which "gives her back" some tiny piece of "herself" from the floor. At bottom left, there's a disconnected hand with polished fingernails, presumably hers, shown holding a mirror-fragment like a piece of jigsaw puzzle. A sliver of white space just below the hand-held fragment brings it into relief, suggesting that the hand is either pulling this piece of glass away or attempting (in apparent futility) to put it back in place, to restore the broken mirror to something resembling wholeness.

If **you** were looking at this photograph as **I** at this very moment **am**—not on the wall of a gallery or in a book or on a computer monitor or cellular screen but while holding it as a postcard between the thumb, middle, and index fingers of your own left hand, with the index extended along the card's edge—then your own hand would, like mine, be visually replicated

---

suffering, protecting wretched sufferers from even more pain than they already feel, then in this case compassionately *hiding* or *withholding* theoretical "truth" automatically becomes the "condition of all truth." But this seeming tension or paradox is actually an old problem in Marxist theory, one solved in advance by Marx himself—for just as he insists that "the point" is not simply to interpret the world but to change it, so the early Marx writes that the political objective of critique or demystification is not simply to destroy people's illusions, but to destroy or abandon or otherwise change "*a condition that require illusions*" (1844/1978: 53). Religion, as Marx quite famously opines, is "the *opium* of the people" (1844/1978: 54), and while, again, "the need to lend a voice to suffering" may be "the condition of all truth" for Adorno, "the criticism of religion is the premise of all criticism" (1844/1978: 54) for the early Marx. But the point of lending a voice to suffering is not simply to offer the sufferer a comforting fix, any more than the point of criticizing religion is stoically to "just say no" to all spiritual narcotics and deny oneself and everyone else the "promise of happiness" they provide. Rather, as Marx writes, "The abolition of religion as the *illusory* happiness of [people], is a demand for their *real* happiness. The call to abandon their illusions about their condition is a *call to abandon a condition which requires illusions*" (1844/1978: 54). "Criticism," Marx continues, "has plucked the imaginary flowers from the chain, not in order that [people] shall bear the chain without caprice or consolation but so that [they] shall cast off the chain and pluck the living flower. The criticism of religion disillusions [people] so that [they] will think, act and fashion [human] reality as [humans] who have lost [their] illusions and regained [their] reason" (1844/1978: 73). The question that will be taken up by Nietzsche and his non-Marxist followers (like Foucault) involves the extent to which life itself might be a condition that for humans absolutely requires illusions, requires art, much more than it demands or even involves "reason" or "truth." The question for Nietzsche is whether all the thinking, acting, and fashioning of human reality of which Marx speaks aren't ultimately *aesthetic* (rather than moral, rational, or veridical) *phenomenon*. We'll be returning to this question.

by that of the woman in the photograph itself. Perhaps this replication implicates us in what Walter Benjamin calls "The Work of Art in the Age of Mechanical Reproduction," since what we hold and behold is not the "original" artwork, imbued with a quasi-sacred "**aura**" of singularity, but the "same" work in its cheaply mass-reproduced commodity form.[4] But this "manual" and "digital" reproduction (of our own hands and fingers) can also raise the unsettling question of whether we "consumers" of contemporary art can ever masterfully "hold" this little picture (like little Ernst holds his reel in the *fort-da*) or whether "the picture" is not holding "us," framing us, containing us, taking us in, cutting off some little piece of **You yourself**—*mon semblable!*—that none of us will ever get back (together with) again.[5]

Kruger's photograph, then, achieves its alienating effects by implicating its viewers and readers in the "self-shattering" message that it both verbally delivers and visually enacts—**You are not yourself**. And so Kruger's piece of jagged edginess not only provides us with the first sentence of our lesson's titular mash-up but also leads us nicely (if that's the appropriate word) to Lacan's essay "The Mirror Stage as Formative of the *I* Function as Revealed in Psychoanalytic Experience." For the first paragraph of Lacan's most famous *écrit* features a discursive fragment of the second portion of the present lesson's title. Here, Lacan writes of a certain "experience"—an early experience of constitutive "misrecognition" or *méconnaissance*—that sets psychoanalytic theory "at odds with any philosophy directly stemming from the *cogito*" (1966b/2006: 75). *Cogito* is of course short-hand for René Descartes' slogan *cogito ergo sum*, "I think, therefore I am," the "root" statement of logically self-reflective self-certainty from which modern Western rationalist philosophy is usually considered to stem. The "experience" of which Lacan speaks, however, involves that fateful historical moment in which the human

---

[4] Writing in the 1930s about photography and cinema as serious but accessible popular arts, Benjamin argues that in the artwork in the modern age suffers disenchantment as it gains democratic mass appeal. In modernity, Benjamin says, art loses its **aura**, both its elitist, aristocratic associations and its hallowed connection to religious ritual. While in the past some paintings were not publically displayed but kept locked away in cathedrals to be seen by only a few, a Hollywood film is of course produced to be viewed by as many as possible. And while today one might still want to make a quasi-religious pilgrimage to, say, the Prado in Madrid to see the Picasso's "Guernica" in all its horrific and "auratic" splendor, no one would go out of her way to see the original print of the latest installment of *Star Wars* or *Saw*. Indeed, with cinema, one might even forego traveling to the radiant multiplex and just wait to have the DVD delivered in the mail with the rest of the junk.

[5] "*Mon semblable!*" is thrown in as an allusion to "*Hypocrite lecteur!—mon semblable— mon frère!*" (hypocrite reader, my twin, my brother), the line from "To the Reader" in Baudelaire's *Les Fleurs du Mal* (Flowers of Evil) that Eliot appropriates in *The Waste Land*.

infant first apprehends its "self," first feebly "grasps" its "own" image, in an "anthropogenetically" reflecting surface.

> This event can take place . . . from the age of six months; its repetition
> has often given me pause to reflect upon the striking spectacle of
> a nursling in front of a mirror who has not yet mastered walking, or
> even standing, but who— though tightly held by some prop, human or
> artificial (what, in France we call a *trotte-bébé*)—overcomes, in a flutter
> of jubilant activity, the constraints of his prop in order to adopt a slightly
> leaning forward position and take in an instantaneous view of the image
> in order to fix it in his mind. (1966b/2006: 75–6)

Now, our initial questions about this little piece of *theatre*—Lacan refers to a mirror *stage* to invoke theatrical performance rather than to designate some "organic" phase or natural plateau of human psychic development— are these: Why does it prompt Lacan to oppose "any philosophy directly stemming from the *cogito*?" How does Lacanian speculation about the psychic consequences of baby's first mirror experience disrupt the Cartesian equation of **epistemological** activity ("I *think*") with **ontological** self-certainty ("therefore I *am*")?[6] What is it about the formation of the "I function" through what Lacan calls "homeomorphic identification" (1966b/2006: 77) that will eventually lead him to make mincemeat of the *cogito* in the following manner?

> I am thinking where I am not, therefore I am where I am not thinking.
> These words render palpable to an attentive ear with what elusive
> ambiguity the ring of meaning flees from our grasp along the verbal
> string.
>   What we must say is: I am not, where I am the plaything of my
> thought; I think about what I am where I do not think that I am thinking.
> (1966e/2006: 430)

Finally, why would a *clinical* psychoanalyst like Lacan—ostensibly devoted to "the healing arts," to the *therapeutic* project of *reducing* human suffering, making people "feel better" about themselves—develop such a painfully bewildering style of writing as what we witness here, a "violent" style that produces in the reader what Jane Gallop calls a "great malaise," an aggressively

---

[6] **Epistemology** is "the branch of philosophy that is concerned with theories of knowledge" (Childers and Henzi 1995: 98), while **ontology**, "literally translated as 'the science of being,'" involves "the study of existence itself" (214). In regard to the *cogito*, Childers and Henzi point out that "Descartes' formulation 'I think, therefore I am,' while a statement of ontology or being, is also fundamentally epistemological" (98).

disintegrative style that causes the typical reader "to feel non-identical to herself as reader" (1985: 117)?

We can address these questions only by continuing to read, however that activity may make us feel. And if our feeling upon attempting to come to terms with Lacan (or any difficult theoretical writer) is anything but placidly oceanic—provoking more alienation than jubilation, more unease than self-confident calm—then our sensations of readerly malaise, of self-divisive dis-ease, may be related to what Lacan considers the infant's experiences of ambivalence and misrecognition when *it* first appears to itself (as an other) upon the mirror stage, on "the threshold of the visible world" (1966b/2006: 77), when it first begins to subject its sense of being-in-the-world to the articulated process by which "the specular *I*" or imaginary ego "turns into the social *I*" (1966b/2006: 79), the subject of the symbolic order. Perhaps Lacan's writing provokes the reader's malaise and alienation all the better to illustrate the point that "malaise and alienation" *are* the subjective conditions of reading and writing *as such*, to better illuminate the poet Artur Rimbaud's grammatically deformed observation (and this is the third source of our lesson's titular pastiche) that "*Je est un autre*"—"I *is* an other" (1871/1966: 304). Perhaps Lacan's style makes the reader feel non-identical to herself as reader because his writings "can be understood only in reference to the truth of 'I is an other,' less dazzling to the poet's intuition than it is obvious from the psychoanalyst's viewpoint" (1966c/2006: 96).

For Lacan, then, the problem with "any philosophy directly stemming from the *cogito*" is that such reflection remains oblivious to this dazzlingly defamiliarizing "truth." Just as Freud (and Nietzsche before him) objected to rationalism's reduction of all psychic activity to intentional consciousness, its indifference to *unconscious* motivations and desires (particularly its own), so Lacan opposes the *cogito*'s seemingly seamless equation of epistemology with ontology, of *meaning* with *being*. For Lacan, as we've read, the thinking subject may very well *desire* to *be*, but it is *required*, instead, to *mean*, ordered to symbolize; meaningful thinking—for all the reasons belabored in previous lessons—always entails a *lack* or *dislocation* of complete being. *To mean* means **not** really, finally, or fully *to be*. So for Lacan it can't be the case that "I think, therefore I am." What the case must be, rather, is that "I think [cognitively participate in meaning only] where I am not [that is, in the symbolic, where I must lack completely real being] . . . I am not [that is, I lack completely real being] where I am the plaything of my thought"— which is nowhere else but in the symbolic.

The ecstatic "truth of self-division" that Lacan and I are driving at here involves the irreducible "splitting of the subject," our unavoidable separation and alienation from ourselves *in language*. Linguistic self-estrangement is unavoidable for Lacan, and for you and I, because (1), like you, I have no "I" to speak of unless I can speak of it, and (2), I can speak and think of myself only by discursively *splitting* myself in two, *scissoring* myself, on the one hand, into the *subject* who performs the speaking and thinking and, on the other, into the potentially losable *object*—the elusive "ring" or "plaything"—of my "own" speech and thought. Whenever I put myself into play; whenever I put myself into words (as I *must*, if I want to participate in human reality); whenever I say, think, or otherwise mean "I," I inevitably (albeit unconsciously) end up with more than one "I" (an embarrassment of r*I*ches). I am thus put into the position of having to play the game of *fort-da* with myself, or at least of having to open myself, playfully or painfully, to the division between signifier and signified, the gap between what I say I am and what I think I mean. Lacan, being Lacan, exacerbates this crack, this fissure, and throws a handsawed bit of *Hamlet* into the breach, by thinking to ask:

> Is the place that I occupy as a subject of the signifier concentric or eccentric in relation to the place I occupy as subject of the signified? That is the question. The point is not to know whether I speak of myself in a way that conforms to what I am, but rather to know whether, when I speak of myself, I am the same as the self of whom I speak. (1966e/2006: 430).

For Lacan, the only valid responses here are: (a) eccentric, and (b) not the same. Because I *is* an other, you are not yourself—all of which means, among other things, that our mutual friend "the *cogito*" just isn't going to cut it anymore, at least not "directly," and certainly not after "the linguistic turn" in the human sciences, not after "language invaded the *universal* problematic and *everything* became discourse" (Derrida 1966/1978: 280).

But let's return, you and I, to the moment of the mirror stage, an "imaginary" event which does seem to complicate the *cogito* to no end but which would also seem to be a scene of cognitive "jubilation" rather than discursive alienation. As we've read, Lacan describes the infant at/upon this stage as a sort of speechless early reader, leaning toward the "first page" of its self-reflection "in a flutter of jubilant activity . . . in order to fix it in his mind." Lacan then repeats the happy adjective, asserting that

> the jubilant assumption of his specular image by the kind of being—still trapped in his motor impotence and nursling dependence—the little man is at the *infans* stage thus seems to me to manifest in an exemplary

situation the symbolic matrix in which the *I* is precipitated in its primordial form. (1966b/2006: 76)

And of course there is cause for celebration, for a bit of the old *"hoopsa boyaboy hoopsa!"* here, for no "little man" of any gender is ever going to make it far in "the visible world" without a sense of identity, a valid ID, or a vehicular *I* of some make or model.[7]

But in Lacan's account, the infant, prior to its premiere upon the mirror stage, *lacks* any *formal* sense of self, doesn't yet possess an ego, is not yet strictly speaking an I, is not yet perceptually coordinated as the subjective locus or pivot of its "own" experience of being-in-the-world. Subjectivity, mind you, depends upon a working sense of differentiation, depends upon knowing the difference "between the *Innenwelt* and the *Umwelt*" (1966b/2006: 78), the inner world and the great outdoors. But as Lacan suggests elsewhere, "the very young child's experience of itself . . . develops on the basis of a situation that is experienced as undifferentiated" (1966c/2006: 91), and, unless I'm very much mistaken, this early situation of experiential undifferentiation bears a close resemblance to our long-lost friend and implacable enemy—*the real*. Let's say that before and outside the montage of the imaginary and the symbolic, before and outside the limits—and the libidinally normalizing *limitations*—of human reality, the infant has all of its "eggs" put into this one oceanic "basket," that the infant has *all* of its sense of *being* situated—cathected or "invested"—in this "sea of yolky enjoyment" (Žižek 1992: 40) that *is* the undifferentiated *real*. Let's say that the infant "in the real" doesn't *know* the difference between subject and object, interior and exterior, can't *tell* the difference between itself and everything else, can't accurately *say* where its self-sameness leaves off and everything else or anything other "officially" begins.

Nor, let's say, does the infant "in the real" have any conception of the way its own prematurely born body actually hangs together. If it happens to see its own hand flapping around in front of its as yet self-unseen face, it still

---

[7] The words "hoopsa boyaboy hoopsa!" appear at the beginning of the "Oxen of the Sun" chapter in Joyce's *Ulysses* (1922/1986: 314); according to Gifford, these words represent "The cry with which a midwife celebrates the birth of a male child as she bounces it to stabilize its breathing" (1988: 408/09). Here, though, against Lacan's *little man*nerisms, let's remember that the child whose image bounces back to it in the mirror isn't necessarily male, and, following the vehicular metaphors employed above, that in some countries an adult female can't legally operate an auto or even obtain a license to drive (see Milani 2011). The point to be driven home here is that it isn't simply natural "breathing" but socio-cultural *gendering* that starts getting stabilized even at such a seemingly "neutral" moment as the mirror stage.

may not visually "grasp" the proper connection of hand to arm to shoulder to "self." Its "own" appendage might register as just another piece of meat swimming in the continuous visual stew, just another blob of perceptual flotsam in the great yolky sea—as, for that matter, might its own mirror reflection, if the infant happens to be exposed to that graceless figure before being developmentally capable of apprehending the image as its "own."

For better and for worse, this oceanic feeling of undifferentiation contracts, dries up, at the moment of the mirror stage. For when the infant, assisted by its human or artificial "prop," first recognizes itself as "an other" in the mirror, first sees the way its own fairly inept bodily movements correspond to those of the fairer shape or sharper image it beholds before it, it arguably "loses" undifferentiation—and loses it *for good.*[8] The infant—*formerly* in the real, now *formally* being hauled out of it—must from now on discern and maintain the *difference* between itself and everything else, must *note* the contrast between figure and background, must come to *know* that "in reality" (as *opposed* to "in the real") it is **not** everything but merely one relatively quite diminished thing, one "miserable glass shell of human individuality" (Nietzsche 1872/2006: 82) among others, what Freud ego-deflatingly calls a "shrunken residue" (1930/1989: 725), a separate and much smaller entity, constitutively discontinuous with everything else in the visible world.

However, beholding for the first time its own head tottering on its shoulders, as well as their connection to its own arms and hands, the infant may now be gratified to see that in the *Umwelt*—in external reality as *represented* in this "other scene" out there—its body *does* seem to hold together in an "ideal" or formally coherent way, or at least in a *much better* way than anything the infant had heretofore imagined. This ideal morphological "unity of self" was imperceptible, unimaginable, in the indifferent time *before* the mirror stage, back "in the real," when and where the infant *will have thus* experienced itself only as a *corps morcelé*, a "body-in-fragments." But as my emphatic and confusing use of the future anterior (the phrase *will have thus*) might suggest, here's where "things" get particularly complicated, logically and

---

[8] The infant loses undifferentiation "for good" in both the "temporal" and the "moral" senses, both "forever" and "for better": for once the infant fixes its distinct image of itself in its mind, once the infant is installed in the imaginary and the symbolic, there's no "going back" to the real for the subject *as* subject, however much the *fantasy* of return might animate a subject's unconscious desire (and in a sense all fantasies *are* this fundamental fantasy, including, perhaps, the fantasy that "all fantasies *are* this fundamental fantasy"). But this fantasmatic return "to an earlier state of things" is both spatio-temporally impossible and "morally" prohibited (since, as we discussed in the previous lesson, primal undifferentiation is "eroto-thanatically" analogous to "incestuous" merger with the maternal).

chronologically, for the newly reflective "little man" (if not for the malaised reader of "The Mirror Stage" essay itself). For if a "fragment" is thinkable *as fragment* only in *differential relation* to the idea of some unbroken unity or whole, then how in the visible world could the infant—*prior* to the mirror stage, *still* residing within an experientially "undifferentiated" situation—be said to imagine itself as a fragmented body? Well, logically and chronologically, it couldn't, and Lacan doesn't exactly say that it does. What Lacan writes is that the mirror stage

> is experienced as a temporal dialectic that decisively projects the individual's formation into history: [it] is a drama whose internal pressure pushes precipitously from insufficiency to anticipation—and, for the subject caught up in the lure of spatial identification, turns out fantasies that proceed from a fragmented image of the body to what I will call an "orthopedic" form of its totality—and to the finally donned armor of an alienating identity that will mark his entire mental development with its rigid structure. (1966b/2006: 78)

Now, to say that the mirror stage is experienced as a *temporal* **dialectic** is to suggest, among other things, that its effects and causes are never *immediately present* but must be read as unfolding in time.[9] In other words, the *narrative*

---

9   **Dialectic** can be provisionally described as a model of conceptual agency that proceeds through confronting (and perhaps even resolving or overcoming) contradiction, particularly the conceptual agent's contradictory self-alienation. When associated with Hegel—or, more precisely, with Hegelianism—the dialectic is often reduced, inaccurately, to an abstract "thesis-antithesis-synthesis" formula and to the notion that any synthesis or unification of opposites becomes a new thesis, which in turn generates another antithesis, which is then overcome, or sublated, by an even greater synthesis, and so on and so on, until ideally all ontological/epistemological contradiction is resolved or subsumed into the rational/conceptual maw of "absolute knowing"—a Hegelian phrase commonly or "vulgarly" understood to represent Hegel's hubristic faith in the philosophical possibility of rationally possessing a totally complete and absolutely unified knowledge of "the ultimate meaning of everything" (Findlay 1971: 93). We will consider Hegelian matters more extensively in our next lesson. But since we are here trying to come to terms with *Lacan* and the dialectic, I will let a few sentences from Fredric Jameson's essay "Lacan and the Dialectic" serve to further provisionally describe the latter term—"At its most general," Jameson writes, "we can call dialectical any thought mode which grasps its objects, terms or elements as subject to definition, determination or modification by the relationships in which they are by definition seized" (2006: 395). Countering the pseudo-dialectic of "vulgar Hegelianism," Jameson writes that the dialectic "is a tormented kind of language which seeks to register incommensurabilities without implying any solution to them by some facile naming of them, or the flattening- out of this or that unified philosophical code" (2006: 375). One might note here that Lacan's "dialectical" writing is not only a "tormented" but a *tormenting* "kind of language." Hence, the "great malaise" produced by Lacan's style, if not, paradoxically, by Lacanian *therapy*, in the clinical experience of which the discovered *lack* of "any solution" to the problems of

of the formation of the *I* function must be read in a sort of temporal loop, backward as well as forward, with an eye toward the phenomenon that Freud calls **Nachträglichkeit**, "deferred action" or "retro-determination" or "retroversive causality." What occurs in a typical episode of psychic *Nachträglichkeit* is that a subject will experience a "new" discovery that retroactively "recodes" the memory of some earlier experience, imbuing the remembered event with a significance (typically a sexual significance) that it previously lacked. This freshly reinterpreted experience then circles back from the past to bear down upon and "pre-recode" the present revelation.

Considering, then, the "bad timing" of the *corps morcèle* in the light of *Nachträglichkeit*, we see that the infant in the undifferentiated real can't cognitively experience itself *at that time* as an insufficient body-in-fragments. This can't be the case because the infant can't *simultaneously* experience undifferentiation *and* insufficiency (since "insufficiency" can be experienced only in *differential* relation to some ideally *sufficient* image). Never having seen its ego ideal before, never having seen its own "up-standing" self up-close and personal, the infant "in the real" can't have the faintest suspicion that there's ever been anything "wrong" with it. It is only *after* the moment of the mirror stage, only *after* the "orthopedic" or *corrective* perception of a totally coherent "body image," that the infant's *earlier* and "innocent" experience of the real is retroactively re-imagined as one of "organic inadequacy" (1966b/2006: 77), of corporeally scattered insufficiency. The *fantasy* of the hellishly fragmented body (Lacan references the paintings of Hieronymus Bosch in this regard) gets retro-projected onto the infant's "lost" situation of undifferentiation, while "the lure of spatial identification," in the form of the *fantasy* of the "ideal-I," gets projected into *its future* as a desirable "dialectical" resolution to what *will have become* the problem of fragmentation. Thus, Lacan writes of "the dialectic syntheses by which [the subject] must resolve, as *I*, his discordance with his own reality" (1966b/2006: 76). The subject of the mirror stage is suspended between the "insufficiency" of a still-present past and the "anticipation" of an attractive future good. The subject is situated between the (bad) *idea* of the fragmented body (which the subject is told, in so many words, that it *should* desire to forget or repress, *should* desire to start moving away from) and the (good) *ideal* of the unified, non-discordant *self*, the *image* of the purely self-identical

contradiction and alienation becomes itself the solution to the problem. In clinical terms, the absolute lack of cure turns into the cure itself. In Slavoj Žižek's Wagnerian terms, the cure involves the realization that "'the wound is healed only by the spear that smote you'" (1993: 165). Meanwhile, in stylistic terms, the "great malaise" produced by Lacan's writing—that is, the speared or smitten reader's feeling of non-identity with herself as reader—paradoxically becomes the very standard of Lacanian well-being.

I (which the subject gets told, in so many words, that it *should* eventually add or shape or live up to).[10]

But as these emphasized *shoulds* should suggest, here's where the "political" or *ideological* aspects of "morphological mimicry" (1966b/2006: 77) come to the foreground. Here's where the little man's "house of mirrors" starts to look like the "department of corrections" that it actually pretty much is. For like everything else in a world that must be made to mean, the imposing ego ideal that appears in a mirror doesn't grow on a tree or fall from the sky but is *produced* through human labor. As we'll see, a mirror is never simply a neutral or objectively reflecting surface but is always "political" to its very tain.[11] The mirror experience functions as the enabling gateway to a whole host of socially produced images, each ready to play its "orthopedic" part in the larger "cultural intervention" (1966b/2006: 79), each lying in wait for its chance to subject the subject to the rigors of "identificatory reshaping" (1966c/2006: 95). In other words, the subject of the mirror stage is always already *subjected* to ideology, and "ideology" is the precise term for and of this *subjection*.

---

[10] It's instructive to read the dynamics of Lacan's mirror stage in relation to Freud's slogan *Wo Es war, soll Ich werden*— "where id was, there ego must be" (1933/2001: 80), or "where it (*Es*) was there I (*Ich*) must come into being." But it's also important to grasp the counter-intuitive coordinates, the weird whens and wheres and theres, of this ego-boosting scenario. If, that is, we apply our habituated, common-sense understanding of the difference between an "I" and an "it"—a pure self and a mere thing, an active subject and an inert object—to the scene of the very young human child situated in front of a mirror, our normal tendency would be to think of the child as being situated on the "spiritual" side of the I/self/subject and the mirror as being on the "material" side of the it/thing/object. In the first moments of the mirror encounter, however, these "sides" are actually reversed—the real living body of the child is, precisely, the soulless and unspiritualized "it," while the ego or "I" initially "resides" in a contraption of deadwood and glass, the mirror as lifeless thing or inanimate object. One of the many paradoxes here is that the infant exits the real and begins to enter human reality by virtue of a formally *mortifying* experience. Or, more precisely, at the crucial moment of the mirror experience, a specter of human reality, launched from the "dead" side of the mirror's surface, enters and inhabits/inhibits the body of the helpless child, so in a sense it's from the position of the mirror image that the *Wo Es war, soll Ich werden* is articulated— where "it," that stupidly living body, is, there "I," a culturally endorsed form, will move, intervene, plant my flag, etc. In their 1999 film, *The Matrix*, the Wachowskis visually literalize this "extimate" movement of cultural intervention: after Neo takes Morpheus's red pill, he sees his own image, at first cracked and then "whole," in a mirror. When Neo reaches out and touches this mirror, its surface begins to liquefy, moving out from the frame and into Neo's space, moving onto his person, covering his hand and arm and creeping quickly up his neck, eventually "invading" his interior by cascading down his open throat. Assuming, consuming, or introjecting his own image, Neo is forced, as it were, to eat himself. In a sense, as we're just about to see, all "subjects of human reality" are similarly force-fed ideology.

[11] The "tain" is the foil or silvered backing applied, by dint of human labor, to a piece of glass (itself produced through labor), thus turning it into a mirror.

II. Ideology is eternal

Although Lacan never employs the word "ideology" in the mirror-stage essay, he nonetheless insists that what the mirror stage represents is not "a natural maturation process" but a "cultural intervention" (1966b/2006: 79). For Lacan, the ideal "specular I" that the infant is encouraged to mimic is a culturally "orthopedic" or *corrective* form, "the root-stock of secondary identifications . . . subsuming the libidinal normalization functions" (1966b/2006: 76). In "Aggressiveness in Psychoanalysis," Lacan suggests that these "secondary identifications" work by virtue of the subject's "introjection of the imago of the parent of the same sex," and he thus stresses "the 'pacifying' function of the ego-ideal: the connection between its libidinal normativeness and a cultural normativeness" (1966c/2006: 95).

Now, boys and girls, what does it mean for Lacan to connect "morphological mimicry" to "libidinal normalization" to "cultural normativeness"? It means that no mirror in the history of the world has ever just "objectively" given back the simple reflection of a "good" little boy or girl anatomically destined to naturally mature and/or libidinally blossom into "normal" heterosexuality. Rather, the mirror functions as a sociocultural "apparatus" that "imposes" and "naturalizes" the vision of an always-already sociocultural subject who had *better* get its act together, who had *better* perform its mimicry correctly, and who had *better* turn out *straight*. For Lacan, the subject's eventual concordance with its "own reality" entails a rather large quantum of fear-based *conformity* with the "pacifying" function of the ego ideal; it involves the coerced internalization of the "appropriate picture," the successful introjection of the image of the parent of the same sex (who, as "successful" parent or effective "prop," must be presumed to have turned out "straight" him-or-herself), and a perpetual identification *with* and docile endorsement *of* all the images of compulsory normativity that a given culture proffers.

The operative critical idea here is that any existing culture, working or doing business as a "system of constraints" (Greenblatt 1995: 227), depends upon the institutional circulation of normativizing images to continue to exist, to work, to "reproduce its conditions of production." This last phrase comes to us from Marx via Louis Althusser, to whose essay "Ideology and the Ideological State Apparatuses" we now turn. For here, Althusser develops an innovative and influential theory of ideology based in no small part on Lacan's insights into the mirror stage.

What Althusser theorizes, however, is not any *particular* ideology, but "ideology in general." In other words, Althusser isn't into analyzing "isms" as codified sets of political ideas or "articles of faith" to which various individuals in a given society might *consciously* subscribe. Nor is he about debunking some specific "ism" as a pernicious piece of Ideological false consciousness." Rather, Althusser sees "ideology in general" both as a pervasively *unconscious* formation and as "a necessary element of 'sociality' itself" (Kavanagh 1995: 314). Ideology in general is "a structure essential to the historical life of societies . . . *indispensable in any society if* [individuals] *are to be formed, transformed and equipped to respond to the demands of their conditions of existence*" (Althusser 1970: 234–5). Because all human individuals are born prematurely, not "fully equipped" to respond to even the most basic existential demands, every stinking one of us *must* be formed and transformed, socialized and cultivated, brought into the fold of human reality in its current historical *form*.[12]

For Althusser, then, the phrase "ideology in general" designates a formal, structural, transhistorical, even "eternal" aspect of *socialization*, that "extraordinary adventure" which "transforms a small animal conceived by a man and a woman into a small human child" (1971: 139–40). Ideology "in general" is now and forever integral to the "humanization of the small biological creature that results from human parturition" (1971: 140). Althusser thus isn't concerned with specific "isms" that turn otherwise perfectly nice people into sinister or tedious "ideologues." Rather, he investigates "ideology in general" as the necessary process that transforms individuals into subjects "in the first place." Althusser is concerned not with ideological *content*, with what some specifically espoused ideology *is*, but rather with the ideological *function*, what "ideology in general" does and how it does it.

---

[12] We can begin to consider the difference between ideology as "false consciousness" and ideology in general as *unconscious* formation by comparing the two versions of the horror film *The Fly*. In both films, a scientist invents a teleportation device that can zap matter from one chamber to another; he intentionally tries the device out on himself and (unintentionally) on the eponymous insect that has lighted into the launch chamber with him; and he emerges from the destination chamber in an altered, "insectified" (or, let's say, "ideologized") form. In Kurt Neumann's 1958 version of the film, the disastrous alteration is quite obvious—the scientist steps out with his human head (his truly human consciousness) missing and with a huge fly-head (i.e., ideological "false consciousness") conspicuously in its place. By contrast, in David Cronenberg's 1986 version, the scientist emerges on the other side of the botched experiment *looking exactly like himself*, but his ideal self-resemblance is preserved only because he has *internalized* the fly (i.e., ideology) at the general, invisible, and *systemic* level of DNA. Later on, the horrifically insectile manifests itself quite visibly, but at least at first, the *invisibility* of the scientist's "inner fly" allows "DNA" to metaphorize ideology as an *unconscious* formation. Cronenberg's treatment of the scientist's dilemma thus implies that the problem of ideology cannot be remedied in an old-school "humanist" fashion—by restoring the true, self-conscious (and now wiser) human head to the human. Actually, given the nasty fate of the tiny human head in Neumann's version (attached to fly, caught in Web, nearly eaten by spider before being smashed by rock), neither *Fly* seems to suggest that the problem of ideology can be remedied at the level of heroic individual effort. In this judgment, as we'll see, both films concur with Althusser.

The first and overarching function of ideology is to *secure* "the reproduction of the conditions of production" (Althusser 1971/2001: 85). By "production" Althusser means the actual making of the world that must be materially made, that must be humanly generated or manufactured (that doesn't grow on trees or fall from the sky). The "conditions of production" include both the "productive forces" (humans in and as their "labor power" to make the world) and "the existing relations of production" (1971/2001: 86)—the cooperative or conflictual relations of these producers (1) to each other; (2) to other humans (in a class society, these would be the *owners* of production, who don't produce but who extract wealth and power from the *workers* who actually do; and (3) to the product(s) or fruit(s) of their labor (all the manufactured objects in the world and, in the largest "materialist" sense, the very history of the world, the very "world history" that they—we— are in the process of producing).

Now, the historical conditions of production or "world-making" are such that they always *necessarily* have to be reproduced—structurally, transhistorically, universally, "eternally," the world *must* be made and remade. Such remaking involves physical, material, and of course sexual reproduction (the producers themselves must be produced—or, as Shakespeare's Benedick crows in *Much Ado about Nothing*, "the world must be peopled!"). It is thus a truth universally acknowledged that "the ultimate condition of production is ... the reproduction of the conditions of production"—or at least Althusser quotes Marx to the effect that "every child knows" (1971/2001: 85) such to be the case. Marxism holds *these* truths to be self-evident—the world must be peopled, and people all over the world always have to *work* to produce the conditions of their self-population. "Labor" in both senses of the word is an absolutely necessary condition of possibility, never a merely historical contingency.

But still one might ask—under what specific and historically contingent conditions do men and women (go into) labor? Leaving aside for the moment the question of the different ways in which "human parturition" might be handled, one can accept the inevitability of labor, can accept that people must work, but nonetheless still wonder—Which people? What sort of work? Under what "working conditions"? And for what actual purpose? Of course, one might *imagine* a world—a "fully human and humanly produced world" (Jameson 2010: 107)—in which the conditions of production were such that the *real* purpose of *all* work was to produce and reproduce equally *humane* and equitably *humanizing* conditions for *all*. Conversely, one might imagine a world in which the real "meaning and purpose" of *everybody's* work everywhere was to produce wealth and power and pleasure for only *some*. But look—one doesn't have to merely "imagine" the latter world. One has only to *recognize contemporary global* capitalist society (or "Planet Money," as I've heard the phrase coined) for what it is and as our very "own reality"— not because we all own it, to be sure, but because *we* actively reproduce *its* conditions of production, simply by "being ourselves," simply by living our purportedly "purpose-driven" lives.[13]

The main purpose driving ideology is, again, to *secure* the reproduction of the conditions of production. But ideological security apparently requires the labor of "making" historically specific and *contingent* conditions *seem unconditional*—necessary, inevitable—to the very producers of those conditions. Making the conditional *seem* unconditional is required whenever it appears that workers will continue to work *only on condition* that their working conditions *appear* to them as unconditional, unquestionable, absolutely inevitable. Without that ideological "job-security"—the job of ideationally securing people in their jobs, in their allotted places on the figurative or actual "assembly line"—these workers might refuse to work. In order to "make" workers (who) work, to make workers (who) "work all by themselves" (i.e., to "make" them without having overtly and physically to *force* them, without having to march them off at gunpoint to labor camps or factories or offices or universities), ideology works to "make" contingent conditions *appear* necessary, to *reproduce* or *represent* contingencies *as* necessities, securing the *reproduction* of the conditions of production by *representing* the contingent as eternal. The dominant effect of this *reproduction/representation* is to render *alternative* working conditions unrepresentable, even unimaginable, to and for the workers themselves.

This work of making the contingent seem eternal involves both *reproduction* and *representation*. It depends, actually, upon a crucial shift from "reproductive systems" (involving the biologically *real*) to "systems of

---

[13] I allude here to "evangelical" blowhard Rick Warren's 2002 best-seller *The Purpose-Driven Life*. I would suggest, however, that in a capitalist society, it doesn't really matter what you *imagine* or *believe* to be the "purpose" driving your life; in a capitalist society, the *real* purpose, the *real* practical effect, of all of your "real life" activities is to create profits for capitalists, to enrich and empower the owners of Planet Money. Not that it always works out that way, but capitalist social reality is *structured* so that that's the dominant intended effect of your actual living, what your living actually *materializes*. In capitalist reality, whatever you may *imagine*, everything that you actually *do*—living somewhere, eating, drinking, being clothed and shod, being entertained and/or educated, staying healthy, staying alive—requires/costs money, and thus *makes* money and power for capitalists. Unless you *are* a capitalist, the work that you do, which makes you *some* money, ultimately makes *more* money for capitalists than it does for you, since you turn most of that money back over to capitalists so that you can continue to *do* all the things mentioned above (i.e., live). So, again, whatever you *imagine* you're purposively doing with your life doesn't really matter; what you're really *doing* with your life is generating wealth and power for capitalists.

representation" (involving the cultural *forms* of human *reality*, pretty much anything comprised of images and/or words). This shift from *systematic reproduction* to *systematic representation* leads us to a second major function of ideology. Althusser writes that to secure the *reproduction* of the conditions of production, ideology "represents the imaginary relationship of individuals to their real conditions of existence" (1971/2001: 109). "Imaginary" here means *imagined*, otherwise than real, and so Althusser clearly implies a discrepancy between representations of "imaginary relations" and non-representationally "real conditions." He suggests, in other words, that people's real conditions of existence might be *otherwise* than what they *imagine* for themselves or *see represented* to them.[14]

But "imaginary" also means *imaged*, comprised of images, involving the social circulation of *pictures*. Karl Mannheim has observed that "a society is possible in the last analysis [only] because the individuals in it carry around in their heads some sort of picture of that society" (1964: xxiii). James Kavanagh writes that "with the important addition of 'and their place in it,'" Mannheim's observation "might serve as a fair introduction to current ideology theory, which tries to understand the complex ways through which modern societies offer reciprocally reinforcing versions of 'reality,' 'society,' and 'self' to social subjects" (1995: 309).

> Ideology designates a rich "system of representations" . . . which helps form individuals into social subjects who "freely" internalize an appropriate "picture" of the social world and their place in it. Ideology offers . . . a fundamental framework of assumptions that defines the parameters of the real and the self . . . Ideology is less tenacious as a "set of ideas" than as a system of representations, perceptions and images that precisely encourages men and women to "see" their specific place in a historically peculiar social formation as inevitable, natural, a necessary function of the "real" itself. (1995: 310)

The basic critical idea here is that men and women, in order to *be* "men" and "women," must be "encouraged" to *see* their allotted places in a particular "social world" as necessary functions of "the real itself" or else they might

---

[14] If you can't bring yourself to imagine a discrepancy between the imaginary relations and the real conditions of your own "purpose-driven" life, consider what happens to Neo in *The Matrix*. Neo "imagines" or "knows perfectly well" that he is Mr Anderson who lives and works and is basically in control of his own life; but when he swallows Morpheus's red pill and "goes through the looking glass," he "awakens" to his real conditions of existence and discovers he is in fact a "coppertop," a passive, plugged-in, quasi-fetal energy source whose only real purpose "in life" is to generate power for "the matrix," the computer-generated "system of representations" in which he "lives" out his imaginary relations.

not want to stay in their places, might not want to keep being what they "are." Encouraging people to just "be themselves" and discouraging them from imagining any other destiny, ideology involves systematically framing/ forming people, keeping them in line and on task, mainly by "giving" them the impression that by staying "on the job" (of being themselves) they are just "doing what comes naturally." *Impressing* us with (and into) our given identities; *representing* our imaginary relations to our real conditions; *offering* "reciprocally reinforcing versions of 'reality,' 'society,' and 'self' [in pictures and in words] to social subjects" (Kavanagh 1995: 309)—all this is ideology's "business."

And ideology is always quite busy, particularly in those intimately "personal" places where ostensibly non-ideological "common-sense" is most loath to find it. "Common sense," as you'll recall, involves the reception/ affirmation of "given meaning," of whatever seems to go without saying, whatever seems perfectly *obvious*, self-evident, clear, right, and true—to anyone with "common sense." But Althusser argues that ideology works its magic by enforcing and reinforcing "common sense," or, as he puts it (and here's the third major ideological function), by imposing certain "obviousnesses as obviousnesses." Althusser writes:

> It is indeed a peculiarity of ideology that it imposes (without appearing to do so, since these are "obviousnesses") obviousnesses as obviousnesses, which we cannot *fail to recognize* and before which we have the inevitable reaction of crying out . . . : "That's obvious! That's right! That's true!" (1971/2001: 116)

For Althusser, ideology (1) *secures* the reproduction of the conditions of production by (2) *representing* people's imaginary relations to their real conditions in a way that (3) *imposes* obviousnesses *as* obviousnesses. By getting social subjects to cough back up its "inevitable" common-sense truisms, ideology offers what Althusser calls "the absolute guarantee that everything really is so, and that on condition that the subjects recognize what they are and behave accordingly, everything will be all right: Amen—'*So be it*.'" (1971/2001: 123).

> This phrase ['*So be it!*'] which registers the effect to be obtained proves that it is not 'naturally' so . . . This phrase proves that it *has* to be so if things are to be what they must be: [i.e.,] if the reproduction of the relations of production is to be assured . . . in the attitudes of the individual subjects occupying the posts which the socio-technical division of labour assigns to them. (1971/2001: 124)

Through this *imposition* of the obvious *as* obvious, ideology gets people to work by getting people to work on their attitudes, on the pictures they carry around in their heads, in order to turn what merely *happens* to be (an historically contingent division of labor) into what "simply" and "obviously" *has* to be (a veritable "force of nature"). In other words, ideology operates in exactly the same "clarifying" way that Roland Barthes says "myth" functions in his 1957 book *Mythologies*. As you'll recall from our introductory chapter, for Horkheimer and Adorno, "False clarity is only another name for myth" (1947/2002: xvii). Similarly, for Barthes, "myth," or ideology—the words can be used interchangeably—is a particularly *clarified* "type of speech," a "purified" or "depoliticized speech," a mode of communicative action whose primary function is to "transform history into nature" (1957/1972: 129). As Barthes writes

> Myth has the task of giving an historical intention a natural justifica-
> tion, and making contingency appear eternal. Now this process is exactly
> that of bourgeois ideology. If our society is objectively the privileged
> field of mythical significations, it is because formally myth is the most
> appropriate instrument for the ideological inversion which defines this
> society: at all the levels of human communication, myth operates the
> inversion of *anti-physis* into *pseudo-physis*. (1957/1972: 142)

To elaborate on this inversion, let's recall that since *"physis"* here means the "raw material" of the natural world, the project of *"anti-physis"* entails the transformative work *on* or *against* "brute materiality" in which humans *must* engage to produce the conditions of their existence, to produce their "world-history." To put this process or project in roughly "dialectical" terms, we can say that if *physis* stands as the negation or antithesis of constitutively humanizing labor, as the negation of human dignity, autonomy, freedom, etc., then labor itself assumes the form of the negation of this negation. *"Antiphysis"* thus expresses the project of the dialectic of freedom, the productive, progressive, and (one can always hope) *liberatory* process of our collectively and cooperatively *making* human history itself—the dialectical project not of intepreting the past but of what Michael Hardt militantly calls "making the present."[15] What Barthes calls *"pseudo-physis,"* then, would thus be a sort of "bogus nature," a "naturalized" reproduction/representation of the laborious production of human reality that effectively "freeze- frames" or reifies it.

[15] As you'll recall from our introductory chapter, Hardt, in the essay called "The Militancy of Theory," writes that "the task of theory is *to make* the present and thus to delimit or invent the subject of that making, a 'we' characterized not only by our belonging to the present but by our making it" (2011: 21).

The "Inversion of *anti-physis* into *pseudo-physis*" thus involves transforming a mutable and (perhaps) progressive *human history* into an immutable and seemingly inevitable *human nature*. And this inversion/transformation is the "very principle of myth" (1957/1971: 129). As Barthes explains:

> What the world supplies to myth is an historical reality, defined . . . by the way [people] have produced or used it; and what myth gives in return is a *natural* image of this reality . . . Myth is constituted by the loss of the historical quality of things; in [myth] things lose the memory that they once were [humanly] made. The world enters language as a dialectical relation between activities, between human actions; it comes out of myth as a harmonious display of essences. . . [Myth] has emptied [human reality] of history and has filled it with nature, it has removed from things their human meaning so as to make them signify a human insignificance . . . In passing from history to nature, myth . . . abolishes the complexity of human acts, it gives them the simplicity of essences, it does away with all dialectic, with any going back beyond what is immediately visible, it organizes a world which is without contradictions because it is without depth, a world wide open and wallowing in the evident, it establishes a blissful clarity: things appear to mean something all by themselves. (1957/1972: 142– 43)[16]

Now, if turning history into nature is the "very principle" of myth, this principle subtends all three of the major functions of "ideology in general" described thus far. There is, however, a fourth function in Althusser's theory, a function which effectively connects the *mythological* work of making "things appear to mean something all by themselves" with the *ideological* work of getting workers to "work all by themselves" (Althusser 1971/2001: 123), that is, without their having to be forced into labor at gunpoint. This function involves "constituting individuals as subjects," imposing the very "category of the subject" as a primary obviousness, and thus eliciting an individual's subjective "self-recognition" as an "inevitable reaction," a "perfectly natural" response.

And here's where Althusser's theory of ideology gets really "personal." He writes that "the category of the subject is constitutive of all ideology" but adds that *"the category of the subject is only constitutive of all ideology insofar as all*

---

[16] In a splendid footnote, Barthes writes "To the pleasure-principle of Freudian man could be added the clarity-principle of mythological humanity. All the ambiguity of myth is there: its clarity is euphoric"—an observation that nicely explains why readers who insist upon "clarity," who like to take their meanings neat, tend to dislike and/or steer clear of theoretical writing—they find its dereifications dysphoric.

*ideology has the function (which defines it) of 'constituting' concrete individuals
as subjects"* (1971/2001: 116).

> It follows that, for you and for me, the category of the subject is a
> primary "obviousness" (obviousnesses are always primary): . . . Like all
> obviousnesses, including those that make a word "name a thing" or "have
> a meaning" (therefore including the obviousness of the "transparency"
> of language), the "obviousness" that you and I are subjects—and that that
> does not cause any problems—is an ideological effect, the elementary
> ideological effect. (1971/2001: 116)

For Althusser, the most elementary ideological effect is the recruitment
or **interpellation** of individuals *as* subjects. Thus, ideological analysis "is
concerned with the institutional and/or textual apparatuses that work on
the reader's or spectator's imaginary conceptions of self and social order in
order to call or *solicit* (or "**interpellate**," as Althusser puts it, using a quasi-
legal term that combines the senses of 'summons' and 'hail') him/her into a
specific form of social 'reality' and social subjectivity" (Kavanagh 1995: 310).
As Althusser puts it:

> Ideology "acts" or "functions" in such a way that it "recruits" subjects
> among the individuals (it recruits them all), or "transforms" the individu-
> als into subjects (it transforms them all) by that very precise operation
> which I have called *interpellation* or hailing, and which can be imagined
> along the lines of the most commonplace everyday police (or other) hail-
> ing: "Hey, you there!" Assuming that the theoretical scene I have imagined
> takes place in the street, the hailed individual will turn around. By this
> mere one-hundred-and-eighty-degree physical conversion, he becomes a
> *subject*. Why? Because he has recognised that "it was *really him* who was
> hailed" (and not someone else). (1971/2001: 118)

In a footnote, Althusser explains that "hailing as an everyday practice subject
to a precise ritual takes a quite 'special' form in the policeman's practice of
'hailing' which concerns the hailing of 'suspects'" (118). And yet, he also
argues that interpellation as an "everyday practice" is always a "police action",
regardless of whether the "hailer" is an actual cop or the "hailed" a guilty
perp. In other words, *anyone* who is *anyone*, anyone who "answers to the
description" of the second-person pronoun in a hailing address—hey, *you*
there!—is ideologically interpellated, effectively constituted or recruited as a
subject. Althusser even includes under the rubric of "ideological subjection"
such "everyday" banalities as answering "it's me" to the question "who's
there?" posed from the other side of a knocked-upon door.

But here, one might well wonder—as long I'm not "suspected" of being a criminal, a maniac, a "terrorist," a "pervert," or some other type of "bad subject," as long as I'm "suspected" only of rather blandly "being myself," what's really so "ideological" about my being constituted as a subject? In Althusser's view, the problem involves "the ambiguity of the term *subject.*" As he writes:

> In the ordinary use of the term, subject in fact means: (1) a free subjectivity, a center of initiatives, author of and responsible for its actions; (2) a subjected being, who submits to a higher authority, and is therefore stripped of all freedom except that of freely accepting his submission . . . The individual *is interpellated as a (free) subject in order . . . that he shall (freely) accept his subjection,* i.e. in order that he shall make the gestures and actions of his subjection 'all by himself'. *There are no subjects except by and for their subjection.* That is why they 'work all by themselves'. (1971/2001: 123)

This ambiguity explains why there's something fundamentally fishy about the category of the subject, why "the 'obviousness' that you and I are subjects . . . is an ideological effect" (1971/2001: 116) —the more self-confidently we "imagine" ourselves as "subjects" in the first sense, the more "freely" we "turn" or screw ourselves into our subjection in the second.

But the larger problem involves the *type* of society by and into which we're screwed. For example, at this historical moment in the dark fields of the republic in which I write, debates about reform of the "health care system" are raging. On the op-ed page of the *New York Times*, a pundit named Matt Miller opines against making the health insurance that covers members of the US Congress available to the American public on the grounds that it "does little to encourage people to be smart health care shoppers" (21 July 2009).

Now, it shouldn't take an Althusserian brain surgeon to diagnose the problem with this symptomatic "encouragement," to recognize "smart health care shoppers" as an ideologically interpellative phrase that basically prescribes and endorses the commodification of all life in the United States. Attempting to make it seem *obvious* that whatever is done about the US health care system *should* "encourage people to be smart health care shoppers," the phrase "encourages" people to envision "health care" itself *only* as a shopping item rather than as, say, oh, I don't know, maybe something like a *human right*. Further, the phrase "encourages" American people to imagine "the American people" themselves *only* as consumers, smart or stupid, with or without purchasing power, rather than as say maybe a collective of

Ten Lessons in Theory

socially empowered citizens with certain *inalienable rights* (i.e., rights that shouldn't be privatized, shouldn't be taken away and then sold back to us as commodities in order to generate abundant monetary health for capitalists). The interpellative phrase "smart health care shoppers" works to *naturalize* "market solutions" to all human problems, to represent private property and the "free market economy" as inevitable functions of the real itself.[17] The phrase reproduces-represents- imposes a world in which, as Fredric Jameson laments, it seems easier to imagine the *end* of the world than to envision the end of capitalism.[18]

Now, as may or may not be "obvious," my point in turning to the journalist's turn of phrase is to connect what occurs "in the text" or "on the page" to the "physical conversion" that transpires in Althusser's theoretical street-scene, wherein the individual turns into a subject simply by turning in response to a policeman's hail. In other words, while the pundit's **hegemonic** hail "hey, American health care shopper!" may seem "merely textual," the phrase is structurally complicit with the cop's more forceful and compelling "hey you there!" The journalist, an editorial agent of an **Ideological State Apparatus**, works in collusion with the cop, a uniformed agent of the **Repressive State Apparatus**, to defend, protect, and serve the private property system.[19]

---

[17] Another example of "mythic" interpellation at work—I was recently on a "commercial flight" from Atlanta to Salt Lake City and noticed an interesting detail in the airline safety instruction video that played prior to take-off. There came the standard moment in the video when we're shown how to behave if "cabin pressure drops" and we suddenly find oxygen-masks dangling in front of us. The video depicted a man properly attaching the mask to his own face before turning to help the young male child, presumably a son, sitting beside him; meanwhile the narrative voice-over instructed us to negotiate our own masks first "before assisting other customers"—not the old "others who might need help" or even "other passengers," but other *customers*. Thus are we instructed to conceive even (or especially) our own children as corporate capitalism conceives/interpellates them and us—as markets. And the point here is not that reading "ideology at work" in the airline's safety video entails discerning some "hidden meaning" or "subliminal message." The "myth" here is anything but subliminal; rather, it's blatant, an imposed obviousness, as clear as the oxygen mask on your face—You and yours are customers; your life is a commercial transaction; don't bother with any other flights of fancy; don't bother imagining alternatives; just relax, sit back, and enjoy the ride. *Amen, so be it.*

[18] "It seems easier for us today to imagine the thoroughgoing deterioration of the earth and of nature than the breakdown of late capitalism; perhaps that is due to some weakness in our imaginations" (Jameson 1994: xii).

[19] Althusser's theory of ideology is indebted to Antonio Gramsci's notion of **hegemony**, which "refers to relationships between classes, specifically the control that the bourgeoisie exerts over the working classes. For Gramsci, hegemonic control is not maintained merely by force or the threat of force, but by consent as well. That is, a successful hegemony not only expresses the interest of a dominant class . . . but also is able to get a subordinate class to see these interests as 'natural' or a matter of 'common sense'" (Childers and Hentzi 1995: 131). Similarly, Althusser's distinction between **Ideological** and **Repressive**

Here, though, let's turn from the theoretical scene of interpellation, which occurs in "the street," with its strong police presence, back to Lacan's earlier "theatrical" scene of mirror-stage recognition, which occurs "in the home," and from which the constabulary would seem to missing. Althusser, however, admits the police into the house, shows *their* warrant to search *your* imaginary premises, when he writes that "the structure of all ideology, interpellating individuals as subjects . . . is *speculary*, i.e., a mirror structure," and that "mirror duplication is constitutive of all ideology and ensures its functioning" (1971/2001: 122).

To see how the "mirror duplication" of the "specular I" functions ideologically, consider the moment in Lacan's account when he writes that the mirror-stage infant is "held tightly by some prop, human or artificial," and that the infant "overcomes . . . the constraints of his prop" to better "take in" the view. Implying that it doesn't really matter whether the "prop" be human or artificial, Lacan suggests *both* that the artificial prop is laboriously human (i.e., the *trotte-bébé* contraption is brought about through human labor, even if our **commodity fetishism** helps us forget that fact) *and* that the properly human is *also* artificial—that is, socially produced through representational labor.[20] The mirrored subject is formed by being *informed* that it *should* "shape up," that it *should* eventually add or live up to the ideal formal totality that it sees before it. But the *agent* of this information is none other than the aforementioned "prop," the primary caretaker (let's say, the mother) who works all by herself, who does her duty and hoists the otherwise incapable one up to eye-level with the mirror and "encourages" it to identify with what it sees. With her own "body language"—her gestures, her looks, her smiles—this supportive

State Apparatuses seems based on Gramsci's "analytical distinction between civil and political society in which the former is made up of voluntary . . . affiliations like schools, families, and unions, the latter of state institutions (the army, the police, the central bureaucracy) whose role in the polity is direct domination" (Said 1978: 7). Althusser distinguishes **Repressive State Apparatuses**, like the police and the army, which work *primarily* by repressive force, from **Ideological State Apparatuses**—churches, schools, families—which function *primarily* by ideology rather than force. He stipulates, however, that the RSAs are not purely repressive—they depend upon ideology "both to ensure their own cohesion and reproduction, and in the 'values' they propound externally" (1971/2001: 98). Nor are the ISAs purely ideological, for "they also function secondarily by repression . . . Thus Schools and Churches use suitable methods of punishment, expulsion, selection, etc., to 'discipline' . . . their flocks. The same is true of the Family" (1971/2001: 98).

[20] "**Fetishism** is the endowment of an object or a body part with an unusual degree of power or erotic allure, as in the cases of cultures that attribute magical powers to idols or human effigies. Use of the term often betrays a skeptical attitude toward such beliefs; thus, Karl Marx coined the term **commodity fetishism** to express the way that capitalist emphasis on the abstract value of commodities conceals the underlying social relations of their producers" (Childers and Hentzi 1995: 109).

"prop" signals a message to the homunculus—"*there* you are—*there's* my good boy!" And the good boy normally responds with a flutter of jubilant activity. All seems well and good with this scenario, everything in its right place, everything perfectly obvious and true. For after all, it's obviously *really him* in the mirror and not someone else.

But while the maternal "prop" seems only to be doing what would "come naturally" to any human mother, isn't mumsy actually following certain stage directions, rehearsing pre- scripted lines, *performing* the duties of "the good mother" as she has *seen* these chores *systematically represented* to her basically all her life? Granted, it does seem more "natural" that the mother should at this juncture utter something like "*there's my good boy*" rather than raise her fist and shout "*Workers of the world unite!*" Nonetheless, when "the good mother" says "*there's* my good boy," all these "obvious" terms are actually shot through with *political* meaning. While "good" may seem to mean *inherently worthy* of any mother's love, it also means *fully compliant* with the prevailing norms of the *polis*, the "historically peculiar social formation" in which tot and mom have to live, with all of its attendant "institutions for the enforcement of cultural boundaries through praise and blame" (Greenblatt 1995: 226).

As for the tot, is it really all that obvious *to him* that it's *really him and not someone else* who's being addressed with the "*there's* my good boy" line? Or is there not already a self-alienating subtext to his prop's orthopedic script? Even in the midst of its jubilant flutter, the infant might begin to get the real picture, to "read" between the lines, to hear the inner voice that effectively says—*there*, reflected in that mirror, not *here*, in your body's immediate experience of itself, is the "good boy"; *that* figure *there* who seems to hang together like a little man-in-full, *he's* the "good boy," *he's* the version of **yourself** that we *like*, that we *recognize*—**not you**, little mister craps-his-pants, **not you**, leaky little *corps-morcèle*, still trapped in your motor impotence and nursling dependence, your yolky enjoyment, polymorphous perversity, and the devil only knows what else.

Small wonder, then, that when **you** look in the mirror and see how the hip-bone's connected to the thigh-bone, **you** hear (and fear) the name of the Lord. But while **you** might believe that in hearing this call and leaning toward this image "in order to fix it" in your mind you are thereby overcoming the constraints of your "prop," what you're actually "leaning into" is an ever more effective system of constraints. Because ideology, my friend, is eternal, there has always been and will always be a correspondence and a complicity between the prop's "there you are!" and the cop's "hey you there!"

III. Aesthetics of resistance?

Is there, then, no possibility of "yours truly" ever resisting or eluding "ideology"? For the Marxist Althusser, this question truly misses the point. Since "ideology in general" is basically synonymous with socialization (the always necessary process of turning little animals into little human beings), and since our species' prematurity at birth ensures that the need for socialization "will always be with us" (as Jesus supposedly said about the poor), "ideology in general" is pretty much eternal, elemental, inescapable, for all individuals—past, present, and future. The truly political question, then, is not whether an individual can somehow heroically resist ideological subjection/interpellation; rather, the only valid political question for Althusser concerns the *historical character* of the society in/to which the individual will be subjected. In the last analysis, Althusser is less concerned with any individual's "personal" transformation than he is committed to the radical transformation of all social relations as a whole:

> In a class [or capitalist] society ideology is the relay whereby, and the element in which, the relation between [people] and their conditions of existence is settled to the profit of the ruling class. In a classless [or communist] society ideology is the relay whereby, and the element in which, the relation between [people] and their conditions of existence is lived to the profit of all [people]. (cited in Kavanagh 1995: 313)

Unlike Althusser, however, some theoretical writers interested in questioning identity *and* effecting political change would settle for less than a classless society, or they desire but don't see the possibility of any such society on the near horizon, or they don't interpret oppression and liberation primarily or exclusively in Marxian economic terms. These theoretical writers do see individual subjectivity as a possible site of resistance to "naturalized" forms of social domination. They understand "personal identity" as the axis of intersection for a *number* of discourses of power, as a nodal point for the reproduction of *various* relations of oppression (including but not limited to economic processes or class). These theorists thus discern liberatory potential— "resistance-value," or what might be called "ref-use value"—in discourses that disturb, subvert, transform, or even abject self-identity, in whatever might unsettle, short-circuit, or reconfigure the regnant human reality, in whatever helps "to fuck shit up" (Halberstam 2006: 824) when it comes to our standard imaginary relations to our real existential conditions.

Michel Foucault, for example, studied arduously with Althusser but never ardently followed Marx. Describing his intellectual training in an interview called "The Minimalist Self," Foucault writes, "I was a pupil of Althusser, and at that time the main philosophical currents in France were Marxism, Hegelianism and phenomenology. I must say I have studied these but what gave me for the first time the desire of doing personal work was reading Nietzsche" (1983/1988: 8).

Now, I would say that this "desire of doing personal work" that Foucault claims to have contracted from reading Nietzsche relates quite intimately to Nietzsche's "antimoral" stance that "only as an *aesthetic phenomenon* are existence and the world *justified*" (1872/2006: 58). I would venture that Foucault's desire to do "personal work" corresponds to what he elsewhere calls "the search for an aesthetics of existence," the "elaboration of one's own life as a personal work of art" (1984/1988: 51). As we read at the end of the preceding lesson, for Foucault, "personal work" as "intellectual work is related to what you could call aestheticism, meaning transforming yourself"; Foucault, as we've read, believes that "this transformation of one's self by one's own knowledge is . . . something rather close to the aesthetic experience" (1983/1988: 14). So, while Althusser's star pupil agrees with his teacher that "the subject is constituted through practices of subjection" (i.e., in politically and economically predetermined ways), Foucault also believes that we subjects of human reality can reconstitute ourselves aesthetically, self-transformatively, "in a more autonomous way, through practices of liberation, of liberty, as in [pre-Christian] Antiquity, on the basis of course of a number of rules, styles, inventions to be found in the cultural environment" (1984/1988: 50–1).

Elaborating on this liberatory stylistics—what I'll call "the will to style"—in an interview titled "On the Genealogy of Ethics," Foucault remarks:

> What strikes me is the fact that, in our society, art has become something that is related only to objects and not individuals or to life. That art is something which is specialized or done by experts who are artists. But couldn't everyone's life become a work of art? (1983/1997: 261)

Asked how his aestheticist perspective differs from the existentialist philosophy of Jean-Paul Sartre, Foucault responds:

> I think that from the theoretical point of view, Sartre [rightly] avoids the idea of the self as something that is given to us, but through the moral notion of authenticity, he turns back to the idea that we have to be ourselves—to be truly our true self. I think the only acceptable

practical consequence of what Sartre has said is to link his theoretical insight to the practice of creativity—and not to that of authenticity. From the [salutary] idea that the self is not given to us, I think there is only one practical consequence: we have to create ourselves as a work of art. (1983/1997: 262)

And when Foucault's interlocutor remarks that his aesthetic work-ethic, which pits style and creativity against morality and authenticity, "sounds like Nietzsche's observation in *The Gay Science* that one should create one's life by giving style to it through long practice and daily work," Foucault concurs, "Yes. My view is much closer to Nietzsche's than to Sartre's" (1983/1997: 262).

Foucault's perspective is indeed closer to Nietzsche's than to Sartre's, or to Althusser's, or, for that matter, to the revolutionary views of Karl Marx. Again, Foucault isn't a Marxist by any measure (he once expressed the desire never to hear the man's name again).[21] But unlike the unabashedly antidemocratic Nietzsche, or the cheerfully slave-owning citizens of classical Antiquity, Foucault comes off as fairly egalitarian in his radical aestheticism, implicitly refusing the idea that "the practice of creativity" should be reserved for some elite cadre of artists/experts within the ruling class. Foucault, that is, seems more sincere than naïve when he poses the "utopian" question—"couldn't *everyone's* life become a work of art?" (1983/1997: 261, my emphasis).

Moreover, Foucault, though not a Marxist, could be considered a sort of historical materialist, at least to the extent that he doesn't believe that anything related to our "personal work," to our human reality, grows on trees or falls from the sky. For Foucault, everything specifically human must involve our old friend *antiphysis*, must involve human "practices" of power and resistance, of discourse and counter-discourse, of subjection and of liberation— practices of creativity that are *simultaneously* "political" and "aesthetic" and that can develop *only* on the basis of "rules, styles, and inventions to be found" nowhere else but in the prevailing "cultural environment," nowhere else but in a cultural language that is by nature *fictional*, nowhere else but in our own making of the present, our own *creative writing* of the "history of the present" (1975/1995: 31).

Perhaps the most conspicuous sign of Foucault's non-Marxist historical materialism is his emphasis on sex, rather than economic class, as a principal vector of oppression and possible self-transformation. In *The History*

[21] "Don't talk to me about Marx anymore! I never want to hear anything about that man again. Ask someone whose job it is. Someone paid to do it. Ask the Marxist functionaries. Me, I've had enough of Marx" (cited in Erbion 1992: 266).

of Sexuality and elsewhere, Foucault famously posits "sex" not as some inherently revolutionary "force of nature" to be repressed or liberated but as a socio-discursive construction, "an especially dense transfer point for relations of power" (1976/1990: 103). Foucault investigates what he calls the "deployment" of sex, the way "sex" is "put into discourse." He analyzes those strategically "discursive orthopedics" (1976/1990: 29) that "encourage" individuals to understand and articulate their "sexuality" as the "truth" of their "identity." For Foucault, there are no "natural" or "inevitable" connections among sexual practices, truth-claims, and identity-formations; rather, the connections among sex, truth, and self are *produced* and *enforced* through disciplinary institutions, discursive implantations, carceral segregations, capillary relays of power, and **panoptical** technologies of self-surveillance.[22] But since all these "police actions" take place *discursively* (they are socially enacted in various institutional, medical, psychological, religious, juridical, pedagogical, and literary discourses— what Althusser would consider ISAs), and because they occur at the level of subjectivity/subjection (what Althusser calls interpellation), these practices of sexual self- policing can be confronted and resisted discursively and subjectively as well, through "practices of creativity," through "deployments" of style and invention. In other words, in Foucault's view, "we" subjects of the social construction of sex don't have to wait for a worker's revolution or for the final breakdown of late capitalism to try to unsettle dominant relations of power, to try to renegotiate sexual identities (or untether "sex" from "identity" altogether), to try to invent new forms of aesthetic existence, new styles of corporeal subjectivity, new ways of orchestrating our "bodies and pleasures" (1976/1990: 159). To re-orchestrate some of Foucault's words in "The Subject and Power"—we don't need Marx to "refuse what we are" and "to promote new forms of subjectivity though the refusal of this kind of individuality that has been imposed on us for several centuries" (1983/2000: 336).

---

[22] In *Discipline and Punish*, Foucault "derives the concept of **panopticism** from a diagram drawn up by the British philosopher Jeremy Bentham in 1791. Bentham's Panopticon was a model prison in which supervisors could observe prisoners in their individual cells without being seen themselves. According to Foucault, this system was effective because prisoners never knew whether or not they were being watched: 'he is seen, but he does not see . . . what matters is that he knows himself to be observed'. Foucault [argues] that this constant sense of surveillance and visibility is what characterizes the development of disciplinary societies *in toto*. In such societies, 'the automatic functioning of power' is guaranteed because individuals police themselves and each other. For Foucault, the notion of individualism in Western society is in fact a direct effect of panopticism. The individual is constructed by having internalized the disciplinary power of penitentiary and/or medicinal discourses, with their numerous methods of segregation and social exclusion. This is why, as Foucault concludes, modern institutions such as hospitals, schools and factories all resemble prisons" (Malpas and Wake 2006: 237).

But while we may not need Marx (or Sartre) for this promotion of the subjectively new, this refusal of the centuries-old, we might very well need *Nietzsche*, as Foucault claims he did, to discover our desire for doing our own "personal work," for undoing the work that's already been done on our persons. For if the authentic and moral "kind of individuality" that Foucault stylistically resists here has in fact been "imposed upon us for several centuries," Nietzsche was one of the first to chafe, rail, and write against the imposition. As for the "individuality" in question, it's clearly more Cartesian than Nietzschean. As you'll recall, we began this lesson by considering Descartes' *cogito ergo sum* as a truth-claim involving both epistemology and ontology, both personal knowing and subjective being. In the purely rational truth of Cartesian self-certainty, I think I know both *that* I am and exactly *what* I am. As we noted, Lacan opposes any philosophy directly issuing from the *cogito* because such philosophy reduces all thinking, and hence all being, to rational consciousness. But Nietzsche also objected to this reduction, this "rationing" or reasonable impoverishment of the "aesthetic phenomena" of human psychical life. In Book V of *The Gay Science*, Nietzsche offers a stingingly "elitist" critique of consciousness, suggesting

> that consciousness does not really belong to man's individual existence but rather to his social or herd nature; that [consciousness] has developed subtlety only insofar as this is required by social or herd utility. Consequently, . . . "to know ourselves," each of us will always succeed in becoming conscious only of what is not individual but "average." Our thoughts are continually governed by the [herd] character of consciousness . . . and translated back into the perspective of the herd. (1887/2006: 367–8)

Translating Nietzsche into a sort of Althusserian Lacanese, we could say that our given or conventional sense of self-understanding is dominated by the ideological character of consciousness, governed by the props and cops of the symbolic order. To "know ourselves" under prevalent "herd" conditions means to tame, police, contain, and domesticate ourselves, to convincingly demonstrate that we have assumed or fixed in our minds all the pictures of libidinal and cultural normativity that pertain to us—the images most *familiar to* and hence most *useful for* the dominant order in its continuous efforts to secure the reproduction of its conditions of production. If this normalization *qua* familiarization is actually all that rationally "knowing ourselves" amounts to, then it's pretty clear that under this epistemological regime any "unfamiliar" aspects of ourselves would have to remain alien, "unknown," unrealized, excluded from consciousness, hustled into the unconscious and/ or projected onto some strange god or abject scapegoat or another.

In Nietzsche's view, maintaining normal everyday consciousness or common sense always depends upon reducing "the strange" to "the familiar." He sees this "will to familiarize" as the very engine of normative epistemology, as "*The* [very] *origin of our concept of 'knowledge.*'" As Nietzsche writes in *Gay Science* under this titular heading:

> I take this explanation from the street. I heard one of the common people say, "he knew me right away." Then I asked myself: What is that the common people take for knowledge? What do they want when they want "knowledge"? Nothing more than this: Something strange is to be reduced to something *familiar*. And we philosophers—have we really meant *more* than this when we have spoken of knowledge? What is familiar means what we are used to so that we no longer marvel at it, our everyday, some rule in which we are stuck, anything at all in which we feel at home. Look, isn't our need for knowledge precisely this need for the familiar, the will to uncover under everything strange, unusual, and questionable something that no longer disturbs us? Is it not the *instinct of fear* that bids us to know? And is the jubilation of those who attain knowledge not the jubilation over the restoration of a sense of security? (1887/2006: 368)

In bringing the hammer down on "knowledge," Nietzsche's writing here adumbrates Althusserian and Lacanian motifs; it features both an ontological scene of common, "street- level" recognition and an epistemological "flutter" of mind-fixing "jubilation," thus grounding the highest flights of metaphysics in the basest instincts of fear. But if Nietzsche here foreshadows Lacan's theory of "paranoic" knowledge, he also sets the stage for performing an abrasively Foucauldian "aesthetics of resistance" to fear-based familiarization, to the anxious expulsion of strange "foreign elements" that still seems to dominate our "everyday" self-understanding. Nietzsche, that is, anticipates not only Foucault's commitment to "aesthetic existence" but Viktor Shklovsky's notion of *defamiliarization* as the defining *aesthetic technique* of all *literary writing* worthy of the name. We'll consider Shklovsky's self-estranging "formalism" at some length in subsequent pages. Here, however, we'll let his main idea— that literary writing *as* literary writing defamiliarizes "the subject" of any literary text—remind us of the underlying thesis of *this* introductory text— that "theoretical writing" is itself a "practice of creativity," that "theory" is not merely a way of "approaching" literature but a way of performing the strangely "personal work" of living one's "life as literature."

Now, having earlier quoted Stephen Greenblatt to the effect that literature is "one of the great institutions for the enforcement" of normative culture as an ideological "system of constraints" (1995: 226, 227), I would be an ass to suggest that "creative" theoretical writing—theory "not *of* literature but *as* literature" (Rabaté 2002: 117)—could ever be *essentially* liberatory, *inherently* resistant to reification, naturalization, libidinal normalization, etc. I would be an ass to think that "theory as literature" could ever work as a sort of permanently subversive riposte or transcendental antidote to "eternal" ideology, could ever stand as what Foucault dismissively calls the "single locus of great Refusal, . . . soul of revolt, source of all rebellions, or pure law of the revolutionary" (1976/1990: 95–6). After all, some of the "greatest" literary works in the world have worked quite diligently to familiarize and naturalize dominant power relations, reinforce given meaning, impose obviousnesses as obviousnesses, and so on. Some "great works of literature" disturb particular aspects of regnant human reality while leaving other matters all too comfortably settled, all too readily known. And *theoretical* writing, like any other kind, can all too quickly become weary, stale, flat, and unprofitable, can lose the capacity to desediment, subvert, or surprise, can fail to keep open that crucial *antiphysical* difference "between things as they are and things as they might otherwise be" (Critchley 1997: 22).

But to the extent that theory can stay aesthetically frosty, can work to remain politically and personally resistant, this kind of writing can invite or provoke all but the most frightened of us to imagine ourselves and "things as they are" otherwise; at its most effective, theoretical writing can make our imaginary relations *and* our real conditions of existence seem strangely unnatural, radically fictional, anything but inevitable. By delivering, among other malaise-inducing messages, the "ontological bad news" that we are not ourselves, that we can never really or "authentically" be ourselves—along with the "glad tidings" that we don't necessarily "have to be ourselves," don't really have "to be truly our true self" (Foucault 1983/1997: 262)— theoretical writing might be able to keep us open, if only just barely, to the possibility of self-alteration, the radical practice of creativity, the secular miracle of change.

Coming to Terms

Critical Keywords encountered in Lesson Five:

culture, aura, epistemology, ontology, dialectic, Nachträglichkeit/
deferred action, interpellation, hegemony, ideological/repressive state
apparatuses, commodity fetishism, panopticism

Part 2

Extimacy: Five Lessons in the Utter Alterity of Absolute Proximity

"This restlessness is us"

—or, the least that can be said about Hegel

Truly to escape Hegel involves an exact appreciation of the price we have to pay to detach ourselves from him. It assumes that we are aware of the extent to which Hegel, insidiously perhaps, is close to us; it implies a knowledge, in that which permits us to think against Hegel, of that which remains Hegelian. We have to determine the extent to which our anti-Hegelianism is possibly one of his tricks directed against us, at the end of which he stands, motionless, waiting for us.

—Foucault (1972: 235)

I. Thesis

Hegel is important. Indeed, for many theoretical writers, the name "Hegel" practically signifies importance itself. In *Hegel: The Restlessness of the Negative*, Jean-Luc Nancy calls Hegel "the inaugural thinker of the contemporary world" and identifies Hegel as "the first to take thought out of the realm of identity" (2002: 3, 55). In *Subjects of Desire: Hegelian Reflections in Twentieth-Century France*, Judith Butler writes that her theoretical work began and still "remains within the orbit of a certain set of Hegelian questions: What is the relation between desire and recognition, and how is it that the constitution of the subject entails a radical and constitutive relation to alterity?" (1999: xiv) Slavoj Žižek, a critical adversary of Butler's, also situates his work in the Hegelian orbit—"Ultimately," he declares, "if I am to choose just one thinker, it's Hegel. He's the one for me . . . He may be a white, dead, man or whatever the wrong positions are today, but that's where I stand" (in Rasmussen 2004).[1] And in *The Future of Theory,* Jean-Michel Rabaté, noting "the almost

---

[1]   Butler critiques Žižek in *Bodies That Matter* (1993); Žižek critiques Butler in *The Ticklish Subject* (1999/2008); Butler, Žižek, and Ernesto Laclau critique and converse with each other in *Contingency, Hegemony, Universality* (2000).

ineluctable Hegelian inflection given to any discourse that presents itself as 'literary theory,'" insists "that a patient reading of Hegel . . . is, if not a prerequisite, at least an essential step on the way to an understanding of theory" (2002: 39, 21).

So, again, Hegel is important, if not, at least in theory, importance itself. And yet, in the preceding pages of *this* discourse, which certainly "presents itself" as literary theory and as a guide to understanding theoretical writing, Hegel is mentioned by name only twice (once in the footnoted gloss on the term "phenomenology" and again in the footnoted gloss on the term "dialectic"). And in fact *most* introductory guides to theory make similarly reductive gestures (or even no gestures at all) toward Hegel, even though practically all of the questions raised in such guides are plausibly situated within the Hegelian ballpark, and even though practically all of the heavy hitters of high theory, from Althusser to Žižek, became the theorists they became by *first* becoming readers, patient or impatient, of Hegel.

We might best explain this relative silence about the hugely important Hegel by considering Fredric Jameson's early warning that "the attempt to do justice to the most random observation of Hegel ends up drawing the whole tangled, dripping mass of the Hegelian sequence of forms out into the light with it" (1971: 306). The problem, that is, facing the writer who would introduce theory, is that even the briefest reference *to* Hegel can transmogrify into a massive treatise *on* Hegel, a gnarly epic narrating the restlessly negative, formally sequential, spirally all-encompassing corpus of Hegelian thinking—a.k.a. "Absolute Knowing"—itself.[2] To avoid getting "totally" caught up in that tangled, dripping, and serpentine mass (Jameson seems to be alluding to Laocoön here), it's safer just to keep one's hole shut and not mention Hegel at all.

But once safety is abandoned, the hazardous mention made, the introductory writer's strategic question still remains—what's the *least* that can justly be said about Hegel? Clearly "Hegel is important" won't do, nor is

---

[2] The "anti-Hegelianism" or desire "to escape Hegel" that Foucault mentions above stems primarily from the perception of Hegel as an abstruse know-it-all who aspires toward or even claims to have arrived at an all-encompassing "Absolute Knowledge" of "the ultimate meaning of everything" (Findlay 1971: 93), a thinker of totality "suspected of totalization, and even of having totalitarian designs" (Malabou 1996/2004: 1). For Žižek, Jameson, Butler, Nancy, Malabou, Johnston, and other contemporary champions of the dialectic, however, "Hegel is the opposite of a 'totalitarian'" thinker" (Nancy 2002: 8); he "is anything but the cheerleader for an omniscient philosophical self-consciousness, for a complete and exhaustive encyclopedic knowledge from whose firm grasp nothing whatsoever can escape" (Johnston 2008: 128). I'll add only that if Hegel were a totalitarian cheerleader, he really wouldn't be "important" to theory, and we wouldn't be including a lesson totally devoted to his writing here.

it sufficient to give in to what Jameson calls "the tripartite temptation" (2010: 19) and reduce the Hegelian dialectic to the old "thesis-antithesis-synthesis" formula *à la* the earlier footnote, since Hegel himself never described his own sense of the dialectic quite so formulaically, and in fact, chafed against the limitations of this Fichtean trinity.[3]

If we had to boil Hegel's thinking down to a single term, other than "dialectic"—and other than "restlessness," which, as Jameson helpfully notes, was "one of Hegel's favorite words" (2010: 21)—that term would probably have to be ***Aufhebung***, or "sublation." But in attempting to do *that* particular word justice we very quickly see our discursive pot boil over, saturating just about "everything" in sight. For in the *Science of Logic*, Hegel asserts that *Aufhebung* or sublation "constitutes one of the most important notions in philosophy" (1812/1998: 194). The word, he writes, has "a twofold meaning," and its duplicity actually constitutes its dialectical operation—"on the one hand [to sublate] means to preserve, to maintain, and equally it also means to cause to cease, to put to an end" (1812/1998: 194). These two "folds" of meaning of course seem mutually opposed, hopelessly contradictory, for how can anything be simultaneously maintained *and* put to an end? But this contradiction, inherent to *Aufhebung*, allows us to consider one of Hegel's most Hegelian premises—to wit, *"everything is inherently contradictory"*

---

[3] Jameson calls the thesis-antithesis-synthesis formula "one of the most notorious and inveterate stereotypes of Hegel discussion," though he allows that Hegel himself "is complicitous in the propagation of this formula, and at least partially responsible for its vulgarization. It is certainly a useful teaching device as well as a convenient expository framework: and is thereby called upon to play its role in that transformation of Hegel's thought into a systematic philosophy—into Hegelianism, if you will . . . [But] even if the tripartite rhythm happens to do justice to this or that local Hegelian insight, it still reifies that insight in advance and translates its language into purely systematic terms . . . Yet the tripartite temptation does not appear out of nowhere, nor does it correspond to nothing [in Hegel] at all. Indeed, it might be considered a relatively awkward codification of what is certainly a far more consistent and coherent Hegelian view of human time, which governs the growth of the individual (*Bildung*) fully as much as the development of history itself" (2010: 18–19). As for the Fichtean origins of the "tripartite temptation," Yirmiyahu Yovel writes that for Hegel, dialectical logic "cannot be formalized, not even by the famous formula 'thesis-antithesis-synthesis' (which is Fichte's, not Hegel's) . . . Fichte constructed his system by triads of the form 'thesis-antithesis-synthesis,' which repeat themselves throughout his systematic work, *The Theory of Science*, as an a priori formula. Though Hegel refrains from using this formula, it has nevertheless been ascribed to him in many textbooks and in the public's mind. It is true that Hegel's system, in its broad lines, also advances a triadic form, but it is different, freer, and without a priori formulaic limitations" (2005: 29). Yovel goes on to suggest that the slogan "'Self-reflection in being-other' is perhaps Hegel's most succinct formulation of a dialectical relation . . . Although the dialectic cannot be squeezed into an a priori formula, when a short characterization is needed, we might prefer to speak of 'self-reflection within otherness' instead of the problematic formula 'thesis-antithesis-synthesis'" (2005: 99).

(1812/1998: 238). And by "*everything*," Hegel *does* mean absolutely everything, for in his book

> there is nothing, nothing in heaven or in nature or mind or anywhere else which does not equally contain both immediacy and mediation, so that these two determinations reveal themselves to be *unseparated* and inseparable and the opposition between them to be a nullity (1812/1998: 178).

So here, our questions become: How does this two-fold meaning of *Aufhebung*—to cancel *and equally* to preserve—relate to the assertion that everything everywhere is contradictory in that there is nothing anywhere that doesn't *equally* contain both **immediacy** and **mediation**? What do "immediacy and mediation" *mean* for Hegel, and why is it so important for him that we nullify their opposition? Why is Yovel correct to say that "absolute immediacy is a myth for Hegel" (2005: 48)? Why is Jameson correct to say that "the whole of Hegel's philosophical production is an elaborate refutation of all possible concepts of immediacy" (2010: 13)?

For Hegel, writes Michael Inwood, "The immediate is unrelated to other things; simple; given; elementary; and/or initial. The mediated, by contrast, is related to other things; complex, explained; developed; and/or resultant" (1992: 184). Thus, for Hegel, developing the understanding that "*everything is inherently contradictory*" entails both *grasping* and *revealing* the inseparability, within the orbit of "everything," of *apparent* immediacy and *actual* mediation; it means *negating* the apparent opposition between the two, so that what appears to be isolatedly unrelated to other things is shown to be totally other-related; what seems simple is shown to be complex; what is normally "taken as a given" demonstrably warrants more sustained explanation; what seems elementary is drawn into secondary, tertiary, and further spirals of rhetorical development; what initially appears to our historical imagination as an absolutely self-identical *origin* is posited instead as a mixed and derived *result*.

"Down-to-earth" examples of all this are forthcoming, but for now let's just say that this *revelation*—*of* and *as* the developmental nullification of opposites—*is* the conceptual *work* of *sublation* and that in Hegel's work it *is* this work that ultimately works through (without entirely *resolving*) the contradiction embedded in *Aufhebung*. For in Hegel's view, mediation "refutes" but doesn't simply *annihilate* immediacy; rather, mediation *dissolves* the immediate *in its given form* and perpetually *transforms* the immediate into *something other than itself*. The given or familiar form is "sublated" rather than destroyed to the extent that something *in* the form that is essential *to* the form *survives* its mediation/transformation into something external to and "alienated" from itself, retaining "something in and of itself" without "self-righteously" resisting self-estrangement. This recourse to self-alienation as destructive transformation explains how sublation equally cancels *and* preserves. The conceptual work of *Aufhebung* consists of grasping the "truth" that *"everything is inherently contradictory"* in that "everything" that *really* "is" only *potentially* "is"; that is, everything that "is" *truly* is, *absolutely* is, *only* by virtue of going through the dialectical process of *remaining* itself (or "winning its truth") by *becoming* (for a moment, or for an ever-extended series of moments) the *negative* of itself, and that nothing—not even "nothing"— can exempt itself from getting "caught up" in the "truth," the "revealed reality," of this universally transformational "sequence of forms." As Hegel posits:

> The True is the whole. But the whole is nothing other than the essence consummating itself through its development. Of the Absolute it must be said that it is essentially a *result*, that only in the *end* is it what it truly is; and that precisely in this consists its nature, viz. to be actual, subject, the spontaneous becoming of itself. (1807/1998: 53)

Now, Hegel turns that loaded phrase *"everything is inherently contradictory"* in the section of the *Science of Logic* called "Doctrine of Essence," and the phrase pops up at a moment in Hegel's exposition that finds him challenging the stale and prejudiced notion that immediate "identity" constitutes the most profound "essence" of "being." As Hegel writes:

> It is one of the fundamental prejudices of logic as hitherto understood and of ordinary thinking, that contradiction is not so characteristically essential and immanent a determination as identity; but in fact, if it were a question of grading the two determinations . . ., then contradiction would have to be taken as the profounder determination and more characteristic of essence. For as against contradiction, identity is merely the determination of the simple immediate, of dead being; but contradiction is the root of all movement and vitality; it is only in so far as something has a contradiction within it that it moves, has an urge and an activity. (1812/1998: 238)

In other words, if *Aufhebung* is inherently contradictory, duplicitous in its unfolding, then so is "everything" else—or at least everything else that in actuality does *unfold*, that actually does *move*, that isn't "dead being," fixed in the immediate "givenness" of determinately self-contained identity. Any "being" that remains fixed maintains the boundaries of its formal necrosis by shrinking from mediation, shirking the duty of self-alienation, refusing to face up to what its own inherent contradictions imply and potentially express. The difference, then, between "identity" and "contradiction" is for Hegel the difference between an ever self-enclosed hypostasis and an ever-expanding expression of self-alienating movement.

> The principle of self-movement . . . consists solely in an exhibition of it. External, sensuous motion itself is contradiction's immediate existence. Something moves, not because at one moment it is here and at another there, but because at one and the same moment it is here and not here, because in this 'here', it at once is and is not. (1812/1998: 239)[4]

What Hegel calls "livingness," then—animation or *Spirit*—is self-movement as "*existent* contradiction itself" (1812/1998: 239). Any "being" that exists, that animatedly *is* "is, in one and the same respect, *self-contained and* deficient, *the negative of itself* (1812/1998: 239). What Hegel on the other hand calls "abstract self-identity" remains fixed "in itself," and it remains fixed because of its refusal to acknowledge its inner deficiency, because of its failure to *fail* to be itself, its inability to let go of itself, to realize itself *in* and *as* the negative *of* itself. Thus:

> Abstract self-identity is not yet a livingness, but the positive, being in its own self a negativity, goes outside itself and undergoes alteration. Something is therefore alive only in so far as it contains contradiction within it, and moreover is this power to hold and endure the contradiction. (1812/1998: 239)

This power to endure contradiction, to hold on to letting go—this capability of *Spirit* to give up "the fixity of its self-positing" (1807/1998: 60), to get outside its own tightly clenched circle and submit itself to alteration—is what Hegel calls negating negativity, "the activity of dissolution," "the tremendous power of the negative" (1807/1998: 59), and so on. But this tremendously negative power is actually nothing but subjective "*Understanding*" as the self-moving/self-dissolving *force* of mediation. In Hegel's understanding,

---

4 Because theorists like Žižek see Hegel's dialectic as anticipating and making possible Lacan's "antiphysical" take on *language*, because Žižek believes that "the Hegelian dialectic begins with a chasm opened up between words and things" (Johnston 2008: 263), it's interesting to note the similarity between what Hegel says here about "the principle of self-movement" and what we earlier saw Lacan say about the movement of the signifier—"The signifier is a unique unit of being which, by its very nature, is the symbol of but an absence. This is why we cannot say of the [signifier] that, like other objects, it must be *or* not be somewhere but rather that, unlike them, it will be *and* not be where it is wherever it goes" (Lacan 1966a/2006: 17). For more on Hegel's anticipations of psychoanalysis, see Mills (2002).

Understanding means (or at least *potentially* means) much more than ideational consumption, more than simply "taking in" existing thoughts and representations "as given"; rather, *Understanding* entails the arduous *work* of "freeing determinate thoughts from their fixity," a *liberatory* work that imparts "spiritual life" (1807/1998: 60) to both the *Understanding* subject and the "substantial" matters understood.[5]

And yet, rather astonishingly, this beneficently and creatively "spiritual life" is for Hegel *inseparable* from the destructive work of death and dismemberment. In a particularly famous moment in the Preface to the *Phenomenology of Spirit*, Hegel writes:

> The activity of dissolution is the power and work of the *Understanding*, the most astonishing and mightiest of powers, or rather the absolute power. The circle that remains self-enclosed and . . . holds its moments together, is an immediate relationship, one therefore which has nothing astonishing about it. But that an accident as such, detached from what circumscribes it . . . should attain an existence of its own and a separate freedom—this is the tremendous power of the negative; it is the energy of thought, of the pure 'I'. Death, if that is what we want to call this non-actuality, is of all things the most dreadful, and to hold fast what is dead requires the greatest strength . . . But the life of Spirit is not the life that shrinks from death and keeps itself untouched by devastation, but rather

5 I use the word "Understanding" here because it's the word Hegel uses in the famous passage from the Preface to the *Phenomenology of Spirit* that you're just about to read. But it's actually a bit misleading to let the word "Understanding" signify the "power and work" of active thinking that Hegel advocates, for typically Hegel lets *Verstand* or "Understanding" stand for exactly the type of ideational consumption—the passive "taking in" of thoughts in their empirical, given, common-sense, or reified form—that is described above. Indeed, "If the strictest formulations of the dialectic often inspire perplexity, annoyance, and refusal, it is because . . . these formulations . . . wish to make understood that they cannot be, as they are, understood by understanding, but rather demand that understanding relinquish itself" (Nancy 2002: 63). For Hegel, effectively dialectical thinking should be understood as the self-overcoming of "Understanding," a relinquishing sublation of certainty and of empiricist common-sense. Thus, Jameson writes that in Hegel's work, "the great movement from *Verstand* or Understanding to *Vernunft* or Reason is grasped as a radical break with common-sense empiricism and with what we may also call reified thinking" (2010: 1), which is why I write that in Hegel's understanding, "Understanding" only *potentially* means something more and other than passive or reified ideational consumption—Understanding, that is, has the potential to radically break with itself, to relinquish itself, but to enact this potential Understanding must "enthusiastically embrace the power of negativity introduced into reality through the internal rupturing of the idiotic, sterile enclosure of consciousness as solipsistic sense-certainty" (Johnston 2008: 263). Without embracing "the power of negativity," which is the power of Understanding itself, Understanding will never become more and other than itself, will never become Reason, but will remain exactly itself, ossified, rigidly if not "idiotically" self-identical.

the life that endures it and maintains itself in it. It wins its truth only
when, in utter dismemberment, it finds itself . . . Spirit is this power only
by looking the negative in the face, and tarrying with it. This tarrying
with the negative is the magical power that converts it into being. This
power is identical with . . . the Subject, which . . . supersedes abstract
immediacy . . . and thus is authentic substance: that being or immediacy
whose mediation is not outside of it but which is this mediation itself.
(1807/1998: 59)

Earlier, in what has been called "the single most important sentence in the
Preface" (Yovel 2005: 16), Hegel writes that "everything turns on grasping
and expressing the True, not only as *Substance*, but equally as *Subject*"
(1807/1998: 52). Hegel also posits that the fact "that the True is actual
only as system, or that Substance is essentially Subject, is expressed in
the representation of the Absolute as *Spirit*" (1807/1998: 55). We can best
understand what Hegel means by these terms by considering "Subject" as
self-consciousness (never mind, for the moment, whose) and "Substance" as
everything supposedly external or alien to self-consciousness; we could also
understand "Subject" as "Spirit" or "Mind" and "Substance" as stuff, objective
"Matter." At first glance, or for what Hegel calls "ordinary thinking," it would
seem that these two determinations are absolutely opposed, that one is the
simple negative of the other, that Spirit is the pure "non-actuality" of Matter,
or that Subject is completely alien to Substance, or, if you like, that the "I"
differs utterly and eternally from the "not-I." But for Hegel, grasping the True
in its totality means realizing that Subject/Spirit "truly is" only through its
developmental actuation or substantiation. Only through the "overcoming
of alienation" (1807/1998: 56) does "Subject" essentially *become* "Substance"
while remaining substantially Subject. Only through Spirit's eventual
realization of "*pure* self-recognition in absolute otherness" (1807/1998: 56)
does inert exteriority become "authentic substance" for, of, and *as* the Subject
of "Absolute Knowing."

II. Antithesis

But what's the deal with "Absolute Knowing"? Since, for Hegel, "the True is
the whole," it follows that the "absolutely true" must be "absolutely whole."
But, for Hegel, nothing can be true or whole without its being *consciously*
and *rationally grasped* to be so. Thus, the "Absolute" can *truly* be, can *totally*
be, only as the *result* of the rational Subject's Substantially and *self-consciously*
becoming itself, *wholly* overcoming its self-estrangement *and knowing*

it, "becom[ing] alienated from itself" and then return[ing] to itself from this alienation" (1807/1998: 61). This absolutely "totalizing" or completely "hetero-tautological" take on Truth can allow readers of Hegel to take this philosopher *either* as a wholly progressive secular **teleological** rationalist for whom human *"reason rules the world"* (1837/1998: 408) *or* as a residually holy-roller Christian **eschatologist** for whom good old "God" still calls the shots—*depending* on how one deals with the question of *to whom* or *to what Power* "self-consciousness" as "Absolute Knowing" finally and properly *belongs,* or depending on whether one takes one's *Spirits* **phenomenologically**, **onto-theologically**, historico-collectively, and/or as a card-carrying Lacanian.[6]

We will return to these questions. But for the moment, let's get back to *Aufhebung.* I've said that its duplicitous unfolding *is* the operation of the dialectic. And, although I've acknowledged that the three-step formula

---

[6] "*Telos* is the Greek word for 'end' or 'goal,' and a **teleology** or **teleological** argument assigns meaning to events by viewing them as progressing toward a goal . . . Many of the most influential philosophies of history in Western thought have been teleological (as is, for example, Christian theology or the philosophy of Hegel)" (Childers and Hentzi 1995: 302). **Eschatology** is the branch of Christian theology concerned with future or final events. **Phenomenology** (once again) involves the analysis of "human consciousness as 'lived experience'" (Childers and Hentzi 1995: 227) and is usually associated with "the canonical three H's of German philosophy" (Rabaté 2002: 47): Hegel, Husserl, and Heidegger. The term **onto-theological** hails from Heidegger and involves his faulting Western metaphysics for limiting the thinking of being (*ontos*) to the idea of God (*theos*) and vice versa. Derrida offers the term "hetero-tautology" as "the definition of the Hegelian speculative" (1980/1987: 301), casting Hegel's "Spirit" as "self-recognition in absolute otherness" as a teleological/tautological/totalitarian process of turning "the other" back into "the same." In distinction to all this, Jameson takes Hegel's "Spirit" to mean the "social collectivity" of human history—the sociohistorical or untranscendably human collective of laboring world-makers in the Marxist or materialist sense. Jameson insists that "we can disambiguate Hegel's discussions by holding firm to the principle that the words Spirit or *Geist,* wherever they appear, have nothing to do with spirituality nor even with consciousness itself as such . . . [Rather], we must . . . hold firmly to the conviction that in Hegel the word 'Spirit' always designates the collective" (2010: 13). Žižek—who likes to call himself a "card-carrying Lacanian"—views Hegel's "Absolute Knowing" not as an all-encompassing grab-bag of final and stable philosophical Truth, nor as the full achievement of a classless society, but rather in the Lacanian "Spirit" of radical loss—Adrian Johnston writes that "as Žižek sees it, Hegel's notorious 'absolute knowledge' (*das absolute Wissen*) amounts to nothing more than the acceptance of the irreducible incompleteness not only of the subjective human understanding of the world . . . but also of the reality of being and of itself. Žižek describes *das absolute Wissen* as involving an experience of 'radical loss,' rather than an intoxicating ascension into omniscience." For Žižek, writes Johnston, "the dialectic arguably involves an insight into the interminability of the restless dialectic movement . . . instead of marking a point at which a stable body of knowledge is consolidated once and for all" (2008: 130–1). As Johnston continues, "According to Žižekian Hegelianism, the Absolute is the absolutely finite. Reaching the vantage point of the Absolute amounts to realizing that there's no seamless transcendent Elsewhere in which the snags and tears in the fabric of experiential reality are magically mended" (2008: 132).

"thesis-antithesis-synthesis" is a sorry way to describe that operation, I will now employ the heuristic formula anyway—after all, as Jameson allows, it's "a useful teaching device" (2010: 18)—in order to draw out several versions of "the Hegelian sequence of forms," one abstractly *logical*, the other comedically *theological*, and the third collectively *world-historical*.

In the *Science of Logic*, Hegel posits that it is impossible to think of the thing or thesis called "being" without also thinking of its non-thing, its antithesis, so-called "nothing." More to the point, Hegel posits the impossibility of thinking "being" itself, "beingness" *as such*, or "being" *in general*, without also thinking of its opposite, the antithetical thought of "nothing" *in particular*. This "nothing in particular" is *summoned* to the thinking (of) being only to be *excluded* from it—it appears only to disappear as the simple, immediate antithesis of "being in general," "being as such." But Hegel, being Hegel, cannot rest content to allow a determination and its negation—in this case, "being" and "nothing"—to settle down into a comfortably fixed or "indifferent" opposition. Understanding that "being" and "nothing" already *infect* each other, that "nothing in particular" negates nothing *but* "being" in general and thus properly *belongs to* "being" as being's *property*, its *own proper* negation, Hegel posits *becoming* as the mo(ve)ment of mediation *between* simple "being" and pure "nothing." In this mediation, "being and nothing each become the other, and so constitute the concept of becoming. Becoming . . . is the 'unity' of . . . both being and nothing, in that becoming is [both] the coming to *be* of what was *not* [and] the ceasing to be of what was" (Inwood 1992: 45). As Adrian Johnston explains:

> For Hegel, the movement of becoming is a result of the inextricable intertwining of being and nothing. In other words, Hegelian becoming is simultaneously the dynamic of being passing into nothing and of nothing passing into being. This two-way dynamic is driven by, among other factors, temporal negativity. The unstoppable movement of time is the passage of nothing into being that forced being to pass into nothing by negating any and every congealed configuration of being(s) . . . Hegel's ontology is one in which all actually existing things are crystallized objectifications of the antagonism between being and nothing. Everything with actual ontological status is in a state of becoming as a materialization of the dialectical oscillation between being and nothing. Consequently, in this ontology, there is neither brute being as inert raw matter (i.e., subjectless substance) nor pure nothing as entirely dematerialized negativity (i.e., substanceless subject)—substance always involves the subject and vice-versa . . . As Hegel repeats, all of existence is an "impure" admixture of these abstract poles: "Nowhere

in heaven and earth is there anything which does not contain within itself both being and nothing" (Hegel 1969, 85), and correlatively but conversely, nowhere in heaven or on earth is there being by itself or nothing by itself. And again, he maintains that *"there is nothing which is not in an intermediate state between being and nothing"* (Hegel 1969, 105). (Johnston 2008: 239–40)

A hell of a long quotation, to be sure—but note in passing how here, as elsewhere in the *Science of Logic,* Hegel simultaneously introduces and negates the opposition between being(s) "in heaven or on earth." Note too how Johnston can pull off his impressive unpacking of the "the dialectical oscillation between being and nothing" *without* giving in to the "tripartite temptation." If we were to yield to that temptation, however, and map the "abstract poles" of this Hegelian "admixture" onto the heuristic formula of the dialectic, we would reductively posit "being" as *thesis,* "nothing" as *antithesis,* and "becoming" as *synthesis,* the negation of the negation. But we would also stress that what keeps this or any other dialectical ball rolling is the conviction that any synthesis must be considered a *new thesis* precipitating *yet another* antithesis, thereby generating the next stage of dialectical synthesis, which becomes a new but restlessly self-contradictory thesis, and so on.

But to see how this transformative sequencing works in less abstractly logical and more "down to earth" terms, let me ask you a question that's out of this world.

Are you, by any chance, "God"?

No, I didn't think so. And I hope and trust you didn't *say* so. But if you did answer that question sanely, then, believe it or not, you manifested something like Hegelian negation, for, as Inwood notes, "The native German for 'negation' is *Verneinung,* from *verneinen* ('to answer "No" (*nein*) to a question, to deny or contradict an assertion')" (1992: 199). Thus, by rationally answering "no" to the crazy question—"are you 'God'?"—you effectively *posit* yourself as the *negation* of God, as God's *antithesis,* as "bad" as that might initially sound.

And it sounds even worse before it starts to sound better. For if "you" stand as the negation of "God," how then stands "God"? Rather unsteadily, as it turns out, at least in Hegel's actively dissolvent *Understanding.* For Hegel really means it when he writes that *"everything is inherently contradictory"* and that there is "nothing in heaven or in nature or mind or anywhere else" that isn't a mix of immediacy and mediation, of being and nothing, including even "God." But how in God's name could "God" possibly be brought down into this dissolute mixture? How can even "God," the very *fixture* of the

Absolute, be posited as an inherently contradictory being that (even up "in heaven") *unfixedly* stands on the unstable grounds of *Aufhebung*?

Well, consider the standard attributes of the Absolute Being in our "ordinary thinking." Conventionally, belief in "God" is staked on the conception of a deity that transcends all human limits, that is immortal and omniscient, that doesn't gain power as He rolls along but is "all-powerful" from the foundational get-go. But a moment's reflection on these "essential" attributes shakes them all up, brings them into trembling contradiction. Immortality, for example, clashes with omniscience, for, strangely enough, an immortal being *can't know* what it feels like to be consciously mortal, to be conscious of mortality, suffering through the actual lived experience of the anticipation of death. Being absolutely all-powerful also abrades omniscience, for an infinitely almighty and exalted being just *can't know* what it really feels like in actual lived experience to be puny, powerless, and forsaken—just a slob, a bum, a loser. Omniscience *alone* is shot through with irony, for the omniscient *can't know* what it really feels like *not to know*, which means that the omniscient is by definition *limited* in knowledge. Paradoxically, then, the omniscient "God" who already knows everything, already knows how it's all going to turn out (at, say, the end of time), thereby *lacks* something that we mere mortals sometimes possess in abundance, and I don't mean ignorance. Rather—and you might already have guessed where this irony is headed (God knows I've planted enough clues)—the Absolutely Omniscient must by definition lack *curiosity*, even the curiosity that killed the cat.

But what say we yield once more to tripartite temptation and take this bizarre notion of an inherently self-contradictory and strangely deficient "God"—a "God" put weirdly at a *deficit in knowledge* by the very virtue of *omniscience*—back to the stereotypical formula? "God" would be the thesis, and, as we've established, you and your ilk would be the antithesis, the negation of "God." Now, the "Almighty God" of some old-time religion might be content to rest or ineffably abide on the safe side of this fixed opposition. But that old-time (or Old Testament) religion (i.e., Judaism) isn't good enough for Hegel. Nor is such divine self-sufficiency good enough for the "deficient" God of the new and "true" religion, for the self-sacrificial *Spirit* that can "*win its truth*" *only* by losing/finding itself in utter dismemberment. To the extent that self-consciousness *of* and *as* inherent contradiction *prods* this "deficient" God into "the restlessness of the negative," this self-prodded God *desires* to overcome the contradiction, to nullify the opposition, between its own divine *thesis* and *your* all-too-human *antithesis*. This restless and infinitely Understanding Spirit not only *has* a desire but essentially *is* this desire to negate the negation by undergoing alteration and *becoming* something other than itself, by coming down to *your* level, by *actually becoming one of you* (no small sacrifice on the Deity's part, you might agree). Only through this sacrificial process can *Spirit* as self-lowered Lord succeed in "winning *its* truth" *and* (if you *do* agree) winning *you* over, winning *all* of you who are in agreement over, or back, if not at the same time, then at the end of time, to be (rapturously) sure. Perhaps, then, the least that can be said about Hegel is simply "Jesus Christ!"[7]

But of course there's nothing simple about *this* moniker, which we can't just drop in praise or take in vain, hoping to let the expletive hang there as the least or last thing that can be said about Hegel. To stop at this particular station would be both to neglect the *ongoing* operation of the dialectic and to ignore the way Hegel's subjectively rationalist philosophy restlessly *supersedes* whatever remains of his substantially religious faith. But since we do have to stop for a vanishing moment before considering that supersession, let's "tarry with the negative" for a while in its "totally" Christian form.

Simply put, and employing the heuristic dialectical formula once again, if God is the thesis and you're the antithesis, *Jesus Christ* would have to be the synthesis. But as we've noted, any synthesis snaps into the position of new thesis, generating yet another antithesis. In this case, however, the *new* antithesis is the *same* one as before, given that *you* (if still sane) would no doubt answer "no" to the question "Are you Jesus Christ?" But we can readily see how *this* contradiction, between you and the Savior of the world, might be sublated, for while you might quite *rationally* deny *being Christ*, you might not *emotionally* deny Christ himself, might not deny "the body of Christ," "the passion of the Christ," and you might very well deny that denial by passionately affirming *being Christian*. But of course when "the devout Christian" becomes the figural synthesis of Jesus and the likes of you, all the non-Christianity "out there" pops up as the new antithesis; Operation Dialectics in its totally and exclusively Christian form thus expands into a world-wide evangelical movement, a missionary crusade that seeks to negate the negation of non-belief by converting (or exterminating) all non-believers. And the absolute *finale* of this dialectical narrative would be that the Absolute Deity that started the whole show will have finally and totally overcome His own self-estrangement. By submitting Himself to "incarnation," by Himself becoming a substantial piece of meat in the very

[7] Jameson notes that Hegel's early writings are concerned with the theological concept of the Trinity, and writes that "the formal similarities of the tripartite dialectic with the theological interpretation of the Trinity have led many interpreters either to locate the origins of the dialectic in these theological reflections or else pronounce Hegel a Christian thinker without further ado" (2010: 120). Yovel notes that "religious interpreters have argued that Hegel gives theology precedence over philosophy because of the structural analogy between dialectical logic and the Christian trinity" (2005: 13). Both Jameson and Yovel believe that "such hermeneutical moves are dubious" (Yovel 2005: 13).

stew of world history that He's spiritually stirring, by sacrificing Himself as flesh and resurrecting Himself as Spirit, the Christian *Dios con carne* lowers Himself into the material world but eventually brings the "best" of the world "back up" with Him (minus, one imagines, the meat). The Deity beats the world's meat, negates what's negative, merely carnal, about the world and reappropriates everything that's "good" about it to Himself—taking it all back up to "heaven" in a cosmically and comedically "hetero-tautological" restoration project. And as for *you,* who don't want to be left behind, it's only by *your* actively negating what's "negative" about yourself (i.e., whatever puts you at odds with Jesus, whatever you would do that Jesus wouldn't)—it's only by *not* denying Christ and actually *becoming* Christian—that you will ever get your sorry self-consciousness hauled back up to heaven.

But, good God, is all of this what *Hegel,* "the inaugural thinker of the contemporary world," actually *believed*? To the extent that he considered Christianity the true *religion* and remained Christian (specifically, Lutheran) in his *religious* beliefs, sure, why not? But to the extent that (his) philosophical concepts sublate (his) religious beliefs, to the extent that Hegel put his ultimate philosophical faith in the power of human Reason, arguing that "Reason is Spirit when its certainty of being all reality has been raised to truth, and it is conscious of itself as its own world, and of the world as itself" (1807/1977: 263), to the extent that Hegel is *the* **Enlightenment** thinker *par excellence,* who justified the Enlightenment's faith in reason's rule of the world in terms of "the human possession of treasures formerly squandered on heaven" (1948: 159), then, no, not so much.[8]

According to Inwood, what Hegel generally believes is that "religion and philosophy have the same content . . . but present it in a different form . . ., e.g. what Hegel presents, in the higher and more perspicuous form of thought, as the emergence of the logical idea into nature, or the overcoming of our natural urges, etc., is presented by Christianity, in the form of conception, as God's creating of the world, or the death of Christ." In Hegel's view, "philosophy is required to translate the conceptions (or 'metaphors') of religion into conceptual thought. Since philosophy involves conceptual thought, it can reflect upon and interpret religion, while religion cannot reflect on or interpret philosophy or, for that matter, art" (1992: 255).

---

[8] "The **Enlightenment** is one of the common names given to the historical period in Europe encompassing roughly the second half of the seventeenth century and the eighteenth century. The word also refers to the major intellectual project of the era, which was described by the philosopher Immanuel Kant as 'man's emergence from his self-incurred immaturity.' Thinkers of the Enlightenment rejected superstition and blind faith, extolled reason, and view it as the crucial means of improvement in all areas of human life" (Childers and Hentzi 1995: 95).

If we think of philosophy's required translation of religion in terms of dialectical stages, stages required *by* the art of the dialectic, then we see that Christianity, which insists on God's becoming (for a limited time) human, sets the stage for Hegelianism, which insists on translating the Christian Deity's historical adventure in self-consciousness into the totally secular story of human Reason's completely coming into its own—with no more squandering of any treasures on heaven. Hegelianism translates the metaphor of the Messiah's salvational sojourn into the concept of human Reason's self-development into Absolute Knowing.

You can, in other words, blame Jesus, or the Absolute's sacrificial decision to become an utterly dismembered "one of us," for Hegel's utterly secularizing representation of Reason *as* Spirit *as* "the likeness of God, the divinity of man" (in Nancy 2002: 101).

III. *Ecce Homo*

But speaking of "man," and of bringing Hegel *completely* "down to earth," speaking, as Marx does, of standing Hegel on his feet rather than on his idealist head, and of revealing the "rational kernel" within the dialectic's "mystical shell" (1873/1978: 302), speaking of bringing the de-deified dialectic to bear on a specifically secular moment in what Hegel calls "*world history* [as] *the progress of the consciousness of freedom*" (1837/1998: 402), let's consider an actual historical scene, a well-known documentary photograph of sanitation workers on strike in Memphis, Tennessee, USA, 1968. This famous photograph depicts a row of marching men confronted by a column of standing men. The marching men are the striking sanitation workers, restlessly "agitating" for non-dehumanizing working conditions; the standing men are the state militia, positioned to control, contain, disperse, perhaps even murder the restless agitators. Except for one conspicuous bearded white guy, each of the marching men is an African American man and thus presumably a descendant of human beings once held in *slavery* in the American South. With no discernible exception, each of the soldiers is a white man, and thus presumably descendent from men who once enjoyed positions of *mastery*, who bought and sold other human beings and/or fought to the death to protect the institution of slavery in the American South. Apparently still employed for institutional protection, each of the standing white soldiers carries a rifle with a fixed bayonet. Demonstrably desiring institutional transformation, each of the marching black strikers carries a sign that bears this message—*I AM A MAN.*

Now, to address the question of what's "Hegelian" about this scenario, we have to ask what *moves* a male human being to make this particular claim— *I AM A MAN*—at this particular *moment* in history, at the *point* of these loaded guns and sharpened knives, at the *risk* of his manhood, his very life. What moves an individual to put his life, his given (biologically male) body, on the line in order to bear a slogan that, *in other historical circumstances* or *for other individual men*, could well be taken as a given, held as an obvious fact, a self-evident truth? And what's the difference between the apparently unnecessary assertion of self-evident maleness and the individual male marcher's claim—apparently *made* necessary *by* world history *as* the progress of the self-consciousness of *freedom*—to be *more* than merely *male*, not an animal, and not a "boy," but actually *a man*?[9]

Let's say that the sentiment behind the marcher's sign *I AM A MAN* can never, has never, simply gone without saying. For:

> Man is Self-Consciousness. He is conscious of himself, conscious of his human reality and dignity; and it is in this that he is essentially different from animals, which do not go beyond the level of simple Sentiment of self. Man becomes first conscious of himself at the moment when— for the "first" time—he says "I." To understand man by understanding his "origin" is, therefore, to understand the origin of the I revealed by speech. (Kojève 1947/1980: 3)

These are the opening words of a speech, an introductory lecture on Hegel, given by the Marxist philosopher Alexandre Kojève in Paris in the 1930s. More specifically, the lecture is a "translation with commentary" of the section of Hegel's *Phenomenology of Spirit* entitled "Autonomy and Dependence of Self-Consciousness: Mastery and Slavery" (or "Lordship and Bondage"). Hegel himself begins that section with the claim that "Self-consciousness exists in and for itself when, and by the fact that, it so exists for another; that is, it exists only in being acknowledged" (1807/1998: 92). And so Lacan, one of the French intellectual luminaries who attended Kojève's lectures, is recognizably waxing Hegelian when he claims that the claim "'I [am] a man' . . . can mean no more than, 'I'm like the person who, in recognizing him to be a man, I constitute as someone who can recognize me as a man'" (1966c/2006: 96).

---

[9] The Memphis sanitation workers were reportedly often referred to as animals— specifically, as "walking vultures." And it is well-known that fully grown African American men were routinely called "boys," and not simply in the American South. For example, consider the line in the 1942 film *Casablanca* in which Ilsa (Ingrid Bergman) casually refers to Sam (Dooley Wilson, then aged 56) as "the boy playing the piano."

Now, what do we recognize these Hegelian "speeches" to mean? What do they reveal about the "I" revealed by the "speech" of the striking sanitation worker on the mean streets of Memphis, 1968, who self-consciously puts his body on the line, his life at risk, in order to recognize himself *being* recognized as being a man, an I, and not your not-I? What does Hegel's famous "master–slave dialectic" tell us about this literally life-risking first-person speech?[10]

The master–slave story begins with the encounter of two beings who would be persons. Each wants from the other the same thing—to be recognized as being *more* than a thing, more than an animal. Each already recognizes its own value to itself, already possesses more than an animal "sentiment of self," and pretty much knows it, but each also recognizes that it needs the other to recognize the same. Thus, neither can rest content with its own private or immediate self-consciousness of its value, and so each must *impose* its desire for recognition upon the other. Each has recognized that "the supreme value for an animal is [only the preservation of] its animal life" and therefore that a "man's humanity 'comes to light' only if he risks his (animal) life for the sake of his human Desire" (Kojève 1947/1980: 7)—that is, the desire for recognition.

> It is in and by this risk that the human reality is created and revealed as reality; it is in and by this risk that it "comes to light," i.e., is shown, demonstrated, verified, and gives proof of being essentially different from the animal, natural reality . . . Man's humanity "comes to light" only in risking his life to satisfy his human Desire [for recognition]— that is, his Desire [for recognition] directed toward another Desire [for recognition]. (Kojève 1947/1980: 7)

Now, if human reality were always already a freely cooperative and egalitarian society, a "risk-free" peaceable kingdom rather than a risky historical business, then our two proto-protagonists would always already safely and effortlessly *"recognize* themselves as *mutually recognizing* one another" (1807/1998: 93), as Hegel describes the ideal scenario. But since human reality isn't a mutual recognition society from the egalitarian get-go, human reality must begin with and as a "fight to the death for pure prestige"—a fight for the honor of being human—a struggle without which "there never would have been human beings on earth" (Kojève 1947/1980: 7).

> A human being can be formed only if at least two [would-be human] Desires confront one another. Each of the two beings endowed with such

---

[10] The risk to life was quite real, for Dr Martin Luther King travelled to Memphis to give his support to the sanitation workers' strike and was assassinated there on 4 April 1968.

a Desire is ready to go all the way in pursuit of its satisfaction; that is, is ready to risk its life—and, consequently, to put the life of the other in danger—in order to be "recognized" by the other, to impose itself on the other as the supreme value [to be *the* man]; accordingly, their meeting can only be a fight to the death. (Kojève 1947/1980: 7)

So, instead of there being two beings who mutually recognize themselves in each other as "fellow human beings," we have this anthropogenetic agon in which one brays "*I'm* the man" to the other's "No, *I'm* the man." But this stubborn fight for prestige, this struggle "to be the man," can't actually be a fight to the literal death, for if one man kills the other then the potential source of the desired recognition is obliterated, and if the other goes all the way and croaks for the cause of recognition then there's nothing but a memory left to be recognized. So what must happen is that one combatant must inexorably impose himself on the other to the extent that the other *gives in* to his fear of death, gives up risking his life, lets the desire for preservation win out over the desire for recognition, and in effect says, "OK, OK, fine, *you're* the man; *you* take history by the reins—I'll just hold on to my merely animal life, such as it is, if you don't mind." And of course the other doesn't mind at all, for the immediate result of this abject surrender is that the victor becomes Lord and Master, while the vanquished other becomes his slave.

But the great irony here is that the Lord, the immediate winner, turns out to be the ultimate loser, the glorious chump of the world-historical process. For the immediate winner wins only self-certain mastery, not the true knowledge of freedom, the absolute knowing that can be attained only through the ironic process of *having been* a slave. It's the master who really gets screwed here because while he wins the recognition he originally desired, he gets this recognition only from someone *he* can't recognize as an equal—the slave. Nor does he win even the resemblance of independence (i.e., prestige), for he obviously depends on both the slave's recognition (which has no value for him) and (more importantly) on the slave's *labor*, for the very enjoyment of his mastery. The master thus screws himself into the "existential impasse" (Kojève 1947/1980: 19) that Hegel calls abstract self-identity, or dead being. "The Master is fixed in his Mastery. He cannot go beyond himself, change, progress" (Kojève 1947/1980: 22). The master loses any desire to "go beyond" his fixed position because all that lies beyond that fixity seems "beneath" him—the position of the slave, which he doesn't want, or death, which he also doesn't want. So, the master simply sits on his prestigious ass and lets the slave do the work of "fixing" and bringing him things to consume.

Meanwhile, the slave is working his ass off to fix things for the master's consumption, to *nourish* the master, to actively *produce* the master's mastery, to produce the wealth and power, the *world* with all its fixings, that the master owns and enjoys. But, crucially, this forced production, this *work* of actively transforming things in the world (preparing them for the immediate enjoyment of the master, who doesn't *have* to work, and so doesn't *get* to change or progress) implies the potentially progressive transformation of everything in this seemingly fixed and given world—including the slave's own given position *as* slave. Here, the slave's historical irony obversely mirrors that of the master's existential dead-end. The master first becomes master by embodying "death, the absolute Lord" (Hegel 1807/1998: 97), by threatening to *be* death *for* the slave, to be the inexorable *force* negating the slave's animal life, only to end up (the master, that is) abstractly stuck in the "dead being" of a fixed identity. The slave's irony, however, involves his freeing himself from his fix, his enslavement, but he liberates himself *only* by subjectively internalizing and objectively materializing exactly what he initially feared *in* the master—*death* as the devastating force of negativity or dissolution, death as the tremendous power of the negative. As Kojève tells the "antiphysical" story:

The Master forces the Slave to work. And by working, the Slave becomes master of Nature . . . In becoming master of Nature by work, then, the Slave frees himself from his own nature, from his own instinct [the animal-instinctual fear of death] that tied him to Nature and made him the Master's Slave . . . The future and History hence belong not to the warlike Master, who either dies or preserves himself indefinitely in identity to himself, but to the working Slave. (1947/1980: 22–3)

The Master can never detach himself from the World in which he lives, and if this World perishes, he perishes with it . . . Only the Slave can transform the World that forms him and fixes him in slavery and create a world that he has formed in which he will be free . . . In transforming the World by this work, the Slave transforms himself, too, and thus creates the new objective conditions that permit him to take up once more the liberating fight for recognition that he refused in the beginning for fear of death. (Kojève 1947/1980: 29–30)

Of course, there's quite a bit more that could be said about this still ongoing fight for recognition, for liberation, for the creation of new objective conditions, if not for a finally andfully egalitarian human reality, a "fully human and humanly produced world" (Jameson 2010: 107) without masters or slaves—or, in Marxist terms, without classes. And indeed, it was Marx who stood Hegel on his feet and transformed Hegel's philosophical narrative of the Spirit's totally overcoming its self-alienation into a fully political story of the social collective's attempt to overcome its alienated labor and positively annul private property. We will address this form of alienation (and its relation to literary formalism) in the next lesson.

But, if we limit ourselves here to flying Hegel back to Memphis, we should at least be able to "read" the photograph of the worker's strike against the warlike masters—those armed myrmidons of white identity, privilege, and prestige—in terms of the classic Hegelian who's who. Not that Hegel told us, two centuries in advance, everything we need to know to *absolutely* grasp or capture this image. Nor can we attribute to Hegel himself any "Absolute Knowing" about world history as the progress of the consciousness of freedom, since he was dumb enough (or sufficiently stuck in his own historical moment) to have considered the African continent a primitive region without history, without any consciousness of freedom, thus without any recognizably human reality whatsoever (and, of course, a number of European "Enlightenment" thinkers thought about "the dark continent" in much the same deplorable way that is, in a way that "we" can all too easily deplore from a smug historical distance).

But if, in a spirit of theoretical militancy, "we" can still think of "contemporary history" or the "making of the present" as involving something resembling progress in the consciousness of freedom, then we might still consider Hegel a productively "inaugural thinker" of our "contemporary world." A "patient reading" of his work might still help us appreciate the *distance* some regions of the contemporary world have come in four decades—from 1968, and an African American man's risking death and dismemberment to hold up a sign saying *I AM A MAN*, to 2008, and a democratic American election that permitted a man of African descent to raise his right hand and say "I am the President." Perhaps the least that can be said about Hegel in our contemporary context is that his restlessly negative reflections might still help us in our attempts to dialectically overcome our own "fundamental prejudices," our own "ordinary thinking" (1812/1998: 238), our reified "belief in the stability and substantiality of what is" (Jameson 2010: 25), or any other fixities of self-positing that continue to afflict us. If "Hegel is important," it may be because his writing continues to provoke the understanding that our "world is precisely what . . . manifests itself as a restlessness" (Nancy 2002: 78). If Hegel is still "close to us," still "waiting for us" (Foucault 1972: 235), it's only to the extent that his work remains "an essential step on the way to an understanding" (Rabaté 2002: 21) that "this restlessness is not only ours, it is itself 'us'" (Nancy 2002: 78).

Coming to Terms

Critical Keywords encountered in Lesson Six:

Aufhebung (sublation), immediacy/mediation, teleology, eschatology, phenomenology, onto-theology, the Enlightenment

"There is no document of civilization that is not at the same time a document of barbarism"

—or, the fates of literary formalism

I. "not a pretty thing"

In Chapter 19 of Voltaire's 1759 novel *Candide*, the eponymous hero and his companion Cacambo find themselves on the outskirts of the South American town of "Surinam, then belonging to the Dutch."

> As they drew near the town, they saw a negro stretched upon the ground, with only one moiety of his clothes, that is, his blue linen drawers; the poor man had lost his left leg and his right hand.
>
> "Good God!" said Candide in Dutch, "what art thou doing there, friend, in that shocking condition?"
>
> "I am waiting for my master, Mynheer Vanderdendur, the famous merchant," answered the negro.
>
> "Was it Mynheer Vanderdendur," said Candide, "that treated thee thus?"
>
> "Yes, sir," said the negro, "it is the custom. They give us a pair of linen drawers for our whole garment twice a year. When we work at the sugar canes, and the mill snatches hold of a finger, they cut off the hand; and when we attempt to run away, they cut off the leg; both cases have happened to me. This is the price at which you eat sugar in Europe." (1759/2009: 95–6)

At the beginning of *Heart of Darkness*, Joseph Conrad has his narrator Marlow matter-of-factly announce that "The conquest of the earth, which mostly means the taking it away from those who have a different complexion or slightly flatter noses than ourselves, is not a pretty thing when you look into it too much" (1902/1996: 21). The rest of Conrad's novel—which follows Marlow into the conquered interior of "the dark continent," into "the horror" of the brutally exploitative ivory business in the Belgian Congo, to the very edge of Mister Kurtz's murderous abyss, and then safely back to European "civilization" again—can be read, and has been read, as an explicit dramatization of this ostensibly anti-imperialist and anti-racist observation.[1] So that at the novel's end, when Marlow sits in Brussels, in the comfortable and "lofty drawing-room" of Kurtz's "intended," and surveys all the "pretty things" that surround him—

> The bent gilt legs and back of the furniture shone in indistinct curves. The tall marble fireplace had a cold and monumental whiteness. A grand piano stood massively in a corner; with dark gleams on the flat surfaces like a somber and polished sarcophagus. (1902/1996)

—the ugly point is driven "home" yet again: The "pretty things" of a given civilization aren't all that pretty, are actually riven with "bloody racist" contradictions, if you look into them "too much," which is why those who get to enjoy the "pretty things" tend not to look into them very much at all.

In Toni Morrison's *Beloved*, we don't have to look too hard at the "things" produced by monumental white civilization to see much that isn't pretty. Late in the novel, Denver, the surviving daughter of Sethe—a character based, as Morrison relates in her foreword to the novel, on "the story of Margaret Garner, a young mother who, having escaped slavery, was arrested for killing one of her children (and trying to kill the others) rather than let them be returned to the owner's plantation" (1987/2004: xvii)—notices a particularly un-pretty thing as she is leaving the house of some "good whitefolks" from whom she is seeking employment.

> Denver left, but not before she had seen, sitting on a shelf by the back door, a blackboy's mouth full of money. His head was thrown back farther than a head could go, his hands were shoved in his pockets. Bulging like moons, two eyes were all the face he had above the gaping red mouth. His hair was a cluster of raised, widely spaced dots made of nail heads. And he was on his knees. His mouth, wide as a cup, held the coins needed to pay for a delivery or some other small service, but he could just as well have held buttons, pins or crab-apple jelly. Painted across the pedestal he knelt on were the words "At Yo Service." (1987/2004: 300)

---

[1] The novel has also been read as a displacement or evasion of Marlow's observation, as a justification for Anglo-Europeans' not looking "too much" into the imperialism and colonialism with which Conrad himself—whom Chinua Achebe famously called "a bloody racist" (1978/1989: 9)—is held to be fully complicit. See Rabinowitz (1996).

You'd have to be a pretty callous reader not to be angered, saddened, and repulsed by this figure, which Morrison depicts as being put on shameless display by some of the "good" (i.e., sympathetic, liberal) "whitefolks" of 1873 Ohio. But if you're the kind of close and unforgetful reader that Morrison wants and warrants, you might let this image of a single "blackboy" *on his knees*, with his head thrown inhumanly back and his "mouth full of money," remind you (particularly if you're acquainted with the properly pornographical meaning of the term "money-shot") of an earlier scene in the novel, involving Paul D's memory of being one of 46 black men on a white-controlled chain-gang in Georgia.

> Chain-up completed, they knelt down. The dew, more likely than not, was mist by then. Heavy sometimes and if the dogs were quiet and just breathing you could hear doves. Kneeling in the mist they waited for the whim of a guard, or two, or three. Or maybe all of them wanted it. Wanted it from one prisoner in particular or none—or all.
> "Breakfast? Want some breakfast, nigger?" "Yes, sir."
> "Hungry, nigger?"
> "Yes, sir."
> "Here you go."
> Occasionally a kneeling man chose gunshot in his head as the price, maybe, of taking a bit of foreskin with him to Jesus. Paul D did not know that then. He was looking at his palsied hands, smelling the guard, listening to his soft grunts so like the doves', as he stood before the man kneeling in the mist on his right. Convinced he was next, Paul D retched—vomiting up nothing at all. An observing guard smashed his shoulder with the rifle and the engaged one decided to skip the new man for the time being lest his pants and shoes got soiled by nigger puke. (1987/2004: 127)

Now, except for the fact that the not-so-pretty "things" presented in these three great moments in literary history—the sweet sugar, the grand piano, the grotesque figurine—are better described as artifacts or commodities than as "documents" or written texts, we might say that these three great authors—Voltaire, Conrad, Toni Morrison—all do a pretty good job of palpably rendering Walter Benjamin's famous observation that "There is no document of civilization that is not at the same time a document of barbarism" (1950/1968: 256).

But because the three "things" represented here are, strictly speaking, less documents than commodities, objects produced by dint of physical rather than merely imaginative labor, we can productively trace Benjamin's axiom back to its source in Marx, specifically in the theory of **alienated labor** that

Marx acts forth in the *Economic and Philosophical Manuscripts of 1844*. There, and as we began to see in our first lesson, Marx argues that it is human labor and *only* human labor—"the *act of production* . . . the *producing activity*" (1932a/1978: 73)—that *creates* human reality, that objectively *produces* "humanity" itself. Marx, being a man of his times, often refers to human reality as "man"—as in "man is not an abstract being, squatting outside the world. Man is *the human world*, the state, society" (Marx 1844/1978: 53), etc. And given his "historical materialist" assumption of the human creation of "man," given his "socialist" assumption of the anthropogenetic nature of all human reality, Marx considers labor, the act of production, to be both the actual "origin of the species" and, at least potentially, "the objectively unfolded richness of man's essential being" (1932a/1978: 88–9).

However, as long as "man" is sufficiently self-benighted and self-impoverished by the world religions "he" has, in fact, created—for "*man makes religion*; religion does not make man" (Marx 1844/1978: 53)—this "objectively unfolded richness of man's essential being" isn't *really* going to get "him" very far or make "*the human world*," the world that "man" *is*, particularly rich. For "religion is indeed man's self-consciousness and self-awareness so long as he has not found himself or has lost himself again" (Marx 1844/1978: 53). But upon "*man's emergence from his self-incurred immaturity*"—as Immanuel Kant puts it in the essay "What is Enlightenment?"—upon, that is, man's learning to "have the courage to use [his] *own* understanding" (Kant 1784/1996: 51) and to *own* his own self-conscious self-awareness, to no longer squander his treasures on deities, "Man, who has found in the fantastic reality of heaven, where he sought a supernatural being, only his own reflection, will no longer be tempted to find only the *semblance* of himself—a non-human being—where he seeks and must seek his true reality" (Marx 1844/1978: 53).

For Marx, "man," in seeking "his true reality," is easily capable of overcoming "his" self-alienation in the "fantastic" sphere of religion or the "idealist" realm of Hegelian philosophy, mainly because these dialectical overcomings can take place in the imaginary, through acts of interpretation. But, "while the philosophers have only interpreted the world," says Marx, "the point must be to change it" (1845/1978: 145), and changing the world by fully overcoming man's self-alienation in the actually *economic* realm is another, much more "down to earth" matter. If under the systems of religion and idealist philosophy the "objectively unfolded richness of man's essential being" is "intellectually" misinterpreted by as yet unenlightened "man" himself, under the private property system of commodity production—a.k.a. capitalism—this "objectively unfolded richness" is quite materially transmogrified, becomes an anything-but-imaginary means of enriching, cultivating, and humanizing *some* men and women at the vital expense of others—at the expense not only of the others' physical labor but, because for Marx labor is *the* essentially humanizing activity of all human beings everywhere in history, of their actual humanity.[2]

Thus, we arrive at what Marx considers the ultimate or global contradiction, the "richest" irony of all time. Instead of the objectively *human* production of a fully *human* world, a fully human society (i.e., socialism), what we observe unfolding under capitalism—if we actually do "look into it"—is the human production of an *inhuman* world, the *social* production of an utterly *reified* reality in which "the *increasing value* of the world of things proceeds in direct proportion [to] the *devaluation* of the world of men," a *reified* reality where the world "which labor produces—labor's product—confronts it as *something alien*, as a *power independent* of the producer" (1932a/1978: 71). In Marx's analysis, the world of private property, the world objectively produced by alienated labor (the world *created* by the workers but *owned* by the capitalists), is a world (and here's where we start to get back to Benjamin) in which

> the more the worker produces, the less he has to consume; the more values he creates, the more valueless, the more unworthy he becomes; the better formed his product, the more deformed becomes the worker; *the more civilized his object, the more barbarous becomes the worker*; the mightier labor becomes, the more powerless becomes the worker; the more ingenious labor becomes, the duller becomes the worker and the more he becomes nature's bondsman . . .
>
> It is true that labor produces for the rich wonderful things—but for the worker it produces privation. It produces palaces—but for the worker, hovels. It produces beauty—but for the worker, deformity . . . It produces intelligence, but for the worker idiocy, cretinism. (1932a/1978: 73, emphasis added)

Now, as an historical materialist, Marx is of course writing here about the entire panoply of production, about all sorts of *reified* social processes, not

---

[2]   In Marx's analysis, workers—that is, those who have no capital, no means of living other than selling their labor power to the capitalists—are alienated in four interrelated ways: They are alienated (1) from the product of their labor (think of laborers in sweat-shops who could not possibly afford to buy the high-end sneakers that they make; (2) from the activity of production (think of the miserable, repetitive, dehumanizing, soul-killing toil of sweat-shop and factory labor, which doesn't seem to resemble the "objectively unfolded richness" of anybody's "essential being"); (3) from other human beings (from the owners and managers, who are always trying to extort more labor out of the worker for less money, and from other workers in a competitive and non-unionized "labor market"); and (4) from their own humanity or "species being," as Marx puts it (since labor is the essentially humanizing activity, alienated labor is essentially dehumanizing).

just about well-formed and "wonderful things" of "beauty" and "intelligence." Benjamin, however, while also writing as an historical materialist, is describing what he specifically calls "cultural treasures," celebrated "things" of beauty and intelligence traditionally thought to possess "intrinsic" literary or aesthetic value—artworks or textual "documents" or literary masterpieces like, say, *Candide,* or *Heart of Darkness,* or (even) Morrison's *Beloved.* The historical materialist, says Benjamin, views *all* such beautifully formed literary achievements "with cautious detachment."

> For without exception the cultural treasures [she] surveys have an origin which [she] cannot contemplate without horror. They owe their existence not only to the efforts of the great minds and talents who have created them, but also to the anonymous toil of their contemporaries. There is no document of civilization that is not at the same time a document of barbarism. (1950/1968: 256)

II. What's the matter with formalism?

In his book *The Significance of Theory,* Terry Eagleton divides "literary critics" into two groups—"those who understand what Walter Benjamin meant" in the passage just quoted "and those who do not." But Eagleton also suggests that:

> you do not need 'theory' to understand the meaning of [Benjamin's] claim; many of those subjected to barbarism, bereft of academic education, understand its meaning perfectly well. You may, however, require theory to work out some of its implications. Benjamin did not presumably mean by his statement that documents of civilization were nothing *but* records of barbarism. He meant that there is a way of reading—difficult and delicate—[by] which [one] can . . . X-ray the text in order to allow to emerge through its affirmative pronouncements the shadowy lineaments of the toil, misery and wretchedness which made it possible in the first place. (1990: 32–3)

For Eagleton, and indeed for most contemporary theoretical writers, the group of literary critics who basically don't get Benjamin, who made not getting Benjamin their critical mission in life, who don't have and who don't seem to want anyone else to have Benjamin's "X-ray" vision into literature, who don't seem to want (anyone) "to look into it too much," tend to be called (or even to call themselves) **formalists** (though not all forms of formalism are equally Benjamin-resistant).

In the remainder of this lesson, we'll consider two versions of literary
formalism that actually had very little to do with each other. On the one
hand, we'll examine Anglo-American Formalism, a.k.a. New Criticism,
the "mono-disciplinary" version that dominated literary studies in English
from just after World War II through the Cold War and Vietnam Eras, but
which was eclipsed by theory in the late 1970s and onward. On the other
hand, we'll consider the earlier Russian Formalism—"a lively and important
interdisciplinary school that flourished around 1920" (Harmon and Holman
2006: 226, my emphasis)—as a version of formalism that in many ways
informs and participates in the later theoretical onslaughts and, unlike New
Criticism, remains relatively cognate and compatible with the analytical
aims of materialist semiotics, with theoretical writing as writing against
reification.

For the Russian formalists, formal study meant "the investigation of the
specific properties of literary material, of the properties that distinguish
such material from material of any other kind" (Eichenbaum 1978/1998: 8).
Russian Formalism assumes that "the object of study in literary science is
not literature but 'literariness,' that is, what makes a given work a literary
work" (Jakobson, in Eichenbaum: 8). The Anglo-American Formalists were
also concerned with isolating the specifically "literary" qualities of literature,
segregating poetic from ordinary language, separating literary art from other
genres, and inoculating literary criticism against infection by other academic
disciplines (such as history or, worst of all, sociology). For the New Critics,
however, formalism meant not only attention to the literariness of literature
but an evaluative description of the literary work as an "organic unity"
whose various parts all contribute to the "total" experience of the whole. But
unlike the Russians, Anglo-American Formalists distanced themselves from
"literary science" and devoted their energies to distinguishing literary study
from scientific observation. Indeed, "the New Critics informed the study of
literature with a concern for traditional religious and aesthetic values of the
kind being displaced by science . . . the values of Christian theology and
idealist aesthetics" (Rivkin and Ryan 1998: 7).

We'll address these "displaced" values later on. First, let's examine some
formal definitions of formalism—and some formal complaints filed against it.
The entry for "Formalism" in Harmon and Holman's *Handbook to Literature*,
for example, begins simply enough with "A term applied to criticism that
emphasizes the form of the artwork." But the entry's author doesn't get much
further before complaining that "The whole form-formal-*formalism* family is
beset by problems of reference." The author observes that it is fairly easy to
discuss form "with a clearly tangible object of culture, such as a cup," but that
with literary artworks, "it is difficult to specify what the form is because plot

may be the form that contains the characters, the characters the form that contains the thoughts and feelings, the thoughts and feelings the form that shapes the diction, the diction the form that shapes the acoustic effects, and so on" (2006: 223–4).

Now, it's fitting that in pointing out formalism's problems of reference, the entry's author distinguishes a cultural object such as a cup from a literary artwork, for to judge from some of their book titles—*The Verbal Icon*, *The Well-Wrought Urn*—the American New Critics did seem to want to frame the literary work as a spatial object. And it's this spatializing and decontextualizing tendency that prompts later, more socially and historically conscientious theorists to howl. Eagleton, for example, complains that in trying "to convert the poem into a self-sufficient object, as solid and material as an urn or icon . . . what New Criticism did, in fact, was to convert the poem in to a fetish" (1983/1996: 42). For the Marxist Eagleton, to *defetishize* a cultural object is to de-reify it, to convert the product to a process, to reveal the underlying social relations that produced the object before it attained the dignity of the fetish. New Criticism is accused of fetishizing poems because its proponents desired to sever sonnets from any social context, and Eagleton here reads "form" as the very emblem of this ahistoricizing severance. For Eagleton, formalism and fetishism are twin symptoms of reification, and he thus calls formalism "a recipe for political inertia, and . . . submission to the political status quo" (1983/1996: 43).

So, let's look at the key ingredients of this recipe for inertia more closely and consider in greater detail formalism's alleged complicity with political submission, with ideological *containment*. In ordinary usage, the word "contain" would seem politically neutral, as for instance when I observe that the red Italian cup that rests beside the laptop on which I write contains coffee. Of course, a Marxist would counter that there's nothing politically innocent about coffee or anything else a writer consumes, since questions of the forces and relations of production, private ownership of land, alienation and exploitation of labor, etc., all bear down upon the immiserating reality underlying the social fact of my fix of caffeine. In other words, Benjamin's observation applies even to the not particularly well-wrought cultural object that contains my last remaining addiction. But, Benjamin's claim notwithstanding, let's say that "this cup contains coffee" *seems* politically neutral in a way that a statement such as, say, "the crowd has been contained" does not. For what was this crowd's desire such that it needed to be contained, and by what "formal" methods? What relations obtain between the formal, seemingly neutral "containment" of coffee in a cup, or characters in a plot, and the more obviously political "containment" of potentially unruly crowds (like, say, those who at the time of this writing have been busy Occupying

Wall Street and other avenues of capitalist hegemony)? What links formal exercises in aesthetic control to regimented demonstrations of political force, compelling the aforementioned submission to the status quo?

The New Critics *did* seem to have some "control issues," as well as a strong investment in preserving—or resurrecting—a status quo. I. A. Richards, for example, writes that "The arts are our storehouse of recorded values. They spring from and perpetuate hours in the lives of exceptional people, when their *control* and *command* of experience is at its highest" (in Bertens 2001: 16). And Cleanth Brooks avers that "the characteristic unity of a poem . . . lies in the *unification* of attitudes into a *hierarchy subordinated* to a *total governing* attitude" (1947/2001: 1361). Now, the terms I've emphasized here—*control, command, unification, hierarchy, subordination, total governance*—all sound sufficiently benign when bathed in an "autonomously" aesthetic or *poetical* light. But the same terms sound more sinister if they are denied their autonomy and reinserted into a historical and political context. For example, this characteristic bit of Brooksian analysis—"The last figure thus seems to me to summarize [Wordsworth's] poem—to offer to almost every facet of meaning suggested in the earlier lines a concurring and resolving image which meets and accepts and reduces each item to its place in the total unity" (1951/2007: 804)—sounds perfectly lovely and critically compelling *until* we are apprised of its author's concurring involvement with the reactionary Vanderbilt **Agrarians**, or until we associate *his* rhetoric of resolution with *their* authoritarian solutions to social problems, their nostalgic desire to return to a traditional hierarchical Southern status quo in which every subordinate knew and obediently accepted his or her "rightful place" (no doubt "At Yo Service") in the total governing unity.[3]

Now, Vanderbilt University, where the Agrarians took their stand, is located in Nashville, Tennessee, not that far from Memphis, the historical setting of the photograph documenting military "crowd control" that we examined in

---

[3] For my money, Eagleton is historically accurate when he associates New Criticism with "irrationalism . . . religious dogma . . . and with the right-wing 'blood and soil' politics of the **Agrarian** movement" (1983/1996: 42). The **Agrarians** were "a group of Southern American writers in Nashville, Tennessee, who published *The Fugitive* (1922–1925), a little magazine . . . championing agrarian regionalism . . . Most of its contributors were associated with Vanderbilt University; among them were John Crowe Ransom, Allen Tate . . . [and] Robert Penn Warren . . . In the 1930s, championing an agrarian economy as opposed to that of industrial capitalism, they issued a collective manifesto, *I'll Take My Stand* . . . The Agrarians were among the founders of the New Criticism" (Holman and Harmon 2006: 11). Some of the Agrarians were also proudly racist—Allen Tate, author of the poem "Ode to the Confederate Dead," is known to have haughtily declined to attend a Vanderbilt social event honoring visiting poet Langston Hughes on the grounds that Hughes was, well, after all, "a Negro" (Baker 1988: 144). Some Agrarians, including Tate, were also open admirers of European fascism—see Brinkmeyer (2009).

the previous lesson on Hegel. As we saw there, we can productively view the *content* of this striking image of striking black workers confronting an armed white militia in politically Hegelian terms. But we could also consider the shot from a purely aesthetic angle, as a formal composition—an autonomous, self-contained, and delicately balanced arrangement of lines, space, light, and shadow—and we could describe and evaluate everything we see that makes the photograph successful *as a photograph* without giving two hoots about the "racially charged" historical context. If we judge the photograph as a literary formalist would want us to judge a poem, we would have to demonstrate our "**disinterestedness**" in such "extrinsic" matters and *exclude* them from our consideration.[4]

For formalism depends upon inclusion and exclusion, upon segregating "intrinsic" from "extrinsic" considerations. As David Richter puts it, "All versions of formalism proposed an 'intrinsic' criticism that defined and addressed the specifically literary qualities in the text, and all . . . began *in reaction* to various forms of 'extrinsic' criticism that viewed the text as either the product of social and historical forces or a document making an ethical statement" (2007: 749, emphasis added). But rather like fetishism, formalism also depends upon historical amnesia; just as the fetishist must forget that he actually *made* the fetish figure in order to endow that figure with magical powers, so the formalist must forget the fact that his own critical activities indeed "began in reaction." This amnesia allows the essentially "reactionary" distinction between "intrinsic" and "extrinsic" to be taken as a positive given and forbids any close scrutiny of the exclusionary manner in which the "intrinsic" as such is produced. In other words, the Anglo-American Formalists assume certain "intrinsically" literary qualities as being simply and independently *there*. The "intrinsically" and essentially literary is thus allowed to assume the "timeless" contours of a Platonic ideal.

Against such idealist essentialism, contemporary theoretical writers argue that the intrinsic *qua* intrinsic can be thought *only* with reference to the extrinsic, that the intrinsic is constituted by exclusion and is thus inescapably *dependent* on that which it excludes (just as the Hegelian Master's mastery depends upon the forced recognition of the working slave, just as the capitalist's private property depends upon the proletariat's alienated labor,

---

4   The term ***disinterestedness*** can be said to originate from Kant's *Critique of Judgment,* but "is perhaps most familiarly associated with the criticism of Matthew Arnold," who used the word "to mean a state of ideal objectivity and neutrality, an impartiality that allows the critic to see an object 'as in itself it really is.'" Disinterestedness is "the cornerstone of an objectivist theory of poetry, which invokes timeless standards of quality." Contemporary theory dismisses the possibility of disinterestedness or objectivity and "emphasizes the imbrications of individuals in language, history, and culture" (Childers and Hentzi 1995: 85–6).

just as the efforts of great minds and talents owe their existence to the
anonymous and often immiserating labor of their contemporaries). There
can, in other words, be no "intrinsic" as such without referential dependence
upon some needed-but-excluded *other*.

And so the ideal of "intrinsic value" falls prey to the deconstructive
principle of *constitutive otherness*. We can see this principle at work in
other dictionary entries on formalism that focus on what formalism self-
definingly excludes. Childers and Hentzi define formalism as "the critical
practice of focusing on the artistic technique of the text or object under
consideration at the *expense* of the subject matter" and write that the term
"has often been applied pejoratively to a number of types of criticism that
emphasize a work's structural design or pattern, or its style and manner—its
form—in *isolation* from its contents" (1995: 116, emphases added); meanwhile Julian Wolfreys informs us that "The formalist approach to literature
is one which, allegedly, *retreats* from any consideration of history, ideology
or context, concerning itself only with the formal aspects of the text" (2004:
142, emphasis added).

Expense, isolation, reaction, retreat—such are the impoverishing terms
of formalism's self-enrichment and self-fortification. But the more serious
problem with formalism involves the way its "literary" exclusions mirror
and abet other, more literal forms of exclusion and containment. In this
sense, we could say that Virginia Woolf pretty much *nails* the main ethical
and political problem with Anglo-American Formalism a few decades
before its full development as a critical school. At the end of the first chapter
of *A Room of One's Own*, after describing being shut out of the library and
shooed off the greens of the all-male enclave she archly calls "Oxbridge"
University, Woolf, effectively demolishing New Criticism before the fact of
its advent, writes that she "thought how unpleasant it is to be locked out;
and . . . how it is worse perhaps to be locked in; and . . . of the safety and
prosperity of the one sex and of the poverty and insecurity of the other and
of the effect of tradition and of the lack of tradition upon the mind of a
writer" (1929/1989: 24). Woolf also preemptively tears formalism a new one
when she writes that:

> Shakespeare's plays . . . seem to hang there complete by themselves
> [which is of course how the New Critics will want the bard's plays to
> hang]. But when the web is pulled askew, hooked up at the edge, torn in
> the middle, one remembers that these webs are not spun in mid-air by
> incorporeal creatures, but are the work of suffering human beings, and
> are attached to grossly material things, like health and money and the
> houses we live in. (1929/1989: 41–2)

With Woolf's "preposterous" assistance, "one remembers" in advance the expense both of excluding others and of isolating the literary work from any concern with the actual social conditions that produced it, "the toil, misery and wretchedness which made it possible in the first place" (Eagleton 1990: 33). The New Critics essentially wanted to segregate literary works from their various contexts in order to talk about literature *as* literature. They invested in "the drawing of distinctions" and assumed not merely the *utility* but the *inevitability* of the distinctions they themselves drew. As Brooks puts it, "Man's experience is indeed a seamless garment, no part of which can be separated from the rest. Yet if we urge this fact of inseparability against the drawing of distinctions, then there is no point in talking about criticism at all. I am assuming that distinctions are necessary and useful and indeed inevitable" (1952/2007: 798–9). As Wimsatt and Beardsley reiterate:

> There is a gross body of life, of sensory and mental experience, which lies behind and in some sense causes every poem, but can never be and need not be known in the verbal and hence intellectual composition which is the poem. For all the objects of our manifold experience, for every unity, there is an action of the mind which cuts off roots, melts away context—or indeed we should never have objects or ideas or anything to talk about. (1954/2007: 815)

But most contemporary theoretical writers hold to the conviction that it is only by radically considering contexts, unveiling occluded political desires, that we have anything critically engaging to discuss. More to the point, most contemporary theorists suspect that the New Critical effort to jettison context arose not simply from the desire to talk brightly about literature "for literature's sake" but, more darkly, from the desire to silence or exclude *other questions*, and that this desire was part and parcel of the need to muzzle *other questioners*—interlocutors and interlopers who didn't physically or psychically resemble the straight, white, upper middle-class, right-wing Christian men who were the New Critics themselves. As Robert Dale Parker points out:

> The new critics' effort to exile social meaning carries (ironically) a social meaning, for it suggests their fear of the changing social world, of conflicts across [the lines of] race, gender, and class. Their vision of unity has no place, literarily or socially, for most of the rest of us. (2008: 25)

The problem with formalism, then, is that it attempts to forget what materialist semiotics and "writing against reification" can never afford *not* to remember—"the work of [the rest of us] suffering human beings."

III. Absolutions of irony

Repeating Virginia Woolf's phrase with a twist, I'm conflating her specifically literary "work" with Eagleton's generally materialist "toil" in order to underscore Benjamin's point that these two *forms* of labor—the sublimely civilized *work* located in the cultural **superstructure**, the barbarically wretched *toil* located in the socioeconomic **base**—are inextricably related.[5] But I also employ Woolf's phrase, and change an adjective to a verb, in order to suggest that "the work of suffering human beings" can be very hard work indeed, given how *insufferable* some of them prove themselves to be. And I confess that what I find most insufferable in Anglo-American Formalism is its obvious indenture to "religious dogma" (Eagleton 1983/1996: 42). As Eagleton points out, "several of the leading American New Critics were Christians" (1983/1996: 42), and as I will argue in what follows, Cleanth Brooks was particularly invested in transubstantiating "new" literary criticism into a quite traditional form of Christian devotion.

In "The Rise of English," Eagleton suggests that "If one were asked to provide a single explanation for the growth of English studies in the later nineteenth century, one could do worse that reply 'the failure of religion'" (1983/1996: 20). What he means here is that "English studies," in picking up the ball that "organized religion" in late Victorian society supposedly dropped, assumed religion's function of maintaining "ideological control" through acting as a sort of "social 'cement'"—providing critical crowd containment, engaging and *binding* readers at the level of "deep-seated a-rational fears and needs", "fostering" in the effectively pacified flock not revolution but "meekness, self-sacrifice and the contemplative inner life" (1983/1996: 20). In other words, says Eagleton, English studies were originally complicit with, not a liberatory break from, the ideological functions of "failed" religion. Like religion, English studies were basically *invented* to help ensure "political inertia and submission to the political status quo" (1983/1996: 43). And one upshot of this mass-opiating complicity of English studies with religion was that some English professors set themselves up as displaced priests whose classrooms became dens of religious genuflection.[6]

---

[5]   "**Base** and **superstructure** are Marxist terms referring to the interdependent and reflexive relationship between the economic foundations of society (base) and the forms of state and social consciousness which inevitably follow that structure" (Childers and Hentzi 1995: 27).

[6]   For Eagleton, "the key figure here is Matthew Arnold" (1983/2001: 21), who in 1880, expressed the belief that "we have to turn to poetry to interpret life for us, to console us, to sustain us" and that "most of what now passes with us for religion . . . will be replaced by poetry (in Bertens 2001: 2). Consider also the language of the British Board of

As for Cleanth Brooks, he begins his 1952 treatise entitled "My Credo" with a list of so-called articles of faith. In one of these, however, he explicitly *dismisses* the idea that literature is "a surrogate for religion" (1952/2007: 798). This dismissal would seem to contradict my assertion that Brooks wanted to turn criticism into formal worship. But, if we look more closely at Brooks' articles of high fidelity (there are, for some reason, 10), we'll see how that contradiction is resolved, if not what for Brooks constitutes the ultimate resolution of all contradiction. To use his own words, "I do not think we can quite shut out the theological overtones" (1951/2007: 802) of Brooks' articles of faith.

The first two of these are "That literary criticism is a description and an evaluation of its object" and that "the primary concern of criticism is with the problem of unity—the kind of whole which the literary work forms or fails to form, and the relation of the various parts to each other in building up this whole." The third and fourth articles—"In a successful work, form and content cannot be separated" because "form is meaning" (1952/2007: 798)—will receive no further commentary here. For it's with the next two axioms that things start to take their theological turn. Brooks believes "that literature is ultimately metaphorical and symbolic" and "that the general and the universal are not seized upon by abstraction, but got at through the concrete and the particular" (1952/2007: 798). He elaborates on these two articles elsewhere, in an essay called "Irony as a Principle of Structure":

> One can sum up modern poetic technique by calling it the rediscovery of metaphor and the full commitment to metaphor. The poet can legitimately step out into the universal only by first going through the narrow door of the particular. The poet does not select an abstract theme and then embellish it with concrete details. On the contrary, he must establish the details, must abide by the details, and through his realization of the details attain to whatever general meaning he can . . . Thus, our conventional habits of language have to be reversed when we come to deal with poetry. For here it is the tail that wags the dog. Better still, here it is the tail of the kite . . . that makes the kite fly.

Education's 1921 "Newbolt Report": "Literature is not just a subject for academic study, but one of the chief temples of the Human spirit, in which all should worship" (in Bertens 2001: 10). And consider I. A. Richards, who like Arnold "saw in poetry an antidote to . . . spiritual malaise," who believed that verse is a means of "overcoming chaos" and that literature "is capable of saving us" (in Bertens 2001: 16). Small wonder, then, that the New Critics, influenced by Arnold and Richards, saw themselves as "disappointed priests seeking in literature for a new Word to replace the one the world had lost" (Richter 2007: 760).

The tail . . . seems to negate the kite's function: it weights down
something made to rise; and in the same way, the concrete particulars
with which the poet loads himself seem to deny the universal to which
he aspires. The poet wants to "say" something. Why, then, doesn't he
say it directly and forthrightly? Why is he willing to say it only through
his metaphors? Through his metaphors, he risks saying it partially and
obscurely, and risks not saying it at all. But the risk must be taken for
direct statement leads to abstraction that threatens to take us out of
poetry altogether.
The commitment to metaphor thus implies, with respect to general
theme, a principle of indirection. (1951/2007: 799)

Now, with this principle of indirection in mind, let's wander back to those
last two "articles of faith." How and why do articles six and seven lead up
to the startling article number eight—"that literature is not a surrogate for
religion" (1952/2007: 798)? Religion hasn't been explicitly mentioned thus
far, so why would Brooks feel the need *at this particular moment* to disavow
the idea that literature surrogates faith? Of course, the idea that poetry
would "replace" religion had been in the belletristic air ever since Matthew
Arnold, and perhaps Brooks simply wanted to dispel it. Basic psychoanalytic
interpretation, however, alerts us to the ways in which a *disavowal* might
indicate an unconscious *affirmation*, and so here Brooks' overt statement
that literature *does not* surrogate religion may indicate his covert desire
that it in some way actually *does* or *should*. And the *placement* of this
disavowal suggests that the *terms* of the surrogacy might be embedded in the
immediately preceding assertions about metaphor and symbol, the universal
and the particular.
What are Brooks' major critical keywords, and how might they indicate
the theological overtones of his operative critical principles? The most
prominent terms are **metaphor, irony, paradox, ambiguity, tension**, and
unity.[7] To take the first two, we might agree with Brooks that a sense of
metaphor and irony are indispensable if one is to read or write literature,
that without them we'd be stuck with only literal or denotative language and
"literature" just wouldn't be happening. However, we need to examine closely
what irony and metaphor ultimately amount to in Brooks' close readings.

---

[7] **Metaphor** is a verbal comparison or analogy based upon similarity. **Irony** "refers to an
expression or event that means something different connotatively from what it means
denotatively"; **paradox** "refers to an expression that combines opposite ideas"; **ambiguity**,
"similar to paradox, refers to suggestively multiple and unsettled meanings"; and **tension**
"refers to connected ideas that pull away from each other without reaching resolution"
(Parker 2008: 16–17). **Unity**, at least for Brooks, is that which finally *stabilizes, contains,
resolves*, and *controls* irony, paradox, ambiguity, and tension.

As we've already read, Brooks sums up modern poetic technique by calling it "the rediscovery of metaphor and the full commitment to metaphor." And yet the rest of the paragraph concerning this rediscovery harps on the difference between universal and particular, abstract theme and concrete detail. If this harping doesn't seem particularly relevant to metaphor, remember that the word "metaphor" stems from the expression "to carry" and that metaphor operates as a form of verbal *transportation*—the basic components of metaphor are **tenor** and **vehicle**, with the former representing the general *substance* of the metaphor and the latter that which *conveys* the tenor. Thus, in the example provided by Aristotle in *The Poetics*—"He was in the evening of his life"—old age is the tenor and "evening" is the vehicle. "He was in the evening of his life" is thus an *indirect* way of saying he's old as hell, a geezer getting close to being a goner.

Brooks thus rightly asserts that the "commitment to metaphor" implies a "principle of indirection." As per Emily Dickinson's instructions to "tell all the truth but tell it slant," the poet cannot say anything directly and forthrightly but must employ metaphorical indirection, and this imperative allows us to see how the universal/particular distinction involves *metaphor*—the universal is the *tenor* of the metaphor and the particular is the *vehicle*.

But why, in an essay the title of which promises a discussion of irony, would Brooks begin with the question of metaphor? Is metaphor in some way a form of irony? Ironically, yes, it seems as if it is, because if we define irony as does Brooks—"irony is our most general term for indicating [the] recognition of incongruities" (1947/2001: 1363), that is, the recognition of a discrepancy between what *seems* and what *is*—then we can indeed read metaphor as a potential field of irony. A particular word may *seem* to mean one thing, but the word can be qualified, contextualized, or "warped and bent" (1947/2001: 1363) to mean something altogether different. Brooks writes that "irony is the most general term that we have for the kind of qualifications which the various elements in a context receive from the context" (1947/2001: 1363). Literally, or denotatively, then, the word "evening" signifies only the later hours of the day; metaphorically, or connotatively, it can mean the latest or last years of a life. But Brooks is right to suggest that there must be a *context* for any single word to assume metaphorical dimensions. The word "evening" cannot be metaphorical "all by itself." Framed in the simple sentence "It was evening," the word still hasn't been sufficiently contextualized to work metaphorically, and if we say only "He was in the evening" it just sounds stupid, as if a word were missing (OK, he was *what* in the evening?). But with the complete sentence—"He was in the evening of his life"—we can grasp the qualification or context that makes the sentence metaphorical, and hence ironical.

For Brooks, both irony and metaphor concern the discrepancy between denotation and connotation, between the literal and the figurative. For him, then, the relationship between the universal and the particular is both ironic and metaphorical. The particular, concrete detail *carries* the universal meaning, and is thus metaphorical, but the particular can only metaphorize the universal if its denotative meaning gets bent, warped, contextualized, qualified. In a successful work, the particular only *seems* to be only particular, literal; ironically, it also signifies something else, something greater—the universal meaning.

OK, but what does all this terminological monkey business have to do with *religion*, with "theological overtones," and with Brooks' seemingly pat disavowal of literature's surrogacy for religious faith?

Let me alert you to the fact that when Cleanth Brooks reads a specific poem, he typically focuses on particular instances of irony and metaphor in order to move toward a *dominant* metaphor or irony that he believes controls or resolves or even *becomes* the poem itself. For example, in Brooks' reading, the "well-wrought urn" that appears *in* Donne's poem "The Canonization" becomes a containing figure *for* all the poem's tensions and ambiguities. This movement toward the *dominant* metaphor in the poem reflects Brooks' desire to arrive at a *resolution* to the poem's ironies, the resolution that Brooks is happy to call the poem's unity—its "total meaning" or "total situation" (1947/2001: 1362). For every little irony *in* the formally accomplished poem, Brooks decrees, there shall be the *dominant* irony *of* the poem, the "principle of structure" that situates the poem as a unified, resolved, aesthetic totality.

But what if there were for Brooks a *single* dominant irony that resolved or unified all the others—a sort of meta-metaphor that ultimately abides outside of poetry but which poetry itself metaphorizes? I think that there is such a metaphor and that Brooks states it fairly directly. I, however, will proceed to it *indirectly* and hark back to the ironic tension between the universal and the particular. Brooks, as you'll recall, announces that the poet can only legitimately "step out into the universal by first going through the narrow door of the particular." Can one not note the structural similarity between that assertion and another, more overtly theological one, which maintains that one can only get to the Father, *indirectly*, by way of the *Son*? I believe that this structural similarity is in fact a *structurating* one for Brooks; I believe that any metaphor or irony that Brooks brings to our attention is itself a metaphor for the *dominant* metaphor, irony, and paradox of Christianity itself—*God* is the universal and *Christ* is the particular; God is the tenor and Christ is the vehicle. Christ *seems* to be just a man, just a slob like one of us, but *ironically*, he's also God. God would *seem* to be almighty and all-powerful, but *paradoxically*, there he is, *ecce homo*, hanging, suffering, dying on the cross. Christ *seems* to be dead, but, lo, he is risen, etc. And through that resurrection, the tension between the human and the divine is resolved, the soul does not perish but is unified with God, etc. But in Christianity this holy harmony is possible only through spiritual indirection, through irony, metaphor, and paradox. Like poets, who can "step out into the universal" only by way of the particular, believers can climb the stairway to the heavenly Father only "by way" of the loving self-sacrifice of the Son.

I would thus hazard to say that Brooks is *lying*, or at least being ironic, when he says that literature is not a surrogate for religion, because the experience of poetry so evidently metaphorizes the experience of Christian faith for him that the two would seem to be as one. Compare two "crucial" paragraphs in "The Language of Paradox":

> For us today, Donne's imagination seems obsessed with the problem of unity; the sense in which the soul is united with God. Frequently, as we have seen, one type of union becomes a metaphor for the other. It may not be too far-fetched to see both as instances of, and metaphors for, the union which the creative imagination itself effects. (1947/1998: 67)
>
> The urn to which we are summoned, the urn which holds the ashes of the phoenix, is like the well-wrought urn of Donne's "Canonization" which holds the phoenix-lovers' ashes: it is the poem itself . . . But there is a sense in which all such well-wrought urns contain the ashes of a Phoenix. The urns are not meant for memorial purposes only, though that often seems to be their chief significance to [historicist or non-formalist] professors of literature. The phoenix rises from its ashes; or ought to rise, but it will not arise for all our mere sifting and measuring the ashes, or testing them for their chemical content. We must be prepared to accept the paradox of the imagination itself; else "Beautie, Truth, and Raritie" remain enclosed in their cinders and we shall end with essential cinders, for all our pains. (1947/1998: 69)

For Brooks, I believe, the paradox of the creative imagination *is* the paradoxical unity offered through the body of Christ: God as man as metaphor for the reunion of the lost soul with its Creator. And though Christ himself is never *directly* mentioned, he certainly seems figured into the phoenix, that great honking symbol of death and resurrection, and even into the *kite* mentioned in "Irony as a Principle of Structure," that holy flying kite which "rises steadily against the thrust of the wind." The kite, you'll recall, is structurally ironic and paradoxical because it has to be weighted down by some tail in order to rise. Likewise, to pin the tail on the Deity,

Christ is ironical and paradoxical because, even though God, he must assume a human form, must load himself down with the particularity of human flesh and blood in order to shed that blood for us, in order to die "for all our pains" and get himself resurrected. And *we*, Brooks preaches, "must be prepared to accept" that paradox or we will all have died and gone to a hell in which words have only denotative meanings, poems fail to add up to organic unities, sociologists blind us with science, students or (worse) tenured colleagues "who have a different complexion or slightly flatter noses than ourselves" ask annoying questions about race, sex, gender, history, politics, imperialism, colonialism, etc.

Now, if, after having sat through this sermon, we return to Brooks' sixth "article of faith"—"that literature is ultimately metaphorical and symbolic"— we might behold that we can warp and bend its language so as finally to stop shutting out the theological overtones—we might say that Brooks' *ultimate* faith is that literature metaphorizes and symbolizes the *Ultimate*, the Absolute, that if for Brooks literature *doesn't* surrogate religion it's only because for him literature *literally is* religion, and that perhaps the final irony about Brooks is that there is, in the end, for his money, absolutely no irony left at all. In the end, that is, Brooks absolves irony of the sin of having been ironic, for what seems to be the dominant sense of irony *in* Brooks' criticism turns out to be the critical domination *of* irony itself, "the labor of controlling incongruities" (Leitch 2001: 1352). In Brooks' work, *openness* to irony noticeably transubstantiates into a stony *invulnerability* to irony:

> Irony, then . . . is not only an acknowledgment of the pressures of context. Invulnerability to irony is the stability of a context in which the internal pressures balance and mutually support each other. The stability is like that of the arch: the very forces which are calculated to drag the stone [of castle or cathedral] to the ground actually provide the principle of support—a principle in which thrust and counterthrust become the means of stability. (1952/2007: 801)

I believe, then, that what makes Brooks literarily formalist is inseparable from what makes him credulously Christian—*ultimately*, he is *not* fully committed to metaphor, tension, irony, ambiguity, or any of that other jazz but rather to what resolves, contains, controls, dominates, stabilizes, and unifies them. For Brooks, the *ultimate* principle of structure is always organic unity, never corrosive irony. He is thus closer in spirit to the preacher than to the poet or the scientist. He would *seem* to side with the poet *against* the scientist in "The Language of Paradox," where he writes that "The tendency of science is necessarily to stabilize terms, to freeze them into strict denotations; the poet's tendency is by contrast disruptive. The terms are continually modifying each other, and thus violating their dictionary meanings" (1947/1998: 62). There would *seem* to be something "proto-deconstructive" about the way Brooks privileges poetry's disruptions and violations over science's tendency to terminological stabilization. Brooks would *seem* eligible for membership in that theoretical club whose charter is to "de-reify the language of thought" (Jameson 2009: 9). And yet, if my reading of Brooks as a reactionary religious acolyte wearing literary critic's clothing is at all persuasive, we can say that Brooks' proto-deconstructive tendencies finally run up against the bulwark of his faith in aesthetic unity, which itself metaphorizes divine unity, and which Brooks hoped would finally ensure sexual, political, racial, and academic unity. In other words, Brooks' faithful formalism is anything but deconstructive and anything but Benjaminian. This formalism ultimately seeks to restabilize whatever disruptions and violations might be effected by poetic language—or by writing about "writing as the very possibility of change" (Cixous 1975/2007: 1646).

IV. Strategies of estrangement

Russian Formalism, however, got along quite well without New Criticism's idealist, theological, and segregationist baggage, which is one reason why Victor Shklovsky's notion of defamiliarization, or *ostranenie*, as developed in the 1917 essay "Art as Technique," can be considered compatible with the work of contemporary theoretical writing.

Shklovsky begins his essay by taking issue with Alexander Potebnya's assertion that "art is thinking in images" (1917/2007: 775). Shklovsky doesn't really mind Potebnya's effort to specify an activity that would define the essential "artiness" of verbal art; he just doesn't think that "thinking in images" quite fits the bill. In particular, Shklovsky objects to Potebnya's assertion that "the purpose of imagery is to help channel various objects and activities into groups and to clarify the unknown by means of the known" (1917/2007: 775)—or at least, he objects to the idea that epistemological clarification amounts to a specifically *aesthetic* use or experience of *language*. Another objection involves the problem of literary history—if imagery is the defining characteristic of poetry, as Potebnya asserts, then a history of poetics would have to account for changes in imagery, whereas poetic images, in Shklovsky's opinion, change very little. Poets, he writes, "are much more concerned with arranging images than with creating them" (1917/2007: 776); verbal artistry, for Shklovsky, thus essentially concerns strategy or *technique*, not creation or clarification.

Furthermore, since imagery is an aspect of both poetry and prose, one can hardly allow imagery to define poetry. Potebnya, says Shklovsky, "ignored the fact that there are two aspects of imagery: imagery as a practical means of thinking, as a means of placing objects within categories; and imagery as poetry, as a means of reinforcing an impression." He clarifies the distinction as follows:

> I want to attract the attention of a young child who is eating bread and butter and getting the butter on her fingers. I call, "Hey, butterfingers!" This is a figure of speech, a clearly prosaic trope. Now a different example. The child is playing with my glasses and drops them. I call, "Hey, butterfingers!" This figure of speech is a poetic trope. (In the first example, "butterfingers" is metonymic; in the second, metaphoric.) (1917/2007: 776)

Now, this distinction between metaphor and **metonymy** will assume a certain importance in the later adventures of literary theory, so let's linger with it for a while. Why, let's ask, does Shklovsky label the first use of "butterfingers" metonymic and the second metaphoric? Why would he consider metaphor (a figure of speech based on similarity or analogy) *poetic* and call metonymy (a figure of speech based on association or contiguity) *prosaic*?

We might say that the first instance of "butterfingers" is metonymic *because* prosaic or "realistic." In the first example, that is, the child *really* does have butter on her fingers, and the physical *contiguity* of the real matter with the actual fingers is mirrored and affirmed by the physical *combination* of "butter" with "fingers" in the trope "butterfingers." In the second example, the child does *not really* have butter on her fingers, but in the metaphor "butterfingers" it's *as if* she did, *as if* the slippery substance had caused her to drop Shklovsky's glasses. Thus, the difference between metonymy and metaphor can be read as the difference between, on the one hand, the prosaic and realistic and, on the other, the imaginative (the *as if*) and the negative (the *not really*). Both instances involve imagery, if you like, but while the first, metonymic usage is prosaic, "journalistic," mere sensory reportage that allows us to "see" what's actually there (butter on fingers), the second, metaphorical usage is poetic, more verbally and cognitively "artistic," an imaginative leap that invites us to envision what's *not* really there (again, butter on fingers).

But there's an irony here, involving *ostranenie*, even if Shklovsky himself doesn't put his finger on it. If I mumble "butterfingers!" at some fumbler whose fingers aren't literally buttered, I have indeed employed metaphor rather than metonymy. But my metaphorical usage isn't, simply by virtue of being metaphorical, necessarily more "poetic" than my metonymically calling a really butterfingered person "butterfingers." Why not? Well, perhaps the metaphor was fresh in 1917, but today, this facile figure is so well-worn and overly lubricated that it's *practically* become what *automatically* slips out of the *average* person's hole in response to seeing another lose her grip. However, it takes a special sort of *idiot* to be so obvious as to dub the *really* butterfingered person a "butterfingers." *Either* our idiot is ignorant of the metaphor and is simply using the metonym to register exactly what he sees, *or* the idiot is more adroitly referring to and *negating* the clichéd metaphorical negation, *as if* to say "Your attention, please. *Ordinarily*, the average person uses the metaphor *butterfingers* to refer *not* to someone with literally buttered fingers but to a fumbler—but look, here I'm with a sort of ostentatious mock-stupidity doing just the opposite, inserting the obviously prosaic metonym in the place of the more familiarly 'poetic' metaphor." In either case, this idiotically "real" use of the metonym "butterfingers" is rather *extraordinary* compared to the average/automatic utterance of the clichéd metaphor. Through over-use and over-familiarity, the metaphor has lost its edge, become practically literal, and so now the metonym—by virtue of a hyper-literal foregrounding of the obvious that disturbs or displaces the familiar—actually creates the *stronger* impression. And since for Shklovsky "poetic imagery is a means of creating the strongest possible impression" (1917/2007: 776), here the realistic metonym could be considered more poetic, more a "work of art," than the standard metaphor.

Shklovsky writes that "by 'works of art' . . . we mean works created by special techniques designed to make the works as obviously artistic as possible" and thus to create "the strongest possible impression." He writes that "poetic imagery" is *one* such impressive technique, but that "as a method it is, depending upon its purpose, neither more nor less effective than other poetic techniques" (1917/2007: 776). His adversary Potebnya's "law of the economy of creative effort" (1917/2007: 777) pertains to modes of perception that involve the least possible mental exertion and to modes of discourse that communicate the most expediently. Again, Shklovsky doesn't mind the application of this law to practical language, but he objects to its being extended to poetry. He writes that "If we start to examine the general laws of perception, we see that as perception becomes habitual, it becomes automatic" and that "all of our habits retreat into the area of the unconsciously automatic" (1917/2007: 778). Such unconscious automatism leads us into a sort of perceptual "algebra," by means of which we do not see objects "in their entirety but rather recognize them by their main characteristics."

> We see the object as though it were enveloped in a sack. We *know* what it is by its configuration, but we *see* only its silhouette. The object, perceived thus in the manner of prose perception, fades and does not

leave even a first impression; ultimately even the essence of what it was
is forgotten . . . The process of "algebrization," the over-automatization of
an object, permits the greatest economy of perceptive effort. (1917/2007:
778, emphases added)

The purpose of *art*, however, is for Shklovsky precisely to disrupt this
"habitualization" and "algebrization" of perceived objects. The purpose of
art is to de-automatize, to dis-habituate, to discomfort, to defamiliarize.
Shklovsky cites a passage from Tolstoy's diary registering the extent to
which our habituation of so much of our daily lives has the effect of *erasing*
our lives' real substance. He writes that in accord with this dismal algebra,
"life is reckoned as nothing" because "habitualization devours" just about
everything. As Tolstoy complains, "If the whole complex lives of many
people go on unconsciously, then such lives are as if they had never been."
For Shklovsky, however, "art exists that one may recover the sensation of life;
it exists to make one feel things, to make the stone *stony*."

The purpose of art is to impart the sensation of things *as they are
perceived and not as they are known*. The technique of art is to make
objects "unfamiliar," to make forms difficult, to increase the difficulty
and length of perception because the process of perception is an aesthetic
end in itself and must be prolonged. Art is a way of experiencing the
artfulness of an object; the object is not important. (1917/2007: 778,
emphasis added)

These passages establish Shklovsky's "formalist" *bona fides*—because only
a formalist would ever privilege technique over content. For Shklovsky,
however, a "form" is not an "organic unity," a "self-sufficient object," a
"spatial figure," a reified "fetish" or article of faith, but rather a "temporal
process" (Eagleton 1983/1996: 42)—"A work is created 'artistically' so that
its perception is *impeded* and the greatest possible effect is produced through
the *slowness* of perception. As a result of this lingering, the object is perceived
not in its extension in space, but, so to speak, in its [temporal] continuity"
(1917/2007: 783). Form, then, is not a perceived *thing* but a "difficult"
perceptual *event*. Thus, for Shklovsky, form is not a means of "containment,"
but rather engages our perceptual *resistance to* containment, particularly
epistemological containment. Art, for Shklovsky, is a struggle *against* our
habitual attempt to "clarify the unknown by means of the known" (1917/2007:
775). What "difficult" forms resist is our normal, ordinary, routine, automatic
ways of *understanding*, of taking the world in. And given the extent to
which we've been "taken in" *by* "normal understanding"—trained to revere
"understanding" or "knowledge" (or "faith" in "truth") above everything

else—perhaps the most "difficult" aspect of Shklovsky's "formalism" is the provocative way he pits art *against* "understanding," the way he distinguishes between the "event" of *seeing* and the "uneventful" act of *knowing*, between *enlivening* aesthetic *perception* and mortifyingly familiar *knowledge*.

Nietzsche, as you'll recall, diagnosed the epistemological drive in terms of the anxious desire to reduce "the strange" to "the familiar." For Nietzsche, the familiar is "what we are used to so that we no longer marvel at it, our everyday, . . . anything at all in which we feel at home," and so, "our need for knowledge [is] precisely this need for the familiar, the will to uncover under everything strange, unusual, and questionable something that no longer disturbs us." For Nietzsche, it is "the *instinct of fear* that bids us to know" and "the jubilation of those who attain knowledge . . . [is] jubilation over the restoration of a sense of security" (1887/2006: 368).

Following Nietzsche, Shklovsky cautions us against the habituating aspects of "secure" knowledge and offers art's strategies of estrangement as a means of recovering sensations and perceptions that we lose or miss through ease, habit, faith, or fear. For Shklovsky, artistic defamiliarization and epistemological clarification are in tension each other, and the former— or perhaps the *formal*—is actively hostile to the latter.

> I personally feel that defamiliarization is found almost everywhere form is found. In other words, . . . an image is not a permanent referent for those mutable complexities of life which are revealed through it; its purpose is not to make us perceive meaning, but to create a special perception of the object—it creates a "vision" of the object instead of serving as a means for knowing it. (1917/2007: 781)

In studying art, then, and particularly "poetic speech," what we find, writes Shklovsky, is "the artistic trademark . . . We find material obviously created to remove the automatism of perception; the author's purpose is to create the vision which results from that deautomatized perception" (1917/2007: 783). Positing "form" as defamiliarization allows Shklovsky to privilege the *temporal* aspects of poetry as "formed speech" (1917/2007: 784) over the *spatial* aspects, which in turn allows us to distinguish Shklovsky's formalism from New Critical fetishism.

But defamiliarization also opens up a way of reading the *history* of poetic perception, and this opening also sets Shklovsky's formalism apart from New Criticism's closed and ahistoricizing "idealist aesthetics." Shklovsky calls poetry "a difficult, roughened, impeded language" (1917/2007: 783) and defines poetry as "*attenuated, tortuous* speech" (1917/2007: 784). Given this definition, we might posit that one aspect of poetry's rough trade would involve "promoting the palpability of signs," deepening "the fundamental dichotomy of signs and objects," as Roman Jakobson will later put it (1960/2007: 856). But another aspect of "torturous" defamiliarization involves what Shklovsky calls "disordering the rhythm" of poetic speech. "The rhythm of prose is an important automatizing element; the rhythm of poetry is not" (1917/2007: 784). And yet Shklovsky quickly points out that rhythmic disordering "cannot be predicted" or systematized—"Should the disordering of rhythm become a convention, it would be ineffective as a device for the roughening of language" (1917/2007: 784).

And here's where history, of a sort, enters the picture. Shklovsky insists that artworks are "works created by special techniques designed to make the works as obviously artistic as possible." But specific techniques or devices don't always or eternally work to make artworks artworks. In the fourteenth century, for Giotto, the specifically new technique that made the painting obviously artistic was **perspective**; in the nineteenth century, for Gauguin, the device that made the painting obviously artistic was the *abolition* of perspective.[8] Or, to go back to "butterfingers"—in a specific historical context, a roughly "prosaic" metonym might be more "artistic" than a smoothly "poetical" metaphor. Some coarse prose might be more palpably "attenuated" than some fluent poetry. One can never predict or permanently decide in advance exactly what it will take for an artist in any genre to make us feel or see, to make the stone stony, to make the painting painterly, to form (or torture) practical language into poetry.

And here's where history of another sort enters the picture. Shklovsky writes that "According to Aristotle, poetic language must appear strange and wonderful; and in fact, it is often actually foreign" (1917/2007: 784). He goes on to cite examples of linguistic, historical, and geographical "foreignnesses" embedded within various poetical practices. For Shklovsky, then, poetic language, by appearing strange and wonderful, allows "foreignness" itself to appear strange and wonderful—rather than, say, bewildering and terrifying. Impeding the reactionary and paranoid habit of "clarifying the unknown by means of the known," poetry—the language of defamiliarization—can serve an ethical political purpose in promoting openness to "the foreign," teaching its readers not to be afraid of "the other" (not, e.g., to automatically assume the "foreigner" to be a "terrorist"). Not that any form of "*attenuated, tortuous* speech" possesses some inherently ethical power to keep

---

[8] In painting, **perspective** is the "method of representing spatial extension into depth on a flat or shallow surface, utilizing such optical phenomena as the apparent diminution in size of objects and the convergence of parallel lines as they recede from the spectator" (Chilvers 1988: 379). Perspective is a technique that gives the illusion of three-dimensional depth to a two-dimensional canvas.

reactionaries from torturing foreigners or to prevent literal exterminations of the unfamiliar. There is no necessary or "intrinsic" relation between aesthetic defamiliarization and a progressive or liberatory ethics of alterity. There is no "specific technique" that can *both* make our artwork "as obviously artistic as possible" *and* permanently keep the documents of our civilization from becoming the registers of our barbarity.

And yet, for some writers, the hope remains that art, in some rough form or another, can still make at least a few stones stony. Or, in other words, the hope remains that an interventional art of the sentence can remain "a crucial element of critical subversion, a political mode [of writing] that is designed to produce a sense of alienation and discomfort in the reader so that newness may enter and alter a defamiliarized world" (Salih 2004: 4).

Coming to Terms

Critical Keywords encountered in Lesson Seven:

alienated labor, formalism, aesthetics, Agrarians, disinterestedness, base/superstructure, metaphor, irony, paradox, ambiguity, tension, unity, tenor/vehicle, metonymy, perspective

Lesson Eight

"The unconscious is structured like a language"

—or, invasions of the signifier

I. Without positive terms

Not everyone buys into "the conviction that of all the writing called theoretical, Lacan's is the richest" (Jameson 2006: 365–6). But for those who are heavily invested in Lacan, the great wealth of his psychoanalytic writing flows from its active trading with semiotics and structural linguistics. Lacan, that is, first "struck it rich" by reading Freud as if Freud had read Saussure, by rethinking Freud's discoveries through Saussure's "linguistic turn," and by cashing in on the claim that "the unconscious is structured like a language" (1973/1981: 203).[1]

Our task in this lesson will be to understand what allows Lacan to stake his signature claim. We've of course already encountered *the unconscious*, the

---

[1] Lacan writes that while "Freud could not have taken into account modern linguistics, which postdates him," Freud's discovery "stands out precisely because, in setting out from a domain in which one could not have expected to encounter linguistics' reign, it had to anticipate its formulations" (1966f/2006: 578). Lacan asserts that when Freud's *Interpretation of Dreams* was published in 1900, "it was way ahead of the formalizations of linguistics for which . . . it paved the way" (1966e/2006: 426); moreover, Lacan notes that "in Freud's complete works, one out of three pages presents us with philological references . . . linguistic analysis becoming still more prevalent the more directly the unconscious is involved" (1966e/2006: 424). In *How to Read Lacan*, Žižek writes that "Lacan started his 'return to Freud' with the linguistic reading of the entire psychoanalytic edifice, encapsulated by what is perhaps his single best-known formula: 'The unconscious is structured as a language.' The predominant perception of the unconscious is that it is the domain of irrational drives, something opposed to the rational conscious self. For Lacan, this notion of the unconscious belongs to the Romantic *Lebensphilosophie* (philosophy of life) and has nothing to do with Freud. The Freudian unconscious caused such a scandal not because of the claim that the rational self is subordinated to the much vaster domain of blind irrational instincts, but because it demonstrated how the unconscious itself obeys its own grammar and logic: the unconscious talks and thinks" (2006: 2–3).

real kernel of Freudian discovery; we've also heard quite a bit about *language*, the central concern of semiotics and structuralism, the study of signs and of sign systems.

But what exactly *is* "a sign" for a semiotician? How, in a structuralist understanding, do sign systems *work*? How does the "structure" in structuralism differ from the "form" in formalism?

In the previous lesson, we witnessed that "form" for a formalist tends to resolve into an ostensibly "singular" *thing* ("organic unity" for Brooks) or *technique* ("defamiliarization" for Shklovsky). According to Robert Dale Parker, however, "we cannot say that structuralism is any one thing" (2008: 40). And the reason we can't say any such thing about structuralism is that structuralism pretty much demolishes the idea of there ever being any *one* thing, any absolutely *singular* element that can *meaningfully* "stand alone," independent of all other units of meaning. So when we read that "if we boil structuralism down to one idea, it is about understanding concepts through their relation to other concepts, rather than understanding them as intrinsic, in isolation from each other" (Parker 2008: 40), we can grasp what distinguishes a structuralist understanding of "textuality in general" from formalism's *intrinsically* "literary" and socially *isolated* text. If we do "boil structuralism down to one idea," it's that there can never be any such thing as one idea, one single "positive term"—it's about "coming to terms" with the realization that "in language there are only differences *without positive terms*" (Saussure 1959: 120); it's about understanding that "language is a system of interdependent terms in which the value of each term results solely from the simultaneous presence of the others" (Saussure 1959: 114).

Now, structuralism's big idea isn't that there's "no such thing" as big ideas, or that meanings "simply don't exist"; rather, the thrust of structuralism is that ideational meanings don't exist *simply*—ideas exist, but they exist *only in language*, and "language being what it is, we shall find nothing simple in it" (Saussure 1959: 122). The structuralist idea is that ideas cannot exist *except* in differential relation to each other. Of course, the underlying ideal of Western metaphysics since Plato has involved the belief that meaningful ideas really do abide in their independently self-present "truth," *prior to* any language that might be used to express, represent, or "stand for" them. But structuralism won't stand for any of that. Structuralism posits that "there are no preexisting ideas" (Saussure 1959: 112), that "no ideas are established in advance, and nothing is distinct"—much less true—"before the introduction of linguistic structure" (Saussure 1972/1986: 110)—"Language," writes Saussure, "has neither ideas nor sounds that existed before the linguistic system, but only conceptual and phonic differences that have issued from the system" (1959: 120).

Language for Saussure is thus necessarily, interdependently, systematic—
"a form and not a substance" (1959: 122). There can't be an "unstructured"
language, any more than there could be an "unstructured" society or an
"unstructured" psychic apparatus. And so the structuralist argument that
"thought is linguistic" and that "concepts cannot exist independently of their
linguistic expression" (Jameson 2004: 403) entails the radical premise that
linguistic structure constitutes *the* fundamental condition of possibility for all
recognizably human reality, social, corporeal, and psychic. "The structuralist
idea is that reality is linguistic and structured, not that there is no reality but
that we construct it, so that there is no reality independent of language." The
structuralist idea is that "language not only describes our world [but] also
produces the world it describes" (Parker 2008: 46).

This conception of language as world-forming is what sets theoretical
writing *after* structuralism apart from preceding or competing literary
criticisms. Regarding structuralism's specific difference from formalism, then,
we can say that if "for the new critics, the goal is to interpret the individual
text," the structuralist goal is "to describe or interpret the larger system"
(Parker 2008: 47–8). And because the structuralist concern *is* with "the
larger system," formalism's more limited focus on the specific "literariness of
literature" seems pretty small potatoes. And yet, while structuralism would
appear to neglect literature's sublime (or starchy) literariness, structuralism's
emphasis on the larger system's "linguistic foundation" arguably extends the
strange *condition* of literature into every corner of human reality; "literature"
thus gains considerably "larger" significance by *losing* the isolated and
elevated status that formalism had bestowed upon it.

In the chapter of his *Structuralist Poetics* called "The Linguistic Foundation,"
Jonathan Culler refers to the structuralist "notion that linguistics might be
useful in studying other cultural phenomena" (1975: 4). By "other cultural
phenomena," Culler means (1) cultural forms that don't traditionally count
as "creative writing" (that aren't poems, novels, plays, etc.) and (2) cultural
phenomena (such as fashion shows or football games) that hadn't previously
appeared to involve "language" to any pertinent extent and so hadn't usually
been considered suitable for linguistic analysis, much less "worthy" of close
reading.

For structuralism, however, *all* cultural phenomena are wide open to
linguistic analysis; moreover, all *phenomena*, even ostensibly "natural"
phenomena, are "actually" always *cultural* objects that warrant being
attentively read. In the key structuralist text *Mythologies*, Roland Barthes
writes that structuralists "take language, discourse, speech, etc., to mean any
significant unit or synthesis, whether verbal or visual: . . . even objects will
become speech, if they mean something" (1957/1972: 110–11). "Every object

in the world," says Barthes, "can pass from a closed, silent existence to an oral state, open to appropriation by society, for there is no law, natural or not, which forbids talking about things" (1957/1972: 109). Culler thus writes that

> the notion that linguistics might be useful in studying other cultural phenomena is based on two fundamental insights: first, that social and cultural phenomena are not simply material objects or events but objects or events with meaning, and hence signs; and second, that they [signs] do not have essences but are defined by a network of relations. (1975: 4)

The first insight is basic to semiology, or semiotics, the "science of signs," while the second is the foundation of structuralism, the analysis of the underlying systemic networks that make meaning, culture, human reality possible. For Culler, however, these twin insights are "inseparable," for "in studying signs one must investigate the system of relations that enables meaning to be produced and, reciprocally, one can only determine what are the pertinent relations among items by considering them as signs" (1975: 4).

> The cultural meaning of any particular act or object is determined by a whole system of constitutive rules: rules which do not regulate behaviour so much as create the possibility of particular forms of behaviour. The rules of English enable sequences of sound to have meaning; they make it possible to utter grammatical or ungrammatical sentences. And analogously, various social rules make it possible to marry, to score a goal, to write a poem, to be impolite. It is in this sense that a culture is composed of a set of symbolic systems. (1975: 5)

OK, so in human reality, everything and everyone is made of rules, composed of signs. But signs, we are told, "do not have essences"; they—and hence presumably we—"are defined by a network of relations." What allows structuralism this disturbingly "anti-essentialist" claim? What makes the claim disturbing in the first place, and for whom? Of course, the claim that *signs* lack essences won't fundamentally disturb anyone who doesn't think much of signs anyway; it wouldn't bother anyone who assumes that the "real truth" of ideas, experiences, or identities preexists any signs that might subsequently be used, like mere tools, to express or describe them. Such a "believer" wouldn't feel spiritually infected by the essencelessness of signs; he would be no more disturbed by the claim that signs lack essences than he would be surprised to hear that his screwdriver or word-processor didn't have a soul; he could readily admit that *signs* don't have essences while still securely holding on to his own, so to speak. But the claim against significant essences could be unsettling for anyone who takes to heart the structuralist premise that signs systematically "create the possibility" for the very reality, the very ideas and very identities, that they are normally thought merely to describe. So given the "existential" stakes involved here, what, again, allows the structuralist to deprive us and our signs of any "essential" natures? What *are* these hungry ghosts called *signs*, anyway—particularly for the semiotician whose job is to study them?

The nineteenth-century American semiotician Charles Sanders Peirce distinguished among **iconic**, **indexical**, and **symbolic** signs. In Peirce's schema, *iconic* signs are mimetic, basically pictographic representations—a crude drawing on a chalkboard could be "iconically" taken to signify, for example, a cat. *Indexical* signs, on the other hand, are effective indices or "indicators" of preexisting natural or physical *causes*—smoke indicates fire, stench indicates rot, etc. Note that an *attempted* iconic sign, like the drawing of the cat on the chalkboard, might be so miserably rendered that no one can possibly make out "what it's supposed to be"; the *failed* iconic sign, however, can still function as an *index* of the merely physical fact that someone has been marking, however ineptly, on the board. But while iconic and indexical signs can be "grasped" or "sensed" by those who can't *read* (a preschooler can recognize a well-drawn kitty, a real cat knows what to make of an emanating odor), a *symbolic* sign, like the *word* "cat," can successfully signify *only* to a reader who knows the *language* in which it is written, in this case English. If a word for "cat" is chalked on the board in some language I can't read, then the marks can signify *indexically* for me (I can take them as indicating that someone has been marking on the board), but not *symbolically* (I can't really tell what the marks symbolize, what they're supposed to *mean*).

For Saussure, all *linguistic* signs, all words, are *symbolic* in Peirce's sense, which means that their *primary* signifying function is neither *iconic* nor *indexical*, that words signify by being *neither* naturally mimetic images *nor* simple indices of physical cause – effect relations. But Saussure inveighs against our using the term "symbol" to "designate the linguistic sign" (1959: 68), because while "*the linguistic sign is arbitrary*"—and we'll be discussing at length the huge implications of *that* little zinger—"one characteristic of the symbol is that it is never wholly arbitrary; it is not empty, for there is the rudiment of a natural bond between the **signifier** and the **signified**. The symbol of justice, a pair of scales, could not be replaced by just any other symbol, such as a chariot" (1959: 67, 68).

For Saussure, "symbol" isn't quite the right word for a word because symbols can still participate in iconic or indexical significations, both of which imply some "natural bond" or physical motivation. But *words* are completely "empty" of and by "nature." The *linguistic* sign, Saussure insists, is not only "antiphysical," in all the senses of that word that we've explored in previous lessons, but *arbitrary*, which means that words are based not on physical nature but on social *convention*, collective agreements. Saussure cautions that the term *arbitrary* "should not imply that the choice of the significr is left entirely to the speaker," for "the individual does not have the power to change a sign in any way once it has become established in the linguistic community." Rather, to say that the signifier is arbitrary means "that it is unmotivated, i.e., arbitrary in that it has no natural connection with the signified" (1959: 69).

Now, Saussure writes that "the principle of the arbitrary nature of the sign . . . dominates all the linguistics of language" and that "its consequences are numberless" (1959: 68). Indeed, the implications of the principle "that there is no fixed bond" (1959: 69) between signifiers and signifieds or signs and referents are probably much more numerous and extensive than Saussure himself might have envisioned. But because the principle of the sign's "arbitrary nature" *has* proven to be so consequential, we need to make sure we understand exactly what Saussure means by it.

In Saussurean terms, a linguistic *sign* couples a *signifier* with a *signified* in order to designate a *referent*. The *signifier* functions as an "acoustic image"; the *signified* is the "concept" that this acoustic image conventionally evokes; while the *referent* is the "real thing" in the world that the *sign* (signifier and signified combined) conventionally designates. In the case of the "cat" inscribed on the chalkboard, the signifier is the *image*, the perceptual *imprint*, of the grouped letters c/a/t, coupled with the phonetic *sound*—kat—that in English conventionally corresponds to those marks. Please note that on the side of the signifier the "image" is *not* your mental vision of some feline but merely your visual perception of this trio of marks, c/a/t, as they appear on the board or page. Note also the absence of any natural, fixed, or inevitable "bond" between the legible mark "c" and the hard "k" sound we are trained to make in English when we perceive that mark; obviously, other languages couple differently imaged marks with that particular sound. Note further that there is no "natural bond" between the *signifier* "cat" and the *signified* concept or mental image of a real cat. If there *were* some natural connection or physical cause – effect relation between them, then the marks "c/a/t" would *inevitably* provoke both the sound "kat" and the mental image of a cat for, say, a Chinese person who didn't read English, just as fire inevitably causes smoke, or rot stench, everywhere in the natural world.

So here's the crux of the matter: the condition of language is such that the linguistic sign has no natural connection, no motivated, iconic, or indexical relation, to anything in the physical world—*and hence neither do we*. This is not to say that neither language nor we, the animals at its mercy, have *any* connection with nature whatsoever; it is only to say that for us, as specifically human beings, there is no *natural* relation, no physically *motivated* connection, between signifiers and signifieds or words and things. What *we* have *instead* of merely natural relations is a shifting ensemble of arbitrary, contingent, *socially conventional* relations. In other words, and once again, what we *have* is only what we ourselves *make*—the ongoing *history* of a world that *must* be made to mean.

Now, as I hope you'll recall from earlier lessons, Roland Barthes refers to *myth* as a "depoliticizing" type of speech that attempts to turn this "history" back into "nature," into a static realm of naturalized significations in which "things appear to mean something by themselves" (1957/1972: 143). Myth in Barthes' sense depends upon a sort of enforced ignorance about the arbitrary, conventional, unmotivated "nature" of the linguistic sign. Myth, in other words, is *politically* motivated to occult language's *lack* of *natural* motivation, to actively depoliticize speech by ignoring or obscuring its purely fabricated social conventionality. Myth attempts to maintain the fiction that language *isn't* fictional, to support the illusion that *linguistic* signs really do function *iconically* or *indexically*; myth, that is, attempts to permanently bond signifiers to signifieds, to make the connection between them seem as natural and inevitable as the indexical connection of smoke to fire or stench to rot.

In other words, myth presents words as if they were *natural facts*, not *social forms*, as if they were completely "positive" terms without any "inmixture of otherness." But Saussure's myth-shattering assertion is that "in language there are only differences. Even more important: a difference generally implies positive terms between which the difference is set up; but in language there are only differences *without positive terms*" (1959: 120). We should understand that a "positive term"—if it existed—would involve a fixed or fundamentally grounded content; a "positive term" would simply and independently be what it is and mean what it means, all by itself, just naturally. But against this myth of terminological positivity, Saussure argues that any word's "content is really fixed only by the concurrence of everything that exists outside it" (1959: 115), that terms "are purely differential and defined not by their positive content but negatively by their relations with the other terms of the system. Their most precise characteristic is in being what the others are not" (1959: 117).

Of course, Saussure is here discussing terms, not real things. He's not suggesting that the "most precise characteristic" of a real cat is that it isn't a hotdog; rest assured that, for all a structuralist cares, a real cat can simply be what it is, positively. But for a structuralist the *signifier* "cat" cannot be a positive term; the signifier "cat" is what it legibly is, means what it visibly/ audibly means, *only* because of its *difference* from other signifiers, "outsiders" that are almost the same but not quite—rat, sat, mat, pat, lat, hat, etc. If linguistic structure is in fact "made" entirely of such micro-differences, if any signifier's most precise characteristic is *not* its positive content but its situation in relation to some other term that it's *not*, then Saussure is justified in claiming that "in language there are only differences without positive terms," that "everything in language is negative" (1959: 120).

All these Saussurean claims are of course the "linguistic foundation" for Culler's unsettling assertion that signs "do not have essences but are defined by a network of relations" (1975: 4). These claims are also the condition of possibility for the anti-essentialist or deconstructive principle of "constitutive otherness" that I mentioned in the previous lesson—that is, the idea that *any* meaningful entity "is what it is" *only* by virtue of its difference from, and dependence upon, other entities. But Saussure may well have sensed the *threat* his principles posed to traditional metaphysics, to "the underlying ideal of Western culture," for, perhaps protecting his own unconscious investment in that very ideal, Saussure backs away from his own "new rule" pretty quickly after having laid it down. Having just said that everything he's said "boils down" to the bold statement that "in language there are only differences *without positive terms*" (1959: 120), Saussure seems to back-paddle—"But the statement that everything in language is negative is true only if the signified and signifier are considered separately; when we consider the sign in its totality, we have something that is positive in its own class" (1959: 120). And as Saussure continues to recant, insisting that the sign in its totality somehow *can* be terminally positive, certain clichés—involving barn doors being shut after horses have bolted, cats being let out of bags, and oddly named eggs falling off their walls—may well pop into the close reader's mind. For once, we *very* close readers have taken to heart Saussure's central claims about language; *nothing* that he says thereafter can put our shattered faith in "positive terms" back together again; *nothing* can restore our previously held idealist belief that signs really do have essences; *nothing* can persuade us that the structuralist slogan "everything in language is negative" *isn't* completely valid for "the sign considered in its totality"—and hence, for human reality considered in *its* totality as well.

Indeed, after Saussure's totally linguistic turn of the screw, *nothing*—not even *the* "nothing" that Hamlet calls "a fair thing to lie between a maid's legs"—has ever been exactly the self-same again.

II. Adventures in metaphor and metonymy

But speaking of legs, and of what lies or doesn't lie between them, did you know that crossing one's legs in a certain fashion—at the ankle, not at the knee—is the single best way "to give the world the assurance of a man" while sitting? I myself was told this once, in so many words. Sitting comfortably enough at my desk in an eighth-grade classroom, minding my own business—albeit crossing my legs the *other* way, *not* at the ankle but at the knee—I suddenly heard a cackle of cultural intervention, the voice of the gender police: a concerned classmate, who happened to be a boy, pointed out to the rest of the class that "Thomas" was "sitting like a girl."

Too bad we weren't studying semiotics in this disciplinary setting. If we had been, I might have been able to respond to my classmate's panoptical observation in some other way than desperately repositioning my signifying limbs, assuming too late the appropriately gendered posture. I might have been able to turn to my interpellating tormentor and ask why he assumed that any particular way of arranging one's legs constituted an *indexical sign* of some preexisting chromosomal *cause*, why he assumed any *natural* bond, *motivated* connection, or *inevitable* relation between the gestural and the genital. I might have pointed out that *signs* of "sitting like" boys or girls are not "positive terms" with fixed, biologically determined contents but are socially conventional signifiers that "mean" *only* in differential relation to each other. I might have suggested that crossing one's legs *one* way signifies sitting "like a boy" *not* because of any single thing that lies between a boy's legs but *only* because crossing them the *other* way signifies sitting "like a girl."

And if these choice words hadn't been enough to earn me an after-school ass-kicking, I might even have announced that since "everything in language is negative" anyway, nothing positively *causal* lies between the legs of *any* human subject, boy or girl. With a precocious nod to Lacan's "Signification of the Phallus," I might have mentioned that nothing "truly" lies between any of our legs *but* lies—contingent *fictions* of sex—regardless of whether any one of us really "has what it takes" down there or not. Or I might have lighted on the word "like" in my classmate's accusation that I was sitting "like a girl" to launch into a discussion of *similarity* and *contiguity* as these physical conditions correspond to the tropes of *metaphor* and *metonymy* in structural linguistics; I might have continued along Lacanian lines and "articulated what links metaphor to the question of being and metonymy to its lack" (1966e/2006: 439).

But setting aside all thoughts of what I might have cleverly said back then, I will now get back on track by launching into—guess what?—a discussion of *similarity* and *contiguity* as they correspond to *metaphor* and *metonymy* in structural linguistics, not only because it is now relatively safe for me to do so, sitting however I like, but because this discussion will take us closer to understanding how the basic elements of Saussurean linguistics allow Lacan to reboot Freud and claim that the unconscious is structured like a language.

We will continue our approach to Lacan's analogy by considering Saussure's distinction between **syntagmatic** and **paradigmatic** relations in language. Saussure insists that "in a language-state everything is based on relations" (1959: 122), but he proposes that linguistic elements "acquire" their relations in two distinct ways. On the one hand, words can "acquire relations based on the linear nature of language because they are chained together." Since language's linearity "rules out the possibility of pronouncing two elements simultaneously," words must be "arranged in sequence on the chain of speaking. Combinations supported by linearity are *syntagms*. The syntagm is always composed of two or more consecutive units" (1959: 123), and syntagmatic combinations are typically arranged sequentially across the **horizontal axis** of language.

Paradigmatic elements, on the other hand, "are not supported by linearity" (1959: 123)—or at least not by a sequentially *horizontal* linearity. But these elements *can be* "associatively" aligned or *imaginatively* "stacked up" on language's **vertical axis**. Paradigmatic or "associative" relations, as Saussure calls them, involve words "that have something in common," that can be "associated in the memory" (1959: 123). While the *real* "scene" of *syntagmatic* relations is their *actual* occurrence on the sequential chain of discourse, the *imaginary* "seat" of *paradigmatic* relations is "in the brain; they are a part of the inner storehouse that makes up the language of each speaker." Thus, *syntagmatic* relations are conspicuously *evident*, can be readily discerned and reported, while *paradigmatic* relations are rather more *obscure*, seem to require stronger powers of memory and imaginative selection. "The syntagmatic relation," writes Saussure, "is *in praesentia*. It is based on two or more terms that occur in an effective series. Against this, the [paradigmatic] relation unites terms *in absentia* in a potential mnemonic series" (1959: 123).

To clarify Saussure's distinction, let's say that a simple declarative sentence such as "This fish is dead" so *effectively presents* its syntagmatic relations, its *horizontally* linear sequence of grammatically and syntactically combined words, that basically, all we have to do to receive this report on piscine morbidity is to grasp conventional grammar and to recognize what the words "fish" and "dead" denote. We don't have to "remember" very much or "imagine" anything at all; we have only to see/hear the words in their "real time" seriality in order to "get the message." But if I were to pick these syntagmatic bones clean and offer up the skeletal sequence ridden with *absences*—as in "This____is____"—then, in order to fill in the blanks, one might *imagine* a potentially towering series of *similar* words *other than* "fish" and "dead," words that have "something in common," nouns or adjectives that could be *selected* from one's mnemonic "inner storehouse" and *inserted* into the positions opened by the absences of "fish" and "dead," that could be *substituted* for "fish" and "dead" (this *bread* is *stale*, this *coffee* is *cold*, this *lesson* is *tedious*, this *tapestry* is *gorgeous*, etc.). And one could *imagine* those series arranged in *vertical* "stacks" above the blank spaces vacated by the dead fish (*bread, coffee, lesson, tapestry* in one stack; *stale, cold, tedious, gorgeous*, in another).

In fact, we pretty much *have to* imagine those vertical, paradigmatic "stacks" of signifiers because—*unlike* the actual and evident *contiguities* and *adjacencies* of the horizontal chain of syntagms, which we don't have to *imagine* but can merely *register*—the paradigmatic "word-towers" are *not really there*: they *must* be imagined, conjured, thought up. While syntagmatic relations depend upon *actual* combinations and contiguities that are *physically* arranged horizontally, *in praesentia,* paradigmatic relations involve *imaginary* substitutions and unifications, *psychically* aligned vertically, *in absentia*. And this distinction between the *physical* and the *psychical*, between the actual and the imaginary, allows the structuralist to align, on the one hand, the syntagmatic—sequential—contiguous—combinative— *horizontal* axis of language with *metonymy* and, on the other hand, the paradigmatic|analogous|selective|substitutive|*vertical* axis of language with *metaphor*.

These alignments are among the most important in structuralist analysis. But Saussure himself doesn't mention metaphor or metonymy by name in his discussion of syntagmatic and paradigmatic relations. And in a sense it was not Saussure but our old *formalist* friend Viktor Shklovsky who laid the foundations for these structuralist alignments when he first distinguished *prosaic* metonymy from *poetical* metaphor. Using structuralist terms to rework Shklovsky's "butterfingers" illustration in the previous lesson, we could say that when the described child has actually gotten butter on her fingers, the employed metonym "butterfingers" is a prosaically *realistic* syntagm, a horizontal verbal sequence combining the word "butter" with the word "fingers" in a way that mimetically reflects/reports the real physical contiguity of substance to flesh in the *present*. But when the clean-fingered child has merely dropped an object—she *doesn't really* have butter on her fingers, it's only *as if* she did—the employed metaphor "butterfingers" is a relatively poetic *imaginative* analogy that substitutes itself for the *absence* of real substance. But if the "present employment" of metaphor really depends upon "the *absence* of real substance," on the *negation* of positive content, then Saussure, without explicitly *naming* metaphor as such, *implies* the utter metaphoricity of language simply by telling us that "everything in language is negative" and that *"language is a form and not a substance"* (1959: 120, 122). Moreover, when he writes that in considering "the relation that ties together the different parts of syntagms . . . one must also bear in mind the relation that links the whole to its parts" (1959: 124), Saussure implicitly describes the function of **synecdoche,** the type of metonym that works by linking parts to wholes, and he thus *nails* the syntagmatic to the metonymic without explicitly naming the latter.

Saussure thus allows us to see the antirealistic "poetry" of *antiphysis* even in the "prosaic" metonym "butterfingers," for in that two-term, syntagmatic composition the *word* "butter" *isn't really* a dairy product any more than the *word* "finger" is really a fleshy digit. In other words, the signifier isn't *really* the signified any more than the sign is *really* the referent. Because in language there are *only* differences without really positive terms, even metonymical terms can be said to *function* metaphorically. But because linguistic differences *must* be strung out along the horizontal or syntagmatic chain of meaning, metaphors themselves are typically *sustained* or *supported* metonymically, in sequential combinations. Finally, since language itself works thanks only to the *interplay* between the paradigmatically metaphorical "poetic" function and the syntagmatically metonymical "prosaic" function, "any attempt to reduce the sphere of the poetic function to poetry [alone] or to confine poetry to the poetic function would be a delusive oversimplification."

Thus spake Roman Jakobson—"a key figure in Russian formalism and a major influence on French structuralism" (Malpas and Wake 2006: 210)—a theoretical writer who indeed seems to meld Shklovsky's "formalist" concerns with Saussure's "structuralist" investigations. For when Jakobson describes "the poetic function of language" in terms of a "focus on the message for its own sake"—that is, excluding any other "factors involved in verbal communication" (1960/2007: 857)—his description resonates with *both* Shklovsky's "formalist" argument that the prolonged process of perceiving a defamiliarizing message "is an aesthetic end in itself" (1917/2007: 778) *and* Saussure's "structuralist" insistence that *"the true and unique object of linguistics is language studied in and for itself"* (1959: 232). This double resonance continues when Jakobson writes that the poetic function "cannot be productively studied out of touch with the general problems of language, and, on the other hand, [that] the scrutiny of language requires a thorough consideration of its poetic function" (1960/2007: 857). What Jakobson calls "the poetic function" would seem to unite Shklovsky's aesthetically "word-roughening" techniques with Saussure's metaphorically "substance-negating" activities, for "by promoting the palpability of signs" (as per Shklovsky's rough-stuff), the poetic function always "deepens the fundamental dichotomy of signs and objects" (1960/2007: 857)—that is, the sign as sign must negate or jettison the object.

Note that in the preceding sentence I've employed what Jakobson calls "the two basic modes of arrangement used in verbal behavior, *selection* and *combination*" (1960/2007: 857). That is, I have *selected* certain words based on their paradigmatic *similarity* and sequentially *combined* those words according to an effectively syntagmatic *contiguity*, imposing Shklovsky's "word-*roughening*" onto Jakobson's "*palpability* of signs" and projecting Saussurean "insubstantiality" onto Jakobson's "fundamental dichotomy." On the one hand, my "verbal behavior" here instantiates what Jakobson calls **metalanguage**—roughly, language about language rather than language about objects. On the other hand, my verbosity would seem to relate to Jakobson's most emphatic description of the poetic function—"*The poetic function projects the principle of equivalence from the axis of selection into the axis of combination*" (1960/2007: 858). Of course, my sentence is "not really" an axial line of poetry at all. And yet, Jakobson's description allows me to speak of my sentence *as if* it were not unrelated to the poetic function, *as if* it somehow involved the interplay of metaphor (the axis of selection) and metonymy (the axis of combination)—even though, strictly speaking, the sentence contains neither metaphor nor metonymy. The fact that Jakobson's description of the poetic function allows me to write about my writing *as if* it were poetry when it's really no such thing underscores his argument that "when dealing with the poetic function, linguistics cannot limit itself to the field of poetry" (1960/2007: 857).

But neither, writes Jakobson—in a key passage that effectively pre-lubricates Lacan's insertion of Saussure into Freud—can linguistics limit itself to the "formalist" focus on "the literariness of literature" when dealing with the interplay of metaphor and metonymy, for

> a competition between both devices, metonymic and metaphoric, is manifest in any symbolic process, be it intrapersonal or social. Thus in an inquiry into the structure of dreams, the decisive question is whether the symbols and the temporal sequences used are based on contiguity (Freud's metonymic "**displacement**" and synecdochic "**condensation**") or on similarity (Freud's "identification and symbolism"). (1956/2001: 1268)

Linking metaphor and metonymy to *all* "intrapersonal" and "social" symbolic processes, as well as to *linguistic* "inquiry into the structure of dreams," Jakobson here effectively paves the way for Lacan's reading of "the 'signifierness of dreams'" (1966e/2006: 424) and thus for his claim that the unconscious is structured like a language. As we learned in our lesson on taking desire literally, Lacan is keenly concerned with what Jakobson calls "the fundamental dichotomy of signs and objects"—he incisively explores *antiphysis*, the *rupture* between signification and "the real" that makes all human reality possible. While he would agree with Roland Barthes that "even objects will become speech, if they mean something" (1957/1972: 110–11), Lacan insists that some ecstatically or traumatically "real thing" *remains missing* whenever objects *or subjects* are ordered to "become" meaningful "speech." And though he would concur with Barthes' statement that "every object in the world can pass from a closed, silent existence to an oral state, open to appropriation by society, for there is no law . . . which forbids talking about things" (1957/1972: 109), Lacan would interject that every object *and every subject* in the world not only *can* but *must* pass from its closed, silent, inarticulate existence to an oral state, open to cultural intervention and social appropriation. Lacan's message is *not* that there's *no* law forbidding our "talking about things" but that there *is* a law that forbids our *not* talking about things, *not* symbolizing them, that outlaws our *not* saying "no" to the real; this law, the symbolic order, prohibits our merely *being* (with or in) certain "real things" rather than differentially *meaning* them, articulately *distancing* ourselves from them.

Exploiting, moreover, the etymology of the word *sex* (from the Latin *secare*, "to cut," as you'll recall), Lacan "sexualizes" this articulate distance, this radical cut away from the real; he posits an "Oedipal" dimension to Saussure's claim that language is the clear-cut "domain of articulations" (1972/1986: 111); he insists that what Jakobson calls "verbal behavior" is always already "sexual behavior" and vice versa. As we've seen, for Lacan, *both* the symbolic order's law against inarticulate, undifferentiated "silence" *and* Saussure's linguistic law of *linearity* that "rules out the possibility of pronouncing two elements simultaneously" (Saussure 1959: 123) are structurally analogous to the paternal law of *lineage,* that "prohibition against incest" which founds all exogamous social orders and which "reveals itself clearly enough as identical to a language order" (1966d/2006: 229).

In "The Instance of the Letter in the Unconscious," Lacan pays homage to Jakobson, whom he duly credits as "one of the leaders of modern linguistics" (1966e/2006: 439). But when it comes to connecting the *terms* of linguistics to basic Freudian keywords, Lacan corrects and expands upon Jakobson to a large degree. As we'll see, Lacan indeed connects *metonymy* to Freudian *displacement,* as Jakobson does above, but he also associates metonymy with *desire* or *lack*; moreover, *unlike* Jakobson, Lacan compares *not* synecdoche but *metaphor* to Freud's *condensation* and to the psychoanalytic **symptom**.[2] Before examining Lacan's corrections, however, we must come to terms with *condensation* and *displacement* as these terms function in Freud's lexicon, specifically in the *Traumdeutung*, the *Interpretation of Dreams*.

Simply put, Freud's premise is that a dream represents the fulfillment of a wish. But dreams being what they are, we shall find nothing simple in them, so Freud's more complicated premise is that a dream represents a compromise formation, the symptomatic *work* of attempting to satisfy *two* mutually incompatible desires at once. On the one hand, there's the dreamer's *unconscious* desire, unconscious because *repressed*, repressed because *incompatible* with the dreamer's socially installed ego-coherence or *conscious* sense of self-esteem; on the other hand, there's the dreamer's desire to *stay asleep*, to remain psychically *undisturbed* by the emergence of any potentially ego-damaging imagery. In Freud's view, human sleep involves the relaxation—but not the complete abnegation—of the *censorship mechanism* that holds repressed desire in place. Thus, when we're soundly asleep, unconscious desire "takes advantage" of our inner censor's vulnerability and surreptitiously attempts to "have its say." The unconscious, rather like Cleanth Brooks' "poet," very much "wants to 'say' something. Why, then, doesn't [it] say it directly and forthrightly?" (1951/2007: 799) Well, because if the unconscious *did* directly "speak itself," its dark matters would most likely set off the censorship mechanism's alarms and wake the sleeping dreamer up. The unconscious therefore "understands" that to allow any dormant *das Ich* to continue dreaming (with ego-coherence altered but still basically intact), and thus to keep its own scandalous message from being abruptly "cut off" in mid-stream, it, the unconscious, must "have its say" only in disguised and distorted *forms*. The unconscious "knows," in other words, that "it"—*das Es*—can have the *substance* of "its say" only *formally*. For the unconscious, like language, "*is a form and not a substance.*" Only as a signifying *structure*, a strangely organized sort of *poetry slam*, and *not* as some formlessly bubbling cauldron of biologically instinctual *nature*, can unconscious desire ever get away with having something like its say.

Let's say that I unconsciously harbor the standard Oedipal desires to "have a father kill'd, a mother stained," as Hamlet ambiguously puts it. If I were to

---

[2] While "in medicine, **symptoms** are the perceptible manifestations of an underlying illness" (as a runny nose is a symptom of the common cold), in psychoanalysis, symptoms are treated not as direct indices of organic maladies but as "unnatural" signs of repressed desires. As writes Dylan Evans, "Lacan follows Freud in affirming that neurotic symptoms are formations of the unconscious, and that they are always a compromise between two conflicting desires. Lacan's originality lies in his understanding of neurotic symptoms in linguistic terms" (1996: 203).

have a dream that "directly and forthrightly" represented the *fulfillment* of those desires—a dream in which I ecstatically decapitated my father and/ or seminally stained my own mother—the image of either atrocity would (let's hope) be disturbing enough to rupture my slumber, because I really don't think I'm the kind of person who would *enjoy* doing or spewing such horrible things. But if I were to dream of sawing off the top of a bottle of *pop*, or of masturbating onto the petals of a chrysanthe*mum*, I would probably be able to sleep right through my own witness of these weird but comparatively placid hieroglyphics—my ego-coherence would be protected and, at the same time, "my" unconscious desire would have had something like "its" say. In my dreams, in other words, I(t) enjoy(s) otherwise.

In the *Traumdeutung*, Freud says that dreams *work* exactly through such distorting mechanisms, through such *condensations* of ideas and *displacements* of enjoyment. Freud uses the word *Verdichtung* or *condensation* to describe the psychic process by which two or more ideas or images are "paradigmatically" compressed into a single *form* (my patricidal dream *condenses* father and bottle; my matri-maculating dream *condenses* mother and flower). He employs the word *Verschiebung* or *displacement* to describe the psychic process by which the "discharge" of forbidden aggression or obscene longing is "syntagmatically" transferred from one element in the dream sequence to another (my daddy-killing dream *displaces* murderous rage away from my father and *onto something else*, a stupid bottle; my mother-soiling dream *transfers* seminal abjection away from my mum and *onto something else*, the lovely petals).

It's all rather *poetic*, wouldn't you say? And even if you wouldn't, Lacan emphatically does, not only stressing the similarity between *condensation* and *metaphor* and associating *displacement* with *metonymy*—

> *Verdichtung*, "condensation," is the superimposed structure of signi-
> fiers in which metaphor finds its field; its name, condensing in itself the
> word *Dichtung*, shows the mechanism's connaturality with poetry, to the
> extent that it envelops poetry's own properly traditional function.
>
> *Verschiebung* or "displacement"—this transfer of signification that
> metonymy displays is . . . represented, right from its first appearance in
> Freud's work, as the unconscious' best means by which to foil censorship.
> (1966e/2006: 425)

—but also insisting on the traumatically *sexual* underpinnings of all enveloping tropes, metaphorical or metonymical, of all symbolic processes, intrapersonal or social, of all unconscious desire taken literally, *à la lettre*.

One way to understand Lacan's "Oedipal" take on metaphorical condensation is to turn again to Saussure's assertion that language's law of linearity
"rules out the possibility of pronouncing two elements simultaneously" (1959:
153). Ordinarily, "realistically" speaking, one could say that this rule against
incest—oops, my bad, I mean, against *simultaneity*, against two "elements"
being pronounced *as/at on(c)e*—generally holds; after all, this is the rule that
compels all *good* writers to keep their letters separate rather than piling them
on top of each other (as in the *bad* experimental "ink-stain" example back in
the lesson on taking desire literally). In a "poetically" condensed metaphor,
however, it's *as if* the rule of linearity were broken by the superimposition
of signifiers. In the Oedipal poetry of my dreams, either one of these dark
inscriptions—"bottle of *pop*" or "chrysanthe*mum*"—would *seem* to break the
syntagmatic rule and would *seem* to allow unconscious desire to enunciate
two elements simultaneously ("as one flesh," so to speak). And this illicit
enunciation transpires without *das Ich* quite catching on to what *das Es* is
actually saying—that *I(t)* really *do(es)* want to have "a father kill'd, a mother
stained."

Another way to understand metaphorical condensation would be to
reconsider the trope from Aristotle that we trotted out in the preceding
chapter, which involved being "in the evening" of one's life. Here, we see
the pronounced *compression* of a lengthy, four-term analogy (as *evening* is
to *day*, so *old age* is to *life*) into a shorter, two-term expression (*evening* of
life). In this metaphorical condensation, the luxury sedan of "as A is to B so
C is to D" becomes the compact two-seater "A of D"—linear sequentiality is
abrogated in that we "jump" directly from A to D; moreover, by virtue of that
"imaginative leap," a certain number of substantially "real terms" are *negated*
or *occulted* from the proposition ("day" and "old age" are *absent* or *missing*
from "evening of life" in much the same way as real butter is nowhere to be
found in Shklovsky's metaphorical "butterfingers").

Note that all these condensations involve the *substitution* of words *for*
other words. *Evening* subs for *old age*; *pop* as bottle subs for *pop* as father;
the final syllable of chrysanthe*mum* stands in for a name bestowed upon my
poor mother, etc. "*One word for another*: this is the formula for metaphor,"
writes Lacan, "and if you are a poet you will make it into a game and produce
a continuous stream, nay, a dazzling weave of metaphors" (1966e/2006:
422). And yet, the *meaningful* continuity of any verbal stream, however
metaphorically dazzling, will always depend upon the horizontal drift of
metonymy, for "metonymy is based on the *word-to-word* nature" of the
syntagmatic thread of verbal behavior. Lacan thus "designate[s] as metonymy
the first aspect of the actual field the signifier constitutes, so that meaning may
assume a place there" (1966e/2006: 421). Because any "meaning" not only

"may" but *must* assume its place *in line*, because the "word-to-word" basis of metonymy can be associated with the *linear* and *sequential* structure of the completely "woven" sentence, and because we *read* sentences not "all at once" but only by *moving* or *transferring* our attention, our perceptual **cathexis** or investment, from one word *to* the next along the chain of contiguous signifiers, Lacan associates the syntagmatic *metonymy* of structural linguistics with the somnambulant *displacement* of the Freudian dreamwork.

Lacan also links the substitutive, word-*for*-word condensations of metaphor with "the very mechanism by which symptoms, in the analytic sense, are determined."

> Between the enigmatic signifier of sexual trauma and the term it comes to replace in a signifying chain, a spark flies that fixes in a symptom—a metaphor in which flesh or function is taken as a signifying element— the signification, that is inaccessible to the conscious subject, by which the symptom may be dissolved. (1966e/2006: 431)

Moreover, Lacan associates the "*word-to-word* nature" of metonymy with "literal" desire. He writes that "the enigmas that desire . . . poses for any sort of 'natural philosophy' are based on no other derangement of instinct that the fact that it [desire] is caught in the rails of metonymy, eternally extending toward the *desire for something else*" (1966e/2006: 431). Desire taken literally is always *desire for something else* because meaning always *lacks* being, because "no signification can be sustained except by reference to another signification" (1966e/2006: 415), because "in language there are only differences *without positive terms*" (Saussure 1959: 120), etc. "Whence we can say that it is in the chain of the signifier that meaning [emptily] *insists*, but that none of the chain's elements [positively] *consists* in the signification it can provide at that very moment" (Lacan 1966e/2006: 419). Mixing, then, the *adventures* of metaphor and metonymy with the *insistence* of the letter in the unconscious, Lacan insists that "there is no other way to conceive of the indestructibility of unconscious desire" than to *imagine* that "it is the truth of what this desire has been in his history that the subject cries out through his symptom" (1966e/2006: 431).

And *that*, for crying out loud, is why Lacan imagines that the unconscious is structured *like* a language. But for Lacan the "crying game" of the "talking cure" involves a fundamental question—a question of the relation between the *idea* that the unconscious is structured *like* a language and the *history* of a subject who has conventionally been expected to posture *like* a boy *or* a girl, to *signify as* a boy *or* a girl, to take its place in *one* line or the *other* whenever two *different* lines *form*. Like linear language for Saussure, sex for Lacan is a form and not a substance; for him, linguistic structure always involves this "binary" question of sexual difference, the metaphorical/metonymical "question of being and . . . its lack" (1966e/2006: 439). As we'll see in the next *section* (another word, come to think of it, like "sex," derived from *secare*), the question of sexual difference is in Lacan's view the question of *being* versus *meaning*, of *being* versus *having* something infamously called . . .

III. "the phallus"—for lack of a worser word

The first thing one wants to say about **the phallus** is that it isn't the penis. It's not an anatomical "object" of any kind, and "still less is it the organ—penis or clitoris—that it symbolizes." Rather, as Lacan insists in "The Signification of the Phallus," "the phallus is a signifier . . . the signifier that is destined to designate meaning effects as a whole, insofar as the signifier conditions them by its presence as signifier" (1966f/2006: 579). The phallus stands for what "meaning effects as a whole" are destined to stand for: namely, that

> man cannot aim at being whole (at the "total personality" . . .) once the play of displacement and condensation to which he is destined in the exercise of his functions marks his relation, as a subject, to the signifier. The phallus is the privileged signifier of this mark in which the role of **Logos** is wedded to the advent of desire. (1966f/2006: 581)[3]

In other words, what "the phallus" means is that Freud's "anatomy is destiny" can pretty much go hang. For the phallus designates the fact that anatomy *isn't* "destiny" for *any* subject of human reality, whether possessed of penis or clitoris; it "means" that whatever any of us has or doesn't, none of us can ever "aim at being whole," at being *all there,* in the "exercise" of our "functions" within the domain of articulation. Because there is no "natural history" of human desire, because our destiny is forever subject to the play

---

[3] "*Logos* is Greek for 'word,' as well as truth, reason, logic, law. Since Plato, logos has stood as the transcendent grounding principle of order and reason that confers meaning on discourse. It constitutes the origin of truth" (Childers and Hentzi 1995: 172–3). Correspondingly, **logocentrism** is "a word coined by Jacques Derrida . . . to describe the form of metaphysics that understands writing as merely a representation of speech, which is privileged because the utterance is present simultaneously to both speaker and listener, a situation that seems to guarantee the transmission of meaning" (Childers and Hentzi 1995: 172). Now, because Lacan couples "the phallus" as a "privileged signifier" with "the Logos" as "origin of truth," he stands accused, by Derrida and others, of being **phallogocentric**, a term which Eagleton suggests that "we might roughly translate as 'cocksure'" (1983/1996: 164). We will, to be sure, have more to say about phallogocentrism later on.

of metaphorical condensation and metonymical displacement, the only "wholes" we can ever "aim at" are grammatically completed sentences—even if no single, fully predicated sentence (and certainly not this one) can ever really satisfy its speaker's desire for completion.

The phallus thus not only "isn't the organ—penis or clitoris—that it symbolizes" but "stands for" nothing other than the fact that *it isn't*. Signifying nothing but its own disappearance, the phallus *isn't* anything and *isn't* everything but "stands for" the fact that "everything in language is negative" (Saussure 1959: 120). Without actually being "a natural fact," the phallus stands for the fact that language is by nature fictional; it really symbolizes nothing but the fact that the symbolic isn't the real. In the most obviously "sexual" terms, the phallus not only isn't the penis but signifies the fact that the *signifier* "penis" *isn't* the *signified* "penis" any more than the *word* "clitoris" gets to be a real clitoris. If words like "penis" and "clitoris" were *really* penises and clitorises, then one could caress, kiss, lick and perchance excite and/or arouse them; one could erotically rub the words together, like sticks, and make a sort of fire. The phallus signifies the fact that *one can't*. The phallus signifies the hard fact that the word "penis" *lacks* a real penis, that the word "clitoris" *lacks* the actual organ. But the phallus also signifies the ostensibly "non-sexual" fact that a *phrase* like, say, "stick of butter" isn't really a stick of butter. In other words, for Lacan, the shadow of the phallus extends across the entire field of signification, designating "meaning effects as a whole" whether any real organs or buttered holes are involved in the signifying act or not—the ostentatiously "sexual" word "phallus" signifies the seemingly "non-sexual" fact that "the signifier" *qua* signifier *lacks* "the signified," that the word *qua* word *lacks* "the real thing," that the subject *qua* subject *lacks* the undifferentiated real. Lacan's phallus is thus the specifically privileged "signifier of lack" *in general*.

The idea that the Lacanian phallus signifies these linguistic negations, these sad-assed "facts of life"—*it isn't, one can't*—means that the phallus is "not unrelated," as Lacan puts it, to the bar that separates signifier from signified in the Saussurean algorithm—

$$\frac{S}{s}$$

—which "is to be read," Lacan writes, "as follows: signifier over the signified, 'over' corresponding to the bar separating the two levels" (1966e/2006: 415). But while Saussure reads the algorithm's horizontal line as *uniting* signifier with signified, comparing "the two levels" to the recto and verso of a single sheet of paper, Lacan likens the same line to a *bar of prohibition*, a significant *barrier* instantiating the aforementioned negations—*it isn't, one can't.* To show the difference between Saussure's paper-thin "line" and his own thicker and longer "bar," Lacan pulls out what he calls Saussure's "faulty illustration" of the signifier/signified dispensation—the signifying word TREE suspended over a horizontal line that *joins* the word to what's below it—an arboreal icon representing the signified *concept* of a tree—and he "replace[s] this illustration with another, which can be considered more correct" (1966e/2006: 416)— the words GENTLEMEN and LADIES situated above a horizontal bar that *separates* them from "the image of two twin doors" below, the floating words indicating alternative *entrances* on the nether side of the bar, the twin doors themselves marking the physically identical but "sexually differentiated" places where "gentlemen" and "ladies" are supposed to go, whenever they really "have to go." As Lacan announces:

> the image of two twin doors . . . symbolize[s], with the private stall offered Western man for the satisfaction of his natural needs when away from home, the imperative he seems to share with the vast majority of primitive communities that subjects his public life to the laws of urinary segregation" (1966e/2006: 417).

Still shaking the Saussurean tree, Lacan goes on to play "scrabble" with the French word *arbre*, anagrammatically transforming it into a *barre* and thus laying bare human reality as the "meaning effect" of primal repression, the laboriously primordial sacrifice of the *real* (and the *arboreal*) to the socio-symbolic order—the domains of articulation, incest prohibition, urinary segregation, and so on. In Lacan's view, the social imperatives of language universally bar our way to any simple and undifferentiated "satisfaction" of "natural needs," so that we "castrated" subjects of the signifier, constitutively *sawed off* from merely animal nature, can't, like lemurs, simply live in, swing from, or piss under trees. Lacan's saw is that everything in language is negative, based on this primordially prohibitive bar, and so everyone who wants to be anyone in our world of words *must* be made to mean, must consent to "castration" as "sexual difference" from the real, *must* abide by the laws of urinary segregation separating LADIES from GENTS, must take *his* or *her* place in *one* line or the *other* in front of the "really identical" twin doors—this is what the phallus, as the "privileged" signifier of lack, signifies for Lacan.

But hold on here—even if we accept linguistic anthropogenesis as radical *antiphysis*; even if we grant that language *must* be articulated and therefore *necessarily* involves an inaugural separation of the speaking subject from the undifferentiated real; even if we swallow the line that being a speaking subject necessarily involves a haunting sense of incompletion, of never really being fully here nor there, *why* in God's name must we think of articulation, separation, incompletion, etc., in the specifically "sexuated" terms of "castration"? Moreover, if we must select a single signifier to signify the fact that the signifier isn't the signified; if we must privilege one symbol to symbolize the fact that symbols aren't real; if we must designate one unit of meaning to designate "meaning effects as a whole," why the fuck does it have to be "the phallus"?

Lacan in fact addresses these questions with a winking nod toward "the fuck," toward *copulation*, both "real" and "literal." As he puts it:

> One could say that this signifier [the phallus] is chosen as the most salient of what can be grasped in sexual intercourse [*copulation*] as real, as well as the most symbolic, in the literal (typographical) sense of the term, since it is equivalent in [discursive] intercourse to the (logical) copula [the "linking" form of the verb "to be"—*is*—is of course called the *copula*]. One could also say that, by virtue of its turgidity, it is the image of the vital flow as it is transmitted in generation.
>
> All of these remarks still merely veil the fact that [the phallus] can play its role only when veiled, that is, as itself a sign of the latency with which any signifiable is struck, once it is raised (*aufgehoben*) to the function of the signifier.
>
> The phallus is the signifier of this very *Aufhebung*, which it inaugurates (initiates) by its disappearance. (1966f/2006: 581)

What we can take this strikingly Hegelian language to mean is that language itself never means anything except by virtue of the real's being stricken with signification. When the symbolic order strikes, signification removes itself from and erects itself above "the real" which disappears from it, which is "primally repressed" or driven into "latency" by it. Once language cuts into the signifiable real, "everything" becomes no longer simply *signifiable* but irrevocably *significant.*

Once language cuts in, "everything" must split along one side or the other of the *horizontal* bar separating the signifier from the signified, and for Lacan this *symbolic* segregation is "not unrelated" to the conventional *social* imperative that "everybody" must flock to the left or right of the *vertical* line separating urinating **LADIES** from **GENTS**. Once language cuts in and we're made to "stand in line" in the public domain of articulation/urination, every erstwhile "total whole" and every formerly "oceanic feeling" *sexually divides* into signifiers and signifieds—signifiers that are *barred* from being signifieds, signs that are *separated* from formlessly immediate experience, words that *bar* us from any *simple* satisfaction of any of our "natural needs when away from home."

Granted, none of the preceding *fully* answers the question of why "the phallus" *must* be "the privileged signifier" of the real's necessary disappearance from signification, but that's because the phallus ensures that nothing can ever *fully* answer that question or fully *satisfy* anyone who asks. Lacan, however, does lay out some strategically *unsatisfying* answers in "The Signification of the Phallus," using his "privileged signifier" to rewrite Freud's basic Oedipal scenario.

To employ a couple of titles, let's say that in Freud's account "The Dissolution of the Oedipus Complex" is brought about by "Some Psychical Consequences of the Anatomical Distinction Between the Sexes." In Freud's terms, "dissolving" one's Oedipus complex involves letting go of one's desire to possess the mother and dispatch the father. *Initially*, all of us polymorphously perverse little children—blithely oblivious to the aforementioned anatomical distinction and its possible psychical consequences—share this *same* desire, "boys" and "girls" *alike* (both, that is, want to "be" with the mother, which means that the little boy's pleasure principle is from a certain perspective already conveniently "heterosexual," the little girl's not so much). *Eventually*, both of "the sexes" will be led to "dissolve" their complexes, albeit for distinctly different reasons, and these contrasting dissolutions pave the way for us to arrive at our "normal" heterosexual masculinity *or* femininity. On the one hand, dissolving the Oedipus complex "like a boy" involves **castration anxiety**—perceiving a body anatomically distinct from his own, misrecognizing absence as violent deprivation (the price paid for some infraction of the rules), fearing similar punishment for his own unruly impulses, the little boy gives up on his mother to safeguard his bodily totality and represses his aggression against the father in favor of a self-protective identification, anxiety thereby assuaged. On the other hand, in Freud's narrative, dissolving the Oedipus complex "like a girl" involves **penisneid** or "penis envy"—perceiving a body anatomically distinct from her own, falling for an unfavorable comparison between her clitoris and the other's more impressive appendage and thus feeling corporeally slighted, the little girl is supposed to *disinvest* libidinally in her own *active* (i.e., "masculine") clitoral self-stimulation in favor of *passive* (i.e., "feminine") vaginal receptivity to outside intervention; she is supposed to give up on her likewise "deficient" ma*ma*, who doesn't seem to have what she lacks either, and turn instead to the fantasy father-figure who apparently *is* better equipped to give her what she really wants—*which*, as it happens, is less a penis per se than what that real organ's "turgidity" and "vital flow" might one fine day spell out—the baby (albeit preferably *with* a penis attached) as the ultimate indexical sign of the big girl's "womanly" fulfillment.

Now, Freud's accounts are obviously quite problematic and have been attacked from a number of fronts, not all of them feminist. But as some feminist theorists have come to recognize, Freud's accounts do possess the great virtue of *being accounts*. In other words, despite that unfortunate "anatomy is destiny" slogan, Freud demonstrably views normative heterosexual masculinity and femininity not as biologically determined outcomes but rather as complicated and fragile "formations of fantasy" for which speculative accounts are precisely what need to be given, even if the accounts themselves are inevitably incomplete and unsatisfactory, no less "fantasmatic" than that which they purport to explain.

Lacan, in any case, rewrites and revises Freud's Oedipal narratives, focusing less on the child's longing *for* the mother and more on its efforts to ascertain and somehow to *be* what it imagines the mother desires. In the Lacanian scenario, the child—boy or girl—still wants its mother, wants her to be its *everything*, but the child also wants to position *itself* to be the mother's *one* and *only* thing, to be the *sole object* of the mother's desire, without any annoying competition. The child's desire to *be* the mother's desire, however, *presupposes* that the mother in fact *desires*, that she wants or *lacks* something, and the phallus is potentially "not unrelated" to the child's pressing question regarding the mother's "enigmatic" desire—*what does she want (me to be)?* Significantly, the phallus enters the picture *if* and *when* this "emotionally necessary" presupposition of maternal lack (she must want *something* if she is to want anything *like me*) gets mapped onto the "standard interpretation" of anatomical distinction that takes the mother to be "castrated" (she seems not to *have* a thing *like that* thing down there). Of course, the "standard interpretation" is not the *only* interpretation available even among perverse little children (or male psychoanalysts); this conjectural reading of maternal "castration" is neither inevitable nor universal—not even for Lacan, who stresses the *fantasmatic* dimension of the "presupposition of lack" and who fully understands that female bodies aren't "non-fictionally" incomplete (they *really* lack lack, as he puts it). Nonetheless, Lacan suggests that *if* maternal lack *is* presupposed, and "if the mother's desire *is* for the phallus, the child wants to be the phallus in order to satisfy her desire" (1966f/2006: 582).

Now, before we jump to any ludicrous suppositions about what being the mother's "little thing" might entail—the child as some sort of supplemental "strap-on" joyously jutting out from maternal loins, for example—let's examine the logic of this "phallic fantasy" more closely. The child in question, boy or girl, in wanting to be what the mother wants, supposedly wants to "complete" the mother by becoming what she *seems* (in fantasy) to lack. Again, this fantasy must presuppose a *wanting* mother in order to generate the corresponding fantasy of the *wanted* child. On the one hand, the *opposing* fantasy of the *unwanting* mother—the "phallic" mother as "total personality"—is basically *unsupportable* for the child, simply because there's no *comforting* or *desirable* place *for* the child to be *in* that fantasy. On the other hand, the fantasy that "the mother's desire *is*" for a single *thing* that the child can somehow *be* "in order to satisfy her desire" isn't going to pan out very well either, at least not if the phallus ends up being her supposed desire, because *another* player's putative possession of this desideratum must *spoil* the child's fantasy of completion. In other words, if "the father" already seems to *have* it, "I" can't possibly *be* it. My bitter recognition that "the father" seems to have what the mother seems to lack pretty much rules out the possibility of *my* ever being the sole object of her desire, rules out her being "my everything" and my being her only thing. And this exclusive rule, if I manage to accept it, ensures that "the phallus" will have functioned *metaphorically* as a veritable *law* of "the father."

This is why Lacan thinks of the "phallic function" in terms of **paternal metaphor** and why I have placed the *name* of the paternal spoiler in ironic or "de-realizing" quotation marks above. For it isn't the *real* father or anything involving that swell fellow's actual "apparatus" that's decisive here. Rather, "the name of the father" figures as a *structural position*, as the third term that seems to *bar* dyadic "completion" in the Oedipally "incestuous" sense, that seems to block any real sexual reunion of mother and child or any "oceanic" merger of the ego with the real. Strictly and metaphorically speaking, no "real father" or "real man" ever need occupy that structural position. Not the real father but the "name of the father" (*nom du père*) functions *as if* it were the "law of the father," *as if* it were the "no of the father" (*non du père*), *as if* the primordial "no to the real" that makes naming necessary and hence human reality possible *issued from* the *loins* and the *lips* of "the father" *at the same time*, the paternal metaphor thus *condensing* what "the father" seems to *have* (the "right answer" to the question of the mother's desire) with what "he" seems to *say* about the child's bid to *satisfy* the mother's desire (*no fucking way!*). It's by virtue of this *metaphorical condensation* of "seeming to have" with "seeming to say" that the *nom/non du père* is "not unrelated" to the phallus that is "not unrelated" to the *bar* that *separates* signifier from signified in Saussure's triadic algorithm.

So the phallus in its "poetical function" as paternal metaphor *substitutes itself* for the mother's desire. This substitution leaves the child, boy or girl, with *nothing to be* (for the mother) and *everything to mean* (including the mothcı). Fuı If she herself respects the *law* of the father, the mother will no longer want the child *to be* her little thing; she will no longer want the child (to want) *to be* with her in a comfortably closed circle of mellifluous sound and sense, homeostatically pleasurable to those two alone but meaningless to the "outside world." Rather, she will want the child not *to be* but *to mean*, to make intelligible sounds that "he"—and the "larger system" that he "stands for"—will be able to understand, to recognize; she will not want the child to be her thing but to substitute words *for* things, even if the very first of those things *was really* her.

The phallus, then, is not a thing but seems to substitute itself for the deprivational fact that words *must* substitute *for* missing persons and lost objects. In other words, the phallus—for lack of a worser word—is nothing but the word that *seems* to stand for the fact that "we must accept castration" (Lacan 2008: 41). And what it *means* "to accept castration" in Lacan's teaching is to accept the fact that we *must* be made to *mean*, that none us of can ever *be* (with or in) or have "the real thing" ever again.

All of which would seem to take us back to the question of "the sexes." For apparently the symbolic order has never allowed all of us boys and girls ever to mean equally "as one." Or at least no symbolic order on record has ever exactly encouraged us to understand our anthropogenetic difference *from the real* except in terms of some putatively "real difference" between "the sexes"—whether the difference be enforced by conventional laws compelling urinary segregation or by other myths that attempt to transform "the history of sexuality" into an essentialized nature. Compelling us to perform cultural contingencies as if they were absolute necessities, the regnant symbolic order *orders* each and every one of us to mean "as" LADIES or GENTLEMEN, "like" boys or girls, in the positive or negative terms of purely masculine or feminine "subject positions."

Addressing the question about *Lacan's* position on these matters involves determining whether his rethinking of Freud through structural linguistics *supports* or *suspends* the regnant symbolic order, whether his work critically *describes* or forcefully *prescribes* phallogocentrism and the workings of the patriarchal unconscious. In "The Signification of the Phallus," Lacan writes that:

> one can indicate the structures that govern the relations between the sexes by referring simply to the phallus' function.
>
> These relations revolve around a being and a having which, since they refer to a signifier, the phallus, have contradictory effects: they give the subject reality in this signifier, on the one hand, but render unreal the relations to be signified, on the other.

This is brought about by the intervention of a seeming [*paraître*]
that replaces the having in order to protect it, in one case, and to mask
the lack thereof, in the other, and whose effect is to completely project
the ideal or typical manifestations of each of the sexes' behavior,
including the act of copulation itself, into the realm of comedy.
(1966f/2006: 582)

Here, Lacan would seem to disabuse us of the notion that the projected
ideals of masculinity or femininity should ever be taken seriously or that he
himself reads any "typical manifestations" of sexuated behaviors as absolute
necessities rather than as broadly comic *contingencies*. In stipulating the way
those manifestations "revolve" around a being, a having, a seeming, etc.,
Lacan, as I take it, means that when the child "accepts castration," accepts
that it cannot "be" (the phallus) for the mother but must make meanings
instead, the child is also made to understand that it must eventually make
"a man" or "a woman" of itself, that it must "mean" or send itself through
one "door" *or* the other, "like" a boy or a girl. The child accepts, however
gradually or grudgingly, that it can't want to end up *being* the phallus for
the mother any longer, but the available and acceptable avenues of *meaning*
are such that the child must *either* (a) want to *want* to *be* like the one who
seems to *have* the phallus, like the one who always seems "to have what it
takes" ("masculine" identification with the actively possessive social position
of the husband/father) *or* (b) want to *want* to *be* like the one who *seems* to
be the phallus *for* another, who always seems "to be there for the taking"
("feminine" identification with the passively possess-able social position of
the "trophy" wife/mother).

Regarding "plan b," Lacan writes, "Paradoxical as this formulation may
seem, I am saying that it is in order to be the phallus—that is, the signifier
of the Other's desire—that a woman rejects an essential part of femininity,
namely, all its attributes, in the masquerade" (1966f/2006: 583). He also writes
that "The fact that femininity finds refuge in this mask . . . has the curious
consequence of making virile display in human beings seem feminine"
(1966f/2006: 584)—a clear enough object lesson for anyone who wants to
follow "plan a."[4] In Lacan's view, however, the anatomically male child isn't
biologically destined to opt for "plan a" any more than the biologically
female child is anatomically destined to go for "plan b." There's nothing (but
fear) to stop a man from wanting "to be" (or) a woman (from) wanting "to

---

[4] For more on the "feminization" of virile display, take a look, so to speak, at my *Male
Matters* (1996).

have." Lacan, that is, concurs with Freud's great line from *Civilization and its Discontents*—"Civilized man has exchanged a portion of his possibilities for happiness for a portion of security" (1931/1989: 752). And given the way our civilization still tends to withhold its love, recognition, and protection from those who deviate from its identificatory rules, it is, for Lacan, "understandable" (albeit anything but "natural") that most "boys" will desire to seem to securely *have* and most "girls" will desire to seem to securely *be* what he, Lacan, seems all too happy to call the phallus.

Whether or not this happy calling makes Lacan a friend of phallogocentrism is a question that we can address by briefly considering the difference, in Lacan's writing, between *necessities* and *contingencies*. Clearly, Lacan views the primordial separation from the real as a *necessary* and *transhistorical* condition for any human reality whatsoever, and he sees "the signifier" as the *necessary* and *transhistorical* mark of that separation or deprivation. Just as clearly, Lacan states that "we must accept castration," allowing "castration" to designate the mark of "primal repression" that always *necessarily* calls or cuts us away from the real. Somewhat less clearly, however, Lacan will suggest that while this "being called away" from the real is structurally *necessary* for all of human reality, the "fact" of our having to keep *calling* that casting call "castration" is historically *contingent* and could conceivably even be dispensed with. Such, at any rate, is what I take Lacan to mean in *Seminar XX* when he writes that for his money "the apparent necessity of the phallic function turns out to be mere contingency" (1975/1998: 94).

Not that it's easy to understand what Lacan "really" means in any of his writings—of all the writing called theoretical, Lacan's is perhaps the most difficult. But Lacan's specific difficulty—so productive of his reader's feelings of bafflement, malaise, and non-self-identity—could be what finally undermines the argument that Lacan not only diagnoses but endorses phallogocentrism or unambiguously wants to enforce the patriarchal law of the father. For if "phallogocentrism" can be taken as a fairly recent word for that "image of perfectly self-present meaning" which has long constituted "the underlying ideal of Western culture" (Johnson 1981: ix); if, as Donna Harraway puts it, the ideal of "perfect communication" and of "one code that translates all meaning perfectly" is in fact phallogocentrism's "central dogma" (1985/2008: 345), then, however "cocksure" he may have been of himself as a man, it would seem hard to justify tagging Lacan's *writing* as phallogocentric, given the ostentatious imperfection and incompletion that pervades his every *écrit*. Perhaps the "fact" that we find nothing but resolute **indetermanence** at the *center* of Lacan's purportedly "modern" or "structuralist" thought can metonymically displace it (and us) into some sort of anti-phallogocentric *postmodernism*—perhaps even into "a queer poststructuralism of the psyche" (Butler 2004: 44).[5] Maybe the fact that Lacan's "center [is one we] cannot hold" is what makes his theoretical writing neither dogmatically *rigid* nor relativistically *limp* but rather excessively *rich*—if not, at the end of the day, "the richest."

Coming to Terms

Critical Keywords encountered in Lesson Eight:

iconic, indexical, and symbolic signs, signifier/signified, syntagmatic/
paradigmatic, horizontal/vertical axes, synecdoche, metalanguage,
condensation/displacement, symptom, cathexis, the phallus, logos,
logocentrism, phallogocentrism, castration anxiety, *penisneid*,
paternal metaphor, indetermanence

---

[5] The word **indetermanence** is used by Ihab Hassan "to designate two central tendencies in postmodernism, indeterminacy and immanence" (Woods 2009: 73). See Hassan, *The Postmodern Turn* (1987). As for Judith Butler's phrase, I use it archly, since for Butler Lacanian psychoanalysis is the *last* place one should look for "a queer poststructuralism of the psyche." My irony has at least one strong queer ally, however—namely, Tim Dean, who in *Beyond Sexuality* argues convincingly *against* Butler's numerous misreadings of Lacan and persuasively *for* the thesis that "in its most fundamental formulations psychoanalysis is a queer theory" (2000: 268). We will be discussing poststructuralism and postmodernism in the next lesson and exploring queer theory in the last.

"There is nothing outside the text"

—or, fear of the proliferation of meaning

I. Given to excess

One of the larger canards in the received wisdom about poststructuralism and postmodernism is that their proponents don't believe in "meaning," don't think it's possible for anyone ever to "mean" anything at all. Both modes of theoretical writing have been branded as "trendy nihilisms" that deny life, language, or literature any significance whatsoever. But this charge of "nihilism" rather badly misses its mark, for, as we will learn in this lesson, poststructuralist and postmodernist writers actually fall quite short of affirming that life, language, and literature have "no meaning." Rather, such writers examine our *fear* that human reality generates far *too many* meanings, produces way *too much* interpretation. They trace and engage—but attempt never to assuage—our pervasive anxieties about *semiotic excess.*

For to return to a key figure who we haven't mentioned in a while, these writers have read their *Nietzsche,* who thought that we should neither "wish to divest existence of its *rich ambiguity"* nor ever "reject the possibility" that the world "*may include infinite interpretations"* (1887/2006: 378, 379). Post-Nietzschean writers hope to preserve and enhance this exceedingly "*rich ambiguity,"* but they also attempt, as did Nietzsche at his diagnostic best, to bring out into the light our persistent "metaphysical" wish to "divest" ourselves of interpretive overabundance; they examine our "imperialist" tendency to reject multiple possibilities and to suppress alternative intelligibilities, our desire to control and contain *difference* and *alterity* in "others" and in ourselves. Far from espousing some lame "disbelief in meaning," then, these writers attempt to expose all the "ideological figure[s] by which one marks the manner in which we fear the proliferation of meaning" (Foucault 1969/1998: 222).

Chief among those fear-based "ideological figures" is arguably "meaning" itself, a word that has been used quite routinely in the "history of metaphysics" to *police* rowdy proliferation, an interpretive police-action allowing certain

readers to imagine that post-Nietzschean infidels "don't believe" in *any*
"meaning" simply because they don't buy any *one* "fixed" interpretation of
what "meaning" means. But other looming figures of fixity include reason,
order, origin, essence, presence, unity, universality, purpose, being, identity,
totality, God, man, center, truth, concept, science, enlightenment, history,
progress, modernity, author, structure, *the* unconscious, and so on. The
general poststructuralist/postmodernist argument is that these figures—each
of which has been purported or relied upon to *guarantee* "meaning," to
enable and enrich (or at least secure and stabilize) our understanding—have
also worked to impede and impoverish creative thought, to limit "the **play**
of signification" (Derrida 1966/1978: 280), to constrict the "liberation of
symbolic energy" (Barthes 1971/1977: 158), to curtail "the free circulation, the
free manipulation, the free composition, decomposition, and recomposition
of fiction" (Foucault 1969/1998: 221), to deny, restrict, or otherwise de-vivify
what Nietzsche himself might have simply called "art."[1]

The more specifically *postcolonial* inflection of this argument (for our
lesson here will also concern postcolonial theory) is that these master
tropes of Western metaphysics have enriched and empowered themselves at
the considerable expense of others—not simply other tropes, but also, and
often brutally, other people—all those who have been "othered" (colonized,
subordinated, abjected, marginalized, exoticized, silenced, exploited,
enslaved) by the dominant "first-world" orders of knowledge, power,
and truth. Thus, Homi Bhabha begins his essay "The Other Question" by
asserting that "an important feature of colonial discourse is its dependence
on the concept of 'fixity' in the ideological construction of otherness"
(1983/1996: 37).

We can't adequately demonstrate here how each and every one of
the figures listed above has participated in "the violence of metaphysics"

---

[1] Because Derrida can be playful when writing about **play**, the play of his writing is
frequently misinterpreted. Niall Lucy writes that "When Derrida writes about 'play',
he doesn't mean 'freeplay' or wanton 'playfulness'. He doesn't mean, 'playing around
with—for the heck of it.'" Rather, writes Lucy, Derrida "makes it clear that 'play' means
something like 'give' or 'tolerance' . . . which works against ideas of self-sufficiency or
absolute completion" (2004: 95). But Lucy also contends that some "US literary critics"
offer wrong-headed readings of Derrida "based on a misinterpretation of Derrida's 'play'
as 'freeplay' or a kind of quasi-Nietzschean 'creativity'" (2004: 94–5). Now, by associating
Derrida's "play" with Nietzsche's "art," as I have above, I would seem to be guilty of
just such a misreading as Lucy describes; I insist upon this overly "free association"
anyway, mainly because, despite Lucy's correction, I remain persuaded that Derrida's
"play" would not have been possible, or givable, or tolerable, without *Nietzsche's* "quasi-
Nietzschean creativity," or at least without what Derrida himself calls the "*Nietzschean*
affirmation . . . the joyous affirmation of a world of signs without fault, without truth, and
without origin which is offered to an active interpretation" (1966/1978: 292).

or operated in the service of ideology and empire. But we *can* note, for example, how the appearance on our list of the words "essence," "God," and "man" underscores the *anti-essentialist, anti-theological,* and *anti-humanist* dispositions of theoretical writing that we first encountered back in our introductory chapter. The fact that the word "truth" gets listed here would seem to indicate that post-Nietzschean theory is also *anti-veridical,* "against truth." And that's actually a true story, for these interpretive strategies do in fact follow Nietzsche in holding that there are no facts, only interpretations, and in experimentally calling into question the actual *value* of what gets called "truth." The distinction between "truth" and "what gets *called* truth" is crucial here, and for post-Nietzscheans, the operative theoretical assumption is that there's actually none of the former outside of the latter—not that there are no truths at all, but rather that there are no truths outside of particular *truth-claims,* which are always rendered in *language,* always put into *words.* In other words, and again, "theory begins . . . at the moment it is realized that thought is linguistic . . . and that concepts cannot exist independently of their linguistic expression" (Jameson 2004: 403).

Or, in still other words, *"there is nothing outside the text"* (Derrida 1967/1997: 158).

Now, an indispensable guide to understanding the paradox of "anti-veridical truth-claims" would be Nietzsche's "On Truth and Lies in an Extra-moral Sense," particularly the following bit of Q&A—

> What then is truth? A moveable host of metaphors, metonymies, and anthropomorphisms: in short, a sum of human relations which have been poetically and rhetorically intensified, transferred, and embellished, and which, after long usage, seem to a people to be fixed, canonical, binding. Truths are illusions which we have forgotten are illusions; they are metaphors that have become worn out and have been drained of sensuous force, coins which have lost their embossing and are now considered as metal and no longer as coins (1873/2006: 117).
>
> Only by forgetting this primitive world of metaphor can one live with any repose, security, and consistency: only by means of the petrification and coagulation of a mass of images which originally streamed forth from the human imagination like a fiery liquid . . . in short, only by forgetting that he himself is an *artistically creating* subject, does man live with any repose, security, and consistency. (1873/2006: 117)

These lines should help us understand the "anti-veridical" bent of post-Nietzschean theoretical writing, to grasp why Nietzsche himself interprets "truth," or what gets called truth, as the implacable *enemy* of "art." For again, in all truth, what we call "truth" exists only in the form of statements, expressions, or truth-claims, which must be made in *language*, which is by nature *fictional*. "Truths" are those initially experimental fictions that have become so *sedimented* or *fixed* for "a people" as to seem metallically *real*, canonical, foundational. For Nietzsche, what "we the people" actually *value* in what we call "truth" is much less *veracity* than *fixity*, "repose," the binding and comforting sense of security against *fiction*, against the wild *proliferation* of fiction, that "knowing the truth" would seem to provide. If (as Nietzsche's story goes) the "eternal verities" could ever be *honest* about themselves, if "an honest truth" weren't a contradiction in terms, then "truth" would just have to fess up to being fiction, simply another form of *art*, and certain *pro-veridical* disciplines—religion, philosophy, history, science—would have to acknowledge their own imaginative, rhetorical, performative, or "literary" statuses as well. *Art* can remain luxuriantly *artistic* while still being completely honest in and about its utter mendacity. But neither "truth" nor its attendant discourses can afford to be truthful about themselves without becoming truly *other* than themselves, *strangers* to themselves. And so, rather like the violent homophobe who attacks in the openly queer individual what he can't admit or abide in himself, the ugly "truth" must maintain itself in its rancorous hostility to *art*, its "constitutive other" or beautiful *semblable*—hence the phrase "the violence of metaphysics."

But just as "truth" operates aggressively against the "symbolic energy" animating the "free circulation" of art, so do *concepts* function repressively against the freeplay of *differences*, against Derridean *différance*.[2] But the key to understanding what Derrida *means* by "différance," or, at least, *a* key to understanding why he insists that "différance" *isn't* a concept, is found once again in "On Truth and Lies," where Nietzsche asks that we critically "consider the formation of concepts."

---

[2] "Perhaps unhelpfully," write Malpas and Wake, "Derrida claims . . . that **différance** is 'literally neither a word nor a concept' and that it 'has neither existence nor essence'. What is clear, however, is that différance derives from the Latin verb *differre* and the French *différer*, which in English has given rise to two distinct verbs: to defer and to differ. Différance incorporates both of these meanings and thus serves to emphasize two key Derridean concerns: with absence rather than presence (full meaning is never present, but is instead constantly deferred because of the différance characteristic of language); and with difference rather than identity . . . In describing différance as the 'systematic play of differences' which is built into language . . . Derrida carries Saussure's theory of language as a system of differences to its most extreme conclusion" (2006: 173). Niall Lucy adds that "the ongoing *movement* of différance disturbs the idea of difference meaning 'a fixed difference'. . . . [T]he disturbance caused by différance [puts] the entire history of metaphysics . . . at risk . . . because difference . . . dislodges the security or self-sufficiency of concepts like truth, presence and identity" (2004: 26).

Every concept arises from the equation of unequal things. Just as it is certain that one leaf is never totally the same as another, so it is certain that the concept "leaf" is formed by arbitrarily discarding these individual differences and by forgetting the distinguishing aspects. This [forgetting] awakens the idea that, in addition to the leaves, there exists in nature the "leaf": the original model according to which all the leaves were perhaps woven, sketched, measured, colored, curled, and painted—but by incompetent hands, so that no specimen has turned out to be a correct, trustworthy, and faithful likeness of the original model. (1873/2006: 117)

Here, Nietzsche takes aim at "conceptual" targets both *political* (the egalitarian democratic movements of his day, which he thought were forcing "the equation of unequal things") and *philosophical* (the arch-idealist Plato, who believed that behind all multifariously existent material realities, like "leaves," there stands a unitary and original *form* or truly ideal model *for* those realities—for example, "leaf"; that all material things are just so many sorry copies of the original model; and that mimetic *representations* of material things are merely copies of copies, many false steps removed from the "truth").

By playing so anti-Platonically in these leaves, however, Nietzsche partially births **deconstruction**, "reversing and displacing" a foundational **binary opposition** of Western metaphysics—good original vs. bad copy.[3] While in

---

[3] Niall Lucy writes that while **deconstruction** "is impossibly difficult to define, the impossibility has less to do with the adoption of a position or the assertion of a choice on deconstruction's part than with the impossibility of every 'is' as such. Deconstruction begins, as it were, from a refusal of the authority or determining power of every 'is', or simply from a refusal of authority in general . . . Or, as Derrida puts it in one of many approximations of a definition of deconstruction, to say that deconstruction consists of anything would be to say it consists of 'deconstructing, dislocating, displacing, disarticulating, disjoining, putting "out of joint" the authority of the "is"' [Derrida 1995: 25]" (2004: 11–12). To "deconstruct" is thus "to open or unsettle the seeming imperviousness of a concept of essence or identity in general, concerning fixed ideas of politics, being, truth, and so on" (Lucy 2004: 12). As for the **binary oppositions** that deconstruction tends to have its way with, note how each of the privileged "master tropes" on our metaphysical list tends to stand over and against its "other" in a hierarchical relationship of dominance: reason/madness, order/chaos, purpose/chance, presence/absence, identity/difference, being/nothingness, god/devil, man/woman, center/margin, truth/error, etc. Derrida argues that Western metaphysics has always depended on maintaining these and other hierarchical binaries. He is principally concerned with the binary pair **speech/writing**, with the way Western metaphysics since Plato has privileged the spoken word, which seems to guarantee the speaker's living *presence* both to himself and his auditors, over the written trace, which seems to imply *absence*, spacing, difference, and death. For Derrida, however, speech is always already infected by every bad thing that writing seems to *represent* (including the "graphic violence" of the *representational* itself). Derrida reads the metaphysical privileging of *speech* as a secondary effect derived from dysgraphia, the basic fear of *writing*.

garden-variety Platonism, "leaf" would be held up as the first and original "cause" over and against those secondary effects called "leaves," Nietzsche here suggests that the putative copies, the leaves—or better, the *differences* among them—actually "come first," and that the *concept* "leaf" is *formed* only by virtue of specific operations of *repression* (arbitrarily discarding individual differences) and *amnesia* (forgetting distinguishing aspects). It is only *after* these operations are performed that their conceptual *effect*—"leaf"—is implanted in our idealist imaginary as the original *cause* of the infinitely multifarious leaves. In our ordinary "metaphysical" thinking, the singularly "good" origin must always causally precede the multiply "bad" copies. In Nietzsche's "proto-deconstructionist" analysis, however, the copies precede and give birth to the origin, which turns out to be a hoary sham—more twilit idol than guiding light.

Before leaving Nietzsche's leaves, however, let's take a brief look at how he treats another prominent figure on the metaphysical list—"reason." Nietzsche begins his critique of philosophical rationalism with his first writing, *Birth of Tragedy*, which diagnoses Greek drama's decline from the "divine" representation of Apollonian and Dionysian "dreams and ecstasies" to the more "stage-manageable" realm of Socratic and Euripidean "ideas and feelings," a more *reasonable kingdom* in which "art is overgrown by *philosophical thought* and forced to cling closely to the trunk of dialectic" (1872/2006: 68).[4] But if Nietzsche begins his critique of rationalism with *Birth of Tragedy*, he brings it to a head in *Genealogy of Morals*, where we find perhaps his pithiest aphoristic truth-claim—"reasons relieve" (1887/1992: 576). To begin to understand Nietzsche's reasons for making

---

[4] I emphasize the phrase *reasonable kingdom* here to pave the way for the following "regicidal" passage from Derrida: "Différance is . . . not a present being, however excellent, unique, principal, or transcendent. It governs nothing, reigns over nothing, and nowhere exercises any authority . . . Not only is there no kingdom of différance, but différance instigates the subversion of every kingdom. Which makes it obviously threatening and infallibly dreaded by everything within us that desires a kingdom, the past or future presence of a kingdom" (1967/1982: 21–2). The "nostalgic" part of us that "desires a kingdom" is, arguably, the part that dreads différance, that fears the proliferation of meaning, and so wants above all else the stability of *fixed* signification, a.k.a. "truth." The "other" part of us is drawn toward what Derrida calls the "*Nietzschean* affirmation" of "active interpretation" (1966/1978: 292). Derrida writes that this "active interpretation . . . substitutes incessant deciphering for the unveiling of truth as a presentation of the thing itself in its presence, etc." What results from this incessant deciphering are "figures without truth, or at least a system of figures that is not dominated by the value of truth . . . Thus, différance is the name we might give to the 'active,' moving discord of different forces, and of differences between forces, that Nietzsche sets up against the entire system of metaphysical grammar, wherever that system governs culture, philosophy, and science" (1967/1982: 18).

this claim, consider that in Nietzsche's analysis we have long channeled our overabundant "symbolic energy" into a series of tense negotiations with the problem of *suffering*. As you'll recall from the discussion in Lesson Four, Nietzsche really couldn't argue with the Buddha's first noble truth—life is *painful*. In Nietzsche's view, we the living can endure quite a lot of pain for quite a long time, even to *no end*; but what we apparently *cannot* endure, not even for a New York minute, is pain to *no purpose*, suffering for *no good reason*. Thus, a large part of our imaginative activities involves creative rationalization, inventing all the *very good reasons* we can come up with, but necessarily forgetting our own acts of invention, pragmatically using these fabricated reasons to explain our suffering to ourselves, blessedly relieving ourselves of the evil of unexplainable sorrow while identifying "the reasonable" and "the relieving" both with each other and with "the good" in and of itself.

A rudimentary example: one aspect of reality that we tend to find insufferable is unfightable injustice—"life isn't fair," horrible things happen to wonderful but powerless people, despicable creeps get away with heinous crimes, and so on. Over time, we've devised our own systems of justice to try to deal with this problem, punishing the guilty and protecting the innocent whenever humanly possible. But because we know that the systems *that we know that we created* don't work *perfectly*—and can't, in any case, medicate the pain we experience when the innocent are slain by "acts of nature"—we must also fantasize *perfect* (if mysterious) systems of justice (God's will, eternal compensations or penalties in the afterlife, the ironclad laws of karma, etc.), systems that *we can't know or acknowledge that we ourselves imagined,* simply because if we *did* know, *they* wouldn't work, wouldn't provide "relief." Nietzsche here joins Marx in thinking of religion as the oldest and most popular *opiate* in world history. Unlike *actual* drugs, however, which "work their magic" regardless of whatever their users might "believe" about them (crystal meth will have its way with me even if I discover that it wasn't cooked up by elves), *imaginary* opiates typically fail to opiate humans who "come to believe" that merely human imaginations *produced* them—"reasons" cease to "relieve" the non-duped who figure out the real reasons behind them.

Hence "God is dead" for the utterly disenchanted, modern, secular, rationalist imagination, which has supposedly left religious fear and superstition behind in the dust of its progress. But Nietzsche's whole argument "against reason" is that "reason" can operate just as narcotically as does religion, dialectically "relieving" its adherents of their sufferings, their pained experience of contradiction, assuaging them of their anxiety that scientific "truth" might relapse into the more ambiguous realities of myth and art. For Nietzsche, the "fundamental secret of science" is that it constitutively misunderstands its own teleological goal: the scientific "search for truth" has always been

> accompanied by a profound *delusion*, which first came into the world in the person of Socrates—the unshakeable belief that, by following the guiding thread of causality, thought reaches into the deepest abysses of being and is capable not only of knowing but even of *correcting* being. This sublime metaphysical madness accompanies science as an instinct and leads it again and again to its limits, where it must transform itself into *art: which is the real goal of this mechanism.* (1872/2006: 71)

For Nietzsche, then, the "reason" worshipped by both modern and classical metaphysics is at root animated by anxiety, by our fear of "the dangerous and cancerous proliferation of significations" (Foucault 1969/1998: 222), our fear that metaphysical truth might metastasize into mad fiction. Like religion, "reason" operates analgesically, spreading the salve of *coherence* on the painful wound of *contradiction*.

> And as always, coherence in contradiction expresses the force of a desire. The concept of centered structure is in fact the concept of a play based on a fundamental ground, a play constituted on the basis of a fundamental immobility and a reassuring certitude, which is itself beyond the reach of play. And on the basis of this certitude anxiety can be mastered. (Derrida 1966/1978: 27)

If, as Nietzsche teaches, "concepts" are the "graveyard of [differential] perceptions" (1873/2006: 121), if "concepts" *per se* express "the force of a desire" to repress or forget the play of différance, then, as Derrida, to whose text we've abruptly cut here, might say, "the concept of centered structure" has long expressed the coercively orthopedic *heart* of that desire. In Derrida's heartbreaking estimation, such forceful expression/repression *is* the center's structural function, or the structure's central function, and *has been* for quite some time, for

> the entire history of the concept of structure, before the rupture of which we are speaking, must be thought as a series of substitutions of center for center, as a linked chain of determinations of the center. Successively, and in a regulated fashion, the center receives different forms or names. The history of metaphysics, like the history of the West, is the history of these metaphors and metonymies. Its

matrix . . . is the determination of Being as *presence* in all senses of this word. (1966/1978: 279)

Now, the "rupture" of which Derrida speaks in this passage would seem to involve the advent of structuralism, "the linguistic turn in the human sciences." *Before* this turn, before this rupture, "the notion of a structure lacking any center represents the unthinkable itself" (1966/1978: 279). *After* the turn, after Nietzsche's insight that the "web of concepts is torn by art" (1873/2006: 121), after Saussure's insight that language is a differential structure without positive terms, the unthinkable materializes itself, tears us a new one. In other words, the unthinkable rupture occurs when it finally dawns upon certain thinkers that human reality is only ever put into writing *and* that writing neither contains nor emanates from a center. "Henceforth," writes Derrida,

> it was necessary to begin thinking that there was no center, that the center could not be thought in the form of a being-present, that the center had no natural site, that it was not a fixed locus but a function, a sort of nonlocus in which an infinite number of sign-substitutions came into play. This was the moment when language invaded the universal problematic, the moment when, in the absence of a center or origin, everything became discourse . . . that is to say, a system in which the central signified, the original or transcendental signified, is never absolutely present outside a system of differences. The absence of the transcendental signified extends the domain and the play of signification infinitely. (1966/1978: 280).

If it was structuralism that first alerted thinkers to this invasion, Derrida thinks that "modern" structuralism, still indentured to an *ancient* metaphysical dream of truth, misread its own differential significance. In "The Structural Study of Myth," for example, Claude Lévi-Strauss asserts that "whatever emendations the original formulation may now call for, everybody will agree that the Saussurean principle of the *arbitrary character of the linguistic sign* was a prerequisite for the accession of linguistics to the scientific level" (1963/2007: 860). On the contrary, poststructuralists would agree that Saussure's principles necessitated the *demotion* of almighty science to the merely *linguistic* level, the *displacement* of all scientific truth into figurative language. And this figural displacement carries with it not only "truth" but any "pro-veridical" discourse aspiring to operate on "the scientific level" or purporting to make "rigorous statements" about any "central" objects of analysis. These "centers" of science include, obviously, "structure" for structuralism, but also "history" for Marxist dialectics and "*the* unconscious" for psychoanalysis. In the essay "Freud and Lacan," for example, Althusser avers that

> Lacan's first word is to say: in principle, Freud founded a *science*. A new science which was the science of a new object: the unconscious. A rigorous statement. If psycho-analysis is a science because it is the science of a distinct object it is also a science with the structure of all sciences. (1971/2001: 135)

For Derrida, however, this "rigorous" presumption of a distinct object as the prerequisite for any science represents the big problem with big science, betraying the metaphysical hangover afflicting the structure of all sciences as well as the "science-ism" of all existing structuralisms.

In Derrida's critique of psychoanalysis, then, Lacan remains a *facteur de la vérité*, a scientific "purveyor of truth" (Derrida 1980/1987: 413) in cahoots with every ascetic idealist in the history of metaphysics from Plato and Hegel to Rousseau and Lévi-Strauss. Coupling, as you'll recall, Saussure with Freud to argue that "the unconscious structured like a language" always involves a *central lack,* Lacan "deprivingly" dictates that "we must accept castration" because "castration" is the bedrock "truth" of desire and the veritable "centre of analytic experience" (Lacan 2008: 41, 53). Writing against the castrating Lacan, Derrida reads Saussure back through Nietzsche to argue that language "more radically" involves not a *central lack*, but a *lack of center.* Derrida thus more generously advocates a "joyous affirmation" that "*determines the noncenter otherwise than as loss of center*" (1966/1978: 292)—a "playful" affirmation that determines the noncenter otherwise than in the *Oedipal* terms of castration and without any *guilt* over "broken immediacy" (1966/1978: 292) with mother/nature or any *nostalgia* for some lost ontological homeland of the real. This "joyous affirmation," writes Derrida, "plays without security." This "active interpretation" *of* interpretation

> affirms play and tries to pass beyond man and humanism, the name of man being the name of that being who, through the history of metaphysics or of ontotheology—in other words, throughout his entire history—has dreamed of full presence, the reassuring foundation, the origin and the end of play. (1966/1978: 292)

One could of course argue with Derrida about the "central significance" of Lacan's writings. As I suggested at the end of the previous lesson, it's possible to affirm Lacan otherwise than as phallogocentric, heterosexist, straight-ahead structuralist blowhard. But as should be clear to anyone who might actually bother to read *Derrida's* most basic writings, his poststructuralist affirmation of "the noncenter" hardly amounts to a nihilistic chucking of all "significance" *tout court*. Rather, Derrida's Nietzschean "affirmation of life" traces what he calls an *"overabundance of the signifier"* (1966/1978: 290).[5] This vital excess can only cause trouble in "a world where one is thrifty not only with one's resources and riches but also with one's discourses and their significations" (Foucault 1969/1998: 221); excessive différance is thus "obviously threatening and infallibly dreaded by everything within us that desires [such a world, such] a kingdom" (Derrida 1967/1982: 21–2). This overabundance of differential signification provokes "anxious" interpreters to circle the wagons around the "fundamental immobility" and "reassuring certitude" of a "center" that can "hold." But this overabundance can also spur *active* interpreters to initiate new methods of paying "tenacious attention to the materiality of human signification" (Chow 2002/2007: 1910), to produce "new concepts to explain how meaning works" (Lucy 2004: 144), novel ways of reading and writing *all* the arts of being human *after* the linguistic turn and *in the absence* of any "transcendental signified."[6]

Derrida, for his part, attempts to "affirm play" *beyond* "man and humanism," *after* the closure of metaphysics. But he hardly imagines that, by virtue of this attempt, he or we can ever simply wash our hands of metaphysics, for any claim "against truth" is still inescapably a truth-claim, and any attempt to rinse oneself clean of the remains of the metaphysical remains, in itself, a metaphysical gesture.

> There is no sense in doing without the concepts of metaphysics in order to shake metaphysics. We have no language—no syntax and no lexicon—which is foreign to this history; we can pronounce not a single destructive proposition which has not already had to slip into the form, the logic, and the implicit propositions of precisely what it had to contest. (Derrida 1966/1978: 280–1)

To "affirm play" thus doesn't mean to imagine that one has completely shaken off the last drops of metaphysics. Rather, for Derrida, to "affirm play" means to let go of the idea that there's ever going to be any really "reassuring

---

[5] "Deconstruction," writes Derrida, "is on the side of the yes, of the affirmation of life" (cited in Benjamin 2006: 81).

[6] Rather than seeming to support an unproductive "us" versus "them" interpretation of interpretation, I hope to have suggested here that the "anxious" and the "active" modes of interpretation can operate simultaneously within the same subject's "interpretive experience." In so suggesting, I am echoing not only points made in note 4 above but also Nietzsche's argument in *Beyond Good and Evil* that "*master moralities* and *slave moralities*" aren't necessary parceled out to "masters" and "slaves" respectively, but can be internally juxtaposed in one individual subject's psyche—"even in the same person, within one single breast" (1886/2006: 356).

foundation" for the signification of human reality, any natural or supernatural locus regulating the proliferation of meaning, any philosophical, political, theological, or poetical "center" that isn't implicated in the all too human *dream* of full presence, the magical "image of perfectly self-present meaning" that is "the underlying ideal of Western culture" (Johnson 1981: ix).[7]

Once play is affirmed, however, Derrida does indeed attempt to extend its domain *ad infinitum*, releasing a swarm of new terms and phrases—différance only one among so many others, like **trace** and **supplement**, that Derrida warrants his own personal dictionary (Lucy 2004)—all in the effort to examine "how meaning works" *without* foundationally fixing it *or* transporting it into some transcendental ether.[8] These Derridean "figures without truth" (1967/1982: 18) cannot be *absolutely foreign* to metaphysics, but they can *defamiliarize* its history—they can never "truly" shake metaphysics off, but they can make its foundational assumptions *tremble*.

Derrida's most infamously tremulous bit of "averidicality" is no doubt the axiom that forms the title of this lesson—*il n'y a pas de hors-texte*—there is no outside-text, or *"there is nothing outside the text"* (1967/1997: 158). This little zinger appears in the section of *Of Grammatology* called "The Exorbitant. Question of Method," which concerns both Rousseau's writings and

---

[7] Speaking of *poetical* "centers," one might say that the line from Yeats's "The Second Coming" to which I've been alluding—"Things fall apart; the center cannot hold" (1920/1983: 187)—rests on the assumption that the very coherence of things depends upon *the* center's absolutely holding. Yeats assumes that for most of his readers it will just make sense—it will be sense itself, as Derrida might say—that if the center cannot hold, things will fall apart. In affirming the noncenter and the absence of the transcendental signified, however, Derrida is no slouching beast; he is not trying to make things fall apart or let all the falcons fly away, not letting loose mere anarchy upon the world or drowning the ceremony of innocence in a blood-dimmed tide. Rather, carrying "Saussure's theory of language as a system of differences to its most extreme conclusion" (Malpas and Wake 2006: 173), Derrida simply proposes an extremely different model of coherence, a radically different way for things to hold together, than that presupposed by "the underlying ideal of Western culture" and by the centered structure of Yeats's poem.

[8] Unlike the Saussurean "sign"—which presupposes a "unity" of signifier and signified and the maintenance of an "active–passive" binary relation between those two components—Derrida's **trace** "functions to unsettle the sign's metaphysical determination" (Lucy 2004: 144). "Although referred to in the affirmative, the trace is actually a lack, the presence of an absence or the absence of presence, the antithesis of the sign" (Malpas and Wake 2006: 261). The **supplement** is not unrelated: "In ordinary language, a supplement is something added to an already complete whole. The possibility of something being added, however, reveals a lack in the original it is meant to complete . . . Derrida extends the contradictory logic of the word 'supplement' in order to interrogate the conventional Western idea that speech, as the original form of language, is merely represented by writing. Derrida argues that the structure of writing is not secondary to, but inextricable from, that of speech itself. This challenges the supposed 'originality' of speech in relation to writing" (Malpas and Wake 2006: 258).

Rousseau's representative and dysgraphic anxieties about the exorbitances of writing in general. For Derrida, however, the methodological question is one "not only of Rousseau's writing but also of our reading." Any writer, writes Derrida,

> writes *in* a language and *in* a logic whose proper system, laws, and life his discourse by definition cannot dominate absolutely. He uses them only by letting himself, after a fashion and up to a point, be governed by the system. And [our] reading must always aim at a certain relationship, unperceived by the writer, between what he commands and what he does not command of the patterns of language that he uses. This relationship is not a certain quantitative distribution of shadow and light, of weakness or of force, but a signifying structure that critical reading should *produce*. (1967/1997: 158)

Derrida attempts to "produce" a method or mode of "reading" (sometimes called deconstruction) which assumes that writers, even great writers, are never the absolutely dominative commanders of language; deconstructive reading tenaciously attends to the differences between command and noncommand that appear in the patterns of language in which all writers, even great writers, participate. As we'll soon see, this Derridean *production* is not unrelated to Roland Barthes' *autopsy* of "the Author" and Michel Foucault's *interrogation* of that august figure, all of which (production, autopsy, and interrogation) were published within the same few tremulously anti-authoritarian years (1967, 1968, and 1969, respectively). But before attending those slightly later funerals for authorial authority, let's consider one of Derrida's explanatory comments about *il n'y a pas de hors-texte*:

> The concept of text I propose is limited neither to the graphic, nor to the book, nor even to discourse, and even less to the semantic, representational, symbolic, ideal, or ideological sphere. What I call "text" implies all the structures called "real," "economic," "historical," socio-institutional, in short; all possible referents. Another way of recalling, once again, that "there is nothing outside the text." That does not mean that all referents are suspended, denied, or enclosed in a book, as people have claimed, or have been naïve enough to believe or have accused me of believing. But it does mean that every referent, all reality, has the structure of a differential trace, and that one cannot refer to this real except in an interpretive experience. The latter neither yields meaning nor assumes it except in a movement of differential referring. That's all. (1988: 148)

Despite, however, this and other lucid explanations of his take on "the text," Derrida is still construed by conventional wisdom to be an "abstruse" nihilist who thought that "all referents are suspended" and that no "interpretive experience" can ever "yield meaning" of any kind or of any value to any reader. Derrida is still understood to have "claimed that language, by its very nature, undermined any meaning it attempted to promote" (Eugenides 2011: 47). But Derrida actually rejects the inherited metaphysical logic that if there's no "center" for everything there can never be any "point" or "meaning" to anything, that if "the center cannot hold" then all arguments must "fall apart." There's quite a significant difference, after all, between claiming that all "meaning" is always "undermined"—whatever *that* means— and promoting the view that no "meaning" ever escapes or transcends its constitutive involvement in "a movement of differential referring." There's a large and loudly honking difference between writing "There is no simple reference" (1972/1981: 206), as Derrida did, and asserting that "there is simply no reference," as Derrida didn't. It was always Derrida's problem that certain people read (him) very selectively, if at all, and that certain readers have trouble envisioning any protocols of reading other than those that protect their own certainties. Reasons relieve, and so, often enough, does reading. In *Of Grammatology*, Derrida writes that a productive (rather than protective) way of reading

> cannot consist of reproducing, by the effaced and respectful doubling of commentary, the conscious, voluntary, intentional relationship that the writer institutes in his exchanges with the history to which he belongs thanks to the element of language. This moment of doubling commentary should no doubt have its place in a critical reading. To recognize and respect all its classical exigencies is not easy and requires all the instruments of traditional criticism. Without this recognition and this respect, critical production would risk developing in any direction at all and authorize itself to say almost anything. But this indispensible guardrail has always only *protected*, it has never *opened*, a reading. (1967/1997: 158)

This passage, had it been carefully read, might have quieted certain academic and journalistic rumors that Derridean "freeplay" = "anything goes," that deconstruction completely evacuates (itself on) "traditional criticism" while "playfully" authorizing itself to say almost anything, or that Derrida considers all "critical productions" equally valid or equally invalid and all "interpretive experience" simply a "meaningless" game. Coincidentally, the passage just quoted happens to appear on the very same page of Derrida's text as *il n'y a pas de hors-texte*, the phrase that launched a thousand claims that Derrida believed all of reality to be "enclosed in a book." Of course, one would have to have actually *opened* and *read* a book by Derrida to understand how many of the slings and arrows of academic outrage against deconstruction were quite beside his points. But then again, one would have to have read (and not just heard rumors about) *Nietzsche* to understand how and why valid points against validity, or truth-claims against truth, or reasonable arguments against reason, might be possible or desirable in the first place; one would need to have read a few key Nietzschean affirmations to understand how deconstruction can be "on the side of the yes, of the affirmation of life" (Derrida, cited in Benjamin 2006: 81), how "interpretive experience" can say "yes" to "life" by affirming no end of "figures without truth" (Derrida 1967/1982: 18); one would have to have read Nietzsche, as Derrida read Nietzsche, to understand how reading and writing can affirm "life" by experimentally calling the "value of truth" into question.

As for Barthes and Foucault, their respective titles—"The Death of the Author" and "What is an Author?"—seemed to distress the late twentieth-century literary cognoscenti even more than Nietzsche's "God is dead" outraged *his* readers at the previous *fin de siècle*. A possible explanation for this difference in distress-levels: most contemporary intellectuals are comfortably atheist or agnostic and either don't very much mind God's being dead or never entertained the notion of one day becoming deities themselves. But many writers (the writer of this very sentence not, in all honesty, exempted) still hold on to the dream of ending up as respected authors or authorities in the dominative and commanding sense that Derrida, Barthes, and Foucault describe and deride. Aspiring masters of meaning may no longer believe in God, but "they still believe in truth," as Nietzsche puts it; they still on some level want (every reader) to bow down before the powerful figure of "the author" as both producer and proprietor of "truth"; they still depend upon the idea of "the author" to grant them serenity, "repose, security, and consistency" (Nietzsche 1873/2006: 119)

Barthes' move "to substitute language itself for the person who until [recently] had been supposed to be its owner" and his assertion that "it is language which speaks, not the author" (1968/1977: 143) both spell a kind of "death" for this patriarchal "Author-God" as proprietary commando, "the father and the owner of his work" (1971/1977: 160). But Barthes doesn't thereby represent actual writers as mere ventriloquist's dummies. The "Author-God" action-figure is arguably dead enough, but for Barthes, this demise hardly means the end of *writing*. For writing "can be read without the guarantee of its father" (1971/1977: 160); moreover, for Barthes, the writer's actual power isn't paternally procreative anyway. The writer's *actual* power is not to *originate* but to *mix*.

> The text is not a line of words releasing a single 'theological' meaning (the 'message' of the Author-God) but a multi-dimensional space in which a variety of writings, none of them original, blend and clash. The text is a tissue of quotations drawn from the innumerable centres of culture . . . The writer can [thus] only imitate a gesture that is always anterior, never original. His only power is to mix writings, to counter the ones with the others . . . Did he wish to *express himself*, he ought at least to know that the inner 'thing' he thinks to 'translate' is itself only a ready-formed dictionary, its words only explainable through other words, and so on indefinitely. (1968/1977: 146)

In Barthes' estimation, the actual purpose of this figure called "the Author" is to please and empower the *critic*, not the active writer or the performative reader. For

> to give a text an Author is to impose a limit on that text, to furnish it with a final signified, to close the writing. Such a conception suits criticism very well, the latter then allotting itself the important task of discovering the Author . . . beneath the work: when the Author has been found, the text is 'explained'—victory to the critic. Hence there is no surprise in the fact that, historically, the reign of the Author has also been that of the Critic, nor again in the fact that criticism (be it new) is today undermined along with the Author. (1968/1977: 147)

In the place of "literature," that once-sacred but now fatally compromised cow milked by Author-God and Victor-Critic alike, Barthes proposes *"writing,"* which

> by refusing to assign a 'secret', an ultimate meaning, to the text (and to the world as text), liberates what may be called an anti-theological activity, an activity that is truly revolutionary since to refuse to fix meaning is, in the end, to refuse God and his hypostases—reason, science, law. (1968/1977: 147)

Barthes goes on to suggest that the "true place" of such "writing" is "reading," that "a text's unity lies not in its origin but in its destination"—namely, the reader, who "is simply that *someone* who holds together in a single field all the traces by which the written text is constituted." Giving a big leg-up to **reception theory** and **reader-response criticism**, Barthes concludes, "Classic criticism has never paid any attention to the reader; for it, the writer is the only person in literature . . . We [however] know that to give writing its future, it is necessary to overthrow the myth; the birth of the reader must be at the cost of the death of the Author" (1968/1977: 148).[9]

Writing a year later than Barthes, Foucault finds nothing fresh in the news about "the disappearance—or death—of the author," which he says "criticism and philosophy took note of . . . some time ago." He suggests, however, that its "consequences . . . have not been sufficiently examined, nor has its import been accurately measured" (1969/1998: 207). As Foucault puts it, in a barb against Barthes and a dig at Derrida, "it is not enough . . . to repeat the empty affirmation that the author has disappeared . . . [or] to keep repeating that God and man have died a common death" (1969/1998: 209), nor is it enough to use "the notion of writing" to "transpose the empirical characteristics of the author into a transcendental anonymity" (1969/1998: 208). Instead, writes Foucault, "we must locate the space left empty by the author's disappearance, follow the distribution of gaps and breaches, and watch for the openings this disappearance uncovers" (1969/1998: 209).

One important historical detail that Foucault uncovers is that "the author" hasn't always represented everything it seems to stand for today, that the "author function" has functioned differently at various moments in the history of "our civilization." "The author function," writes Foucault, "does not affect all discourses in a universal and constant way."

> In our civilization, it has not always been the same types of texts that have required attribution to an author. There was a time when the types of texts we today call "literary" . . . were accepted, put into circulation, and valorized without any question about the identity of their author . . . On the other hand, those texts we now would call scientific . . . were accepted in the Middle Ages, and accepted as "true," only when marked with the name of their author. "Hippocrates said," "Pliny recounts" . . . (1968/1994: 212)

---

[9] Elsewhere, Barthes writes that overthrowing the myth of the Author "requires that one try to abolish . . . the distance between writing and reading . . . by joining them in a single signifying practice." He compares this joining to a moment in "the history of music"—before the age of mechanical reproduction and hence of music's *passive* consumption—"when 'playing' and 'listening' formed a scarcely differentiated activity" because "practicing amateurs" (1971/1977: 162) had to be able to read and play the music on an instrument to be able to listen to it. As for **reception theory** and **reader-response criticism**, these are "concerned with both the aesthetic and the historical aspects of reading, i.e., the ways in which readers use texts for pleasure, and how readings alter and shift through history" (Malpas and Wake 2006: 245).

Today, of course, the situation is reversed—while we can't tolerate the idea of a great literary work without some illustrious personage designated as its author, we routinely "impersonalize" scientific discourses in the very gesture of granting their authority ("evolutionary biology says," "according to quantum physics," etc.) without giving that grant a second thought.

Foucault's most characteristic arguments here, however, involve the *ideology* of the "author function," the relationship between, on the one hand, the circulation of discourses that are thought to have "authors" and, on the other, the coercively panoptical operations of knowledge and power. When, for example, we read at the beginning of Foucault's treatise that "the coming into being of the notion of the 'author' constitutes the privileged moment of individualization in the history of ideas, knowledge, literature, philosophy, and the sciences" (1968/1994: 205) we should recall that while for some of us "individualization" might sound like a sweet deal, for Foucault, it's essentially a *disciplinary* process, a sour means of reproducing power relations. As he admonishes elsewhere, "Do not demand of politics that it restore the 'rights' of the individual, as philosophy has defined them," for "the individual is the product of power" (Foucault 1972/1983: xiv). "Individualization" for Foucault is related to (albeit not completely identical with) ideological "interpellation" à la Althusser, which, as you'll remember, involves turning "individuals" into docile bodies who "work all by themselves," as if they were centers of rights and initiatives, as if they were *free*.[10] If, historically, "discourses" have become *unfree*, have become "objects of appropriation" or ownership, then their "authors," the "individuals" who can be held responsible for them—who "own" them or can be made to "own up" to them—aren't exactly free either but are always already "subjects" of discipline and control. In other words, "authors" are brought into being so that discourses might be better brought into custody; or, discourses are attributed to "authors" so that the latter can more effectively be located, incarcerated, and/or killed.

> Texts, books, and discourse really began to have authors . . . to the extent that authors became subject to punishment, that is, to the extent that discourses could be transgressive. In our culture (and doubtless in many others), discourse was not originally a product, a thing, a kind of goods; it was essentially an act—an act placed in the bipolar field of the sacred

[10] While there's no room here for a full explication of the tension between Foucault's analytics of power and Althusser's theory of ideology, suffice it to say that Foucault associates Althusser with just the sort of "Freudian-structuralist-Marxism" from which he wants to free himself: "I have," he proclaims, "never been a Freudian, I have never been a Marxist, and I have never been a structuralist" (1983/1998: 437).

and the profane, the licit and the illicit, the religious and the blasphemous. Historically, it was a gesture fraught with risks before becoming goods caught up in a circuit of ownership. (1969/1998: 212)

Relating Foucault's observation to relatively recent cultural clashes, we might ask against *whom* the Ayatollah Khomeini of Iran could have issued his famous *fatwa* if *The Satanic Verses* (1988) had been attributed only to "the anonymity of a murmur" (Foucault 1969/1998: 222) and not to the transgressively blasphemous Salman Rushdie.

Foucault of course begins and ends the essay called "What is an Author?" with a question attributed to Samuel Beckett—"'What does it matter who is speaking'"? (1969/1998: 205). Someone like Foucault might reply not simply that it never matters who's speaking, that we should never take the question seriously at all, but rather that it is *only* the Ayatollahs of coercive culture—and culture is always to some degree coercive—who are duty-bound to take the question of "who is speaking" *deadly* seriously. For if we "keepers of the culture" can't ascertain which particular "who" is in fact speaking, how can we know exactly which individual we should want to punish or silence or kill?

Foucault himself wasn't into killing off "the author." Nor was he interested in torturing and interrogating that figure, forcing it to reveal its inner "authenticity" or express its "deepest self" (1969/1998: 222). But Foucault *did* want to "change the subject," to "reexamine the privileges of the subject" and call into question "the absolute character and founding role of the subject." Foucault didn't want to water-board "the author," but he advocated "depriving the subject (or its substitute) of its role as originator" and favored "analyzing the subject as a variable and complex function of discourse" (1969/1998: 220-1). Because "the author" has long (but not always) functioned as one of the most highly privileged "substitutes" for "the subject" *qua* originator in "our civilization," Foucault thinks that it's high time to address "the 'ideological' status of the author" and "reverse the traditional idea" of the author function.

> We are accustomed . . . to saying that the author is the genial creator of a work in which he deposits, with infinite wealth and generosity, an inexhaustible world of significations. We are used to thinking that the author is so different from all other men, and so transcendent with regard to all languages, that, as soon as he speaks, meaning begins to proliferate, to proliferate indefinitely.
>
> The truth is quite the contrary: the author is not an indefinite source of significations that fill a work; the author does not precede

the works; he is a certain functional principle by which, in our culture, one limits, excludes, and chooses; in short, by which one impedes the free circulation, the free manipulation, the free composition, decomposition, and recomposition of fiction. In fact, if we are accustomed to presenting the author as a genius, as a perpetual surging of invention, it is because, in reality, we make him function in exactly the opposite fashion . . . The author is . . . the ideological figure by which one marks the manner in which we fear the proliferation of meaning. (1969/1998: 221–2)

As this passage should make crystal clear, Foucault didn't scoff at "meaning" or fear its proliferation. He obviously didn't completely discount "the truth," either, since he doesn't seem to mind telling us what it is.[11] And if it's true that we have turned "the author" into an overly privileged "principle of thrift in the proliferation of meaning," Foucault truly feels that we no longer have to be quite so "thrifty" with our "discourses and their significations" (1969/1998: 221), that "our civilization" can now afford to dethrone "author" and "subject" as original, eternal, transcendent, inexhaustible *sources* of signification, that it really wouldn't kill us to begin thinking of these figures, and of ourselves, as variable and complex functions of discourse.

Foucault's proposals are thus remarkably compatible with Derrida's and Barthes' writings about "a writing that can know no halt" (Barthes 1968/1977: 147). But maybe it's that very compatibility that makes all *their* writings about *all that writing* threatening to and dreaded by all our inner Ayatollahs, by everything within us that fears *semiotic excess* and wants to fix meaning, to bring writing to a halt, everything within us that desires to be "the author" or to bow down before that seemingly generous and extravagant but actually quite austere figure. Just as our inherited *metaphysical* assumption has been that the center must hold in order for everything to hang together, our traditional *literary* assumption has been that in order to love language and appreciate great writing, to affirm *fiction* and value its meaning, we pretty much had to believe in "the author." The truth, as we for some reason still call it, may be quite the contrary, and the deconstruction of these conventional assumptions might radically renew our appreciation, and our affirmation, of the fiction that we write, the fictions that we are.

---

[11] Though Foucault necessarily speaks of "the truth" in a phrase like "the truth is quite the contrary," his thinking about truth remains Nietzschean, which is to say that his thinking remains quite contrary to the idea that *the* truth exists, that there can ever be *one* truth for good and for all. For as he insists in "An Aesthetics of Existence," "I believe too much in truth not to suppose that there are different truths and different ways of speaking the truth" (1984/1988: 51).

II. "What are we calling postmodernity?"

Not that it should matter who's speaking here, but it just happens to be Foucault, admitting or perhaps feigning ignorance about postmodernity in a 1983 interview—"What are we calling postmodernity? I'm not up to date" (Foucault 1983/1998: 447). Foucault's interlocutor, one Gerárd Raulet, thus finds himself in the ironic position of having to bring Foucault, reputedly one of postmodernism's principle perpetrators, up to speed on the debate between Jürgen Habermas and Jean-François Lyotard about the viability of the so-called **project of modernity** and the emancipatory potential of what we're still calling postmodernity.

For the German Habermas, the "project of modernity" begins with eighteenth-century "Enlightenment" rationalism; it involves "the belief, inspired by modern science, in the infinite progress of knowledge and in the infinite advance towards social and moral betterment" (Habermas 1980/2001: 1749). Though he recognizes that "the 20th century has shattered this optimism," Habermas believes that we should still "try to hold on to the *intentions* of the Enlightenment, feeble as they may be" rather than "declare the entire project of modernity a lost cause" (1980/2001: 1754). Upholding the goal of a transparently "communicative rationality" operating within and governing "all spheres—cognitive, moral-practical, and expressive" (1980/2001: 1754), Habermas thinks that we should want to continue with the "progressive" modern project, which he considers "incomplete" but still completely worthwhile. He thus labels Derrida and Foucault as postmodern "young conservatives" (1980/2001: 1758) who have prematurely abandoned the progressive project out of an irrationalist Nietzschean aestheticist extravagance and a fetishistic investment in the notional expenditures of Georges Bataille.

On the French side of the debate, Lyotard also notes "the disappearance of this idea of progress within rationality and freedom . . . a sort of decay in the confidence placed by the last two centuries in the idea of progress." For Lyotard, "this idea of progress as possible, probable or necessary was rooted in the certainty that the development of the arts, technology, knowledge and liberty would be profitable to mankind as a whole." But Lyotard thinks that contemporary thinking has become deeply distrustful of the very idea of "mankind" as a unified "whole," and rightly so. Lyotard finds it no longer salutary to sustain the modern "belief that enterprises, discoveries and institutions are legitimate only insofar as they contribute to the [total] emancipation of mankind" (1986/2001: 1612–13). Calling this modern faith in the complete emancipation of everybody a **metanarrative**—a grand or master narrative, overarching and monolithic—Lyotard famously characterizes *postmodern* skepticism as a radical "incredulity towards metanarratives" (1984: xxiv). For Lyotard, postmodern reality comprises incommensurable "language games," a Humpty-Dumpty host of differential *micro*-narratives that the modernist *metanarrative* can no longer put back together again— "Only the transcendental illusion (that of Hegel [or of Sartre]) can hope to totalize [these language games] into a real unity" (1979/1984: 81).[12] But Lyotard warns that "the price to pay for such an illusion is terror," and he thus links the transcendental dream of "completing" the project of modernity to the totalizing and totalitarian schemes of modern history.

> The nineteenth and twentieth centuries have given us as much terror [and as much totality] as we can take. We have paid a high enough price for the nostalgia of the whole and the one, for the reconciliation of the concept and the sensible, of the transparent and the communicable experience . . . [and] for the [attempted] realization of the fantasy to seize reality . . . Let us [thus] wage a war on totality; let us be witnesses to the unpresentable; let us activate the differences and save the honor of the name. (Lyotard 1979/1984: 82)

Having summarized this French–German debate, Raulet explains to Foucault that "Postmodernity is a breaking apart of reason . . . Postmodernity reveals, at least, that reason has only been one narrative among others in history; a grand narrative, certainly, but one among many, which can now be followed by other narratives" (in Foucault 1983/1998: 447). But Foucault surprisingly responds that he's "never clearly understood what was meant in France by the word 'modernity'" in the first place. Nor does he know "what Germans mean by modernity."

> Neither do I grasp the kind of problems intended by this term—or how they would be common to people thought of as being "postmodern." While I see clearly that behind what was known as structuralism, there was a certain problem—broadly speaking, that of the subject and the recasting of the subject—[I] do not understand what kind of problem is common to the people we call "post modern" or "poststructuralist." (1983/1998: 448)

Now, at this point, you might very well be thinking—if Michel Foucault himself didn't quite get "modernity" or "postmodernity," what fat chances

---

[12] In his 1960 *Critique of Dialectical Reason*, Sartre stated that his philosophical goal was "to establish that there is one human history, with one truth and one intelligibility—not by considering the material content of this history, but by demonstrating that a practical multiplicity, whatever it may be, must unceasingly totalize itself through interiorizing its multiplicity at all levels" (1960/1976: 69).

for understanding have I? I would answer by saying that whatever is meant by "modernity" or "structure," Foucault is essentially correct—they aren't simply different words for the same set of problems. And so while *post*modernism and *post*structuralism are "problematically" related—both involve "following" Nietzsche, questioning science, calling truth's bluff, changing "the subject," interrogating the absolute primacy of "reason," activating the play of differences, protecting the proliferation of meaning, and so on—they aren't exactly the same theoretical phenomenon. We've read that poststructuralism takes the specific findings of structural linguistics (the arbitrary and differential nature of the linguistic sign) to their most "extreme" conclusions. Here, we'll see how postmodernism involves a different but related set of dilemmas and extremities.

Let's begin by considering three mutually implicated aspects of "modernity," so as to better address the question of what the "post" in "postmodernity" might entail. Let's say that these three aspects—let's call them socioeconomic *modernization*, philosophical *modernity*, and aesthetic *modernism*—all involve *new and different* ways of coming to terms with the fact that the world must be made to mean. Socioeconomic *modernization* involves shifts in what a Marxist would call the mode of production—new ways of making wealth, goods, services, tools, machines, technologies, laws, wars, institutions, weapons, governments, nations, states, and empires, what Marx himself calls the "uninterrupted disturbance of social conditions" (1888/1978: 476). Philosophical *modernity* involves developing new modes of conceptualizing, rationalizing, critiquing and/or justifying the intellectual processes of making sense in and of modernization as uninterrupted social disturbance. And aesthetic *modernism* involves new ways of making and responding to the work of *art* within *modernity/modernization*.

Modernization is the "oldest" of these three aspects. Indeed, as Marshall Berman points out, "vast and increasing numbers of people have been going through it for close to five hundred years" (1988: 15).[13] Berman writes that

> The maelstrom of modern life has been fed from many sources: great discoveries in the physical sciences, *changing* our images of the universe and our place in it; the industrialization of production, which *transforms* scientific knowledge into technology, *creates* new human environments and *destroys* old ones, *speeds up* the whole tempo of life,

---

[13] We can avoid undue befuddlement about the word "postmodern" by not mistaking "the modern" for the contemporary, the present day, or even the twentieth century. Western culture has been in "the modern" for quite a while. Shakespeare, for example, is an "early modern" writer.

generates new forms of corporate power and class struggle; immense
demographic *upheavals*, severing millions of people from the ancestral
habitats, *hurtling* them half-way across the world into new lives; rapid
and often *cataclysmic* urban growth; systems of mass communication,
dynamic in their development, enveloping and binding together the
most diverse people and societies; increasingly powerful national
states, bureaucratically structured and operated, constantly *striving* to
expand their power; mass social movements of people, and peoples,
challenging their political and economic rulers, striving to gain some
control over their own lives; finally, bearing and *driving* all these people
and institutions along, an ever-expanding, drastically *fluctuating*
capitalist world market. In the twentieth century, the processes that
bring this maelstrom into being, and keep it in a state of *perpetual
becoming*, have come to be called "modernization." (1988: 16, my
emphases)

The "dynamic" words that I've emphasized in Berman's description—
changing, hurtling, striving, challenging, driving—can all be summed up in
that last phrase, "a state of *perpetual becoming*." And this state of perpetual(ly)
becoming (modern) could be negatively compared to the sense of relatively
"static being" or uninterrupted non-disturbance that we now associate (rightly
or wrongly) with the *pre-modern* or medieval "life-world," in which there
really didn't seem to be much happening, in which everything and everybody
basically seemed to *stay put*—no great discoveries; no big changes in images
of *our* place in the cosmos or *one's* place in the "natural order"; no radical
transformations in knowledge effected or even desired (particularly not by
the church); no appreciable social mobility, much less mass demographic
upheaval; no moveable type, printing presses, or mass communications; no
particularly successful challenges to autocratic rulers; no acceleration, no
movement, no change.

Or, in a word, no *capitalism*—Berman is right to say that it's "finally"
capitalist markets driving "the maelstrom of modern life" *only* in the sense
that he *lists* the capitalist engine last. But it was arguably the transition in
Western Europe from *feudal agrarianism* to *mercantile capitalism* that got
this ball of "perpetual becoming" or "uninterrupted disturbance" rolling in
the first place. It was arguably the shift from immovable to *moveable* capital,
from arable *land* to investable *money* as the *primary basis* of wealth in Europe,
which initiated all the increasingly rapid "movement and change" that we
now associate with modernization. This shift helped precipitate the various
revolutions (scientific, industrial, and sociopolitical) by virtue of which the
rulers of the *ancien regime* (the titled monarchs of the *landed* aristocracy and the

stony patriarchs of the crumbling church) were suddenly or gradually forced to cede power to the more secular and democratic mercantile bourgeoisie.

But more than political economy, more than an exchange of money and power, is at stake in the "modern" triumph of "movement and change" over feudal–medieval stability and stasis. There began to dawn, in the eighteenth and nineteenth centuries in Europe, the *philosophical* sense that perpetual "movement and change" were revolutionary *values in themselves*, inherently utopian, leading somewhere pretty good or even supremely good for everybody; in other words, there began to form the optimistic conviction that all these ever-accelerating upheavals were not just aleatory economic transitions profitable for the rising bourgeoisie alone, but morally progressive developments that would turn out to be "profitable to mankind as a whole" and would, in fact, lead to a final and total "emancipation of mankind." In place of the relatively "frozen" or cyclical sense of time and history supported by feudal agrarianism (cyclical because still allegorizing seasonal cycles of planting and harvest), modern *philosophers* began to substitute a linear, dynamic, and dialectically progressive sense of human temporality and historicity. Moreover, in place of the anti-ameliorative ideology of "original sin" promulgated by a medieval church that condemned all talk of *worldly* self-improvement as hubristic heresy (no "redemption" for the fallen save through God's mercy; no final happiness for select humans except in heaven, and so on), modern philosophy served up the purely *secular* idea of rational Enlightenment as mankind's "original destiny" (Kant 1784/1996).[14]

We might note a sort of merger between "acquisitive" economic modernization and "inquisitive" philosophical modernity in a claim made by our old friend Hegel, one of the great promoters of perpetual becoming. In "The Positivity of the Christian Religion," Hegel suggests that the principle imperative of Enlightenment rationality is to justify "the human possession of treasures formerly squandered on heaven" (1795/1948: 159). In the Enlightenment, that is, those who dared to think *for* themselves began thinking that we should start thinking *of* ourselves and should *keep* our most

---

[14] In 1784, Immanuel Kant defined Enlightenment as *"man's emergence from his self-incurred immaturity. Immaturity* is the inability to use one's own understanding without the guidance of another. This immaturity is *self-incurred* if its cause is not lack of understanding, but lack of resolution and courage to use it without the guidance of another. The motto of enlightenment is therefore: *Sapere aude* [from Horace: 'dare to be wise']. Have the courage to use your *own* understanding" (1784/1996: 51). When Kant goes on to say that "One age cannot enter into an alliance on oath to put the next age in a position where it would be impossible for it to extend and correct its knowledge . . . or to make any progress whatsoever in enlightenment [for] this would be a crime against human nature, whose original destiny lies precisely in such progress" (1784/1996: 54), the phrase "original destiny" seems a rather pointed jab against the doctrine of *original sin* and against anyone still immature enough to fall for it.

treasured thoughts *to* ourselves, in our own orbit, rather than squandering them on exorbitant fantasies like "God" and "heaven." Enlightenment humanists thus attempted to give us all permission to start loving, helping, and believing in ourselves *directly*. Short-circuiting the old *other-worldly* route, Enlightenment humanist thinkers stopped projecting all the great powers of love and salvation onto the Deity and disinvested in the after-life as the only conceivable site for the final acquisition of happiness or the total accomplishment of our own ameliorative goals, all of which could be worked out in *this world* through the progressive use of Reason.[15]

And so began for Western Europe the languid and sinister blooming of the dream of a totally *rational* and totally *organized* human self-possession. Justifying our complete ownership of treasures once squandered on the divine, hoping to gain a conceptually controlling interest in "the maelstrom of modern life," philosophical modernity attempts a total "realization of the fantasy to seize reality" (Lyotard 1979/1984: 82). From the postmodern perspective, however, the end results of this grab at reality's fleeting ring have proven rather mixed. Not that Enlightenment humanism has produced only unmitigated disaster for humans; not that there hasn't been *some* recognizable "progress within rationality and freedom" in the Western world in the last 200–500 years, but the twentieth century in particular has shattered the blithe assumption that our taking up the dare to think for ourselves would *necessarily* advance us all toward "social and moral betterment"; it has darkened the optimistic view of human history as the inevitably beneficent upward expansion of Man's Reason.

For tooling along in the blind spot of Enlightenment's Sunday morning drive is none other than our friend Thanatos, the good old-fashioned death instinct, which you don't have to be a licensed psychoanalyst to discern busily at work in all teleological fantasies indentured to "nostalgia for the whole and the one," whether the fantasies be sexual, secular, philosophical, or religious, harbored by political left or right. God knows there's more than a touch of suicidal desire in the fantasy of sending oneself to heaven, else "the Everlasting" wouldn't have "fix'd His canon 'gainst self-slaughter," as Shakespeare had Prince Hamlet complain in the "early modern" year 1603. And, as Walter Benjamin observed in 1936, "mankind" as the collective subject/object of mechanical modernization has reached such a degree of self-alienation "that it can experience [even] its own destruction as an aesthetic pleasure of the first order" (1936/1968: 242). But of course the pleasures of totally human

---

[15] Compare Marx—"The criticism of religion disillusions man so that he will think, act, and fashion his reality as a man who has lost his illusions and regained his reason; so that he will revolve about himself as his own true sun. Religion is only the illusory sun about which man revolves so long as he does not revolve about himself" (1844/1978: 54).

destruction, subjective and objective, failed to remain merely *aesthetic* in the mid-twentieth century; indeed, only a few years after Benjamin's suicide, these irresistible urges from "beyond the pleasure principle" became *real* in a substantially "new and different" way. *If* the modern metanarrative involves the fantasy of humanly (not humanely, but humanly) possessing *all* the treasures formerly squandered on heaven, and if *one* of the great powers humans had heretofore attributed to the Deity was the capacity to reduce the world to rubble and ash, then one developing plot-line of modernity's big story reaches its climax in 1945, when we for the first time held the *real* power of world-destruction in our own trembling hands. Perhaps the postmodern condition really begins with the bombings of Hiroshima and Nagasaki. Or perhaps it begins somewhere in the "unpresentable" distance between Auschwitz as an *industrial* mode of genocide and Hiroshima as a *technological* form of mass destruction. To be sure, the new American petard was an inspired *scientific* advance over the old European ovens, but one wouldn't exactly call it progress *qua* "social and moral betterment."

So much, then, for the question of how we got to the "post" in *philosophical* postmodernity—few philosophers whole-heartedly believe in the modern metanarrative any longer, and incommensurable language (and war) games are still proceeding without morally progressing. If pro-modernist stalwarts complain that postmodernity involves all the social fragmentation and malaised alienation of "the maelstrom of modern life" but without the *hope* of total reunification and emancipation that alone makes it all bearable, the postmodernist rejoinder is that this totalizing "hope" is itself irredeemably implicated in various totalitarian daydreams of a unified "life-world" hygienically cleansed of all contaminating "others" (Jews, queers, capitalists, immigrants—name your poison). The darkest side of the dialectic of Enlightenment is purely instrumental reason, the racist/fascist "male warrior" fantasy of global purification in which freedom's just another word for nothing left to kill.[16] For philosophical postmodernists, then, the only "good war" left is Lyotard's war against totality.[17]

---

[16] See Klaus Theweleit (1987). Or read Freud, who in 1930 observed that it was not "an unaccountable chance that the dream of German world-dominion called for anti-semitism as its complement; and it is intelligible that the attempt to establish a new, communist civilization in Russia should find its psychological support in the persecution of the bourgeois. One only wonders, with concern, what the Soviets will do after they have wiped out their bourgeois" (1930/1989: 752).

[17] Bellicosely inscribing "an ironic political myth faithful to feminism, socialism, and materialism," Donna Haraway writes in her "Cyborg Manifesto" that postmodern feminists "do not need a totality in order to work well. The feminist dream of a common language, like all dreams for a perfectly true language, of perfectly faithful naming of experience, is a totalizing and imperialist one. In that sense, dialectics too is a dream language, longing to resolve contradiction" (1985/2008: 324, 342).

But if the preceding explains the *philosophical* "postmodern turn," how might we answer the question of "postmodernization"? How do we deal with the idea of human reality "after the end" of modernization when modernization clearly hasn't ended? After all, there's still a lot of "perpetual becoming" *qua* technological innovation going on in the world, so perhaps the term "postmodernization" is descriptive only in regard to certain "futuristic" fictions like George Miller's 1981 film *The Road Warrior*, which depicts the coming exhaustion of petro-industrial society as a bloody struggle between nomadic hordes dueling over the last dribbles of fossil-fuel in a post-apocalyptic wasteland; or James Cameron's 1984 film *The Terminator*, which suggests technology's relentless continuation of its own "project" even after human civilization has ended; or David Foster Wallace's 1996 novel *Infinite Jest*, which represents the consumer society of the very near future as being so fatally addicted to entertaining itself and so indifferent to a progressive or even linear conception of time and history that its calendar years are no longer consecutively numbered but corporately sponsored, named after illustrious commodities (Year of the Whopper, Year of Glad, Year of the Tuck's Medicated Pad, etc.).

But, to think less speculatively about what "postmodernization" might mean for us today, we might think in terms of a particular paradigm shift from *industrial mechanics* to *digital technology* within the contemporary mode of production itself; we might consider, that is, the way technology seems to have superseded industry as the socioeconomic *dominant* of our global civilization; and we might ponder the changes in the experiential *character* of our present "life-world" consequent to this transition. The transition itself involves not only the specters of mass *destruction* (as in the Auschwitz to Hiroshima itinerary cited above) but the "indetermanances" of mass *transportation* and mass *communication* as well. Consider that while the paradigmatic contraption of "the modern age" is arguably the *engine* (steam, locomotive, automobile, jet), the paradigmatic conveyance of the postmodern condition is surely the *screen* (cinematic, televisual, digital, terminal). Consider as well that the shift from the former to the latter effectively and profoundly *inverts* and *compresses* human space/time relations. While the modern *engine* still serves to move bodies (and/as commodities) through space at ever-increasing speeds, the postmodern *screen* serves to bring commodified *images* of bodies and commodified *information* about commodities in ever-quickening tempos to increasingly *stationary* or stay-at-home bodies. While our engines might still take us to work, or play, or war, our screens bring all of that business back home to us in a hi-def 3D nanosecond. While we still have asphalt highways upon which to drive our fossil-fueled or hybrid automobiles, the "information superhighway" (to use a now rather dated phrase) is a much more important and culturally dominant thoroughfare. And while we may still want to drive our hybrids *really fast*, the speed of our hard-drives and search engines has become our infinitely more *vital* consideration.

Indeed, today, everything *vital* seems to have gone terminally *virtual*, which is why Jean Baudrillard considers "the postmodern" as the age of the **simulacrum**, *"the desert of the real itself"* (1983: 2).[18] But because the "engine" driving both modern/industrial and postmodern/technological "movement and change" is still very much the production of wealth and power for the ruling/owning class—rather than, say, the positive annulment of private property and the dawn of a classless society—the Marxist Fredric Jameson designates and castigates postmodernism as "the cultural logic of late capitalism" and laments quite a number of its cultural turns. In addition to mourning "the death of the subject," Jameson bemoans what he calls the "eclipse" of lively **parody** by dead-pan **pastiche**. Both are forms of stylistic mimicry, but while parody, says Jameson, "mocks the original" style in a satiric spirit of collectively normative judgment, casting "ridicule on the private nature of . . . stylistic mannerisms and their excessiveness and eccentricity with respect to the way people normally speak or write," pastiche is spiritless "speech in a dead language."

> It is a neutral practice of . . . mimicry, without parody's ulterior motive, without the satirical impulse, without laughter, without that still latent feeling that there exists something *normal* compared with which what is being imitated is rather comic. Pastiche is blank parody, parody that has lost its sense of humor. (1988/2007: 1957, 1958)

A particularly unamusing form of pastiche for Jameson is the "nostalgia film," which displays its "pathological" indifference to developmental social transformation by transporting outdated cinematic styles into contemporary settings (as in Lawrence Kasdan's 1981 film *Body Heat*, which Jameson takes as "distant remake" of Billy Wilder's 1944 *film-noir* classic *Double Indemnity*) or by beaming futuristic technologies into a mythic past, as in George Lucas's heavily archetypified *Star Wars* saga ("Long ago, in a galaxy far far away . . ."). To Jameson, it seems

> exceedingly symptomatic to find the very style of nostalgia films invad- ing and colonizing even those movies today which have contemporary

---

[18] A **simulacrum** is a copy for which there is no original. The term is as old as Plato. But while for Plato, the simulacrum is an aberration, for Baudrillard, it's the order and general rule of the day, for in postmodernity simulation "is the generation by models of a real without origin or reality: a hyperreal" (1983: 2).

settings, as though, for some reason, we were unable today to focus our own present, as thought we had become incapable of achieving aesthetic representations of our own current experience. But if that is so, then it is a terrible indictment of consumer capitalism itself—or, at the very least, an alarming and pathological symptom of a society that has become incapable of dealing with time and history. (1988/2007: 1960)

Nor is Jameson amused by postmodern architecture, which, like the nostalgia film, tends to glom together different and incongruent historical styles without any sense of historical progression, and which, like pastiche in general, makes no normative judgments about its contextual urban surroundings and, worse, expresses no particular desire to transform them. For Jameson, the "great monuments of the International Style" that epitomized modernist architecture could be critically distinguished from their surrounding cities; moreover, "the act of disjunction was violent, visible, and had a very real symbolic significance," for this stylistic gesture

> radically separates the new utopian space of the modern [building] from the degraded and fallen city fabric, which it thereby explicitly repudiates (although the gamble of the modern was that this new utopian space . . . would fan out and transform [the whole urbanized world] eventually by the power of its new spatial language). (1988/2007: 1962)

The postmodern building, however, expresses neither critical judgment nor any ameliorative will to power beyond its own design parameters and is "content" to let the fallen city lie—"no further effects—no larger protopolitical utopian transformation—are either expected or desired" (1988/2007: 1962).

But if conditions are alarmingly bad with postmodern structures when considered from the outside, things get even worse, even more indifferent to utopian transformation, when you pass through the entrances into their bewildering interiors. Jameson, that is, has even less fun being lost in the funhouses of consumer capitalism than he does with postmodern pastiche, and he singles out as the worst architectural offender John Portman's Los Angeles Bonaventure Hotel, a "mini-city" that "ideally ought not to have entrances at all (since the entryway is always the seam that links the building to the rest of the city that surrounds it), for it does not wish to be a part of the city" (1988/2007: 1962). The Bonaventure is a "postmodern hyperspace" in the lobby of which "it is quite impossible to get your bearings." It is also the structure in which Jameson himself lost his bearings (as academic rumor has it) while trying to find his panel at a Modern Language Association convention being held there. Generalizing from his own interpretive experience of alienated dislocation, Jameson comes to his "principal point":

> that this latest mutation in space—postmodern hyperspace—has finally succeeded in transcending the capacities of the individual human body to locate itself, to organize its immediate surroundings perceptually, and to map cognitively its position in a mappable external world . . . This alarming disjunction between the body and its built environment . . . can itself stand as the symbol and analogue of that even sharper dilemma, which is the incapacity of our minds, at least at present, to map the great global, multinational and decentered communicational network in which we find ourselves caught as individual subjects. (1988/2007: 1963)

For Jameson's money, then, we have splendid reasons to fear postmodern "proliferations of meaning" at every level, for they are all driven by the "ahistoricizing" logic of late capitalism, in the "perpetual present" of whose invisible hand we still find ourselves caught. For Jameson, the only intellectually valid way to bite the hand that feeds us postmodern culture is constantly to obey what he calls "the imperative of all dialectical thought" and to "always historicize!" (1981: 9)—a slogan that for minds less dialectically supple than Jameson's (or for that matter Marx's) seems to boil down to constantly diagnosing *every* cognitively mappable social ill as a symptom of "the global offensives of capital" (Ahmad 1996: 284).[19]

---

[19] In *The Political Unconscious*, where he designates "always historicizing" as "the imperative of all dialectical thought" (1981: 9), Jameson also writes that "to think dialectically is to invent a space from which to think . . . two identical yet antagonistic features together all at once . . . to identify [the] twin negative [or reactionary/ideological] and positive [or progressive/utopian] features of [any] given phenomenon" (1981:224)—even, presumably, the phenomenon of global capitalism itself, for in this description of dialectical thinking Jameson is following and lauding Marx, who in the *Communist Manifesto*, identified both the positive/progressive/utopian and the negative/ideological/reactionary aspects of the mercantile bourgeoisie's ascent. Though he, of course, emphasizes the negative, Marx doesn't fail to mention the positive. For example, railing against early capitalism's already global/colonial offensives, Marx writes that "the bourgeoisie, by the rapid improvement of all instruments of production, by the immensely facilitated means of communication, draws all, even the most barbarian, nations into civilization . . . It compels all nations, on pain of extinction, to adopt the bourgeois mode of production; it compels them to introduce what it calls civilization into their midst, i.e., to become bourgeois themselves. In one word, it creates a world after its own image" (1888/1978 477). But that Marx sees this compulsory creation as simultaneously negative/reactionary/ideological *and* positive/progressive/utopian is made clear in the very next passage, where Marx writes that "the bourgeoisie has subjected the country to the rule of the towns. It has created enormous cities, has greatly increased the urban population as compared with the rural, *and has thus rescued a considerable part of the population from the idiocy of rural life*"

Of course, one might wonder if Jameson himself isn't less "historicizing" here than overly generalizing about the current "incapacity of our minds." After all, not every "individual human body" in the world gets hopelessly lost in the Bonaventure or its utopia-indifferent analogues, and some individual subjects (who are neither venture capitalists nor schizoid consumers) can cognitively map postmodern hyperspace reasonably well. One might think, moreover, that a Marxist with *populist* leanings (though that's not exactly the sort of intellectual Jameson is) would smile upon certain *aesthetic* practices of postmodernism, practices which do their best to overturn given hierarchies and to subvert all the regnant "highnesses" of "elitist" culture. As Jameson notes, aesthetic postmodernisms "emerge as specific reactions against the established forms of *high* modernism . . . which conquered the university, the museum, the art gallery network and the foundations"; they efface "key boundaries or separations, most notably the older distinction between *high* culture and so-called **mass** or **popular culture**," so that in postmodernism "the line between *high* art and commercial forms seems increasingly difficult to draw" (1988/2007: 1956, emphases added). This difficulty in drawing the line, however, which often energizes the populist academic left, seems only to distress Jameson, for insofar as he remains within the **Frankfurt School** tradition of profound suspicion toward mass culture (rather than the **Birmingham** tradition of cautiously celebrating the popular), Jameson of course wants art and thought to keep their critical distance from commerce. In other words, he would concur with Habermas that "when the containers of an autonomously developing cultural sphere are shattered, the contents get dispersed. Nothing remains from a

(1888/1978: 477, emphasis added). To think dialectally with Marx here is to see that Marx is simultaneously critiquing *and endorsing* this anti-idiotic rescue operation—to think dialectically is to hold on to the condemnation of all "the offensives of global capital"—including bourgeois imperialism/colonialism—while not losing sight of the fact that Marx actually does prefer civilization, even bourgeois civilization, to feudal barbarity, urbanity to idiocy, science to superstition, and so on; in other words, while he frequently expresses reverence for an earlier "artisanal" (as opposed to industrial) mode of production, Marx just isn't all that nostalgic for "the feudal relations of property" that have been "burst asunder" or the "ancient and venerable prejudices" that have been "swept away" by the "colossal productive forces" unleashed by capitalism's "uninterrupted disturbance of all social conditions" (1888/1978: 476). To think *undialectically*, on the other hand, is to imagine that "Marxism" always and everywhere equals an unequivocating knee-jerk "anti-capitalism"; to think undialectically is to think that if Marx were alive today, he would whole-heartedly endorse the preservation of certain contemporary superstitions, barbarisms, and idiocies on the grounds that the idiots in question are not just being idiots but heroically "resisting Western hegemony" and fighting back against "the offensives of global capital."

desublimated meaning or a destructured form; an emancipatory effect does not follow" (1980/2001: 1756).[20]

But here, a question of cultural and intellectual authority emerges—who gets to decide what *counts* as a bona fide "emancipatory effect"? An "effect"—a discernible change in the interpretive experience of "the subject," a particular activation of difference or liberation of symbolic energy or desedimenting shift in cultural innovation—that might well seem emancipatory, salutary, productive, or maybe just interesting to an Ihab Hassan or a Donna Haraway won't cut much mustard in a strictly Marxist metanarrative that views any changes as "legitimate only insofar as they contribute to the [total] emancipation of mankind" (Lyotard 1986/2001: 1613) or only insofar as they help to bring about "the revolutionary transformation of social relations as a whole" (Jameson 1988: 53). Emancipatory effects in the fields of gender and sexuality, for example, will forever register as small potatoes for any

---

[20] In general, **popular culture** can be understood as culture that is actually produced *by* "the people" and which expresses their "authentic" desires. **Mass culture**, by contrast, is commodified stuff that is mass-produced *for* "the people" by the "culture industry," which reifies and exploits their desires. We can distinguish mass from popular culture by considering the different attitudes that the **Frankfurt** and **Birmingham Schools** take toward them. The name "Frankfurt School" refers to the Institute for Social Research founded in Frankfurt in 1923. Key members include Benjamin, Adorno, Horkheimer, Herbert Marcuse, and, in a second generation, Habermas. In the Frankfurt School view, writes John Fiske, "the industrialization of culture and the development of the mass media had destroyed all traces of authentic popular or folk culture . . . The culture industries . . . were crucial in enabling capitalism to saturate people's experiences and consciousness so thoroughly as to leave no space in which to experience a noncapitalist identity or consciousness"—the consciousness of being anything other than a consumer. "The culture industries, then, were the means by which capitalism could erase any possibility of opposition and thus social change . . . They commodified people by erasing their consciousness of all needs or desires except those that could be satisfied by commodities" (1995: 324). Cultural theorists in the Birmingham School tradition (associated with Birmingham University's Centre for Contemporary Cultural Studies and with the work of Richard Hoggart, E. P. Thompson, Raymond Williams, and Stuart Hall) view the Frankfurt School's "critical pessimism" as "ultimately elitist because it saw people as the helpless, passive victims of the system, and denied them any agency of their own." The Birmingham "school of thought agrees with all the criticism of industrial capitalism" launched from Frankfurt "but disagrees with the claimed totality of their effectiveness." The Birmingham tradition "rejects the assumption that the people have no resources of their own from which to derive their coping strategies, their resistances, and their own culture." For Fiske, contemporary popular culture is unproductive but still creative—it "is typically bound up with the products and technologies of mass culture, but its creativity consists in its ways of using these products and technologies, not in producing them" (Fiske 1995: 325). For Jameson's nuanced and dialectical reading of the high/mass culture divide, see his "Reification and Utopia in Mass Culture" (1979), in which he argues that any given cultural phenomenon, high or mass, negotiates social anxieties by simultaneously staging antagonistic (reifying vs. utopian) desires and by representing imaginary resolutions to real contradictions.

Marxist meta-narrator in relation to the always much meatier dialectic of history as class antagonism. Indeed, for those who imagine themselves as the firmest adherents to the trunk of the Marxist dialectic, steadfast opposition to the predations of late capitalism and Western neo-imperialism sublates all "other" considerations, so that any new developments within postmodernity will be suspected as the free market's latest ruse, and even the most retrograde and *anti-modern* practices of sexual oppression in non-Western or "Third World" regions (female genital mutilation, murderous persecution of gays and lesbians, *fatwas* against advocates of "gender mixing," "honor killings" of young women, compulsory veiling of all women, and so on) can be countenanced, since the religious police or indigenous goon-squads who enforce these traditions can be viewed as defending their cultures against **globalization**, resisting colonization by the neoliberal West.[21]

We'll return to this problem in the next section, which attends somewhat more closely to postcolonial theory. Let's conclude this section, however, by taking up in greater detail the two aspects of *aesthetic* postmodernism that Jameson singles out—the reaction against "high modernism" and the effacement of the boundary between "high" and "mass" culture.

It's easy enough to cognitively map "high modernism" in terms of periods and players—its time-frame stretches from just before World War I

---

[21] **Globalization** is "a term drawn from economics to refer to the dominant model of contemporary manufacture, consumption and political systems within capitalist societies. Rather than focusing upon the needs of a local or national market, the globalized approach considers the world or 'global village' as its end user. Because such an audience encompasses a wide range of peoples and values, globalized practices inevitably use models of 'best fit'. Many times these values reflect a corporation's Western origin, with the result that some critics accuse globalization of favouring Western interests and norms" (Malpas and Wake 2006: 195). As for "honor killings," these "are widely reported in the Middle East and South Asia, but in recent years they have taken place in Italy, Sweden, Brazil, and Britain. According to Navi Pillay, the United Nations High Commissioner for Human Rights, there are 5,000 instances annually when women and girls are shot, stoned, burned, buried alive, strangled, smothered and knifed to death by fathers, brothers, sons, uncles, even mothers in the name of preserving family 'honor.'" (*New York Times*, 13 July 2010, A22) Given such figures, I, for one, have to confess, in full knowledge that I will not in certain corners of theory-world ever be forgiven, that I read, say, Aimé Césaire's "searing" critique of colonialism—his discourse "about societies drained of their essence, cultures trampled underfoot, institutions undermined . . . religions smashed . . . [and] extraordinary *possibilities* wiped out" (1955/1972: 21) *by* colonialism—with somewhat less sympathy than I otherwise might. Given the figures on "honor killings" and other atrocities, I confess to wanting to play a self-consciously Western-devil's advocate and ask about the extraordinary possibilities wiped out *by* these very societies, cultures, institutions, and religions *themselves*, to ask why certain traditionally vicious, lethal, and misogynist practices deserve *not* to be undermined, trampled, and smashed, even if the tramplers *are* the imperial forces of modernization, colonization, globalization, "Western interests and norms," "hegemonic Western feminism," and so on. I ask this unforgiveable question, frankly, out of a profound fatigue with the resolutely

to Just after World War II (with the greatest wave cresting in the period *entre deux guerres*). Its most prominent practitioners would include Picasso, Braque, Mondrian, Matisse, Rothko, and Pollock in the visual arts; Stravinsky, Schoenberg, Webern, and Berg in music; and Eliot, Joyce, Pound, Woolf, Faulkner, Stevens, and Hemingway, etc., in literature. What characterizes all these aesthetic practices at their heights is the relentless will to experimentation and innovation, the need to draw a line between *current* artistic procedures and those immediately *preceding*, the imperative (as per Ezra Pound's famous slogan) to always "make it new." Aesthetic modernism involves "the vertiginous work" of questioning all the given "rules of image and narration," so that "all that has been received, if only yesterday . . . must be suspected" (Lyotard 1979/1984: 79). Aesthetic *postmodernism* thus involves the work that must be done when modernist practices themselves become the all too given, received, established, when formerly vertiginous work no longer provokes even the slightest unease, much less vertigo, in the viewer, listener, or reader. In other words, postmodernism "occurs" when the aesthetic value of experimentation is itself (experimentally) called into question, which is what Lyotard means when he "preposterously" says that modernism had to be postmodernist in order to *stay* modernist—"A work can become modern only if it is first postmodern. Postmodernism thus understood is not modernism at its end but in the nascent state, and this state is constant" (1979/1984: 79).

undialectical sort of anticapitalist postcolonial theorist (see note 19 above) for whom to "always historicize" means always to blame *only* Western capitalism/imperialism/militarism—never indigenous patriarchal religions, never Hindu tradition, never Judeo-Christianity, never Islam—for retrograde misogynist and homophobic violence in and out of the so-called Third World. Sara Suleri, for example, in an article published in *Critical Inquiry*, describes some "murderous and even obscenely ludicrous" punishments administered against young women under so-called Hudood Ordinances in Pakistan in the 1980s and then provides the standard "historicizing" explanation—"It is not the terrors of Islam that have unleashed the Hudood Ordinances on Pakistan," she concludes, "but more probably the US government's economic and ideological support of [General Mohammad Zia-ul-Haq's] military regime" (1992: 768). Just to be clear, though I have no desire to absolve the US government from "probable" involvement in the unleashing of the idiotic ordinances in question; I'm only saying that I consider quite undialectical the claim that Islamic tradition had *nothing* to do with their issuance. Or let's say that I find Suleri and some others (like Chandra Mohanty, to whom we owe the phrase "hegemonic Western feminism" and whose critique of that phenomenon we'll consider in the next chapter) guilty of what Slavoj Žižek calls "over-rapid historicization," which "makes us blind to the real kernel which returns as the same through diverse historicizations/symbolizations" (1989: 50). In this case, the "real kernel" is global misogynist violence, which "returns as the same" in a number of seemingly diverse cultural contexts, and which "always historicizing" *qua* always blaming capitalism never seems to adequately explain or contain.

But let's linger with the question of modernism's nascence. Habermas is correct to say that the modernist "movement" in painting and literature began "in the mid-nineteenth century" when "color, lines, sounds and movement ceased to serve primarily the cause of representation," when "the media of expression and the techniques of production became the aesthetic object" (1980/2001: 1755). But how do we account for this modernist *non servium* to the cause of representation? In a sense, Western painting has always served that cause in some form or another, but what Habermas means is that the self-defining gesture of modernist art is to abjure *verisimilitude*, to decline "realistic" representation.

In terms of the history of *painting* in the West, we can say that the cause of representational realism was first taken up by Giotto in the fourteenth century, with his development of *perspective*, the specific technique that gives the viewer of a painting the "realistic" impression of three dimensions, of *depth* within the scene depicted in the frame. *Before* Giotto, European painting, however otherwise vivid, was noticeably "flat" in a number of senses—spatially two-dimensional (and so somewhat "cartoonish" from our perspective); temporally anachronistic (for the painter wasn't expected to accurately "frame" any single moment of historical time); facially expressionless and thematically "monotonotheistic" (for the painter's job was not to capture human emotion but to depict identifiable allegorical figures from Christian mythology). For some time *after* Giotto, Western art may have remained religiously *themed*, but it became ever more realistically *framed*. And European painting continued in its servitude to verisimilitude, obeying the rules of perspective and serving the cause of representation, even as it dropped religious content and joined the party trying to justify the human possession of treasures formerly squandered on heaven.

Painting continued to adhere to the rules of spatio-temporal realism, that is, until it entered the age of mechanical reproduction and confronted the new reality of the *camera*, a little mechanical invention capable of serving "the cause of representation" much more faithfully and meticulously than painting ever could. Painting, from then on, in order to serve the cause not of verisimilitude but of *painting*, had to abandon realistic representation, had to perform aesthetic feats of which the camera would be incapable; painting had to distinguish itself *from* mechanical photography by turning its own *autonomy*, its own specifically *painterly* "techniques of production," into the very *content* of its self-presentation. What the modern "abstract" painting conveys to its viewer is not the artist's power to serve up a slice of real life, but rather the essential "painterliness" of painting itself. And one of the first steps in establishing painting's autonomy by breaking the rules of pictorial realism was the abolition of perspective (as in Gauguin), followed in short order by the conspicuous foregrounding of the brushstroke (Van Gogh, Cézanne), the flattening out of multiple perspectives effected by the cubists (Picasso and Braque), and finally the jettisoning of even minimally mimetic content (the pristine geometries of Mondrian, the color fields of Rothko, the pure action paintings of Pollock, and so on).

All of these painterly breaks with realism (and breaks with the immediately *preceding* breaks with realism) were precipitated by modernism's flight from photography.[22] It isn't that modernism dismissed photography or cinema as art-forms in their own right; rather, modernist painting staked its autonomy as an art-form on its critical distance from "the cause of representation" as served *by* these new media. Given this steady rejection, however, it should be relatively easy to see what's postmodern in the painterly *embrace* of photography represented by the "photorealism" of Chuck Close or some of the work of Gerhardt Richter—in a sense, both painters paint their *rejection* of painting's rejection of the photographic image. If, moreover, the "essential virtue" of high modernism was its "staying power" against the "spreading ooze of Mass Culture" (Macdonald 1957/1998: 35)—against advertising jingles, standardized Hollywood schlock, pulp fiction, kitsch, porn, comics, television, rock'n roll, and so on—then it's relatively easy to see what's postmodern in "pop art," in Andy Warhol's promiscuously lithographed Campbell's Soup cans, Elvis Presleys, and Marilyn Monroes, the replicated comic book panels of Roy Lichtenstein, or the porn-inspired statuary of Jeff Koons.

But the "relative ease" with which postmodern art can be seen, consumed, or "used" is, for some, the very heart of its problem. Jameson, again, writes that postmodernism's effacement of the boundary between high and mass culture "is perhaps the most distressing development of all from an academic standpoint, which has traditionally had a vested interest in preserving a realm of high or elite culture . . . and in transmitting difficult and complex skills of reading, listening and seeing in its initiates" (1988/2007: 1956). And yet, from a radically different academic standpoint—that of the branch of contemporary critical inquiry known as **cultural studies**—it's a mistake of the highest order to think that "difficult and complex skills of reading, listening and seeing" aren't needed to negotiate with mass and/or popular culture or that the consumers of such culture are merely manipulated dupes who don't know how to read, listen, or see. A decidedly postmodern academic phenomenon, cultural studies takes its cues rather indiscriminately from all manner of Marxist social theory (Frankfurtean, Birmingha-mian, Althusserian, Gramscian); from feminism and gender studies; from

---

[22] I rehearse here arguments about modern art first made by Clement Greenberg. See Clark (1982).

Derridean speculation on difference and Foucauldian analytics of power; and, particularly, from the early semiological acrobatics of Roland Barthes, who demonstrated back in his 1957 text *Mythologies* that "difficult and complex skills of reading" could be quite productively lavished on such items of contemporary French popular culture as professional wrestling, striptease, Citroëns, and soap-powders.

But here we can let Barthes be our bridge to the question of postcolonial theory as an "anti-Western" extension of European poststructuralism and postmodernism.[23] For a major political reality informing Barthes's writing in the 1950s is the French colonial presence in Indochina and Algeria. Indeed, in *White Mythologies*, Robert Young argues "that the historical roots of poststructuralism are to be found not in the crisis of European culture associated with the student revolts of 1968, but in the Algerian struggle against colonialism ten years earlier" (cited in Gikandi 2004: 99). So it isn't exactly irrelevant that one of Barthes's more dazzling semiotic performances in *Mythologies* involves deciphering the cover-image of a *Paris-Match* magazine showing a "Negro in a French uniform . . . saluting, with his eyes uplifted, probably fixed on the tricolor" (1957/1972: 116). The cover is of course operating "mythologically," in Barthes's sense, attempting to "turn history into nature" by imposing a "depoliticized" image of social reality upon the very reality of the social. And Barthes says that he sees "very well" what this mythic cover attempts to "depoliticizingly" signify:

> that France is a great Empire, that all her sons, without any colour discrimination, faithfully serve under her flag, and that there is no better answer to the detractors of an alleged colonialism than the zeal shown by this Negro in serving his so-called oppressors. (1957/1972: 116)

Barthes understands fully well that French colonialism is more than simply "alleged," that French imperialism isn't all that great and that the "so-called oppressors" are so called for excellent empirical reasons. He understands that Anglo-European colonialism and imperialism are *real* social structures, the *actual* socioeconomic sources of "the steady immiseration of the large majority of the world's population" (Lazarus 2004b: 27). But later on in his performance, when Barthes insists that what this naturalizing image of the saluting African constitutively occludes is nothing but "the contingent,

---

[23] In *Postcolonialism: An Historical Introduction*, Robert Young presents postcolonial theory "as an extension of anticolonial movements in the 'Third World,' arguing that poststructuralism developed as an anti-Western strategy 'directed against the hierarchal cultural and racial assumptions of European thought'" (Gikandi 2004: 99; Young 2001: 67).

historical, in one word: *fabricated*, quality of colonialism" (1957/1972: 143), that "one word: *fabricated*" turns out to be a fighting word, adumbrating postcolonial studies as the site of some particularly difficult and complex struggles over the proliferation of meaning in a "Third World" that, like any other world, must be made to mean. As we'll eventually see, the *agon* of postcolonial studies pits "Third World" intellectuals who "always historicize" from a critical position of epistemological realism against those purportedly less political theorists who take a woefully "cultural" approach to the fabrications of empire—and who thus, according to their realist adversaries, end up "endorsing the cultural claims of transnational capital itself" (Ahmad 1996: 285).

III. "something strange to me, although it is at the very heart of me"

We'll begin with two quite different theoretical writers, both heavily influenced by Foucault, who describe their respective objects of inquiry in such remarkably similar terms that "the celebrated Foucauldian nexus between knowledge and power becomes clear in the arenas of both colonial relations and gender relations" (Bahri 2004: 205). The one, Edward Said, describes his object of analysis as "a logic governed not simply by empirical reality but by a battery of desires, repressions, investments and projections" (1978: 8); the other, Eve Sedgwick, describes hers as "an array of acts, expectations, narratives, pleasures, identity-formations, and knowledges" (1990: 29). Said is of course describing **Orientalism**, "the imaginative examination of things Oriental . . . based more or less exclusively upon a sovereign Western consciousness out of whose unchallenged centrality an Oriental world emerged" (1978: 8), while Sedgwick is examining "*something* legitimately called sex or sexuality," something that "is all over the experiential and conceptual map" and which represents "the full spectrum of positions between the most intimate and the most social, the most predetermined and the most aleatory, the most physically rooted and the most symbolically infused, the most innate and the most learned, the most autonomous and the most relational traits of being" (1990: 29).

Both theorists, then, address a certain "*something*" that is not *simply* empirically *real* but is so constitutively "constructed" or "fabricated" as to require constant and complex mapping and remapping. Said assumes "that the Orient is not an inert fact of nature. It is not merely *there*, just as the Occident itself is not just *there* either. We must take seriously Vico's great observation that men make their own history, that what they can know is

what they have made, and extend it to geography" (1978: 4–5). Sedgwick
follows Freud and Foucault in extending Vico's great observation to human
sexuality; Sedgwick assumes that "the distinctly sexual nature of human
sexuality has to do precisely with its excess over or potential difference from
the bare choreographies of procreation," and she stresses that "the definitional
narrowing-down in this century of sexuality as a whole to a binarized calculus
of *homo-* or *hetero*sexuality is a weighty fact but an entirely historical one"
(1990: 29, 31). Following Said and Sedgwick, then, we can note that neither
Orientalism nor sexuality, neither geographical nor sexual "orientation," is
merely empirical, natural, or inevitable; all of our orientations are inextricably
caught up in the graphic, the rhetorical, the fabricated, "the constructed, the
variable, the representational" (Sedgwick 1990: 29); all are inscribed in the
sociohistorical nexus of *asymmetrical* "knowledge and power" relations.

As Deepika Bahri points out, "the power of representation as an ideological
tool" is such that "those with the power to represent and describe others
clearly control how those others will be seen" (2004: 205). Hence, for Said,
Orientalism is a powerful representational/ideological tool.

> Orientalism can be discussed and analyzed as the corporate institution
> for dealing with the Orient—dealing with it by making statements
> about it, authorizing views of it, describing it, by teaching it, settling it,
> ruling over it: in short Orientalism is a Western style for dominating,
> restructuring and having authority over the Orient. I have found it useful
> here to employ Michel Foucault's notion of a discourse . . . to identify
> Orientalism. My contention is that without examining Orientalism as
> a discourse one cannot possibly understand the enormously systematic
> discipline by which European culture was able to manage—and even
> produce—the Orient politically, sociologically, militarily, ideologically,
> scientifically, and imaginatively during the post-Enlightenment period.
> (1978: 3)

Sedgwick similarly employs Foucault's notions to consider "sex/sexuality"
discursively, as a corporate institution for representing and dealing with
bodies and pleasures both "normal" and "perverse," both within and beyond
the "bare choreographies of procreation." For Foucault, human sexuality
is not a timeless natural/instinctual force that can be repressed but a
historico-discursive deployment that can be systematically managed or even
produced. And for Foucault, sex *has* been produced, particularly "during
the post-Enlightenment period," as "an especially *dense transfer point for
relations of power*" (1976/1990). For Foucault and Sedgwick, then, sexual
identities or orientations are always social representations rather than merely

empirical facts—like the Occident and the Orient, "heterosexuality" and "homosexuality" are no more "merely *there*" than is the "binarized calculus" that produces and reduces them.

Now, the point of this mutual articulation of the postcolonial critic Said with the queer theorist Sedgwick is that, precisely in being transfer points for relations of power, colonial and sexual relations are also particularly dense transfer points *for each other*, and that all these power transfers can be facilitated and contested, analyzed and discussed, in the cultural and political arenas of representation/fabrication. Arguably, all the dominant fictions to date have attempted to ensure that Orientalism—as "a *distribution* of geopolitical awareness" and an "*elaboration*" of a "basic geographical distinction" in which "the world is made up of two unequal halves, Orient and Occident" (Said 1978: 12)—is wedded to institutional heterosexism and misogyny. In other words, we can observe what Donna Haraway calls "the close ties of sexuality and instrumentality" (1985/2008: 340) in the ongoing work of culturally constructing both colonial and sexual relations. And we have only to glance at a few scenes from classical Hollywood cinema to see with what success the Occident fabricates itself in and as the sovereign hetero-masculine "hero" and constructs the Oriental "other" as the passively feminized, the criminally abject, and/or the treacherously queer.

Consider, for example, the entrance of dandy criminal Joel Cairo (Peter Lorre)—announced by strains of Levantine "snake-charming" music simultaneously whimsical and sinister—into the office of detective Sam Spade (Humphrey Bogart) in Walter Huston's 1941 film *The Maltese Falcon*. Cairo's calling card reeks of gardenia, while his cane-handling antics none too subtly suggest oral/anal receptivity to penetration. He carries multiple "false" passports, and hence has no single "true" national origin or identity, but there's no mistaking the various global and sexual "regions" we should suppose Mr Cairo to represent. Nor should we doubt that the violence our Western hero and straight arrow Sam Spade inflicts against those "regions"— Middle Eastern but fully nether—is justified, if not desired: when Cairo angrily objects to being struck by Spade, the detective coolly responds, "when you're slapped, you'll take it and like it."

Or consider Howard Hawks' 1946 film *The Big Sleep*. Here, detective Philip Marlowe (Bogart again) finds himself having to snoop into a rare bookstore that is actually a front for a criminal ring of blackmailing pornographers. To prepare for this reconnoiter, Marlowe conducts research in the Hollywood Public Library, arming himself with knowledge about a "Chevalier Audubon 1840" and a *Ben Hur* 1860 "with an erratum on page one-sixteen." When the young bespectacled female librarian tells Marlowe that he doesn't "look like a man who would be interested in first editions," Marlowe asserts his hard-boiled private dick-iness with the retort that he also "collects blondes in bottles." But when he's just about to enter his target, Geiger's Rare Books, Marlowe realizes that to play his part convincingly he really should look rare and bookish himself, so pushes up the brim of his hat and pulls his sunglasses down his nose and begins behaving in the mincing, effeminate, and bitchy way that codes him as queer as per the standard performative conventions of 1940s Hollywood film.

It's an apt disguise, for it turns out that Geiger is not exactly a "real man" himself but rather a homosexual with a "shadow" (a young male consort and "gunsel" named Carol), not to mention a glass eye and a "Charlie Chan moustache." But that last detail is only one of the very many that serves to "Orientalize" Geiger and his enterprises, for his bookstore is positively saturated with Asian artifacts and decorations. He's got Buddhas out the wazoo, so to speak, and all these Oriental motifs are brought into even stronger relief when Marlowe pulls out of Geiger's and trots across the street to the opposing and conspicuously Occidentalized "Acme Bookstore." Here, our hero drops his queer act, straightforwardly reveals himself as "a private dick on a case," and so gets some straight information and (we infer) some straight sex from the knowledgeable and accommodating proprietress (Dorothy Malone)—and all with a presidential seal of approval, for there's a legitimizing portrait of, not Buddha, but FDR himself, looking down on these upstanding heterosexual citizens from the Acme Bookstore's wall.

In the counterfeit presentment of two bookstores, then, we behold a spectacularly "binarized calculus," an active distribution of both geopolitical and eroticized awareness—on the Acme side of the street, we find a stronghold of knowledge and power; we find truth, justice, and the American way (of having sex); while on the Orientalized side, we find only criminal deception, perversion, artifice, and ignorance (the "girl in Gieger's bookstore" doesn't know anything about books, while glass-eyed Geiger reportedly "affects a knowledge of antiques and hasn't any"). If "Acme" is the pinnacle, the very top, then Geiger, like Cairo, is clearly a bottom. Thus, does Hollywood at its heights put the ass in Asiatic, insert itself and its powers of representation into every open orifice in the Oriental market, a colonizing gesture if there ever was one.[24]

If, however, you were to stop me here with the suggestion that I "get real"; if you were to insist upon firmly distinguishing cultural or merely representational colonization from "the real thing"; if you were to point out that no actual Asians were harmed in the making of these films, whereas untold

---

[24] For more on *The Big Sleep* in particular and Hollywood Orientalism, in general, see White (1988).

numbers are steadily immiserated by the unfabricated onslaughts of capitalism, then you would be missing Bahri's point about "the power of representation as an ideological tool." But you might well complain about my using these or any other cinematic examples anyway, citing them as sorry signs of the misbegotten *"culturalist* emphasis in postcolonial studies" (Lazarus 2004a: 9). You might dislike the way I've chosen to frame this discussion, taking my insistence upon serving up Said and Sedgwick side by side as symptomatic of the standard bourgeois Western male intellectual's incapacity to think of "the Orient" or "the Other" except in the "exotic" terms of sex, or the sexy terms of culture. After all, isn't it just like a postmodernist/cultural studies/queer theory type to revert, in what should be a serious discussion of postcolonialism, to the relative safety of campy close readings of Humphrey Bogart films to the exclusion of any consideration of history, social context, political economy, or "the international division of labor" (Bahri 2004: 201)? And isn't it all too predictably Eurocentric to keep employing the Frenchman Foucault to critically limn Orientalism when *that* perpetrator of non-Marxist historicism might very well have been not only a "young conservative," as Habermas calls him, but even a "new Orientalist," as per the analysis of Ian Almond (2007)?

These questions stem from the serious reservations certain Marxist critics hold about some of the most prominent postcolonial theorists, who are perceived as being overly indentured to the poststructuralist/postmodernist idea "that language (in the broad sense) is not only world-disclosing but also world-constituting" (Lazarus 2004a: 11). Said himself is even a bit suspect for ever having employed the discursive theories of Michel "I have never been a Marxist" Foucault. But the main culprits here seem to be Gayatri Spivak and Homi Bhabha—Spivak, the translator of Derrida whose difficult representations of the unrepresentability of **subaltern** speech "come close to fetishizing difference under the rubric of incommensurability" (Lazarus 2004a: 10), and Bhabha, whose own "postcolonial perspective resists the attempt at holistic forms of social explanation" (Bhahba 1994: 173)—a resistance considered by Marxists to be "constitutively anti-Marxist" (Lazarus 2004a: 4)—and whose dense ruminations on **hybridity** and **liminality** are thus, according to his adversaries, really only consumerist celebrations complicit with the global offensives of late capitalism.[25] Aijaz Ahmad writes that

> the entire logic of the kind of cultural 'hybridity' that Bhabha cele-
> brates presumes the intermingling of Europe and non-Europe in a

---

[25] The term **subaltern** "designates non-elite or subordinated social groups. It problematises humanist concepts of the sovereign, autonomous subject, since the subaltern has been overlooked in the accounts of and by the elite. The subaltern emerges not as a positive identity complete with a sovereign self-consciousness, but as the product of a network of differential, potentially contradictory identities" (Woods 2009: 49). **Hybridity** and

context already determined by advanced capital, in the aftermath of colonialism . . . The underlying logic of this celebratory mode is that of the limitless freedom of a globalized marketplace that pretends that all consumers are equally resourceful and in which all cultures are equally available for consumption, in any combination that the consumer desires . . . This playful 'hybridity' conceals the fact that commodified cultures are equal only to the extent of their commodification. At the deepest level, however, the stripping of all cultures of their historicity and density . . . produces not a universal equality of all cultures but the unified culture of a Late Imperial marketplace that subordinates cultures, consumers and critics alike to a form of untethering and moral loneliness that wallows in the depthlessness and whimsicality of postmodernism—the cultural logic of Late Capitalism, in Jameson's superb phrase. (1996: 290)

For Marxists like Ahmad, however, the *main* problem with the hybrid intermingling of poststructuralism, postmodernism, and postcolonialism is that this theoretical mash-up seems to demolish the very possibility of intellectual *critique* in the sense that Marxism inherits from the Enlightenment tradition. Faithfully representing that tradition, Neil Lazarus writes that "our methodological assumption would be that it is always in principle (and indeed in practice) possible to stand outside any given problematic in order to subject its claims to scrutiny. This, of course is the classical notion of critique as encountered in Immanuel Kant and exemplified most significantly for radical scholarship in Karl Marx's various critiques" (2004a: 12). Also privileging radical scholarly exteriority, Ahmad critiques the following formulation from Spivak's *Outside in the Teaching*

---

liminality are terms Bhabha uses to "stress the mutual interdependence and construction of selfhood that exists between a colonizer and a colonized person." For Bhabha, **hybridity** "refers to a 'third space' or 'in-between space' which emerges from a blend of two diverse cultures or traditions, like the colonial power and the colonized culture" (Woods 2009: 51), though Bhabha insists that hybridity "is not a third term that resolves the tension between two cultures" (Bhabha 1994: 113), that its purpose is to intervene "in the exercise of authority not merely to indicate the impossibility of identity but to represent the unpredictability of its presence" (1994: 114), and to terrorize authority "with the *ruse* of recognition, its mimicry, its mockery" (1994: 115). **Liminality**, writes Woods, "derives from the Latin word 'limen' meaning 'threshold', and like 'hybridity' refers to an 'in-between space' . . . of symbolic interaction, which is distinguished from the more definite notion of a 'limit.'" Woods also comments that "Bhabha's concept of hybridity fits the poststructuralist attack on totalites and essentialisms" (2009: 52), for Ahmad, however, this "fit" links Bhabha's postcolonialism to an "apocalyptic anti-Marxism" that "playfully" abolishes "nationalism, collective historical subjects and revolutionary possibility as such" (Ahmad 1996: 283).

Machine—"This impossible 'no' to a structure which one critiques, yet inhabits intimately, is the deconstructive philosophical position, and the everyday here and now of 'postcoloniality' is a case of it" (1993: 281)—by describing Spivak's variance from Said, for whom "the line of demarcation between the so-called colonial and postcolonial intellectuals was that the 'colonial' ones spoke from positions imbibed within metropolitan culture while 'postcolonial' ones spoke from *outside* those positions" (1996: 277, 278). Now, since "the deconstructive philosophical position" that Spivak promotes does, in principle and in practice, question *all* lines of demarcation and *all* resulting positions or dispositions, deconstruction and the general "consent to theoretical postmodernity" (Ahmad 1996: 283) would indeed seem to disturb, if not destroy, the Enlightenment ideal of a *pure* critical *exteriority*, the traditional scholarly ideal of speaking "truth"—even "truth to power"—from some absolutely objective outside.

But do deconstruction and postmodernism in their exceedingly Nietzschean inheritance truly kill the switch on "critique" altogether? Must "critique" always establish its Enlightenment *bona fides*, its *pure* exteriority to its problematic, to count as having *any* resistant or transformative value, any potential for generating any emancipatory effects whatsoever? Can scholars not attempt to critique particular structures that they could never help but intimately inhabit? Is there nothing but untethered moral loneliness to be gained from an "extimate" critique of (but still in) postmodern indetermanance? The postmodern/poststructuralist answer to these questions is that there's no compelling reason, after all, why the lack of pure exteriority, the "interpretive experience" of liminal hybridity, or the actually lived "coincidence of utter alterity with absolute proximity" (Žižek 1999/2008: 368) should stop anyone from addressing a problematic, subjecting competing truth-claims to scrutiny, or exposing a particular logic as being "governed not simply by empirical reality but by a battery of desires, repressions, investments and projections" (Said 1978: 8).

But perhaps, in a spirit of postmodern modesty, a responsible scholar in and of "the everyday here and now" really should stop short of imagining that he or she addresses any problematic from some Archimedean point purely exterior to it, much less that the "subject position" or cognitive encampment from which one launches one's critique is itself anything other than an all-too-human battery of desires, repressions, investments and projections, "something strange to me, although it is at the very heart of me" (Lacan 1986/1992: 71). In other words, in the interests of "getting real," of being responsive *to* (neither completely outside *of* nor utterly complicit *with*) our times, one might cease dreaming that one can finally hoist one's critical fabrications up the long flagpole of transcendence and into the immaculate ether of some purely exterior "truth." One might call time-out (or even game-over) on this metaphysical dream, this fantasy of truly seizing reality, without thereby sacrificing theoretical militancy, without admitting surrender, capitulation, or defeat. Perhaps deconstruction as radically "extimate" critique—beginning "from a refusal of the authority or determining power of every 'is'" (Lucy 2004: 11), committed to the cause of "dislocating, displacing, disarticulating, disjoining, putting 'out of joint' the authority of [any] 'is'" (Derrida 1995: 25)—*is* "constitutively anti-Marx*ist*" or an exercise in "apocalyptic anti-Marx*ism*," to repeat the words of Lazarus and Ahmad. But such a critique could never hope to remain proliferatively deconstructive while at the same time *totally* opposing the emancipatory project of modernity or *absolutely* dispossessing itself from what Derrida calls the "spiritual inheritance" of Marx.[26]

Such, one might say, would be the "anti-metanarrative" lesson of deconstruction, the "extra-moral" moral of the postmodern story. And "hence"—as Foucault *did* say at the end of an essay called "Truth and Power"—"the [ongoing] importance of Nietzsche" (1977/2000: 133).

Coming to Terms

Critical Keywords encountered in Lesson Nine:

Difference, deconstruction, binary opposition, speech/writing, reception theory/reader response, project of modernity, metanarrative, simulacrum, parody/pastiche, mass/popular culture, Frankfurt/Birmingham Schools, globalization, cultural studies, Orientalism, subaltern, hybridity, liminality

---

[26] Derrida speaks complexly, but affirmatively of this inheritance throughout *Specters of Marx* (1994). Marxists of various stripes speak complexly but not always affirmatively of Derrida in *Ghostly Demarcations* (Sprinker, ed., 1999).

"One is not born a woman"

—on making the world queerer than ever

I. My (male feminist) credo

In her feminist landmark *The Second Sex*, Simone de Beauvoir asserts that "one is not born, but rather becomes, a woman" (1949/1989: 267). One might think that Beauvoir's claim, issued over 60 years ago, would be relatively uncontroversial—at least among educated adults performing something like intellectual work in the public sphere—today. If, that is, one has understood, as per our early lessons, that human reality *must* be *made* to *mean*, and that our species' prematurity at birth necessitates that no little animal at the mercy of language is ever born already fully *humanized*, much less "essentially" *gendered*, then the question of whether or not one "agrees" with Beauvoir's observation is pretty much a no-brainer. Or if one has grasped Lacan's argument that "Woman does not exist" (1975/1998: 7)— that *women* exist but that "Woman" is a product of male fantasy, a symptom of what Roland Barthes calls "this disease of thinking in essences, which is at the bottom of every bourgeois mythology of man" (1957/1972: 75)—then one should be able to recognize that a newly born human female hasn't quite yet "lived up" to the expectations of masculinist fantasy or gotten very far in "the process of assuming, taking on, identifying with the positionalities and meaning effects specified by a particular society's **gender** system" (De Lauretis 1994: 302). One might well *imagine* the female infant's "womanly" *potential*, but as our old pal Hegel puts it, "when we want to see an oak . . . we are not satisfied to be shown an acorn instead" (1807/1977: 7). Or one might point out that if "woman" is our standard English term for an *adult* human female, then to call a newborn human female "a woman," to purport that anyone can be *born* as a fully grown *adult*, is *preposterous*, in the literal sense of that word.

And yet, "preposterous" is exactly the word that an adult female has recently used, in the pages of *The New York Times Book Review*, to describe Simone de Beauvoir's signature claim. In her review of a new translation of

The Second Sex, a woman named Francine du Plessix Gray calls Beauvoir's "one is not born a woman" a "preposterous assertion" which—get ready— "will be denied by any mother who has seen her toddler son eagerly grab for a toy in the shape of a vehicle or a gun, while at the same time showing a total lack of interest in his sister's cherished dolls" (2010: 7)—as if any and all mothers everywhere in all of human history had beheld nothing else but this particular scenario of playtime preferences; as if all *fort-da* games ever played, all eager grabbing or bored letting go of manufactured objects on the part of our littlest animals, were always attributable only to their innate and unmanufactured natures, not to those protocols of "nurture" or socialization from which no *human* playtime has ever been immune; or as if no "nurturing" mother had ever done her duty to the reality principles of patriarchy by actively *discouraging* a toddling son's interest in any dolls other than "G. I. Joe" action figures or by vigilantly squelching a barely ambulant daughter's desire, as expressed through the available playthings, to one day drive a car or shoot a gun or use a tool or write a book, her desire to *be* something other *than* a cherished doll, plaything, or trophy herself, to *do* something else *with* herself, with her life, if she chooses, than make and care for those little living dolls called babies.

And of course there's a point—a certain logic and sagacious foresight— to this protective maternal discouragement. After all, there's little point in letting little girls actively play with toy trucks in a society (such as Saudi Arabia) where big girls can't legally drive anyway. There's little point in letting little girls actively play with their own clitorises in cultures where even those excessive "little toys" are one fine day to be taken away from them, so that they might become marriageable young women, the toys and/or tools of men. There's little point in letting a little girl even pretend to be literate or educated, to read or to write, in settings such as Pakistan or Afghanistan, where, reportedly, a little girl might get acid thrown in her face on her way to school as Taliban-style punishment for the "obscenity" of being a little girl on her way to school.[1] Maybe there's little point in allowing a little

---

[1] "Acid," reports Declan Walsh, "is the preferred weapon of vindictive men against women accused of disloyalty or disobedience. Common in several Asian countries, acid attacks in Pakistan grew sharply in number in 2011, to 150 from 65 in 2010, although some advocacy workers said the increase stemmed largely from better reporting" (*The New York Times* 10 April 2012: A1). Although acid may be the "preferred weapon" of such men against women and girls, bullets can also produce the desired effect, for as Walsh more recently reports from Karachi, Pakistan, "At the age of 11, Malala Yousafzai took on the Taliban by giving voice to her dreams. As turbaned fighters swept through her town in northwestern Pakistan in 2009, the tiny schoolgirl spoke out about her passion for education—she wanted to become a doctor—and became a symbol of defiance against Taliban subjugation. On Tuesday [9 October 2012], masked Taliban gunmen

American girl to pretend to be interested in math and science—to play with a toy microscope or a real calculator—in a culture where male presidents of prestigious universities casually attribute the relative scarcity of women in the highest echelons of scientific research to "innate" differences in men's and women's cognitive abilities.[2] Or, as Virginia Woolf suggests with her hypothetical account of "Shakespeare's sister" in *her* feminist landmark *A Room of One's Own*, there would be little point for "a woman in Shakespeare's day" to have had Shakespeare's gifts as a writer, his "natural" and "innate" talent or genius for writing, for "any woman born with a great gift in the sixteenth century would certainly have gone crazed, shot herself, or ended her days in some lonely cottage outside the village, half witch, half wizard, feared and mocked at" (1929/1989: 48, 49).

One fears that these elementary tutorials in what Toril Moi calls "sexual/ textual politics" are lost on the likes of Francine du Plessix Gray, or on anyone who would mockingly call Beauvoir's claim that one is not born a woman "preposterous" and then trundle out the playpen observations of "any" old ahistorical "mother" as airtight evidence supporting the charge. Gray, to be fair, also maintains that Beauvoir's claim has been "disputed by certain feminist scholars, who would argue that many gender differences are innate rather than acquired" (2010: 7)—but she doesn't bother telling us who these "certain" feminist scholars are, nor upon what empirical research they base their certainties, nor upon what theoretical premises they base their claims to

answered Ms Yousafzai's courage with bullets, singling out the 14-year old on a bus filled with terrified schoolchildren, then shooting her in the head and neck . . . Doctors said that Ms Yousafzai was in critical condition at a hospital near Peshawar, with a bullet possibly lodged close to her brain. A Taliban spokesman, Ehsanullah Ehsan, confirmed by phone that Ms Yousafzai had been the target, calling her crusade for education rights an 'obscenity'. 'She has become a symbol of Western culture in the area; she was openly propagating it,' Mr Ehsan said, adding that if she survived, the militants would certainly try to kill her again. 'Let this be a lesson.'" (*The New York Times* 10 October 2012: A1).

[2]   I refer to comments made in 2005 by Lawrence Summers, then president of that great "symbol of Western culture" called Harvard University. And yes, following Walter Benjamin's "There is no document of civilization that is not at the same time a document of barbarism" (1950/1968: 256), I am "wildly" suggesting a line of continuity between the Taliban's barbaric assaults against women and girls in Afghanistan and Pakistan and Summers' more civilized, but still discouraging words in Cambridge, Massachusetts, taking both the actions and the words as documents of patriarchy as a global structure in dominance, as indications, to quote Virginia Woolf quoting Lady Stephen, of "how few people really wish women to be educated" (1929/1989: 20n1) even now. And, just to be clear, I am *not* citing the Taliban's actions as some "hegemonic Western feminist" rationalization for the United States' continuing military occupation of Afghanistan or its military drone operations in Pakistan—though, to be quite honest, I'll admit that, while I would likely be saddened by the sheer stupid waste of it all, I wouldn't exactly be overcome with grief or guilt if I were to read that some sort of American ordnance had taken out Mr Ehsanullah Ehsan.

being feminist. Of course, one is not born, but rather *becomes*, a feminist—or then again maybe one doesn't.

But what *does* it mean for any individual subject to become not "a woman" or even a feminist activist but an actively *feminist theoretical writer*? What follows here, in answer to this question, is, in warped imitation of Cleanth Brooks, of all people, a sort of "My Credo" regarding what *feminist theorizing* "means to me." First of all, though, given the gendered credentials of the "me" here in question, given that I was not born female and have thus far completely failed to become a woman, let's stipulate that one need not be, become, or have ever been a woman to engage in feminist theorizing.[3] Conversely, let's observe the obvious point that just being female doesn't pre-qualify anyone to be a feminist. Moreover, let's emphasize the second word in the phrase feminist *theorizing* to indicate that not all theorizing is informed by political feminism any more than all feminism or feminist literary criticism is demonstrably "theoretically aware."[4]

Of course, one is never born "theoretically aware," either, but I believe that to *become* theoretically aware *as* a feminist, and to *become* responsibly feminist *as* a theorist, one must learn to negotiate with a few basic critical ground rules. Thus, as per my credo, and to further warp the words of Mr Cleanth Brooks, "here are some articles of faith I could subscribe to" (1952/2007: 798). To become a feminist theorist, one must learn:

(1): *To become relentlessly anti-essentialist, except maybe when it's "strategi-cally" productive not to be.*

As Diana Fuss explains, essentialism in general philosophical terms involves "belief in the real, true essence of things, the invariable and fixed properties which define the 'whatness' of a given entity," while essentialism in the cognitive domain of sex and gender involves "the idea that men and women . . . are identified as such on the basis of transhistorical, eternal, immutable essences." While theory in general is "anti-essentialist" in that it rejects "any attempts to naturalize human nature" (Fuss 1989: xi), *feminist* theory in particular is anti-essentialist in that it rejects any attempts to naturalize and thereby eternalize historical social inequalities and asymmetries of power in the lived experience of sex and gender. Feminist theory assumes that human sex and gender are never essential facts of nature but are only ever materialized in the socio-symbolic, in the *social* realm of *signs*, and signs, as you'll recall from our lesson on structuralism,

[3] For discussions of the problem of men and/in feminism, see Thomas (2002) and (2007).
[4] In *Sexual/Textual Politics: Feminist Literary Theory*, Moi claims that Sandra Gilbert and Susan Gubar, authors of *The Madwoman in the Attic*, are "theoretically aware" (1985: 61)—and then sets about demonstrating that they pretty much aren't.

"do not have essences but are defined by a network of relations" (Culler 1975: 4). Hence, for feminist theory, neither "woman" nor "man" can ever be "essentially natural" identities; gender itself can never be anything other than "a socially imposed division of the sexes" (Rubin 1975/2007: 1675), "a social category imposed upon a sexed body" (Scott 1988: 32), and no "body that matters" can ever *have* or *express* a "gender identity" except by virtue of signification, symbolic practices. But as Gayle Rubin points out in *her* landmark feminist text "The Traffic in Women," all significant "expressions" of gender constitutively involve suppressions, repressions, and oppressions that are anything but naturally ordained:

> Far from being an expression of natural differences, exclusive gender identity is the suppression of natural similarities. It requires repression: in men, of whatever is the local version of "feminine" traits; in women, of the local definition of "masculine" traits. The division of the sexes has the effect of repressing some of the personality characteristics of virtually everyone, men and women. The same social system which oppresses women in its relations of exchange, oppresses everyone in its insistence upon a rigid division of personality. (1975/2007: 1675)

For Judith Butler, however, this insistence on rigid sexual division works itself out, or doesn't, not through "expression" as normally understood but rather via **performativeness** or **performativity**. Indeed, for Butler, who in the 1990s became anti-essentialism's most prominent feminist champion, "the distinction between expression and performativeness is crucial" (1990: 192). To understand this crucial distinction, however, we should first "distinguish 'the performative' in the linguistic sense from 'performance' as public exhibition." We should then observe that "speech-act theorist J. L. Austin distinguishes **performative utterances**, which 'perform the action they describe,' from **constantive utterances**, which 'describe a state of affairs and may be true or false'" (Childers and Hentzi 1995: 222). In *Gender Trouble: Feminism and the Subversion of Identity* (1990), Butler subversively applies the idea of the linguistic performative to articulations of identity, arguing that outright "expressions" of identity—such as "I am a straight white man"—can never be *constative* utterances, merely describing some already existing gendered, sexed, and raced "self," but are rather utterly *performative*, actually bringing into (relatively fragile) social existence that which they purport to describe (in "my" case, straight white manliness). In Butler's account, I never substantially *am* a straight white man; I only ever performatively repeat—and with no small amount of flop sweat—an approximation of a culturally produced ideal of straight white manliness, an ideal that is itself always only a copy for which there was never any "true original." For Butler, "gender is performative," by which she means

> that no gender is "expressed" by actions, gestures, or speech, but that the performance of gender produces retroactively the illusion that there is an inner gender core. That is, the performance of gender retroactively produces the effect of some true or abiding feminine [or masculine] essence or disposition so that one cannot use an expressive model for thinking about gender . . . Gender is produced as a ritualized repetition of conventions, . . . [a] ritual [that] is socially compelled in part by the force of a **compulsory heterosexuality**.[5] (1997: 144)

With, however, her analysis of "drag" or "female impersonation" as a deconstructive imitation of a purportedly "true gender" that is itself shown to be only ever imitation, Butler in ways collapses the distinction between the linguistic performative and "performativity" in the sense of public exhibition.

> When a man is [publically] performing drag as a woman, the "imitation" that drag is said to be is taken as an "imitation" of femininity, but the "femininity" that he imitates is not [ordinarily] understood as being itself an imitation. Yet if one considers that gender is acquired, that it is assumed in relation to ideals which are never quite inhabited by anyone, then femininity is an ideal which everyone always and only "imitates." Thus, drag imitates the imitative structure of gender, revealing gender itself to be an imitation. (1997: 145)

For Butler, in other words, when it comes to gender, it's all drag all the time, not only "when a man is performing drag as a woman," but whenever "a man *is*" or "a woman *is*"—period. Given the imitative structure of all gender, whenever a man *is*, whenever a man's a man, that man is only ever "caught in the act" of male impersonation, performing drag as a man, so that "a man is" is not a constative utterance (any more than, say, crossing one's legs in a specific manner while sitting is the "natural expression" of some "inner gender core"). Given gender's imitative structure, there's never any *real* difference between *being* a man or a woman and *acting like* a woman or a man, whether we men and/or women like it or not.

And in fact Butler's performative theories are not to everyone's liking. Some see her work as symptomatic of a baleful move within the academy

---

[5] **Compulsory heterosexuality** is a term used by Adrienne Rich (1980) "to suggest that heterosexuality, though commonly understood as a natural and personal 'preference,' is actually shaped and imposed upon women by society" (Childers and Hentzi 1995: 53).

from a specifically feminist focus on "women's studies" to an overly general "gender studies" or to a not always discernibly feminist "queer theory" (both moves facilitating yet more discussion from, about, and between *men*, not infrequently to the exclusion of women). Others, such as Joan Copjec (1994), Slavoj Žižek (1999/2008), Tim Dean (2000), and yours truly (2008), disagree with Butler's take on Lacan (or think that Butler, who frequently critiques Lacan, seems not to have actually read very much Lacan). Still others attack Butler for being too "theoretical" and hence insufficiently "political," if not actually *immoral*, some even going so far as to assert that Judith Butler—brace yourself here—"collaborates with evil." In her assault on Butler in the pages of *The New Republic*, Martha C. Nussbaum pillories the woman she calls "The Professor of Parody," rips into this evil academic's "hip quietism," and rather noisily proclaims that "Hungry women are not fed by this, battered women are not sheltered by it, raped women do not find justice in it"—with "this" and "it" here standing for the seemingly "cheerful" but actually cynically debilitating "Butlerian enterprise" of highfalutin theory. "Feminism," says Nussbaum, "demands more and women deserve better" (1999: 45) than Butler's "fancy words on paper" (1999: 37). Of course, Nussbaum is technically absolutely correct—hungry women are *not* fed, etc., by reading the theoretical works of Judith Butler. But then, one might wonder exactly how the hungry, battered, and raped women of the world *are* substantially assisted or protected by moralistic attacks on the evil Judith Butler published in the pages of *The New Republic*.

However, Nussbaum's unfancy if not rather puritan "words on paper" allow us to consider more seriously the question of whether feminist anti-essentialism enables or disables political action or agency on the part or behalf of *women*. Feminism, after all, is necessarily, even *essentially*, a political project—it *must be about change*. And so, some wonder what in the world "anti-essentialism" ever really changes, what politically "emancipatory effects" really follow from buddying up with Butler at theoretical drag bars or lolling around with Denise Riley examining the moniker "Woman" and forever asking *Am I that Name?* (1993). How does all this essence-less inquiry *really* help get anything politically salutary accomplished for women as an "identitarian grouping" (Bahri 2004: 209) of oppressed human beings? If in our desire to avoid "essentializing," we become reluctant to say *what* or even that "a woman" truly is, basing our reluctance on the deconstructive imperative to refuse "the authority or determining power of every 'is'" (Lucy 2006: 11) that there is, then how can "we" claim that "she" *is* truly oppressed (hungry, held down, battered, raped) or ever really fight against her oppression?

Now, the political aim of anti-essentialist feminism is of course to resist patriarchal oppression by refusing to fix meaning—specifically, by subverting the purportedly "biologically determined" meanings of the word "woman." But (if I can begin to tap into some critically queer resources here) there's also a sort of anti-metaphysical ethic of non-violence involved in proliferating the term "woman" in the same destabilizing way that queer theorists proffer "queer" as "an identity without an essence" (Halperin 1995: 62). Just as poststructuralists and postmodernists follow Nietzsche in questioning the value of "truth," this queerly anti-identitarian ethic radically questions the value of "the self," even if the "self" in question is the vaunted experiential self of collectively feminist **identity politics**, the sacrosanct "self" that, as the saying goes, supposedly "speaks truth to power."[6] For as Leo Bersani argues, "the sacrosanct value of selfhood accounts for human beings' extraordinary willingness to kill in order to protect the seriousness of their statements." The self, writes Bersani, is actually no more than "a practical convenience," a way to get things done; but when "promoted to the status of an ethical ideal, it is a sanction for violence" (1990: 4), a way to get people killed. To avoid sanctioning violence, particularly violence against "the other," one must learn to take oneself ironically. The ethically ironic trick that one must play or perform on oneself involves utilizing "the self" only as a "practical convenience"—not as an essential truth or locus of absolute authenticity but rather as a strategic fiction, and always without taking identity or identity-statements (or identity politics) seriously enough ever to kill or die for.

Even though the queer theorist Bersani and the Marxist feminist deconstructive postcolonial critic Gayatri Spivak are far from addressing the same set of problems, perhaps Bersani's ethically ironic stance toward "the self" can be productively related to what Spivak famously calls **strategic essentialism** in relation to "the group." For the principle trick of strategic essentialism would be to remain theoretically anti-identitarian while mobilizing as much essentialist identity as is *practically convenient* to form a politically effective identitarian grouping. As Deepika Bahri explains, Spivak considers it possible for feminists

> to avoid the pitfalls of biological determinism or formulaic fixity while continuing to use essentialism in a self-conscious and meditated fashion. Spivak describes the tactical and deliberate use of essentialist typology as "strategic essentialism": "a strategic use of positivistic essentialism in a scrupulously visible political interest" (1996: 214). Although it is

---

[6] The phrase **identity politics** is used in contemporary critical debates to capture "the sense of identity offered by one's membership in groups that have suffered oppression on the basis of gender, race, class, or sexual preference" (Childers and Hentzi 1995: 148).

undesirable to accept any positivistic or deterministic notion of identity, Spivak nevertheless allows for its contingent use in a specific and well-defined context for the work being undertaken. (2004: 209)

Whether anti-essentialist or strategically essentialist, however, feminist theorists, as *feminist* theorists, all recognize that there is a great deal of political work still to be undertaken. Even if they grant the possibility of "performative interpretation, that is, of an interpretation that transforms the very thing that it interprets" (Derrida 1994: 51), feminist theorists still understand that revolutionary change in human sexual relations isn't going to happen simply on Judith Butler's or Jacques Derrida's interpretive say-so. But as feminist *theorists*, most also take to heart Donna Haraway's postmodernist point that even "the *feminist* dream of a common language, like all dreams for a perfectly true language, of perfectly faithful naming of experience, is a totalizing and imperialist one" (1985/2008: 342, my emphasis). At the very minimum, and unlike Gray's purportedly "feminist scholars," *feminist theorists* acknowledge that human sex and gender are performative to the marrow—bodily matters, perhaps, but matters of cultural signification nonetheless, always in excess of "the bare choreographies of procreation" (Sedgwick 1990: 29) or the "bare bones" of chromosomal variance. Even, that is, if there turn out to be empirically provable "innate" differences between human males and females, we'll still have to *talk* about what these differences *mean* and what, if anything, we want to *do* about them in relation to the question of what sort of world we want to live in. Yes, like non-human animals, human *males* and *females* are indeed made of flesh and blood and X and Y chromosomes and such, but, unlike non-human animals, "women" and "men" are made of *signs*, which neither have essences nor grow on trees nor fall from the sky. And the fact that the signs of gender have been to some extent denaturalized and demystified by feminist theory leads me to *my* credo's next article faith; to wit, that to become feminist in one's theorizing and theoretically aware in one's feminism, one must learn:

(2) *To become relentlessly anti-theological: no gods (or goddesses), no masters— no exceptions.*

"Man," says Marx, "makes religion" (1844/1978: 53), but, being a man, he forgot to add—"in order to maintain systemic male dominance." For just as there's no document of civilization that doesn't also document barbarism, there is no documented "world religion" to date that hasn't been invented by men in order to serve oppressively patriarchal purposes. This "radical" observation—which should be obvious to anyone who's not a religious adherent (to the cause of male dominance)—isn't nullified by the fact of no few women's "willing participation" in their own "spiritual" oppression, much less by the fact that certain people consider themselves "feminist," but nonetheless remain adhered to some patriarchal religious institution or another, no doubt in hopes of "reforming" it (i.e., inserting a few tokens of female authority into the overarching structure of male dominance but basically leaving that structure ideologically intact, i.e., with some phallic deity or another fixed at the fantasized center). I confess that my own powers of sympathy are strained by these remarkable (but not miraculous) powers of adherence, and that I quite frankly see no intellectually respectable way to reconcile feminist theory with any of the available andro-monotono-theisms. In other words—sorry, boys and girls, but if we want to grow up to become real-world feminist theorists, then we've got to get over "God," even if we can't get rid of grammar.

Well, I'm afraid that I've just alluded to Friedrich Nietzsche yet again, specifically to his dig at the "pitiable God of Christian monotono-theism" (1888b/2006: 491) and to his fear "that we are not getting rid of [this] God because we still believe in grammar" (1888a/2006: 464). My allusions aren't at all inappropriate to a discussion of gender, however, for the immediately preceding sentence in *Twilight of the Idols* reads, "'Reason' in language: oh what a deceitful old woman!"—by which quip Nietzsche, according to his editors, is not simply being ageist and misogynist but rather "exploiting the fact that the grammatical gender of the word for reason in German (*die Vernunft*) is feminine" (Pearson and Large 2006: 464n21).

We'll come back to this matter of *gender* and grammar anon. Here, let's tarry with Nietzsche's point about God and grammar, or "Reason in language." Let's observe that every grammatically correct and completely predicated sentence must include a subject and a verb, a subject which is the legible *cause* of the action that the sentence *effectively* describes. Nietzsche suggests, however, that this arbitrary grammatical rule is the unacknowledged legislator of the "reasonable" philosophical assumption that any *effect* must have a *cause* and for the "reasonable" theological assumption that any *creation* must have a *creator*. In sum, Nietzsche here ascribes sublime theological belief to mere grammatical prejudice. Of course, this ascription doesn't mean that a prescriptive grammarian can't be a howling atheist, any more than my claim that a feminist theorist must be "anti-theological" turns every militant atheist into a feminist. Nietzsche's writing does, however, suggest that "getting rid of God" remains a problem of *writing*, and a problem of *authority*, for all animals at the mercy of language.

No coincidence, then, that the word "anti-theological" hails, as we've read, from Roland Barthes' "The Death of the Author." As you'll recall, Barthes calls *writing* "an anti-theological activity" that basically bumps off "God and all his hypostases" by refusing "to fix meaning" (1968/1977: 147). But it isn't just any old writing that "deicidally" refuses fixity. It certainly isn't "male writing" that refuses phallic divinity by refusing to demonize feminine sexuality. It is, rather, "a *new insurgent* writing"—a "writing the body" or *écriture feminine*—that inscribes this explicitly feminist refusal to fix meaning. In *her* feminist landmark "The Laugh of the Medusa," Hélène Cixous writes:

> I mean it when I speak of male writing. I maintain unequivocally that there is such a thing as *marked* writing; that, until now . . . writing has been run by a libidinal and cultural—hence political, typically masculine—economy; that this is a locus where the repression of women has been perpetuated, over and over, more or less consciously, and in a manner that's frightening since it's often hidden or adorned with the mystifying charms of fiction; that this locus has grossly exaggerated all the signs of sexual opposition . . . , where woman has never *her* turn to speak—this being all the more serious and unpardonable in that writing is precisely *the very possibility of change*, the space that can serve as a springboard for subversive thought, the precursory movement of a transformation of social and cultural structures. (1975/2007: 1646)

Writing of sexually opposed ways of writing, Cixous celebrates the writing called *écriture feminine* as "the very possibility of change," and she describes its opposite, "male writing," as repressive and mystifying fiction that works *against* change, that tries to keep all its meanings fixed, all its canards in a row. But here, we might pause to ask—isn't all this "writing the body" stuff borderline "essentialist"? Isn't Cixous buying into biological determinism, writing as if *any* writing from *any* female body is inherently revolutionary while any male script remains innately phallogocentric? *On the one hand*, Cixous *is* clearly and intentionally writing about "writing, from and toward women" (1975/2007: 1647)—she is writing (from and toward) the female body, the masturbating, menstruating, maybe child-bearing (or maybe not—your choice, says Cixous), the literally and figuratively *lactating* body of "woman." "There is always within her at least a little of that good mother's milk," writes Cixous, "She writes in white ink" (1975/2007: 1647). "By writing her self, woman will return to the body . . . Write your self. Your body must be heard" (1975/2001: 1646), etc. *On the other hand*, Cixous doesn't count all writing by any female as automatically *écriture feminine* by a long shot. Nor does she think that all *male* bodies are biologically determined to just keep pumping out the custard of phallogocentrically "male writing." In "The Laugh of the Medusa," she notes "inscriptions of femininity" in the work of "Colette, Marguerite Duras . . . and Jean Genet" (1975/2007: 1646n4), while elsewhere she writes extensively on feminine inscription in her *Exile of James Joyce* (1968/1980). Despite, then, certain menstrual and milky appearances, there's ultimately nothing *biologically* essentialist about Cixous' *écriture feminine* (in other words, she gets metaphor—she understands that the word "milk" isn't really milk, that the word "real" isn't the real, etc.). I would also suggest that there's nothing *theologically* essentialist about *écriture feminine* either, for Cixous' Medusa, though obviously a conscientiously un-demonized figure of mythic resistance, isn't exactly "a goddess."

And neither is Donna Haraway's socialist-feminist sci-fi **cyborg**.[7] For at the end of her landmark "Manifesto for Cyborgs," having pretty much pulled the plug on certain naturalizing, techno-phobic, and residually religious forms of feminist discourse, Haraway flat-out claims that she "would rather be a cyborg than a goddess" (1985/2008: 349). And to *my* atheist ear, Haraway also begins the essay on an anti-theological note, calling her manifesto "an effort to build an ironic myth faithful to feminism, socialism, and materialism" and then following with this irreligious (*and* ungrammatical) fragment— "Perhaps more faithful as blasphemy is faithful, than as reverent worship and identification" (1985/2008: 324). She goes on to call her essay

> an argument for *pleasure* in the confusion of boundaries and for *responsibility* in their construction . . . an effort to contribute to socialist-feminist culture and theory in a post-modernist, non-naturalist mode and in the utopian tradition of imagining a world without gender, which is perhaps a world without genesis, but maybe also a world without end. The cyborg incarnation is outside salvation history. (1985/2008: 325)

Haraway's non-salvational cyborg is a "cybernetic organism, a hybrid of machine and organism, a creature of social reality as well as a creature of fiction." And yet, it pleases Haraway to confuse the boundary between social reality and fiction, even science fiction, for "Social reality is lived social relations, our most important political construction, a world-changing fiction" (1985/2008: 324). What links Haraway's poly-sci-fi cyborg to Cixous'

[7] "A contraction of 'cybernetic organism', a cyborg is any self-organizing system which combines organic and mechanical parts . . . The word was coined by Manfred Clynes and Nathan S. Kline in their 1960 *Astronautics* article "Cyborgs and Space' . . . However, critical theory did not explore the implications of the cyborg until the American socialist-feminist Donna Haraway wrote her seminal 'Cyborg Manifesto' (1985). Haraway reinscribed the cyborg as a political and theoretical idea which could disrupt conventional binary oppositions, such as human/animal and organism/machine. Because the cyborg is a hybrid or mixture, it suggests an alternative to unifying, homogeneous concepts, such as 'Woman'" (Malpas and Wake 2006: 166).

laughing Medusa to Barthes' anti-theological "scriptor," and perhaps even to Nietzsche's overflowing Dionysus, is this happy blasphemy against identity, this ironic belief in human reality as world-changing fiction, in writing as "the very possibility of change" in and of a world that must be made to mean. And yet, as much *pleasure* as we might take in the confusion of boundaries, we must, as Haraway observes, also take *responsibility* for their construction. Thus, as every good boy and girl must tirelessly point out, not everybody in the world—particularly the "Third World"—has the luxury of reading fiction or writing the body or proliferating sexy theory. And this point leads to my penultimate article of faith, which is that to become feminist in one's theorizing, one must:

(3) *Become relentlessly "anti-universalizing" in one's radically critical endeavors, except when to do so effectively disables one's radically critical endeavors.*

With apologies to Cixous, we do have to observe that a good bit of the "ink" spilt in the name of feminist theory has been pretty "milky" (that is, Anglo-Eurocentrically "white") and that anti-essentialist, anti-identitarian feminism has taken its share of hits from certain critical race and postcolonialist quarters. In "Postmodern Blackness," for example, bell hooks describes (without exactly endorsing) the way she says

> black folks respond to the critique of essentialism, especially when it denies the validity of identity politics[,] by saying, "Yeah, it's easy to give up identity, when you got one." Should we not be suspicious of postmodern critiques of the "subject" when they surface at a historical moment when many subjugated people feel themselves coming to voice for the first time [?] (1989/2007: 2012)

And Gayatri Spivak famously and effectively hangs Cixous and (particularly) Julia Kristeva out to dry in "French Feminism in an International Frame" (1981).

But perhaps the most relentless postcolonialist critique of Anglo-Eurocentric feminist theory is Chandra Mohanty's "Under Western Eyes: Feminist Scholarship and Colonial Discourses," which steadily argues against "a universalist theory of women's oppression," rightly insists "on the heterogeneity of the lives of 'Third-World' women," and passionately "pleads for an interrelational analysis that does not limit the definition of the female subject to gender and does not bypass the social, class, and ethnic coordinates of those analyzed" (Bahri 2004: 213). Mohanty writes that her project involves "deconstructing and dismantling" what she calls "hegemonic 'Western' feminisms" while "building and constructing" what she calls "autonomous, geographically, historically, and culturally grounded feminist concerns and strategies" (1991/2008: 381). Of course, at the time of its writing, Mohanty's essay represented a sorely needed intervention into the overly universalizing, overly generalizing, blinkeredly ethnocentric, and even discernibly racist tendencies of middle-class white Western feminisms.[8] And Mohanty helpfully specifies that even in her non-Western woman's eyes, "Western feminist discourse and political practice is neither singular nor homogeneous in its goals, interests, or analyses" and that her reference "to 'Western feminism' is by no means intended to imply that it is a monolith" (1991/2008: 381–2).

But what seems problematic about Mohanty's project—at least to *this* conspicuously pale male feminist theorist (and please remember that it's "my credo" you're reading here, and that *my* credo needn't necessarily be yours)—is the way the project potentially "dismantles" not simply the "hegemonic Western-ness" but the *feminism* of purportedly "hegemonic 'Western' feminism," the way its insistence on always historically contextualizing and culturally *grounding* feminist strategies could work to bring those very strategies crashing *to* the ground. If, on the one hand, Western feminist theory has been, as Mohanty rightly charges, often quite guilty of what Slavoj Žižek calls "over-rapid universalization," which "produces a quasi-universal Image whose function is to make us blind to its historical, socio-symbolic determination," then, on the other hand, Mohanty herself might be indulging in what Žižek calls "over-rapid historicization," which "makes us blind to the real kernel which returns as the same through diverse historicizations/ symbolizations" (Žižek 1989: 50). And if the "real kernel which returns as the same" here is, simply put, the systematic oppression of women *by men*, then a *searing* critique of "a universalist theory of women's oppression"—of the oppression, that is, of women everywhere *by men* everywhere—can end up effectively *sparing* men, *acquitting* us (and the socio-symbolic systems we construct and maintain in our own image) of the very charge of oppression, thus inadvertently *endorsing* patriarchal discourses and oppressive political practices. I'm not suggesting here that Mohanty *intends* to endorse male dominance (in fact I'm quite sure that she doesn't), but rather that her over-rapid historicizations in the essay called "Under Western Eyes" might effectively blind her readers to what my self-admittedly Western eyes nonetheless take to be the "real kernel."

For example, Mohanty writes that we must avoid *universally* casting "women as victims of male violence" and that "male violence" itself "must be theorized and interpreted *within* specific societies, in order both to understand

<hr>

[8] Mohanty discusses the time of the essay's writing, some of the feminist responses to it, and her current thinking about it, in "'Under Western Eyes' Revisited" (2003).

it better and to effectively organize to change it" (1991/2008: 386–7); to more effectively organize toward change, says Mohanty, we must "theorize male violence within specific societal frameworks, rather than assume it as a universal fact" (1991/2008: 402). Now, on the one hand, as a subject supposed to be male, and hence supposedly supposed by feminism to be violent, I suppose I should be grateful for the presumption of innocence that Mohanty, in the interests of sociohistorical specificity, here provides me and my likes, and I suppose I should take full advantage of the opportunity she affords me to claim myself as a non-violent exception to the rule. I can also appreciate that her intended motive here is to rescue "Third World women" from their prescribed roles as victims of universal male violence, so as to afford these women greater political agency. On the other hand, this feminist man has to ask—are there any societies anywhere in which patriarchy, or systemic male dominance, isn't still pretty much the *de facto* if not the *de jure* lay of the land, in which female agency isn't *still* at least something of a *threat* to the idea of male authority, and in which authoritarian male violence against women *isn't* always a strong possibility, an assumed prerogative of "male identity," if not a universal then at least a fairly pervasive fact? And if there *aren't* any such societies, wouldn't that absence suggest that "male violence against women" is a big honking part of what Žižek calls the "real kernel," a legitimately "trans-societal" concern for "strategically universalizing" feminist analysis?[9] Mohanty apparently thinks not, for in her analysis, it is *not* systemic male dominance, but rather universalizing "Western feminist discourse" that "ultimately robs" Third-World women "of their historical and political *agency*" (1991/2008: 398). Mohanty's analysis can thus be read as effectively protecting (non-Western) patriarchy while handing "hegemonic Western feminism" an enormous amount of power over Third World women.[10]

---

[9] Cf. the "strategically universalizing" gesture in note 2 above, where I focus on a specifically "real kernel which returns as the same in diverse historicizations" by suggesting lines of continuity running back and forth between Afghanistan's vicious Taliban, Harvard's more genteel Lawrence Summers, and all those who really didn't want women to be educated back in the days of Virginia Woolf's Lady Stephen.

[10] It might be worth noting that, as represented in Mohanty's essay, this purportedly quite powerful "hegemonic Western feminist" bloc—powerful enough to "rob" all Third World women of all political agency—amounts to a small number of not particularly well-known academics writing for an obscure feminist publishing house called Zed Press. On the one hand, in pointing this out, I'm certainly not suggesting that feminists can't possibly write in a way that's complicit with the ideological project of Orientalism, or that "mere" representations don't have real effects on real people's lived experience; on the other hand, there may be limits to the power and reach of "hegemonic" representation, and while Western feminists may represent Third World women in a way that seems to "rob" them of political agency, women in the Third World probably have whatever political agency they have or don't have, regardless of what a handful of Western feminists may be writing about them.

As for the "contextualization" upon which Mohanty unwaveringly insists—she writes that "while Indian women of different religions, castes, and classes might forge a political unity on the basis of organizing against police brutality toward women . . . an *analysis* of police brutality must be contextual." But one wonders exactly *which* explanatory contextual details a feminist analyst really needs to know to "better understand" *and better oppose* such "complex realities" (1991/2008: 396) as state-sanctioned male brutality against women. There can be little doubt that Mohanty both opposes and wants to render more "understandable" statist/misogynist/masculinist violence in India and elsewhere, and yet, there are times when the definitional line separating "the understandable" from "the justifiable" can seem precariously thin—or again, there are times when an overly contextualized analysis of "complex realities" might blind us to the "real kernel."

One (male) feminist analyst of masculinity (and organizer against male violence) has written that "under patriarchy, the cultural norm of male identity consists in power, prestige, and prerogative *as over and against* the gender class women. That's what masculinity is. It isn't something else" (Stoltenberg 1974/2004: 41). And yet, Mohanty often writes as if patriarchal masculinity (at least in "the Third World") really were "something else." She rather astoundingly argues against the "universalizing" feminist theory in which "patriarchy is always necessarily male dominance" and in which "religious, legal, economic, and familial systems are implicitly assumed to be constructed by men" (1991/2008: 397). But again, *this* anti-theological male feminist wants to know—who or what else does Mohanty *think* "constructed" these "systems"? God? Does she think they grew on trees or fell from the sky? If Mohanty demonstrably doesn't want (us) to consider "male violence against women" as a universal problem, a "real kernel which returns as the same through diverse historicizations" (Žižek 1989: 50), or if she really doesn't (want us to) see how "patriarchy" really has and still does *equal* systemic "male dominance" everywhere and always (even if not all men get to be dominant, even if not all men are treated equally in or by this system), then her project, for all its vaunted and welcomed anti-universalist value, arguably falls short of the basic minimum requirements of radical feminist critique (which, in order to be radical, should, in my view, neither over-urgently universalize nor over-hastily historicize). Moreover, if Mohanty really doesn't think patriarchal "religious, legal, economic, and familial systems" are constructed by men (to serve the purposes of systemic male dominance), then her discourse falls somewhat short of what Said in *Orientalism* calls "Vico's great observation that men make their own history, [and] that what they can know is what they have made" (1978: 4–5). Finally, particularly invested, as she seems to me, in denying that *religious* systems are "construct~d by men" (she lets the adjective "religious" appear first on her list of systems), Mohanty seems to disregard even Marx's most basic historical materialist observations that "Man makes religion" and that the "criticism of religion is the *prerequisite* of *all* criticism" (1844/1978: 53, my emphases). One suspects, in other words, that *unlike* Donna Haraway's radically ironic cyborg myth, Mohanty's sincere crusade against hegemonic Western feminist universalism may on some fundamental level be more "faithful" to religion, and hence to patriarchy, than to "feminism, socialism, or materialism" (Haraway 1985/2008: 324).

But look, I'm not an idiot—I am quite fully aware of the fact that Gayatri Spivak has "famously described British intervention in the Sati [or wife-burning] practice in India as 'white men saving brown women from brown men'" (Bahri 2004: 200; Spivak 1988: 297). And so I also understand quite well that *my* intervention into Mohanty's scorchingly critical practices in "Under Western Eyes" opens me to charges of just being a white man attempting to save white women (and white theory) from a brown woman, if not of being nothing more at the end of the day than a violently identitarian masculinist posing as a feminist, a man all too willing, if not to kill, then at least to kick discursive ass in order to protect the seriousness of his own ethnocentrically and anti-religiously biased statements—statements, like "real feminism sees no use-value in religion," to paraphrase what I've asserted above, that may themselves have no real use-value for feminists, and which may indicate that my most fundamental political commitment is to Nietzschean atheism (or to my own cleverness) rather than to feminism, postcolonial critique, anti-capitalist struggles, or even, for that matter, social justice. All I might say in response to these quite serious charges is that if I truly believe that social justice entails my attempting to read and write theory as a feminist, and that if I discern what I take to be a non-feminist or potentially anti-feminist undercurrent in anyone's otherwise sympathetic critique of feminist theory, then I feel duty-bound to point it out—a feminist man's gotta do what a feminist man's gotta do to expose over-hasty historicization and to try to keep all our eyes peeled for the "real kernel." Or I might stress once again that this is after all only *my* credo—you'll have to get your own, and, just as Mohanty's critique hasn't become a particularly valuable part of mine, mine might very well not become a credible part of yours.

But rather than attempting to support my charges against Mohanty with further evidence that I could draw from "Under Western Eyes," or further refute what I imagine would be her charges against me, I will veer away from the problem of feminism's *ethnocentrism* (which I think white Western feminist theory, *after* Spivak, Mohanty, bell hooks, and others, has basically bent over backward to politically correct) and turn instead to that of feminism's **heteronormativity**.[11] And this turn leads me to the end of my credo and to my last remaining article of faith—to wit, that in order to live up to its most radically and globally transformative promises, in order to keep writing (as) the very possibility of change, feminist theory must

(4) *Do its part to help "make the world queerer than ever."*

II. "The future is kid stuff"

In her *other* feminist landmark "Thinking Sex," Gayle Rubin compares the analytical *limitations* of feminism to those of Marxism and concludes that "Feminism is no more capable than Marxism of being the ultimate and complete account of all social inequality." She writes that "Marxism is probably the most supple and powerful conceptual system extant for analyzing social inequality" but that "attempts to make Marxism the sole explanatory system for all social inequalities have been dismal exercises." While Marxism *best* confronts *class* antagonisms, Rubin writes, "Feminist conceptual tools were developed to detect and analyze gender-based hierarchies," and "to the extent that these [hierarchies] overlap with **erotic stratifications**, feminist theory has some explanatory power."[12]

> But as the issues become less those of gender and more those of sexuality, feminist analysis becomes irrelevant and often misleading. Feminist thought simply lacks angles of vision which can encompass the social organization of sexuality. The criteria of relevance in feminist thought

[11] Lauren Berlant and Michael Warner write that "by **heteronormativity** we mean the institutions, structures of understanding, and practical orientations that make heterosexuality not only coherent—that is, organized as a sexuality—but privileged. Its coherence is always provisional, and its privilege can take several (sometimes contradictory) forms; unmarked, as the basic idiom of the personal and the social; or marked as a natural state; or projected as an ideal or moral accomplishment. It consists less of norms that could be summarized as a body of doctrine than of a sense of rightness produced in contradictory manifestations—often unconscious, immanent to practice or institutions. Contexts that have little visible relation to sex practice, such as life narrative and generational identity, can be heteronormative in this sense, while in other contexts forms of sex between men and women might *not* be heteronormative. Heteronormativity is thus a concept distinct from heterosexuality" (1998/2007: 1722).

[12] We can best consider what Rubin means by **erotic stratifications** by considering the diagram she provides in "Thinking Sex," which charts the way heteronormativity separates "Good" sex from "Bad." The "best" sex is "normal, natural, healthy, holy, heterosexual, married, monogamous, and reproductive" while the "worst" is "abnormal, unnatural, sick, sinful, 'way out,'"—anything involving "transvestites, transsexuals, fetishists, sadomasochists," and/or the exchange of money. The point of Rubin's diagram is that "most people mistake their sexual preferences for a universal system that will or should work for everyone. This notion of a single ideal sexuality characterizes most systems of thought about sex . . . including feminism and socialism" (1984/2008: 294).

do not allow it to see or assess critical power relations in the area of sexuality. In the long run, feminism's critique of gender hierarchy must be incorporated into a radical theory of sex, and the critique of sexual oppression should enrich feminism. But an autonomous theory and politics specific to sexuality must be developed. (1984/2008: 314)

And in fact such a theory *has* been developed by various cultural and political analysts who see their work as not (only) Marxist and not (only) feminist but (also) **queer**.[13] What is now commonly known as **queer theory** develops as a "critique of sexual oppression" *qua* social *normativity*—queer theory develops by *distilling* the lessons of Marxism, feminism, postmodernism, poststructuralism, psychoanalysis, semiotics, and gay/lesbian studies while at the same time *distinguishing* itself from those movements by *exposing* their investments in heteronormativity and/or identity politics. Queer theory advocates a "thorough resistance to regimes of the normal" and attempts to "make the world queerer than ever" (Warner xxvi, xxvii) through such anti-identitarian resistance. Thus, on the one hand, queer theory

> is interested in any and all acts, images, and ideas that "trouble," violate, cross, mix, or otherwise confound established boundaries between male and female, normal and abnormal, self and other. In a limited sense, the goal is to create more space for and recognition of the various actions performed daily in a social landscape blinded and hostile to variety. But the broader goal is a general troubling, and an attempted unfixing, of the links between acts, categories, representations, desires, and identities. (Leitch 2001: 2487)

On the other hand, queer theory

> views with postmodern skepticism the minoritizing conception of sexuality that undergirds gay liberation and women's liberation (and hence academically institutionalized gay studies and women's studies

---

[13] The word **queer** has appeared a number of times already in this book, but I've strategically deferred a specific gloss until now. Carla Freccero writes that the term **queer**, "as taken up by political movements and by the academy, has undergone myriad transformations and has been the object of heated definitional as well as political debates . . . It is a term that [has] something to do with a critique of literary critical and historical presumptions of sexual and gender (hetero) normativity, in cultural contexts and in textual subjectivities. It also has something to do with the sexual identities and positionalities, as well as the subjectivities, that have come to be called lesbian, gay, and transgender, but also perverse and narcissistic—that is, queer. At times, *queer* continues to exploit its productive indeterminacy as a word used to designate that which is odd, strange, aslant; in this respect, . . . all textuality, when subjected to close reading, can be said to be queer" (2006: 5). For somewhat "historicizing" accounts of the emergence of the term "queer" in the academy, see Thomas (2000) and (2009).

too) . . . Feminism and gay liberation based their claims for political participation and radical equality . . . on the foundation of *identity* . . . By contrast, queer theory and politics begin from a critique of identity and of identity politics, inspired primarily by Foucault's analysis of the disciplinary purposes that sexual identities so easily serve. (Dean 2000: 223)

Thus, taking on what Berlant and Warner call the hard "labor of ambiguating categories of identity" (1995: 345), queer theorists offer up the fighting words "queer" and "queerness" as *differing* from not only "straight" and "straightness" but from gay, lesbian, etc., insofar as these terms function as clear markers of sexual *identity*. For "queer" is "less an identity than a *critique* of identity. . .a site of permanent becoming" (Jagose 1996: 131). "Queerness" involves "the open mesh of possibilities, gaps, overlaps, dissonances and resonances, lapses and excesses of meaning where the constituent elements of anyone's gender, of anyone's sexuality aren't made (or *can't* be made) to signify monolithically" (Sedgwick 1993: 8). For "queer," writes David Halperin, "is by definition *whatever* is at odds with the normal, the legitimate, the dominant. *There is nothing in particular to which it necessarily refers*. It is an identity without an essence" (1995: 62). "Queerness," writes Lee Edelman, "can never define an identity; it can only ever disturb one." Queerness is "what chafes against 'normalization,'" what "deliberately sever[s] us from ourselves, from the assurance, that is, of knowing ourselves" (2004: 17, 6, 5).

Queerness is thus "obviously threatening and infallibly dreaded by everything within us that desires a kingdom," a fixed and knowable identity. I hope that you will recognize not only *that* but *why* I just swapped the word "queerness" for Derrida's dreaded différance. And, I hope that you will understand both that and why différance, like queer, *is* one of those troubling words that troubles "is" itself, that, once again, "begins . . . from a refusal of the authority or determining power of every 'is'" (Lucy 2006: 12) that there is. In this authoritarian and identitarian sense, "is" *is* its own kingdom. But "there is no kingdom of différance" (Derrida 1967/1982: 21–2); there is no kingdom of the queer.[14]

---

[14] "*Queer*, in its deconstructive sense, designates a kind of Derridean *différance*, occupying an interstitial space between binary oppositions . . . This use of *queer* finds its energy from the way the term works to undo the binary between *straight* and *gay*, operating uncannily between but also elsewhere. *Queer*—precisely by marking out the space and time of *différance*—can thus show how the two, gay and straight, are inter-implicated and how they differ from themselves from within . . . Meanwhile, *queer* can also be a grammatical perversion, a misplaced pronoun, the wrong proper name; it is what is strange, odd, funny, not quite right, improper. Queer is what is and is not there, what disaggregates the coherence of the norm from the very beginning" (Freccero 2006: 18–19).

Heteronormativity, however, is a big "fucking" kingdom, a *vast* kingdom in which all real "fucking" is retroactively ruled over by its idealized product or result—"King Baby," the ideological figure of "the Child" through which heteronormativity perpetuates its reign by attempting to ensure that "the future" is always "kid stuff." Now, the first chapter of Lee Edelman's *No Future: Queer Theory and the Death Drive* is called "The Future is Kid Stuff." There, speaking for queers, queerness, and queer sexuality—and speaking quite provocatively in favor of associating all three with the death drive—Edelman writes:

> On every side, our enjoyment of liberty is eclipsed by the lengthening shadow of a Child whose freedom to develop undisturbed by encounters . . . with an "otherness" of which its parents, its church, or the state do not approve, uncompromised by any possible access to what is painted as alien desire, terroristically holds us all in check and determines that political discourse conform to the logic of a narrative wherein history unfolds as the future envisioned for a Child who must never grow up . . . That Child, immured in an innocence seen as continuously under siege, condenses a fantasy of vulnerability to the queerness of queer sexualities . . . The Child, that is, marks the fetishistic fixation of heteronormativity: an erotically charged investment in the rigid sameness of identity that is central to the compulsory narrative of **reproductive futurism**. And so, as the radical right maintains, the battle against queers is a life-and-death struggle for the future of a Child whose ruin is pursued by feminists [and] queers. (2004: 21–2)

But Edelman goes on to argue that it isn't just the "radical right" that enforces this "compulsory narrative of reproductive futurism"; it isn't just the "moral majority" that insists on sacrificing everybody's libidinal and aesthetic liberty to the future good of the permanent Child (an idealized figure of "imaginary unity" that, as Edelman points out, has little enough to do with actual children); the radical *left* and even some in the gay/lesbian community *also* get in on the act, bowing heads to singer "Whitney Houston's rendition of the secular hymn, 'I believe that children are our future,' a hymn we might as well simply declare our national anthem and be done with it" (2004: 143). For Edelman, moreover, the identity politicians of the gay/lesbian community are never more indentured to the "pro-procreative ideology" (2004: 12) of reproductive futurism than when they *deny* the religious right's hysterical slanders against those who engage in non-procreative or queer sex, when they dispute the idea that queers really do embody "a drive toward death that entails the destruction of the Child" (2004: 21).

Now, Edelman isn't saying that queers *qua* queers literally desire to sexually murder real children, as per extremist right-wing fantasy. Nor is he saying that queer politics shouldn't fight against homophobic conservative slander and dogma. But what he is saying is perhaps no less startling and abrasive.

> Without ceasing to refute the lies that pervade . . . right-wing diatribes, do we also have the courage to acknowledge, and even to embrace, their correlative truths? Are we willing to be sufficiently oppositional to the structural logic of opposition—oppositional, that is, to the logic by which politics reproduces our social reality—to accept that figural burden of queerness . . . of the force that shatters the fantasy of Imaginary unity, the force that insists on the void [that is] always already lodged within, though barred from, symbolization: the gap or wound of the Real that inhabits the Symbolic's very core? Not that we are, or ever could be, outside the Symbolic ourselves: but we can, nonetheless, make the choice to accede to our cultural production as figures—within the dominant logic of narrative, within Symbolic reality—for the dismantling of such a logic and thus for the death drive it harbors within. (2004: 22)

What's at stake in Edelman's provocative argument is the oppositional relation between "the queerness of queer sexuality" and the "meaning" of sociality itself. He argues that our current symbolic reality is a "collective fantasy that invests the social order with meaning by way of reproductive futurism" and "bestows the imprimatur of meaning-production [only] on heterogenital relations" (2004: 28. 13). Reproductive futurism depends upon a "meaningful" libidinal investment in the ideological figure of "the Child" and on vigilantly protecting that figure from all queer figurations. It isn't just "the Child" but "meaning" itself that must be protected from the queer, who/which embodies the destruction of heteronormative "meaning." But "the queer" isn't simply "the homosexual," the gay man or lesbian woman, but rather *anyone* whose gender or sexuality "can't be made to signify monolithically" (Sedgwick 1993: 8), *anyone* for whom "the distinctly sexual nature of human sexuality has to do precisely with its excess over or potential difference from the bare choreographies of procreation" (Sedgwick 1990: 29). Reproductive futurism is a "pro-procreative ideology" that attempts to reduce not only "the meaning" of human sexuality, but the meaning of "meaning" itself to those bare choreographies. This ideology maintains, as the narrator of P. D. James's *The Children of Men* puts it, that "sex totally divorced from procreation" is "meaninglessly acrobatic" (in Edelman 2004:

13); this ideology tells us—quite stupidly—that to engage in such "sterile" shenanigans is to behave like an animal.[15] Reproductive futurism tells us:

> "If there is a baby, there is a future, there is redemption." If, however, there is *no baby* and, in consequence, *no future*, then the blame must fall on the fatal lure of sterile, narcissistic enjoyments understood as inherently destructive of meaning and therefore as responsible for the undoing of social organization, collective reality, and inevitably, life itself. (Edelman 2004: 12–13)

Edelman argues that queerness demands something other than simply denying responsibility for the destruction of "meaning," something other than the attempt to earn "a place at the table" of heteronormative "social organization" and become full-fledged members of a "collective reality" determined and driven by reproductive futurism. There might be a place-setting waiting for any good homosexual who buys into heteronormative "meaning-production," but the "structural mandate" of reproductive futurism is always that s/he "who refuses the Child *be* refused . . . be projectively reviled" (2004: 45), punitively abjected. Edelman thus wants queers to resist the regimes of the normal by accepting "the figural burden of queerness," by accepting responsibility for the destruction of "meaning" and the abject "undoing of social organization," by happily embodying that symbolic reality's inner void and its death drive to the hilt. If "the sacralization of the Child . . . necessitates the sacrifice of the queer" (2004: 28), then for Edelman, a real insistence on queerness by queers—as per the in-your-face AIDS-activist slogan "we're here, we're queer, get used to it"—necessitates nothing short of a massive cluster "fuck you" to the Child, which obscene discursive gesture Edelman is more than happy to provide (and with which we will rather rudely and abruptly end this lesson). After reviewing some standard antigay-rights sentiments issued by religious representatives of church and state sanctioned sociality, Edelman writes that

> Queers must respond to the violent force of such constant provocations not only by insisting on our equal right to the social order's prerogatives [i.e., the benefits of matrimony], not only by avowing our capacity to

---

[15] The situation is, of course, just the opposite, for animals as a lot are pretty much incapable of divorcing sexual activity from reproductive imperatives, while our divorce from nature is what's anthropogenetic, constitutively humanizing, for us. Ironically, then, the queerest sex is the most productively human/humanizing, and reproductive futurism, which attempts to naturalize sex, to rob sexual activity of its specifically human meanings, is actively dehumanizing in its hostility to the queer.

promote that order's coherence and integrity [by serving in the military], but also by saying explicitly what [Cardinal Bernard] Law and the Pope [John Paul II] and the whole of the Symbolic order for which they stand hear anyway in each and every expression or manifestation of queer sexuality: fuck the social order and the Child in whose name we're collectively terrorized; fuck ["the sun will come up tomorrow"] Annie; fuck the waif from *Les Mis*; fuck the poor, innocent kid on the Net; fuck Laws with both capital ls and with small; fuck the whole network of Symbolic relations and the future that serves as its prop. (2004: 29)

Coming to Terms

Critical Keywords encountered in Lesson Ten:

Gender, performativity, performative/constative utterances, compulsory heterosexuality, identity politics, strategic essentialism, *écriture feminine*, cyborg, heteronormativity, erotic stratifications, queer, queer theory, reproductive futurism

---

In the End: Theory is (not—) Forever

As you might imagine, not everyone in even the queer academic community applauded *No Future*'s abrasive, antisocial, f-bombing barrage.[1] But to me it seems entirely appropriate to bring not only the preceding lesson in gender-troubling queer theory but all 10 of our theoretical lessons to an end with Edelman's incomparable negativity. It seems meet and fitting for us to *end* our theoretical narrative with Edelman's queerly affirmative nod toward the *death drive*, for we've learned a few lessons here about the strange relations between narrative writing and our unconscious desire for "the end." In the beginning, we were subjected to some unsettling lessons in "anthropogenetic" textuality, alienating interpretations of our polymorphously perverse geneses; if we learned those early lessons sufficiently, if we *read* those lessons and all that followed *closely* enough, then perhaps here, in the end, we can understand what queer theorist Carla Freccero means when she seriously suggests that "all textuality, when subjected to close reading, can be said to be queer," why she writes that "if one were being playfully adjectival . . . one might call English departments departments of queer studies", why she both seriously and playfully holds theory and literature, or theory *as* literature, to be "always already queer" (2006: 5, 18, 13). For like "queerness," theory and literature offer themselves as "site[s] of permanent becoming" (Jagose 1996: 131), discursive activities that "can never define an identity" but "can only ever disturb one" (Edelman 2004: 17).

And to return one last time to the titles of our identity-disturbing lessons in theory, we might suggest that that in the end they're all kind of "queer," that "queerness" in its most current usage effectively addresses what's been at stake all along in this strange set of defamiliarizing axioms—that the world must be made to mean; that meaning is only the polite word for pleasure (whether that pleases us or not); that language is by nature fictional, as are we, the animals at its mercy; that our desires are thus never purely instinctual or merely biological but must always be taken literally, to the letter; that we are consequently **not** quite ourselves today, and weren't yesterday, and, bet your bottom dollar, still won't be "tomorrow" (even if the sun does come up); that restless negativity is therefore the actual substance of our subjectivities, what we anti-essentially are; that even our most highly valued documents of

---

[1] See, for example, Hall (2006), Halberstam et al. (2006), and Dean (2008). But see also Ruti (2008).

civilization will probably always also document our yawping barbarisms, if only because the unconscious, with all its aggressions, "desires, repressions, investments and projections" (Said 1978: 8) is structured like a language; that there's consequently nothing for us outside the text, which means that we are never *born* human, much less gendered, but always have to *become* human (though not necessarily always so narrowly gendered or so monolithically sexuated) in a world that, precisely because it always must be made to mean, could always be made to mean more queerly.

Maybe "queerness" in Edelman's "antisocial" and "antifuturistic" sense can serve for a while as the last best "critical keyword" for the occluded but constitutive *negativity* of all human reality after the linguistic turn—the restless force of negativity that pervades the centerless core of "what theory does"—so that what it means in Edelman's "demeaning" terms "to accept the figural burden of queerness . . . of the force that shatters the fantasy of Imaginary unity, the force that insists on the void [that is] always already lodged within, though barred from, symbolization: the gap or wound of the Real that inhabits the Symbolic's very core" could be intimately related to what it means in Lacan's terms "to accept castration" (2008: 41), to accept "the endless perpetuation of the subject's desire" (1966d/2006: 262), or to what it means in Adorno and Horkheimer's terms to "negate reification" (1947/2002: xvii), or to what it means in Culler's terms to always take "meaning as a problem rather than a given" (2007: 85), or even to what it means in Hegelian parlance to embrace dissolution, to "tarry with the negative," to engage with "the tremendous power of the negative" so as to free all of our "determinate thoughts from their fixity" (1807/1998: 59, 60).

Throughout these 10 lessons, I've insisted that theoretical writing—writing about "writing as the very possibility of change" (Cixous 1975/2007: 1646)—involves a thoroughgoing refusal to fix meaning, a perpetual attempt "to dereify the language of thought" (Jameson 2009: 9). At the risk of seeming to reify this very refusal of fixity, of letting this "refusal to fix meaning" become *the* fixed meaning of theory itself, I will end by stating my own interpretive desire to perpetually connect this "refusal to fix" to whatever "resistance to regimes of the normal" we can muster, to perpetually fix this "refusal to fix" to our ongoing political and aesthetic project of making "the world queerer than ever" (Warner 1993: xxvi, xxvii). The world, let's say, is always already queerer than ever, but only because it still always has to be made that way, still has to be *written* that way—by us. For to rewrite the words from Jean-Luc Nancy that appeared at the end of our lesson on Hegel, this queerer-than-ever "world is precisely what . . . manifests itself as a restlessness"—this globally restless and eternally queer negativity is "not only ours" but "is itself 'us'" (Nancy 2002: 78), all of us, every single one of us, living or dead—strangely enough.

For Hegel, let's recall, though no longer living, still writes that "something moves, not because at one moment it is here and at another there, but because at one and the same moment it is here and not here, because in this 'here', it at once is and is not" (1812/1998: 239). And Lacan, let's remember, though likewise no longer alive, still writes of the written letter not "that, like other objects, it must be *or* not be somewhere but rather that, unlike them, it will be *and* not be where it is wherever it goes" (Lacan 1966a/2006: 17).[2] And so maybe the queerest thing about us animals at the mercy of moving letters will *always* be that "we're here" and *we're not* wherever we end up going. And perhaps "the activities that have come to answer to the nickname *theory*" (Culler 2007: 1) can serve, if only for the passing moment, as our queerest, our strangest, our strongest way of "coming to terms" with this (no) future, this eternally returning affirmation, in the present that we're making, of the future of the word—"no."

Which is what I think I mean when I write that in the end "theory is (not—) forever," an inscription I'm sure I mean to be taken three ways— theory *is* forever; theory is *not* forever; and theory *is* this perpetual *not—is* this restlessness of the negative, *is* this refusal of the authority of every is that there is—forever (or at least for as long as "human reality" is still a going concern and not yet a total goner). What I think I mean by writing "theory is (not—) forever" is that all theoretical writing is "always already queer" to the extent that "theory never stops coming back" (Rabaté 2002: 10) as the personal and collective site of our permanent(ly) becoming (undone), so that, at least in theory, "we never stop losing 'the fixity of [our] self-positing'" (Nancy 2002: 79). Like any productive unfixity, like any "possibility of change," like anything that restlessly moves—like "all textuality," like all writing, like all of "us"—theory is *here*, and it's *queer*, and, at the same time, it's *not*.

So I'm tempted in this penultimate paragraph simply to trot out the old activist taunt "get used to it!" once again and consider my work done. But if theory is indeed (not—) forever, then *this work*, our arduous "attempt to dereify the language of thought," our protracted "labor of ambiguating categories of identity," can never be quite so tidily finished. For any "terms" with which we could ever fully "come to terms" would not be effectively theoretical terms, and any writing that we could ever get comfortably

---

[2] Hegel, Lacan, and basically all the dead writers who ever lived can be said to "still write," to still *be* writing, by virtue of the literary convention that bids us describe "what has been written" in the present tense, as if we'd just seen a ghost. This apparitional aspect of all textuality is more or less what I was getting at back in the introduction when I referred to "the undead," to "everyone who still participates in human reality, if only in the *spectral* form of writing."

"used to" would not be specifically theoretical writing, would not be the radical "practice of creativity" (Foucault 1983/1997: 262) to which it's been my great pleasure to introduce you here. For to revisit some rude and radical statements about theory that appeared at the beginning of this introduction, isn't the "whole point" of theory not to get used to anything but rather, in Judith Halberstam's words, "to fuck shit up" (2006: 824)? Isn't the *aim* of theory to produce or provoke "insights which completely shatter and undermine our common perceptions" (Žižek 2006: ix)—those perceptions of the present to which we've gotten all too commonly accustomed? And isn't "the task of theory . . . *to make* the present and thus to . . . invent the subject of that making, a 'we' characterized not only by our belonging to the present but by our making it" (Hardt 2011: 21)? If our actively and provocatively "making the present" is indeed the perpetual "task of theory," as Michael Hardt proposes in "The Militancy of Theory," then our having gotten used to any present that presently is could only mean our having gotten off task, our having settled for taking the meanings of the present, the past, and the future, as reified givens rather than as ever-startling problems.

So perhaps we'd best get used to *not* getting used to the activities nicknamed "theory." And perhaps getting used to *never* getting used to theoretical writing means nothing more or less than taking the full measure of Foucault's militant wisdom and joining him in (still) thinking (about thinking) that "there are times in life when the question of knowing if one can think differently than one thinks and perceive differently than one sees is absolutely necessary if one is to go on looking and reflecting at all" (1986: 7).

Reference Matters

Achebe, Chinua (1978/1989), "An Image of Africa: Racism in Conrad's *Heart of Darkness.*" In *Hope and Impediments: Selected Essays*. New York: Doubleday.

Adorno, Theodor (1966/2007), *Negative Dialectics*, translated by E. B. Ashton, New York: Continuum.

Ahmad, Aijaz (1996), "The Politics of Literary Postcoloniality." In *Contemporary Postcolonial Theory*, edited by Padmini Mongia, 276–93. London: Arnold.

Almond, Ian (2007), *The New Orientalists: Postmodern Representations of Islam from Foucault to Baudrillard*, London and New York: I.B. Tauris.

Althusser, Louis (1971/2001), *Lenin and Philosophy and other essays,* translated by Ben Brewster, New York: Monthly Review Press.

Badmington, Neil, and Julia Thomas, eds. (2008), *The Routledge Critical and Cultural Theory Reader*, London and New York: Routledge.

Bahri, Deepika (2004), "Feminism in/and postcolonialism." In *The Cambridge Companion to Postcolonial Studies*, edited by Neil Lazarus, 199–220, Cambridge: Cambridge university Press.

Baker, Houston, et al. (1988), "The Afro-American Writer and the South." In *The Southern Review and Modern Literature 1935-1985*, edited by Lewis P. Simpson, James Olney, and Jo Gulledge, Baton Rouge, La.: Louisiana State University Press.

Barthes, Roland (1957/1985), *Mythologies*, translated by Annette Lavers, New York: Hill and Wang.

—(1964/1972), *Critical Essays*, translated by Richard Howard, Evanston: Northwestern University Press.

—(1966/1977), "Introduction to the Structural Analysis of Narratives." In *Image, Music, Text,* translated by Stephen Heath, 79–124. New York: Noonday.

—(1968/1977), "The Death of the Author." In *Image, Music, Text,* translated by Stephen Heath, 79–124. New York: Noonday.

—(1971/1977), "From Work to Text." In *Image, Music, Text,* translated by Stephen Heath, 155–64. New York: Noonday.

—(1975), *The Pleasure of the Text*, translated by Richard Miller, New York: Noonday.

—(1981), *Camera Lucida: Reflections on Photography*, translated by Richard Howard, New York: Noonday.

Baudrillard, Jean (1983), *Simulations*, translated by Paul Foss, Paul Patton and Philip Beitchman, New York: Semiotext(e).

Beauvoir, Simone de (1949/1989), *The Second Sex*, translated by H. M. Parshley, New York: Vintage.

Beckett, Samuel (1955), *Three Novels: Molloy, Malone, The Unnamable*, New York: Grove Press.

Benjamin, Andrew (2006), "Deconstruction." In *The Routledge Companion to Critical Theory*, edited by Simon Malpas and Paul Wake, 81–90. New York: Routledge.

Benjamin, Walter (1936/1968), "The Work of Art in the Age of Mechanical Reproduction." In *Illuminations: Essays and Reflections*, edited by Hannah Arendt, translated by Harry Zohn, 217–53. New York: Schocken.

—(1950/1968), "Theses on the Philosophy of History." In *Illuminations: Essays and Reflections*, edited by Hannah Arendt, translated by Harry Zohn, 253–64. New York: Schocken.

Berlant, Lauren, and Michael Warner (1995), "What Does Queer Theory Teach Us About X?" *PMLA* 110(3): 343–9.

—(1998/2007), "Sex in Public." In *The Critical Tradition: Classic Texts and Contemporary Trends*, 3rd edition, edited by David Richter, 1721–33. Boston and New York: Bedford/St. Martin's.

Berman, Marshall (1988), *All That Is Solid Melts Into Air: The Experience of Modernity*, New York: Penguin.

Bersani, Leo (1990), *The Culture of Redemption*, Cambridge, MA: Harvard University Press.

Bertens, Hans (2001), *Literary Theory: The Basics*, New York and London: Routledge.

Bérubé, Michael (2011), "The Science Wars Redux," *Democracy: A Journal of Ideas* 19: 64–74.

Bhabha, Homi (1994), *The Location of Culture*, New York and London: Routledge.

—(1996), "The Other Question." In *Contemporary Postcolonial Theory*, edited by Padmini Mongia, 37–54. London: Arnold.

Bloom, Harold (1994), *The Western Canon*, Harcourt Brace.

Brinkmeyer, Robert (2009), *The Fourth Ghost: White Southern Writers and European Fascism, 1930-1950*, Baton Rouge, La.: Louisiana State University Press.

Brooks, Cleanth (1947/1998), "The Language of Paradox." In *Literary Theory: An Anthology*, edited by Julie Rivkin and Micheal Ryan, 28–39. Oxford: Blackwell.

—(1951/2007), "Irony as a Principle of Structure." In *The Critical Tradition: Classic Texts and Contemporary Trends*, 3rd edition, edited by David Richter, 799–807. Boston and New York: Bedford/St. Martin's.

—(1952/2007), "My Credo: Formalist Criticism." In *The Critical Tradition: Classic Texts and Contemporary Trends*, 3rd edition, edited by David Richter, 798–9. Boston and New York: Bedford/St. Martin's.

Brooks, Peter (1977/2007), "Freud's Masterplot." In *The Critical Tradition: Classic Texts and Contemporary Trends*, 3rd edition, edited by David Richter, 1161–71. Boston and New York: Bedford/St. Martin's.

Butler, Judith (1990), *Gender Trouble: Feminism and the Subversion of Identity*, New York and London: Routledge.

—(1991/2007), "Imitation and Gender Insubordination." In *The Critical Tradition: Classic Texts and Contemporary Trends*, 3rd edition, edited by David Richter, 1707–19. Boston and New York: Bedford/St. Martin's.

—(1993), *Bodies That Matter: On the Discursive Limits of 'Sex*,' New York: Routledge.

—(1997), *The Psychic Life of Power: Theories in Subjection*, Stanford: Stanford University Press.

—(1999), *Subjects of Desire: Hegelian Reflections in Twentieth-Century France*, New York: Columbia University Press.

—(2004), *Undoing Gender*, New York and London: Routledge.

Butler, Judith, Ernesto Laclau, and Slavoj Žižek (2000), *Contingency, Hegemony, Universality: Contemporary Dialogues on the Left*, New York: Verso.

Carr, David (1987), *Interpreting Husserl: Critical and Comparative Studies*, Dordrecht, The Netherlands: Martinus Nijhoff Publishers.

Césaire, Aimé (1955/1972), *Discourse on Colonialism*, translated by John Pinkham, New York and London: Monthly Review Press.

Childers, Joseph, and Gary Hentzi, eds. (1995), *The Columbia Dictionary of Modern Literary and Cultural Criticism*, New York: Columbia University Press.

Chilvers, Ian, and Harold Osborne, eds. (1988), *The Oxford Dictionary of Art*, Oxford: Oxford University Press.

Chow, Rey (2002/2007), "The Interruption of Referentiality: Poststructuralism and the Conundrum of Critical Multiculturalism" In *The Critical Tradition: Classic Texts and Contemporary Trends*, 3rd edition, edited by David Richter, 1910–19. Boston and New York: Bedford/St. Martin's.

Cixous, Hélène (1968/1980), *The Exile of James Joyce*, New York: Riverrun Press.

—(1975/2007), "The Laugh of the Medusa." In *The Critical Tradition: Classic Texts and Contemporary Trends*, 3rd edition, edited by David Richter, 1643–55. Boston and New York: Bedford/St. Martin's.

Clark, T. J. (1982), "Clement Greenberg's Theory of Art," *Critical Inquiry* 9(1): 139–56.

Conrad, Joseph, (1902/1996), *Heart of Darkness*, edited by Ross C. Murfin, Boston: Bedford.

Copjec, Joan (1994), *Read My Desire: Lacan Against the Historicists*, Cambridge, MA: MIT Press.

Critchley, Simon (1997), *Very Little…Almost Nothing: Death, Philosophy, Literature*, London: Routledge.

Culler, Jonathan (1975), *Structuralist Poetics: Structuralism, Linguistics and the Study of Literature*, London: Routledge.

—(1997), *Literary Theory: A Very Short Introduction*, Oxford: Oxford University Press.

—(2007), *The Literary in Theory,* Stanford, California: Stanford University Press.

—(2011), "Afterword: Theory Now and Again," *South Atlantic Quarterly* 110(1): 223–30.

Dean, Tim (2000), *Beyond Sexuality*, Chicago: University of Chicago Press.

—(2008), "An Impossible Embrace: Queerness, Futurity, and the Death Drive." In *A Time for the Humanities: Futurity and the Limits of Autonomy*, edited by James Bono, Tim Dean, and Ewa Ziarek, 122–40. New York: Fordham University Press.

De Lauretis, Teresa (1994), "Habit Changes," *Differences: A Journal of Feminist Cultural Studies* 6(2/3): iii–iviii.

DeLillo, Don (2001), *The Body Artist*, New York: Scribner.

Derrida, Jacques (1966/1978), "Structure, Sign, and Play in the Discourse of the Human Sciences." In *Writing and Difference*, translated by Alan Bass, 351–70. Chicago: University of Chicago Press.

—(1967/1982), "Differance." In *Margins of Philosophy*, translated by Alan Bass, 3–27. Chicago: University of Chicago Press.

—(1967/1997), *Of Grammatology*, corrected edition, translated by Gayatri Chakravorty Spivak, Baltimore: Johns Hopkins University Press.

—(1972/1981), *Disseminations*, translated by Barbara Johnson, Chicago: University of Chicago Press.

—(1972/1981), *Positions*, translated by Alan Bass, Chicago: University of Chicago Press.

—(1980/1987), *The Post Card: From Socrates to Freud and Beyond*, translated by Alan Bass, Chicago: University of Chicago Press.

—(1988), "Towards an Ethics of Discussion." In *Limited Inc*, Evanston, IL: Northwestern University Press.

—(1994), *Specters of Marx: The State of the Debt, the Work of Mourning, and the New International*, translated by Peggy Kamuf, New York: Routledge.

—(1995), "The Time is Out of Joint," translated by Peggy Kamuf, in *Deconstruction is/in America*, edited by Anselm Haverkamp, New York: New York University Press.

—(2008), *The Animal That I Therefore Am*, edited by Marie-Louise Mallet, translated by David Wills, New York: Fordham University Press.

Eagleton, Terry (1983/1996), *Literary Theory: An Introduction*, 2nd edition, Minneapolis: University of Minnesota Press.

—(1990), *The Significance of Theory*, Oxford: Basil Blackwell.

Edelman, Lee (2004), *No Future: Queer Theory and the Death Drive*, New York: Columbia University Press.

Eichenbaum, Boris (1978/1998), "Introduction to the Formal Method." In *Literary Theory: An Anthology,* edited by Julie Rivkin and Michael Ryan, 7–14. Boston: Blackwell.

Erbion, Didier (1991), *Michel Foucault*, translated by Betsy Wing, Cambridge, MA: Harvard University Press.

Eugenides, Jeffrey (2011), *The Marriage Plot*, New York: Farrar, Strauss, and Giroux.

Evans, Dylan (1996), *An Introductory Dictionary of Lacanian Psychoanalysis*, London and New York: Routledge.

Farias, Victor (1991), *Heidegger and Nazism*, Philadelphia: Temple University Press.

Findlay, John (1971), "Hegel's Use of Teleology." In *New Studies in Hegel's Philosophy*, edited by Warren E. Steinkraus, 92–107. New York: Holt, Rinehart, and Winston.

Fiske, John (1995), "Popular Culture." In *Critical Terms for Literary Study*, 2nd edition, edited by Frank Lentricchia and Thomas McGlaughlin, 321–35. Chicago: University of Chicago Press.

Foucault, Michel (1963/1998), "A Preface to Transgression." In *The Essential Works of Foucault, 1954-1984, vol II: Aesthetics, Method, and Epistemology*, edited by James D. Faubion, translated by Robert Hurley, 69–88. New York: The Free Press.

—(1966/1973), *The Order of Things: An Archeology of the Human Sciences*, New York: Vintage.

—(1967/1998), "Nietzsche, Freud, Marx." In *The Essential Works of Foucault, 1954-1984, vol II: Aesthetics, Method, and Epistemology*, edited by James D. Faubion, translated by Robert Hurley, 269–78. New York: The Free Press.

—(1969/1998), "What is an Author?" In *The Essential Works of Foucault, 1954-1984, vol II: Aesthetics, Method, and Epistemology*, edited by James D. Faubion, translated by Robert Hurley, 205–22, New York: The Free Press.

—(1972), *The Archeology of Knowledge & The Discourse on Language*, translated by A. M. Sheridan Smith, New York: Pantheon.

—(1972/1983), preface to Gilles Deleuze and Felix Guattari, *Anti-Oedipus: Capitalism and Schizophrenia*, translated by Robert Hurley, Mark Seem, and Helen R. Lane, Minneapolis: University of Minnesota Press.

—(1975/1995), *Discipline and Punish: The Birth of the Prison*, translated by Allan Sheridan, New York: Vintage.

—(1976/1990), *The History of Sexuality: An Introduction*, translated by Robert Hurley, New York, Vintage.

—(1977/2000), "Truth and Power." In *The Essential Works of Foucault, vol III: Power*, edited by James D. Faubion, translated by Robert Hurley, 111–33. New York: The Free Press.

—(1983/1988), "The Minimalist Self." In *Politics Philosophy Culture: Interviews and Other Writings 1977-1984*, edited by Lawrence D. Kritzman, translated by Alan Sheridan, 3–16. New York: Routledge.

—(1983/1997), "On the Genealogy of Ethics: An Overview of Work in Progress." In *The Essential Works of Foucault, 1954–1984, vol I: Ethics, Subjectivity and Truth*, edited by Paul Rabinow, translated by Robert Hurley, 253–80. New York: The Free Press.

—(1983/1998), "Structuralism and Post-structuralism." In *The Essential Works of Foucault, 1954-1984, vol II: Aesthetics, Method, and Epistemology*, edited by James D. Faubion, translated by Robert Hurley, 433–58. New York: The Free Press.

—(1983/2000), "The Subject and Power." In *The Essential Works of Foucault, vol III: Power*, edited by James D. Faubion, translated by Robert Hurley, 326–48. New York: The Free Press.

—(1984/1988), "An Aesthetics of Existence." In *Politics Philosophy Culture: Interviews and Other Writings 1977-1984*, edited by Lawrence D. Kritzman, translated by Alan Sheridan, 47–56. New York: Routledge.

—(1986), *The Uses of Pleasure: Volume 2 of The History of Sexuality*, translated by Robert Hurley, New York: Vintage.

Freccero, Carla (2006), *Early/Queer/Modern*, Durham: Duke University Press.

Freud, Sigmund (1907/1989), "Creative Writers and Daydreaming." In *The Freud Reader*, edited by Peter Gay, 436–42. New York: Norton.

—(1915/1989), "Repression." In *The Freud Reader*, edited by Peter Gay, 568–71. New York: Norton.

—(1920/1989), "Beyond the Pleasure Principle." In *The Freud Reader*, edited by Peter Gay, 594–625. New York: Norton.

—(1930/1989), "Civilization and its Discontents." In *The Freud Reader*, edited by Peter Gay, 722–71. New York: Norton.

—(1933/2001), "New Introductory Lectures on Psychoanalysis." In *The Standard Edition of the Complete Psychological Works of Sigmund Freud, Vol. XXII*, edited and translated by James Strachey, 7–184. London: Vintage.

Fuss, Diana (1989), *Essentially Speaking: Feminism, Nature & Difference*, New York and London: Routledge.

Gagnier, Regina (1991), *Subjectivities: A History of Self-Representation in Britain, 1832-1920*, Oxford: Oxford University Press.

Gallop, Jane (1985), *Reading Lacan*, Ithaca: Cornell University Press.

Garber, Marjorie (2003/2008), "Who Owns 'Human Nature'?" In *The Routledge Critical and Cultural Theory Reader*, edited by Neil Badmington and Julia Thomas, 422–42. New York: Routledge.

Gibson, Andrew (2006), *Beckett and Badiou: The Pathos of Intermittency*, Oxford: Oxford University Press.

Gifford, Don (1988), *Ullysses Annotated: Notes for James Joyce's Ulysses*. Berkeley: University of California Press.

Gikandi, Simon (2004), "Poststructuralism and postcolonial discourse." In *The Cambridge Companion to Postcolonial Studies*, edited by Neil Lazarus, 97–119. Cambridge: Cambridge University Press.

Gray, Francine du Plessix (2010), "Dispatches from the Other: A new translation of *The Second Sex*," *New York Times Book Review*, May 30: 6–7.

Greenblatt, Stephen (1995), "Culture." In *Critical Terms for Literary Study*, 2nd edition, edited by Frank Lentricchia and Thomas McGlaughlin, 225–32. Chicago: University of Chicago Press.

Habermas, Jürgen (1980/2001), "Modernity—An Incomplete Project." In *The Norton Anthology of Theory and Criticism*, edited by Vincent B. Leitch, 1748–59. New York: Norton.

Halberstam, Judith, et al. (2006), "Forum: Conference Debates the Antisocial Thesis in Queer Theory," *PMLA* 121(3): 819–36.

Hall, Donald E. (2003), *Queer Theories*, New York: Palgrave MacMillan.
—(2006), "Imagining Queer Studies Out of the Doldrums," *Chronicle Review,* 15 September.
Hall, Stuart (1982/1998), "The Rediscovery of Ideology." In *Literary Theory: An Anthology*, edited by Julie Rivkin and Michael Ryan, 1050–64. Boston: Blackwell.
Halperin, David (1995), *Saint Foucault: Towards a Gay Hagiography*, Oxford: Oxford University Press.
Haraway, Donna (1985/2008), "A Manifesto for Cyborgs: Science, Technology, and Socialist Feminism in the 1980s." In *The Routledge Critical and Cultural Theory Reader*, edited by Neil Badmington and Julia Thomas, 324–55. New York: Routledge.
Hardt, Michael (2011), "The Militancy of Theory," *South Atlantic Quarterly* 110(1): 19–35.
Harmon, William, and Hugh Holman (2006), *A Handbook to Literature*, 10th edition, Upper Saddle River, NJ: Pearson/Prentice Hall.
Hassan, Ihab (1987), *The Postmodern Turn: Essays in Theory and Culture*, Columbus, Ohio: Ohio State University Press.
Hegel, G. W. F. (1795/1948), *Early Theological Writings*, translated by T. M. Knox, Chicago: University of Chicago Press.
—(1807/1977), *The Phenomenology of Spirit*, translated by A. V. Miller. Oxford: Oxford University Press.
—(1807/1998), "The Phenomenology of Spirit." In *The Hegel Reader,* edited by Stephen Houlgate, 45–124. Oxford: Blackwell.
—(1812/1998), "Science of Logic." In *The Hegel Reader,* edited by Stephen Houlgate, 175–250. Oxford: Blackwell.
—(1837/1998), "Philosophy of History." In *The Hegel Reader,* edited by Stephen Houlgate, 400–16. Oxford: Blackwell.
Heidegger, Martin (1947/1977), *Basic Writings*, edited by David Farrell Krell, New York: Harper Collins.
hooks, bell (1989/2007), "Postmodern Blackness." In *The Critical Tradition: Classic Texts and Contemporary Trends*, 3rd edition, edited by David Richter, 2009–13. Boston and New York: Bedford/St. Martin's.
Horkheimer, Max, and Theodor W. Adorno (1947/2002), *Dialectic of Enlightenment: Philosophical Fragments*, edited by Gunzelin Schmid Noerr, translated by Edmund Jephcott, Stanford, California: Stanford University Press.
Inwood, Michael (1992), *A Hegel Dictionary*, Oxford: Blackwell.
Jagose, Annamarie (1996), *Queer Theory: An Introduction,* New York: New York University Press.
Jakobson, Roman (1956/2001), "Two Aspects of Language and Two Types of Aphasic Disturbances." In *The Norton Anthology of Theory and Criticism*, edited by Vincent B. Leitch, 1265–69. New York: Norton.
—(1960/2007), "Linguistics and Poetics." In *The Critical Tradition: Classic Texts and Contemporary Trends*, 3rd edition, edited by David Richter, 852–59. Boston and New York: Bedford/St. Martin's.

Jameson, Fredric (1971), *Marxism and Form: Twentieth Century Dialectical Theories of Literature*, Princeton: Princeton University Press.

—(1979), "Reification and Utopia in Mass Culture," *Social Text* 1(1): 130–48.

—(1981), *The Political Unconscious: Narrative as Socially Symbolic Act*, Ithaca: Cornell University Press.

—(1988), *The Ideologies of Theory: Essays 1971-1986: Volume Two: The Syntax of History*, Minneapolis: University of Minnesota Press.

—(1988/2007), "Postmodernism and Consumer Society." In *The Critical Tradition: Classic Texts and Contemporary Trends*, 3rd edition, edited by David Richter, 1956–65. Boston and New York: Bedford/St. Martin's.

—(1994), *The Seeds of Time*, New York: Columbia University Press.

—(2004), "Symptoms of Theory or Symptoms for Theory?" *Critical Inquiry* 30(2): 403–8.

—(2006), "Lacan and the Dialectic: A Fragment." In *Lacan: The Silent Partners*, edited by Slavoj Žižek, 365–97. New York: Verso.

—(2009), *Valences of the Dialectic*, New York: Verso.

—(2010), *The Hegel Variations: On the Phenomenology of Spirit*, New York: Verso.

Johnson, Barbara (1981), Translator's Introduction to *Dissemination*, by Jacques Derrida, Chicago: University of Chicago Press.

Johnston, Adrian (2008), *Žižek's Ontology: A Transcendental Materialist Theory of Subjectivity*, Evanston: Northwestern University Press.

—(2009), *Badiou, Žižek, and Political Transformations: The Cadence of Change*, Evanston: Northwestern University Press.

Joyce, James (1922/1986), *Ulysses*, edited by Hans Walter Gabler. New York: Vintage.

Kant, Immanuel (1784/1996), "An Answer to the Question: What is Enlightenment?" In *From Modernism to Postmodernism*, edited by Lawrence Cahoone, 51–7. Cambridge, MA: Blackwell.

Kavanagh, James (1995), "Ideology." In *Critical Terms for Literary Study*, 2nd edition, edited by Frank Lentricchia and Thomas McGlaughlin, 306–20. Chicago: University of Chicago Press.

Kojève, Alexandre (1947/1980), *Introduction to the Reading of Hegel*, Ithaca: Cornell University Press.

Kristeva, Jula (1982), *Powers of Horror: An Essay on Abjection*, translated by Leon S. Roudiez, New York: Columbia University Press.

Lacan, Jacques (1966a/2006), "Seminar on 'The Purloined Letter.'" In *Écrits: The First Complete Translation in English*, translated by Bruce Fink, 6–48. New York: Norton.

—(1966b/2006), "The Mirror Stage as Formative of the I Function as Revealed in Psychoanalytic Experience." In *Écrits: The First Complete Translation in English*, translated by Bruce Fink, 75–81. New York: Norton.

—(1966c/2006), "Aggressiveness in Psychoanalysis." In *Écrits: The First Complete Translation in English*, translated by Bruce Fink, 82–101. New York: Norton.

—(1966d/2006), "The Function and Field of Speech and Language in Psychoanalysis." In *Écrits: The First Complete Translation in English,* translated by Bruce Fink, 197–268. New York: Norton.

—(1966e/2006), "The Instance of the Letter in the Unconscious or Reason Since Freud." In *Écrits: The First Complete Translation in English,* translated by Bruce Fink, 412–44. New York: Norton.

—(1966f/2006), "The Direction of the Treatment and the Principles of Its Power." In *Écrits: The First Complete Translation in English,* translated by Bruce Fink, 489–542. New York: Norton.

—(1966g/2006), "The Signification of the Phallus." In *Écrits: The First Complete Translation in English,* translated by Bruce Fink, 575–84. New York: Norton.

—(1966h/2006), "The Position of the Unconscious." In *Écrits: The First Complete Translation in English,* translated by Bruce Fink, 703–21. New York: Norton.

—(1973/1981), *The Seminar of Jacques Lacan. Book XI, The Four Fundamental Concepts of Psychoanalysis, 1964,* edited by Jacques Alain-Miller, translated by Alan Sheridan. New York: Norton.

—(1975/1991), *The Seminar of Jacques Lacan. Book I: Freud's Papers on Technique, 1953-1954*, edited by Jacques Alain-Miller, translated by John Forrester. New York: Norton.

—(1975/1998), *The Seminar of Jacques Lacan. Book XX, On Feminine Sexuality, the Limits of love and Knowledge, 1972-1973 (Encore),* edited by Jacques-Alain Miller, translated by Bruce Fink, New York: Norton.

—(1986/1992), *The Seminar of Jacques Lacan. Book VII, The Ethics of Psychoanalysis, 1959-1960*, edited by Jacques-Alain Miller, translated by Dennis Porter, New York: Norton.

—(2008), *My Teaching,* translated by David Macey, London: Verso.

Laplanche, Jean, and Jean-Baptiste Pontalis (1974), *The Language of Psychoanalysis*, translated by Donald Nicholson-Smith, New York: Norton.

Lazarus, Neil (2004a), "Introducing Postcolonial Studies." In *The Cambridge Companion to Postcolonial Literary Studies,* edited by Neil Lazarus, ix–xii. Cambridge: Cambridge University Press.

—(2004b), "The global dispensation since 1945." In *The Cambridge Companion to Postcolonial Literary Studies,* edited by Neil Lazarus, 19–40. Cambridge: Cambridge University Press.

Leitch, Vincent, et al., eds. (2001), *The Norton Anthology of Theory and Criticism*, New York: Norton.

Lévi-Strauss, Claude (1963/2007), "The Structural Study of Myth." In *The Critical Tradition: Classic Texts and Contemporary Trends*, 3rd edition, edited by David Richter, 859–68. Boston and New York: Bedford/St. Martin's.

Lucy, Niall (2004), *A Derrida Dictionary*, Oxford: Blackwell.

Lyotard, Jean-François (1979/1984), *The Postmodern Condition: A Report on Knowledge*, translated by Geoff Bennington and Brian Massumi, Minneapolis: University of Minnesota Press.

—(1986/2001), "Defining the Postmodern." In *The Norton Anthology of Theory and Criticism*, edited by Vincent B. Leitch, 1612–15, New York: Norton.

Macdonald, Dwight (1957/1998), "A Theory of Mass Culture." In *Cultural Theory and Popular Culture: A Reader*, 2nd edition, edited by John Storey, 22–38. Athens, GA: University of Georgia Press.

Malabou, Catherine (1996/2005), *The Future of Hegel: Plasticity, Temporality and Dialectic*, New York: Routledge.

—(2004/2008), *What Should We Do with Our Brain?*, New York: Fordham University Press.

Malpas, Simon, and Paul Wake (2006), *The Routledge Companion to Critical Theory*, London and New York: Routledge.

Marx, Karl (1844/1978), "Contribution to the Critique of Hegel's *Philosophy of Right*: Introduction." In *The Marx-Engels Reader*, 2nd edition, edited by Robert C. Tucker, 53–65. New York: Norton.

—(1845/1978), "Theses on Feuerbach." In *The Marx-Engels Reader*, 2nd edition, edited by Robert C. Tucker, 143–5. New York: Norton.

—(1873/1978), "From the Afterword to the Second German Edition of *Capital*." In *The Marx-Engels Reader*, 2nd edition, edited by Robert C. Tucker, 299–302. New York: Norton.

—(1888/1978), "Manifesto of the Communist Party." In *The Marx-Engels Reader*, 2nd edition, edited by Robert C. Tucker, 469–500. New York: Norton.

—(1932a/1978), "Economic and Philosophical Manuscripts of 1844." In *The Marx-Engels Reader*, 2nd edition, edited by Robert C. Tucker, 66–125. New York: Norton.

—(1832b/1978), "The German Ideology." In *The Marx-Engels Reader*, 2nd edition, edited by Robert C. Tucker, 146–202. New York: Norton.

McLaughlin, Thomas (1995), "Introduction." In *Critical Terms for Literary Study*, 2nd edition, edited by Frank Lentricchia and Thomas McGlaughlin, 1–10. Chicago: University of Chicago Press.

Milani, Farzaneh (2011), "Saudi Arabia's Freedom Riders," *The New York Times* June 13, A21.

Mills, Jon (2002), *The Unconscious Abyss: Hegel's Anticipation of Psychoanalysis*, Albany: State University of New York Press.

Mohanty, Chandra Talpade (1991/2008), "Under Western Eyes: Feminist Scholarship and Colonial Discourses." In *The Routledge Critical and Cultural Theory Reader*, edited by Neil Badmington and Julia Thomas, 324–55. New York: Routledge.

—(2003), "'Under Western Eyes' Revisited: Feminist Solidarity through Anti-Capitalist Struggle," *Signs* 28(2): 499–535.

Moi, Toril (1985), *Sexual/Textual Politics: Feminist Literary Theory*, New York and London: Routledge.

—(2000), "Is Anatomy Destiny? Freud and Biological Determinism." In *Whose Freud? The Place of Psychoanalysis in Contemporary Culture*, edited by Peter Brooks and Alex Woloch, 71–92. New Haven: Yale University Press.

Morrison, Toni (1987/2004), *Beloved*, New York: Vintage.

Nancy, Jean-Luc (2002), *Hegel: The Restlessness of the Negative*, translated by Jason Smith and Steven Miller, Minneapolis: University of Minnesota Press.

Negri, Antonio (2005), *Time for Revolution*, New York: Continuum.

Nehamas, Richard (1987), *Nietzsche: Life as Literature*, Cambridge, MA: Harvard University Press.

Nietzsche, Friedrich (1872/2006), "The Birth of Tragedy from the Spirit of Music." In *The Nietzsche Reader*, edited by Keith A. Pearson and Duncan Large, 42–87. Oxford: Blackwell.

—(1873/2006), "On Truth and Lie in a Nonmoral Sense." In *The Nietzsche Reader*, edited by Keith A. Pearson and Duncan Large, 114–23. Oxford: Blackwell.

—(1886/2006), "Beyond Good and Evil." In *The Nietzsche Reader*, edited by Keith A. Pearson and Duncan Large, 311–61. Oxford: Blackwell.

—(1887/1974), *The Gay Science,* translated by Walter Kaufmann. New York: Vintage.

—(1887/2006), "The Gay Science, Book V." In *The Nietzsche Reader*, edited by Keith A. Pearson and Duncan Large, 362–84. Oxford: Blackwell.

—(1887/1992), *On the Genealogy of Morals,* in *The Basic Writings of Nietzsche*, edited by Walter Kaufmann, New York: Modern Library.

—(1887/2006), "On the Genealogy of Morals." In *The Nietzsche Reader*, edited by Keith A. Pearson and Duncan Large, 390–446. Oxford: Blackwell.

—(1888a/2006), "Twilight of the Idols." In *The Nietzsche Reader*, edited by Keith A. Pearson and Duncan Large, 456–85. Oxford: Blackwell.

—(1888b/2006), "The Anti-Christ." In *The Nietzsche Reader*, edited by Keith A. Pearson and Duncan Large, 486–99. Oxford: Blackwell.

—(1901/1968), *The Will to Power*, translated by Walter Kaufmann, New York: Vintage.

Nussbaum, Martha C. (1999), "The Professor of Parody: The Hip Defeatism of Judith Butler," *The New Republic* 220(8): 37–45.

Parker, Robert Dale (2008), *How to Interpret Literature: Critical Theory for Literary and Cultural Studies*, New York and Oxford: Oxford University Press.

Pearson, Keith Ansell, and Duncan Large, eds. (2006), *The Nietzsche Reader*, Oxford: Blackwell.

Phillips, Adam (1999), *The Beast in the Nursery: On Curiosity and Other Appetites*, New York: Vintage.

Rabaté, Jean-Michel (2002), *The Future of Theory*, Oxford: Blackwell.

Rabinowitz, Peter J. (1996), "Reader Response, Reader Responsibility: *Heart of Darkness* and the Politics of Displacement." In Joseph Conrad, *Heart of Darkness: Complete, Authoritative Text with Biographical and Historical Contexts, Critical History, and Essays from Five Contemporary Critical Perspectives*, 2nd edition, edited by Ross C. Murfin, 131–47. Boston: Bedford.

Rasmussen, E. D. (2004), "Liberation Hurts: An Interview with Slavoj Žižek," *Electronic Book Review,* http://electronicbookreview.com/thread/endconstruction/desublimation.

Richter, David, ed. (1999), *Falling into Theory: Conflicting Views on Reading Literature*, Boston and New York: Bedford/St. Martin's.

—(2007), *The Critical Tradition: Classic Texts and Contemporary Trends*, 3rd edition, Boston and New York: Bedford/St. Martin's.

Riley, Denise (1993), *Am I That Name?: Feminism and the Category of Woman in History*, Minneapolis: University of Minnesota Press.

Rimbaud, Artur (1871/1966), *Complete Works and Selected Letters*, edited by Wallace Fowlie, Chicago: University of Chicago Press.

Rivkin, Julie, and Michael Ryan, eds. (1998), *Literary Theory: An Anthology*, Oxford: Blackwell.

Rubin, Gayle (1975/2007), "The Traffic in Women: Notes on the 'Political Economy' of Sex." In *The Critical Tradition: Classic Texts and Contemporary Trends*, 3rd edition, edited by David Richter, 1664–82. Boston and New York: Bedford/St. Martin's.

—(1984/2008), "Thinking Sex: Notes Towards a Radical Theory of the Politics of Sexuality." In *The Routledge Critical and Cultural Theory Reader*, edited by Neil Badmington and Julia Thomas, 281–323. New York: Routledge.

Ruti, Mari (2008), "Why There Is Always a Future in the Future: Queer Theory and the Death Drive," *Angelaki: Journal of the Theoretical Humanities* 31(3): 113–26.

Salih, Sarah, ed. (2004), *The Judith Butler Reader*, Oxford: Blackwell.

Said, Edward (1979), *Orientalism*, New York: Vintage.

Sartre, Jean-Paul (1960/1976), *Critique of Dialectical Reason*, translated by Alan Sheridan Smith, London: New Left Books.

Saussure, Ferdinand de (1959), *Course in General Linguistics*, edited by Charles Bally and Albert Sechehaye, translated by Wade Baskin, New York: Philosophical Library.

—(1972), *Course in General Linguistics*, edited by Charles Bally and Albert Sechehaye, translated by Roy Harris, La Salle, Illinois: Open Court.

Scott, Joan (1988), *Gender and the Politics of History*, New York: Columbia University Press.

Sedgwick, Eve Kosofsky (1990), *Epistemology of the Closet*, Berkeley: University of California Press.

Shklovsky, Viktor (1917/2007), "Art as Technique." In *The Critical Tradition: Classic Texts and Contemporary Trends*, 3rd edition, edited by David Richter, 775–84. Boston and New York: Bedford/St. Martin's.

—(1993), *Tendencies*, Durham: Duke University Press.

Smith, Jason (2002), "Introduction: Nancy's Hegel, the State, and Us." In Nancy (2002), *Hegel: The Restlessness of the Negative*, translated by Jason Smith and Steven Miller, Minneapolis: University of Minnesota Press.

Spivak, Gayatri (1981), "French Feminism in an International Frame," *Yale French Studies* 62: 154–62.

—(1988), "Can the Subaltern Speak?" In *Marxism and the Interpretation of Culture*, edited by Cary Nelson and Lawrence Grossberg, 271–316. Urbana: University of Illinois Press.

—(1993), *Outside in the Teaching Machine,* London and New York: Routledge.

—(1996), *The Spivak Reader,* edited by Donna Landry and Gerald MacLean, London and New York: Routledge.

—(1999), *A Critique of Postcolonial Reason: Toward a History of the Vanishing Present,* Cambridge, MA: Harvard University Press.

Sprinker, Michael, ed. (1999), *Ghostly Demarcations: A Symposium on Jacques Derrida's Specters of Marx,* New York: Verso.

Stevens, Wallace (1937/1982), "The Man With The Blue Guitar." In *The Collected Poems,* New York: Vintage.

Stoltenberg, John (1974/2004), "Toward Gender Justice." In *Feminism and Masculinities,* edited by Peter Murphy, 41–9. Oxford: Oxford University Press.

Suleri, Sara (1992), "Woman Skin Deep: Feminism and the Postcolonial Condition," *Critical Inquiry* 18: 756–69.

Surin, Kenneth (2011), "Introduction: 'Theory Now'?", *South Atlantic Quarterly* 110(1): 3–17.

Theweleit, Klaus (1987), *Male Fantasies, Volume One: Women, Floods, Bodies, History,* translated by Stephen Conway, Minneapolis: University of Minnesota Press.

Thomas, Calvin (1996), *Male Matters: Masculinity, Anxiety, and the Male Body on the Line,* Urbana and Chicago: University of Illinois Press.

—(2000), *Straight with a Twist: Queer Theory and the Subject of Heterosexuality,* Urbana and Chicago: University of Illinois Press.

—(2002), "Re-enfleshing the Bright Boys: How Male Bodies Matter to Feminist Theory." In *Masculinity Studies and Feminist Theory: New Directions,* edited by Judith Kegan Gardiner, 60–89. New York: Columbia University Press.

—(2007), "Men and feminist criticism." In *A History of Feminist Literary Criticism,* edited by Gill Plain and Susan Sellars, 187–208. Cambridge: Cambridge University Press.

—(2008), *Masculinity, Psychoanalysis, Straight Queer Theory: Essays on Abjection in Literature, Mass Culture, and Film,* New York: Palgrave Macmillan.

—(2009), "On Being Post-Normal: Heterosexuality After Queer Theory." In *The Ashgate Research Companion to Queer Theory,* edited by Noreen Giffney and Michael O'Rourke, 17–32. Farnham UK: Ashgate.

Voltaire (1759/2009), *Candide,* translated by Nourse, edited by Eric Palmer, Toronto: Broadview Press.

Warner, Michael (1993), "Introduction." *Fear of a Queer Planet: Queer Politics and Social Theory,* edited by Michael Warner, Minneapolis: University of Minnesota Press.

White, Susan (1988), "Male Bonding, Hollywood Orientalism, and the Repression of the Feminine in Kubrick's *Full Metal Jacket,*" *Arizona Quarterly* 44(3): 121–44.

Wimsatt, W. K., and Monroe Beardsley (1954/2007), "The Intentional Fallacy." In *The Critical Tradition: Classic Texts and Contemporary Trends,* 3rd edition, edited by David Richter, 811–18. Boston and New York: Bedford/ St. Martin's.

Wittig, Monique (1981/2007), "One Is Not Born a Woman." In *The Critical Tradition: Classic Texts and Contemporary Trends*, 3rd edition, edited by David Richter, 1637–42. Boston and New York: Bedford/St. Martin's.

Wolfreys, Julian (2004), *Critical Keywords in Literary and Cultural Theory*, New York: Palgrave Macmillan.

Woods, Tim (2009), *Beginning Postmodernism,* 2nd edition, Manchester and New York: Manchester University Press.

Woolf, Virginia (1929/1989), *A Room of One's Own*, New York: Harcourt Brace.

Yeats, William Butler (1920/1983), "The Second Coming." In *The Poems of W. B. Yeats*, edited by Richard J. Finneran, New York: Macmillan.

Young, Robert (1990), *White Mythologies: Writing History and the West*, London and New York: Routledge.

—(2001), *Postcolonialism: An Historical Introduction*, Oxford: Blackwell.

Yovel, Yirmiyahu (2005), *Hegel's Preface to the Phenomenology of Spirit*, Princeton: Princeton University Press.

Žižek, Slavoj (1989), *The Sublime Object of Ideology*, New York: Verso.

—(1992), *Looking Awry: An Introduction to Jacques Lacan through Popular Culture*, Cambridge, MA: October Books.

—(1993), *Tarrying with the Negative: Kant, Hegel, and the Critique of Ideology*, Durham, NC: Duke University Press.

—(1994), *Metastases of Enjoyment: Six Essays on Women and Causality*, New York: Verso.

—(1999/2002), "The Matrix; or, the Two Sides of Perversion." In *The Matrix and Philosophy: Welcome to the Desert of the Real*, edited by William Irwin, Peru, Illinois: Open Court.

—(1999/2008), *The Ticklish Subject: The Absent Centre of Political Ontology*, New York: Verso.

—(2006), *The Parallax View*, Cambridge, MA: MIT Press.

—(2007), *How to Read Lacan*, New York: Norton.

Index

Parker, Robert Dale 2n. 1, 157, 160,
173–4
parody/pastiche 95, 229–30
paternal metaphor 196–7
Pearson, Keith Ansell 17n. 9, 256
Peirce, Charles Sanders 176
penisneid (penis envy) 194
performative/constative utterances
54n. 5, 251–2, 255
performativity 251–2
perspective 170, 236–7
phallogocentrism xx, 190n. 3, 197,
199, 210, 257
phallus xx, 190–200, 190n. 3
phenomenology 22, 22n. 16, 116,
126, 133n. 6
Phillips, Adam xvi, 37, 41
Picasso, Pablo 93n. 4, 235, 237
pigs 25
Pillay, Navi 234n. 21
Plato (Platonism) 74n. 14, 155, 173,
190n. 3, 205–6, 205n. 3,
210, 229n. 18
pleasure/reality principles xvi, 34–47,
39n. 1, 53, 64–7, 109n. 16,
194
political xiii, xviii–xix, 4, 12,
17–18, 18n. 12, 20–1,
20n. 15, 32, 41, 88–90,
90nn. 1, 3, 101–2,
112n. 19, 114–17, 121,
144, 153–4, 156–8,
165, 170–1, 178, 205, 212,
224–6, 227n. 17, 230,
234n. 21, 238–43, 250,
253–5, 257–8, 258n. 7,
260–3, 261n. 10, 265–7,
265n. 13, 272
Pollock, Jackson 235, 237
polymorphous perversity 74, 74n. 12,
114, 194, 271
Pontalis, Jean-Baptiste 63n. 3, 66n. 4
Portman, John 230
Potebnya, Alexander 165–7

Pound, Ezra 235
prematurity at birth (human) 32, 34,
61, 97, 103, 115, 247
primal scene 79, 79n. 20
principium individuationis 61n. 1
project of modernity 221–2, 246

queer (queer theory) ix, xiv,
xx–xxii, 12, 23, 32,
76n. 16, 200, 204, 227,
241–3, 247, 253–4,
264–70, 265n. 13, 266n. 14,
269n. 15, 271–3

Rabaté, Jean-Michel xiv, xviii,
xxii, 3, 22n. 16, 121, 125,
133n. 6, 145, 273
Rabinowitz, Peter J. 147n. 1
Ransom, John Crowe 154n. 3
Rasmussen, E. D. 125
rat 179
Raulet, Gerárd 221–2
real/imaginary/symbolic xvii, 30–3,
31n. 4, 43, 43n. 3, 51, 60,
62–5, 62n. 2, 68–9, 69n. 7,
86, 95, 97–8, 98n. 8, 207,
268, 272
reception theory/reader
response 217, 217n. 9
recognition (misrecognition) 29n. 3,
40–3, 65, 76, 90n. 3, 93, 95,
98, 107, 109–10, 113–14,
120, 125, 132, 133n. 6,
140–4, 155, 194, 199,
243n. 25
referent 52, 52n. 2, 169, 177, 183,
213–14
reification xii, 2–4, 2n. 1, 6–8,
12, 20–2, 22n. 16, 24, 85,
90n. 3, 109n. 16, 121,
152–3, 157, 165, 272
repetition compulsion 66
representational pleasure 36–8,
42–3, 47

White, Susan   242n. 24
Wilder, Billy   229
Williams, Raymond   233n. 20
Wilson, Dooley   140n. 9
Wimsatt, W. K.   157
Wittig, Monique   12
Woods, Tim   200n. 5, 243n. 25
Woolf, Virginia   xix, 156–8, 235,
        249, 261n. 9
Woolfreys, Julian   17, 156
word-presentations   xvii, 64
Wordsworth, William   154
world *see* human reality

Yeats, William Butler   212n. 7
Young, Robert   238, 238n. 23
Yovel, Yirmiyahu   127n. 3, 128,
        132, 137n. 7

Žižek, Slavoj   xiii–xv, 2, 6–7, 6n. 2,
        19n. 14, 23, 41n. 2, 43,
        45, 46n. 5, 48, 59, 61n. 1,
        62, 70, 72, 84, 87, 97,
        99n. 9, 125–6, 125n. 1,
        126n. 2, 130n. 4, 133n. 6,
        172n. 1, 234n. 21, 245, 253,
        260–2, 274